THE WORKING-CLASS INTELLECTUAL IN EIGHTEENTH- AND NINETEENTH-CENTURY BRITAIN

The Working-Class Intellectual in Eighteenth- and Nineteenth-Century Britain

Edited by

ARUNA KRISHNAMURTHY
Fitchburg State College, USA

ASHGATE

Published by
Ashgate Publishing Limited
Wey Court East
Union Road
Farnham
Surrey, GU9 7PT
England

Ashgate Publishing Company
Suite 420
101 Cherry Street
Burlington
VT 05401-4405
USA

www.ashgate.com

British Library Cataloguing in Publication Data
The working-class intellectual in eighteenth- and nineteenth-century Britain
    1. Working class writings, English – History and criticism 2. English literature – 18th century – History and criticism 3. English literature – 19th century – History and criticism 4. Working class – Great Britain – Intellectual life – 18th century 5. Working class – Great Britain – Intellectual life – 19th century 6. Great Britain – Intellectual life – 18th century 7. Great Britain – Intellectual life – 19th century
    I. Krishnamurthy, Aruna
    820.9'920624

Library of Congress Cataloging-in-Publication Data
The working-class intellectual in eighteenth- and nineteenth-century Britain / edited by Aruna Krishnamurthy.
    p. cm.
Includes bibliographical references and index.
ISBN 978-0-7546-6504-5 (alk. paper)
    1. Working class—Great Britain—History—18th century. 2. Working class—Great Britain—History—19th century. 3. Working class—Great Britain—Intellectual life. 4. Intellectuals—Great Britain—History—18th century. 5. Intellectuals—Great Britain—History—19th century. 6. Great Britain—Intellectual life. I. Krishnamurthy, Aruna.
    HD8390.W674 2009
    305.5'62094109033—dc22

2008036682

ISBN: 978-0-7546-6504-5

Mixed Sources
Product group from well-managed forests and other controlled sources
www.fsc.org Cert no. SA-COC-1565
© 1996 Forest Stewardship Council
FSC

Printed and bound in Great Britain by
MPG Books Ltd, Bodmin, Cornwall.

Contents

Notes on Contributors

Rob Breton has recently joined the faculty of Nipissing University as Assistant Professor of English. He has also recently published a book—*Gospels and Grit: Work and Labour in Carlyle, Conrad, and Orwell*—with the University of Toronto Press. His current work is focused on the British nineteenth-century working-class novel.

William J. Christmas is Professor of English at San Francisco State University where he teaches courses in eighteenth-century British literature and culture. He is the author of *The Lab'ring Muses: Work, Writing, and the Social Order in English Plebeian Poetry, 1730–1830* (Delaware, 2001), and editor of Volume 1 of the series *Eighteenth-Century English Labouring-Class Poets* (Pickering & Chatto, 2003). He is currently working on revising the poetry section for Volume 3 (1700–1800) of *The Cambridge Bibliography of English Literature*.

Julie F. Codell is Professor of Art History, Film and Media Studies, and English at Arizona State University where she is also an affiliate in Asian Studies and Women's Studies. Her interdisciplinary articles on Victorian culture and India under the Raj have appeared in many scholarly journals, 25 anthologies, and 9 encyclopedias. She wrote *The Victorian Artist* (Cambridge, 2003), edited *The Political Economy of Art* (Fairleigh Dickinson University Press, 2008), *Genre, Gender, Race, and World Cinema* (Blackwell, 2007), *Imperial Co-Histories* (Fairleigh Dickinson University Press, 2003) and special issues of *Victorian Periodicals Review* on the 19th-century press in India (2004) and Victorian art and the press (1991). She co-edited (with L. Brake) *Encounters in the Victorian Press* (Palgrave Macmillan, 2004) and (with D.S. Macleod) *Orientalism Transposed* (Ashgate, 1998), now being translated into Japanese (Hosei University Press, 2008). She is currently editing *Photography and the Imperial Durbars of British India* (2009) and preparing books on Victorian material culture in art and on British coronations in Delhi, 1877–1911, a project for which she received fellowships from the American Institute of Indian Studies, Getty Foundation, National Endowment for the Humanities, and Huntington Library.

Alice Jenkins is a lecturer in English at the University of Glasgow. Her research interests are mainly in the nineteenth century, especially in literature and science. She is the co-editor with Juliet John of *Rethinking Victorian Culture* (Macmillan, 2000) and *Rereading Victorian Fiction* (Macmillan, 2000). Her *Gerard Manley Hopkins: A Literary Sourcebook* was published by Routledge in 2006 and her monograph *Space and the 'March of Mind': Literature and the Physical Sciences in Britain, 1815–1850* is forthcoming with Oxford University Press. She has published articles on Michael Faraday, Mary Somerville, and other figures in nineteenth-century science, as well as on a range of topics in contemporary science fiction.

Aruna Krishnamurthy is Assistant Professor in the English Department at Fitchburg State College in Massachusetts. She has published a number of essays on the topic of the working-class intellectual on figures such as Friedrich Engels, William Cobbett and Mary Collier. Her research interests include themes of class and Empire in the long eighteenth century.

Luke R.J. Maynard received his MA in English from the University of Western Ontario in 2004, and is currently a PhD candidate at the University of Victoria. His work focuses mainly on J.R.R. Tolkien, especially the narrative and textual evolution of Middle-Earth. His other interests include eighteenth-century satire of the British Isles, the Gothic novel, the poetry of the Beat Generation, and the narrative and poetic possibilities of alternative storytelling media ranging from graphic novels to Flash and hypertext.

Ian Peddie's work ranges widely across British and American culture. He has published numerous articles on subjects such as American poetry and prose, popular music, in addition to interviews with a number of authors. He contributed to and edited the collection *The Resisting Muse: Popular Music and Social Protest* and he is currently editing two volumes on contemporary popular music and human rights as well as completing a book that examines representations of class in twentieth-century American culture.

Kathryn Prince is an Assistant Professor in the Department of Theatre at the University of Ottawa. Her main research interest is the post-Renaissance reception and performance of Shakespeare, a broad topic on which she has published a book and numerous articles.

Richard Salmon is a senior lecturer in the School of English, University of Leeds, where he teaches Victorian and Romantic period literature, which also form his research interests. He has published books on Henry James and W.M. Thackeray (forthcoming), as well as numerous articles on various aspects of Victorian literature and culture. He is currently working on a book about Victorian representations of authorship.

Sambudha Sen is affiliated with the Department of English, the University of Delhi. He is the author of *Khaki Shorts and Saffron Flags* (with four others) (1996) and *Dickens's Novels in the "Age of Improvement"* (2000). He has also edited *Mastering Western Texts* (2002). Sen's essays on the fiction of Dickens and Thackeray have appeared in *ELH and Nineteenth Century Literature*. He has been awarded several fellowships which include the Foundation

Fellowship (Clare Hall, Cambridge, 1996), Andrew Mellon Fellowship (1999, The Huntington Library, Pasadena), A Bellagio Residency (2001) and the Leverhulme visiting fellowship 2006, at the Anglia Ruskin University at Cambridge. Sen is working on book length project called *Dickens, Thackeray and the Making of a Popular Novelistic Aesthetic*.

Monica Smith Hart is Assistant Professor of English in the Department of English, Philosophy, and Modern Languages at West Texas A&M University. Her research focuses on class and national identity in romantic and victorian verse.

Acknowledgments

First and foremost, I would like to thank the many contributors to this volume. During the course of our many correspondences, our relationship has grown from that of colleagues to friends. I am grateful for their patience as this book went through its many phases, as well as their receptiveness to my suggestions for revisions. I also want to thank Ann Donahue at Ashgate for her encouragement and patience with the project. Her efficiency and support have been invaluable.

I am especially thankful to my husband, Rahul, and my children, Trisha and Nikhil, for their many sacrifices that made it possible for me to complete this work. I am also very grateful to our parents for their encouragement and support throughout the process. I dedicate this book to my family.

Chapter 1
Introduction

Aruna Krishnamurthy

I will tell you, according to my judgment, what is the line of conduct by which we may obtain [liberty]. It is not by tumult. It is not by violence. It is by reason; by turning our serious attention to facts and principles; by bold and determinate investigation, not to be checked by idle threats, nor turned aside by actual danger.

—John Thelwall

The intellectual spoke the truth to those who had yet to see it, in the name of those who were forbidden to speak the truth: he was conscience, consciousness, and eloquence.

—Michel Foucault

At the height of the Reform Movement of 1832, the Chartist "Corn Law Rhymer" Ebenezer Elliot raised a question that simultaneously approved and revised the production and reception of nineteenth-century Romantic literature: "Poetry is impassioned truth; and why should we not utter it in the shape that touches our condition most closely—the political?"[1] The import of Elliot's question is two-fold: not only that poetry, as a complex personal statement, should respond to politics and become a political utterance, but also, "why should we [i.e. the working classes] not utter it?" The question, signaling as it does, a double transformation—of the working classes through literary self-expression, and literary culture through the political ideals of the working class—forms the critical matrix for this collection of essays that unites two categories—"working class" and "intellectual"—within the social and cultural landscape of eighteenth and mid-nineteenth-century Britain.

Both categories—working class and intellectual—have their own distinct "trailing clouds of etymology."[2] Though the word "intellectual" appeared sporadically in the early nineteenth century, it did not acquire the capacity to

---

[1] Quoted in Martha Vicinus, *The Industrial Muse* (New York: Barnes and Noble, 1974), 94.

[2] Leon Fink et. al. use this term to discuss the category of intellectual: "'Intellectuals,' like most social and political concepts, is constituted by a history of changes in which attempts to define and identify its instances involves an ongoing process of conceptual transformation, expanding, contracting, bending, breaking, establishing, and reestablishing meaning." *Intellectuals and Public Life: Between Radicalism and Reform*, eds Leon Fink, Stephen T. Leonard, and Donald M. Reid (Ithaca: Cornell University Press, 1996), 3–9.

denote a discrete social category until the 1870s.[3] In Zygmunt Bauman's analysis, the rise of the intellectual is linked with the "power/knowledge syndrome" of the Enlightenment which underwrote "a new type of state power with resources and the will necessary to shape and administer the social system according to a preconceived model of order; and the establishment of a relatively autonomous, self-managing discourse able to generate such a model complete with the practices its implementation required."[4] Even more well known is Foucault's vaguely paranoid version of an expert-run society in which knowledge is power, which leads him to declare, "[m]aybe the target ... is not to discover who we are, but to refuse what we are."[5] These essays contribute to the current debates about the shape and function of the intellectual by locating that figure within a class, specifically working class, determination. The dilemma of the Foucauldian intellectual, of turning critique into social action, knowledge into power, is shared by every example of the working-class intellectual, but it is James Epstein's definition of "intellectual" that allows immediate access to that figure in the eighteenth and nineteenth centuries. According to Epstein, rather than viewing the intellectuals as a "distinct social group drawn from certain sections of society involved in 'intellectual' work—the clergy, writers, artists, university professors, certain professionals—and acting with a relatively high degree of independence with regard to their political and social allegiance or identification, it is better to think in a predominantly functional sense of an intellectual as someone who assumes the role of persuader, consciously producing or conveying ideas to a public."[6] The figures that populate these essays—threshers, orators, poets, musicians, scientists, journalists, novelists—though varied in form and function, cohere around the common ground of persuading their very diverse readers and audiences towards a consideration of working-class realities.

The story of the formation of the working class has a long and distinguished lineage in the discipline of history.[7] As a category, "working class" displaced

---

3   Look at T.J. Heyck, "From Men of Letters to Intellectuals: The Transformation of Intellectual Life in Nineteenth-Century England," *The Journal of British Studies*, Vol. 20, No. 1 (Autumn, 1980), 158–183.

4   Zygmunt Bauman, *Legislators and Interpreters: On Modernity, Post-Modernity and Intellectuals* (New York: Polity Press, 1987), 2.

5   Michel Foucault, "Intellectuals and Power" in *Power/Knowledge: Selected Interviews and Other Writings, 1972–1977*, eds and trans. Colin Gordon, et al (New York: Pantheon Books, c1980), 216.

6   James Epstein, "Bred as a Mechanic: Plebeian Intellectuals" in *Intellectuals and Public Life.*

7   Various historians have attempted to deal with the topic of British working-class radicalism from different perspectives. I borrow from D.G. Wright's pithy discussion of some of the positions in *Popular Radicalism: The Working-Class Experience, 1780–1880* (London and New York: Longman, 1988): E.P. Thompson builds upon Gramsci's transactional model, and configures change around the idea of 'moral economy' and 'customary consciousness,' in *Customs in Common* (London: Merlin Press, c1991) a theme

an earlier terminology of "lower ranks" and came into common parlance after the failure of the1832 Reform Movement,[8] in response to the unprecedented impoverishment of the countryside and the displacement of 'lower orders' into urban areas that accompanied creation of industrial England.[9] While the details differ, historians have consistently favored the period from 1790s to 1830s to identify a *sui generis* tradition of working-class presence in the political and public sphere. Most famously, E.P. Thompson and his circle have celebrated the late eighteenth century in terms of a monumental transformation of popular culture brought about by the convergence of disparate radical traditions of coffeehouses, taverns and Dissent, which set the stage for nineteenth century-working class radicalism.[10] While it is indisputable that the potent combination of political and literary conflict of these years yields fertile ground for investigating the rise of the working-class intellectual, the essays in this collection suggest that the plot begins as far back as the early eighteenth century within the "republic of letters"[11] that (at least in theory) valued literacy over class. Working largely within a patronage economy and for a select subscription readership, "laboring" poets such as Stephen Duck, Ann Yearsley, Mary Collier and many others, though cut off from the politics of dissent, creatively manipulated the neo-classical idiom to infect eighteenth-century

---

that will be discussed in some detail in this essay. Harold Perkin prefers to localize the idea of causes and extend it outside economic determinations, where complex inter-relationships between social structures are given a large role in the formation of the working-class consciousness in *The Origin of Modern English Society 1780–1880* (London, 1969). John Foster (who has been called a "platonist marxist" by Thompson) deploys a Leninist model of analysis and identifies discrete stages in the growth of the working classes from a purely economic struggle to an intellectual one in *Class Struggle in the Industrial Revolution* (London, 1974). Gareth Stedman Jones's analysis delinks the idea of a revolutionary class from its anti-capitalist activity in his book, *The Languages of Class* (Cambridge: Cambridge University Press, 1983). Craig Calhoun valorizes the idea of local communities against a unified class theory, while rejecting the idea that class identities would supersede all other considerations in *The Question of Class Struggle* (Oxford: Oxford University Press, 1982).

[8]   See Asa Briggs, "Middle-Class Consciousness in English Politics, 1780–1846," *Past and Present*, No. 9 (April, 1956), 65–74.

[9]   According to D.G. Wright, "by 1780 the language of ranks and orders slowly began to be replaced by the language of class, so that by mid-nineteenth century the old terminology, though still in use, was being substituted by then categorizations 'working classes,' 'middle classes' and 'aristocracy,' or, even more precisely, 'working class' and 'middle class.' Such a change in linguistic usage implicitly recognized that social conflict had become focused on the clash of interests arising from the distribution of wealth, income and power." 2–3.

[10]   E.P. Thompson, *Making of the English Working Class* (New York: Viking, 1964).

[11]   Roger Chartier describes the "republic of letters" as "a concept that united the lettered and the learned, through correspondence and through print" that was "founded on the free engagement of the will, on equality among its interlocutors, and on the absolutely disinterested exercise of the intellect." *The Cultural Origins of the French Revolution* (Durham, NC: Duke University Press, 1991), 26.

literature with the subversive energy of class conflict. In their writings, the central theme that dominates the later tradition of working-class writers, the challenge of plotting working-class identity and its accompanying narrative outside of middle-class determinations, is articulated very effectively, though indirectly. By placing the early and mid-eighteenth century narratives within the putative "making" of working-class identity, I want to suggest a rewriting of that historiography; here, the working-class intellectual in the role of the persuader is recognizable through his or her ability to negotiate between two antithetical affiliations—one proceeding from the intellectual mode of operating within the lexicon of the public sphere, and another, that engages with the reality of class conflict, and renders the worker's experiential and cultural modalities as inherently hostile to that of the public sphere. Further, the insertion of the figure of the intellectual into the larger story of the formation of working-class identity allows for a tripartite rendering of that history—the early eighteenth-century moment that saw the rise of a sporadic but comprehensible "tradition" of working-class poets who wrote for a select readership and within conventional modes and genres; the 1790s era of the radicalized artisan who innovatively adapted the universalistic language of the bourgeois public sphere to the demands of an indigent and restless constituency of readers; and the Chartist era of the 1830s, where the working-class intellectual consolidated the identity of the working classes within a multi-generic, counter hegemonic narrative that reinserted indigenous oral traditions into print culture. In charting the trajectory described, we follow Michael McKeon's approach towards class. According to McKeon, while class (in Marx's discussion) "describes a very particular historical reality, whose particularity is registered by ... class consciousness," as a "simple abstraction" it also functions as an "abstract term to describe a socioeconomic relation and conflict that is generally characteristic of all human societies." Following McKeon, the essays in the collection envision class not "as two distinct categories impinging on each other but a single category comprehended in its temporal multiplicity."[12]

Stephen Duck's now famous "The Thresher's Labour" marks the origin point of the "laboring poets" tradition of the eighteenth century. Published in 1730, the poem appropriates and subverts the seventeenth-century georgic's celebration of agrarian production and industriousness by highlighting the realities of strenuous and under-compensated labor in the fields, glimpsed in lines such as these:

> In briny streams our sweat descends apace,
> Drops from our locks, or trickles down our face.
> No intermission in our works we know;
> The noisy threshall must forever go. ... [13]

---

[12]　Michael McKeon, *The Origins of the English Novel: 1600–1740* (Baltimore: John Hopkins University Press, 1987), 163.

[13]　Stephen Duck, "The Thresher's Labour," in *The Thresher's Labour by Stephen Duck and The Woman's Labour by Mary Collier*, eds E.P. Thompson and Maria Sugden (London: Merlin Press, 1989), ll.42–45.

One of the debates that surrounds the legacy the laboring poets (and lower-class writers that precede them) [14] and is pertinent to this collection, is the difficulty of gauging the precise nature of their involvement with the laboring community on the one hand, and their pursuit of poetry on the other, and the points at which the two come together. John Goodridge polarizes the evaluation of these poets along a materialist vs. aesthetic axis, where elevating the worker's subaltern status devolves upon diminishing his/her poetic achievements:

> Literature was not usually available to these writers, who latched on to whatever texts were available, and their natural first subject matter was their 'situation' in society, which dominated their waking lives (their time, resources and opportunities to read and write). But this does not mean that they had no other aspiration than to record the social history of their lives; and even less that their poems are not poetry, with its characteristics of abstraction, idealization, structural and rhythmic patterns, but merely records. [15]

One of the fallouts of gaining visibility within the eighteenth-century patronage system is the suspicion that has followed these writers from the eighteenth into the twentieth century that they were working in self rather than collective interest. There is, after all, a difference between writing for one's patrons and subscribers and writing for one's people. William J. Christmas reminds us that "many laboring poets saw their writing as means to social advancement, and many used their access to print culture to better themselves economically and socially ... [and] [a]s a group, these poets faced stiff opposition from authors of the gentlemanly classes who often voiced their concerns in the periodical press." [16] The success of the plebeian poets in the literary marketplace was almost entirely dependent upon their ability to exemplify the ideal of a "rustic" or "natural" genius or "heaven-taught ploughman," appellations that most of these poets share. For the plebeian poets,

---

[14] Carey McIntosh extends the problem of middle class influence on working class narratives to the popular literatures of the day: "For example, look at *The London Spy* (1698), a popular (fictitious) tour guide to the sights and sounds of the London underworld by Ned Ward, a tavern-keeper of lower class origins. ... But the first three sentences of *The London Spy* make rambunctious allusion to Diogenes, Socrates, Aristotle, Virgil, and Descartes. The book falls squarely within a family of Renaissance genres grouped by Frank Chandler as "anatomies of rougery:" beggar-books (most popular in the early sixteenth century); cony-catching pamphlets (the tricks of London con men and pickpockets, all the rage in the 1590s); and prison tours (from 1600). ... There is no doubt that Ward was trying to appeal to a popular readership, that is, to sell as many copies of his book as possible, but the language of *The London Spy* derives more from literary than authentic lower-class sources. *Common and Courtly Language: The Stylistics of Social Class in Eighteenth Century English Literature* (University of Pennsylvania Press: Philadelphia, 1986), 14.

[15] John Goodridge, *Rural Life in Eighteenth-Century English Poetry* (Cambridge University Press: Cambridge, 1996), 17.

[16] William J. Christmas, *The Lab'ring Muses Work, Writing, and the Social Order in English Plebeian Poetry, 1730–1830* (Newark and London: University of Delaware and Associated University Presses, 2001), 20.

to be a rustic genius meant the ability to at once affirm and erase one's identity as a worker; at the textual level, it meant incorporating the reality of underpaid labor but confining it within established poetic conventions such as the georgic or the pastoral, and at the social level, to be included in polite circles, but only as an object of curiosity.[17] Joseph Spence's amazement at Stephen Duck's ability to rise above his circumstances underscores the plebeian poet's sense of displacement that accompanied his ascendancy within polite circles (and which may well have contributed to his suicide later): "Stephen read [*Paradise Lost*] over twice or thrice with a Dictionary, before he could understand the Language of it thoroughly. ... Indeed it seems plain to me, that he has got *English* just as we get *Latin*."[18] The cost of worldly success for these poets was a double estrangement—from the polite circles of the patrons and from their own community of workers. For instance, Duck's attempts at self-education between spells of threshing in the field were (perhaps understandably) met with skepticism by his wife, who confided to her neighbors "that her Husband dealt with the Devil, and was going mad because he did nothing all day but talk to himself, and tell his Fingers."[19] Similarly, Mary Leapor, the daughter of a gardener who dabbled in versification was met with suspicion from her neighbors who complained that as a child "she always chose to spend her leisure Hours in Writing and Reading, rather than in those Diversions which young People generally chuse," and were concerned that she "should overstudy herself, and be mopish."[20]

But despite these critical caveats, it is possible to locate Duck's writings at the helm of a novel tradition of working-class letters. As Gustav Klaus shows, the effect of Duck's example on other laborers of the age, such as the bricklayer Robert Tatersal and washerwoman Mary Collier, was considerable.[21] In his "The Bricklayer's Miscellany," Tatersal pays homage to Duck when he asks

> Since Rustic Threshers entertain the Muse
> Why not Bricklayers too their Subjects chuse?

Though Tatersal, like his predecessor Duck, walks the thin line between social mobility and class resentment, the range of literary styles of later writers such as

---

[17] Raynor Unwin links this hostility towards the laboring poet of the eighteenth century with the privatizing of land that replaced an earlier paternalism with class hostility: "[D]uring the eighteenth century there was an increasing reluctance to allow class barriers to be overridden. If a man was born to manual labour the analogy of breaking a horse to the collar young applied. To be a contented labourer it was considered a disaster to be literate. The apprenticeship to husbandry should be one of practical application." *The Rural Muse: Studies in the Peasant Poetry of England* (London: Allen and Unwin, 1954), 48.

[18] Quoted in Raynor Unwin, 51.

[19] Quoted in Unwin, 49.

[20] Quoted in Bridget Hill, *Women, Work, And Sexual Politics In Eighteenth-Century England* (Oxford: B. Blackwell, 1989), 208.

[21] Gustav Klaus, *The Literature of Labour: Two Hundred Years of Working-Class Writing* (New York: St. Martin's Press, 1985).

Ann Yearsley, James Woodhouse and Robert Burns who fall into this tradition of laboring poets, suggests a consolidation and diversification of the laboring-poet tradition. Furthermore, this tradition has a distinctive feature: in the absence of a communitarian idiom (such as one based on universal rights and liberties that defined the 1790s), these poems, while open to the charge of self-interest, are remarkable in their unfiltered images of working conditions; no one who has read Duck's "The Thresher's Labour" and Collier's "The Woman's Labour" can forget the hardnosed farmer and unsympathetic mistress who control their workers. The individualized lament and resentment of these poems are linked directly to the workaday realities of an exploitative economy and the many human agents of that economy, a motif that sometimes gets obscured by the universalist rhetoric of the late eighteenth century. That these articulations are capable of conducting their own indigenous working-class critiques of political economy is readily apparent in Collier's poem, an anti-georgic that ends with the hard-hitting image of "industrious bees" that

> ... do hourly strive
> To bring their Loads of Honey to the Hive;
> Their sordid Owners always reap the Gains
> And poorly recompense their Toil and Pains. (243–246)

All three essays on plebeian poets of the eighteenth century in this collection attempt to rescue the writings of these poets, both from the arbitrations of the eighteenth-century critic, as well as the standardized expectations of working-class radicalism in the twentieth century.[22] William Christmas breaks fresh ground in eighteenth-century scholarship by stepping away from Duck's already canonical "The Thresher's Labour" to consider his more controversially conciliatory poems in *Poems on Several Occasions*. Through numerous close readings Christmas shows how Duck uses the popular Horatian Ode as his poetic material, but rather than merely "translating" the odes, imaginatively reinvents them. For Christmas, Duck's ability to imitate in this way that characterizes the best of neoclassical verse testifies to the emergence of an authentic and autonomous poet who is able to challenge his loss of his poetic identity as a rustic genius. Monica Smith shifts the narrative of the working-class intellectual towards Ann Yearsley, the milkmaid turned poet. While laboring men and women had much in common in terms of their marginalized status within gentlemanly culture, the female plebeian poet

---

[22] For instance, while remarking upon the progression of working-class self-expression from the conventional poetry of Duck and others in 1730s to the lyrical, subjective writings of Yearsley's generation of poets in the 1770s, Klaus notices that "once again, the plebeian poets were merely following tendencies which had been initiated by the forerunners of the Romantics. The impression therefore remains that even though they were opposed to certain elements of established poetic theory, they were still rooted in it. And that is why their works do not represent a completely autonomous current within the development of the national literature." Gustav Klaus, 20.

may be seen as the bearer of a distinct identity defined by gendered as well as class realities. In evaluating the contribution of plebeian poets such as Mary Collier, Mary Leapor, Ann Yearsley, Elizabeth Hands and others, Donna Landry, reading them through the lens of materialist feminism, declares that while "textual traces of elite literary culture overdetermine the site of [their own] textual production," the female tradition "cannot be so easily deracinated, so easily accommodated in the higher social ranks; they tend to remain poor and laboring until their deaths, though some improvement in their circumstances may result from publication."[23] Smith extends Landry's analysis by appraising the ways in which Yearsley both aligns herself with middle-class women such as her patroness Hannah More in privileging education, but also appropriates that demand to address a plebeian consciousness. Yearsley's privileging of the ideal of education in *Poems on Several Occasions* (reminiscent of Duck's project of "imitating" Horatian odes), rather than being symptomatic of middle-class values, acquires a new radical significance when read against the contentious atmosphere of the late 1800s with its manifold voices arguing against the education of the lower classes. Luke Maynard's essay revisits the much-debated legacy of Robert Burns who has variously represented working-class, middle-class and "local-class" (i.e. Scottish) realities. In many ways Burns presents the ideal case for the eighteenth-century laboring intellectual, the self-taught farmhand who successfully (both in worldly and ideological terms) challenges eighteenth-century and romantic literature by yoking class and ethnic identity with vernacular traditions of the Scottish people and adapted the politics of Dissent to that project. But rather than revisiting the theme of Burns's allegiances with his various constituencies, Maynard examines the possibility of a "hybridized" viewpoint (borrowed from gender theorists such as Helene Cixous and Bonnie Zimmerman) that shows how Burns destabilizes the analytical binary itself through his poetry.

The economic and intellectual challenge mounted against the *ancien regime* through the republic of letters is now a well-established narrative within eighteenth-century scholarship.[24] Jurgen Habermas's analysis seamlessly links the economic, political and cultural aspects of the eighteenth century to investigate the "structural transformation of the public sphere:" in this narrative, the creation of a free-market economy emerges through the establishment of civil society through

---

[23]   Donna Landry, *The Muses Of Resistance: Laboring-Class Women's Poetry In Britain, 1739–1796* (Cambridge: Cambridge University Press, 1990), 13–14.

[24]   Ann Goldgar charts the transformation of the bourgeois public sphere as follows: "Shift from the seventeenth-century model to the eighteenth century one is that of the introduction of overt political elements into the republic of letters: from inwardness to social issues, extension of the community of republic of letters into the whole of society. This is the background along with the growing commerce against which we may trace the growth of the English middle class. The flourishing of book trade and print culture necessitated the expansion of the republic of letters from its previous form." *Impolite Learning: Conduct and Community in the Republic of Letters, 1680–1750* (New Haven: Yale University Press, 1995), 2.

an antiauthoritarian and inclusive lexicon that emphasized the "parity of common humanity."[25] The formation of the bourgeois public sphere is inseparable from the rise of a culture of intellectualism whose symbiotic relationship is highlighted by Nancy Fraser as follows:

> [The idea of the public sphere] designated a specific kind of discursive interaction. Here the public sphere connoted an ideal of unrestricted rational discussion of public matters. The discussion was to be open and accessible to all, merely private interests were to be inadmissible, inequalities of status were to be bracketed, and discussants were to deliberate as peers. The result of such discussion would be public opinion in the strong sense of a consensus about the common good.[26]

In Britain, the formation of what Jon Klancher calls "the society of the text" through the proliferation of public journals and Whiggish clubs "cement[ed] an audience of divergent social ranks as equal interlocutors, and galvaniz[ed] a new audience previously unrepresented in the universe of public discourse."[27] While popular magazines of the age, such as *The Gentleman's Magazine*, *Monthly Magazine*, and *Bee* empowered the "commonwealthman" figure of the eighteenth century through the medium of "public opinion,"[28] they sparked off a parallel tradition that is of interest to working-class historians. The parity of common humanity and the task of disseminating public opinion combined with the anti-authoritarian rhetoric of the bourgeois public sphere in order to generate a collective counter-hegemonic working-class identity. This narrative—central to E.P. Thompson's *Making of the English Working Classes*—emphasizes the ways in which intellectual activity transforms an inchoate and 'plebeian' crowd into a 'working class' through an appropriation of the eighteenth-century republic of letters. It is this process that

---

[25] Jurgen Habermas, *Structural Transformation of the Public Sphere*, trans. Thomas Burger and Frederick Lawrence (Cambridge, MA: MIT Press, 1989).

[26] Nancy Fraser, "Rethinking the Public Sphere : A Contribution To The Critique Of Actually Existing Democracy," in *Habermas And The Public Sphere*, ed. Craig Calhoun (Cambridge, MA: MIT Press, c1992), 113.

[27] Jon Klancher, *The Making of English Reading Audiences, 1790–1832* (Madison, WI: University of Wisconsin Press, 1987), 24.

[28] Journals such as *The Gentleman's Magazine* constructed ideals of liberty around the figure of the "independent Whig" defined in 1751 by "Cato" as an anti-authoritarian ideologue, who "scorns all implicit faith in the State, as well as the Church. The Authority of Names is nothing to him; he judges all men by their Actions and Behaviour, and hates a Knave of his own Party, as much as he despises a Fool of another. He consents not that any Man or Body of Men, shall do what they please. He claims a right of examining all public Measures and, if they deserve it, of censuring them. As he never saw much Power possessed without some Abuse, he takes upon him to watch those who have it; and to acquit or expose them according as they apply it to the good of their country, or their crooked Purposes." Caroline Robbins, *The Eighteenth-Century Commonwealthman* (Cambridge: Cambridge University Press, 1959), 120.

underlies the rise of the London Corresponding Society in the 1790s, whose leaders, such as 'Citizen' John Thelwall—artisan-turned-intellectual—advocated that the true meaning of liberty must be located in an "[active] energy of mind" ... [which] must be fought among "thronged and promiscuous audiences," "in theatres and halls of assembly" against Godwin's "solitary abstraction" of philosophic thought.[29]

But while these ideas became more pronounced under the radical leadership of Dissenters, by no means do they represent an exclusive narrative of working class in the eighteenth century.[30] The linking of the categories of working class and intellectual in terms of their common origins in the eighteenth-century milieu allows us to develop a symbiotic (rather than a merely serendipitous) relationship between them—the rise of working-class identity is coterminous with the incursions of working-class men and women into the intellectual sphere of eighteenth- and nineteenth-century Britain. To shift from the plebeian poets to late-eighteenth-century urban poets such as Thelwall, and later, Chartists, reveals lines of continuity and change. Writing in the atmosphere of Dissent and for a readership made literate through Sunday schools, the new working-class writer became a "critic" and eagerly assumed the task of unearthing, in Foucault's words, "a whole set of knowledges that have been disqualified as inadequate to their task or insufficiently elaborated: naive knowledges, located low down on the hierarchy, beneath the required level of cognition or scientificity."[31] Nineteenth-century poet laureate Robert Southey's exemplifies the new spirit when he both affirms and questions the earlier tradition of plebeian poetry, in an attempt to locate an authentic working-class tradition. According to Southey,

---

[29]   John Thelwall, *The Politics of English Jacobinism: Writings of John Thelwall*, ed. Gergory Claeys (Pennsylvania State University Press, 1995), 93–94.

[30]   Since this essay will not be looking at the Dissenters in detail, I use Albert Goodwin's analysis of their legacy to summarize their contributions to eighteenth-century radicalism: "Adequately endowed by their own denominational trust funds, ably staffed by tutors and ministers of wide culture and diversified scientific attainments, and closely connected with Scottish universities, several of these [Dissenting] academies ... had devoted themselves not only to the training of Dissenting ministers, but had also attracted an elite of the aristocratic or professional laity, by offering their pupils a wide general education in modern subjects. Designed in this respect to provide for the needs of those who would later occupy responsible positions in commerce or administration, as well as for the practical education of the landed gentry, their curricula included the study of science, English literature and *belles lettres*, modern languages, history, political theory and economics. ... these institutions trained the remarkable generation of distinguished theologians, scholars and scientists, headed by Dr. Joseph Priestley and Dr. Richard Price, collectively known as Rational Dissenters, who paved the way for modern Unitarianism and won the contemporary repute of being the fomenters of modern English radicalism." *The Friends of Liberty: The English Democratic Movement in the Age of the French Revolution* (Cambridge, MA: Harvard University Press, 1979), 69–70.

[31]   Michel Foucault, *Power/Knowledge: Selected Interviews and Other Writings, 1972–77*, ed. Colin Gordon (New York: Pantheon Books, c1980), 82.

[a] process, indeed, is observable, both in the verses of Woodhouse and Stephen Duck, which might be looked for, as almost inevitable: they began by expressing their own thoughts and feelings, in their own language; all of which, owing to their stations in life, had a certain charm of freshness as well as truth; but that attraction passes away when they begin to form their style upon some approved model, and they begin to produce just such verses as any person, with a metrical ear, may be taught to make a receipt.[32]

This process of questioning and self-affirmation reaches its apogee in the Chartist era, with the creation of a literary subculture that self-consciously battled for its dominance in the literary and political field. In the electrified atmosphere of the years leading up to 1848, Mary Leman Gillies is able to assert: "It is now fairly a race between the classes; and I fancy that the energetic sons of the people, such as can write *The Purgatory's Suicide*, and *The Baron's Yule*, with the few hours that they ring from toil, or snatch from rest, will out-run the college-taught and castle-protected sons of fortune."[33] It is precisely this coming together of class experience and intellectual activity, and its potential to simultaneously transform intellectual and working-class culture of the age, that (like Ebeneezer Elliot) Thomas Cooper advocates in the Chartist Manifesto of 1850, in "To the Young Men of the Working Classes:"

[it is] a matter of the highest necessity, that you all join hands and head to create a literature of your own. Your own prose, your own poetry ... would put you all the more fully in possession of each other's thoughts and thus give you a higher respect for each other, and a clearer perception of what you can do when united.[34]

It is also interesting to note that at the other end of the spectrum, the creation of a radical working class was accompanied by the conversion of the "man of letters" into an "intellectual" who is both intimately linked with and set apart from this new class of readers. According to Heyck, these new men of letters "were expected to be useful, as entertainers, providers of an anodyne, or, most significantly, as moral leaders and guides ... . [and were] expected to help the audience through the troubles of economic, social, and religious change."[35] In his new role as a social critic the intellectual sought to close the gap between himself and his readers: as Heyck says, the mid-nineteenth century writers "knew their audiences, and understood how ideas and rhetoric would resonate in their readers' minds."[36] The writings of Alexander Somerville and William Cobbett, for example, are interesting for studying the effects of this familiarity with an

---

[32]   Robert Southey, *The Lives and Works of the Uneducated Poets*, ed. J.S. Childers (London: n.p., 1925), 118.

[33]   Quoted in Klaus, 139.

[34]   Quoted in Vicinus, 108–109.

[35]   Heyck, 160.

[36]   Ibid.

impoverished audience upon the lexicon of classical republicanism. [37] It is not coincidental that this version of the intellectual—termed by Carl Boggs as the "Jacobin intellectual"—gained ascendancy in the late eighteenth century, in the same socio-cultural terrain that frames Thompson's *Making of the English Working Class*. According to Boggs, the Jacobin intellectual, capturing Romantic and Enlightenment strains of rationalism and reformation found his or her identity by radically redefining an earlier lineage of intellectuals:

> The type of intellectual predominant in preindustrial society was the detached, genteel, cleric or scholar who monopolized the traditional forms of discourse. While appearing in some respects to stand "above" class divisions, this stratum was the bearer of hegemonic ideologies that justified aristocratic power, the monarchy, and the church. With the revolutionary turbulence of late eighteenth and nineteenth century Europe, the traditional intellectual gave way, at crucial junctures, to the Jacobin mode of intellectual whose historical debut arrived with the French revolution and whose political role in countries like the United States, Italy, and Russia was also decisive. [38]

The new image cast intellectuals "as Promethean agents of social transformation or, less frequently, of stability and order."[39] A closer consideration of Boggs's analysis suggests the relevance of Gramsci's rather elusive categories of the "traditional" and "organic" intellectual that are pertinent for this collection as well. If traditional intellectuals (linked with feudal society) are defined by their specialized role as professional and political mediators who sequester and maintain "knowledge" outside of structures of power—or, in Gramsci's words, "put themselves forward as autonomous and independent of the dominant social group"—the organic intellectual (linked with civic/bourgeois society), emerges from within a particular class, forges a direct link between knowledge and power, and becomes instrumental in shaping class identity through the deployment of that knowledge. Gramsci further emphasizes that "[o]ne of the most important characteristics of any group that is developing towards dominance is its struggle to assimilate and to conquer 'ideologically' the traditional intellectuals, but this assimilation and conquest is made quicker and more efficacious the more the group in question succeeds in

---

[37]   See my "'Assailing the THING': Politics of Space in William Cobbett's *Rural Rides*," in *Romantic Textualities*, No. 7 (December, 2001) that examines how William Cobbett in his *Rural Rides* (1821–1830) transfigures the rural topos of early-nineteenth-century England into a dystopia of Enclosures and taxation. But rather than the language of political economy employed by working-class journals, Cobbett uses a civic-humanist frame of reference that equates the disintegration of working-class communities with the loss of a paternal and hierarchical society. I argue that Cobbett's politics of nostalgia is significant despite its obvious limitations as it generates an organic and "physical" narrative that not only gives a human face to the disadvantaged worker, but also questions the abstract and "rational" method of Malthus and middle-class political economy.

[38]   Carl Boggs, *Intellectuals and the Crisis of Modernity* (SUNY Press, 1993), 3.

[39]   Boggs, 16.

simultaneously elaborating its own organic intellectuals."[40] Viewed from this lens, the Jacobin intellectual seems to be poised for the realization of class-in-itself.

But, interestingly, Gramsci's analysis of the English situation reveals a peculiar alliance between the traditional and organic intellectual that, in a sense, collapses the gap between the two. According to Gramsci,

> In England ... [t]he new social grouping that grew up on the basis of modern industrialism shows a remarkable economic-corporate development but advances only gropingly in the intellectual-political field. There is a very extensive category of organic intellectuals—those, that is, who come into existence on the same industrial terrain as the economic group—but in the higher sphere we find that the old landowning class preserves its position of virtual monopoly. It loses its economic supremacy but maintains for a long time a political-intellectual supremacy and is assimilated as "traditional intellectuals" and as a directive group by the new group in power.[41]

Historians of the British working class have cast this residual presence and enormous influence of the (pre-industrial) lexicon of classical republicanism— glimpsed in the "commonwealthman" figure—in radical circuits in terms of the "peculiarities of the English," a theme to which I will return. In Isaac Kramnick's analysis, the rhetoric of classical republicanism "conceives of human beings as political animals who realize themselves only through participation in public life ... concerned primarily with the public good, *res publica*, or commonweal, not with private or selfish ends."[42] The unlikely alliance between upper-class leaders such as Sir Francis Burdett and Henry "Orator" Hunt and the working-class crowd that characterized much of early-nineteenth-century radicalism can be made seen as the outcome of the rhetoric of classical republicanism that trickled from Dissent into the lives of working men.[43] But classical republicanism, though providing the

---

[40]   Antonio Gramsci, *Selections from Prison Notebooks*, eds and trans. Hoare and Smith (New York: International Publishers, 1978), 10.

[41]   Gramsci, 18.

[42]   Isaac Kramnick, *Republicanism and Bourgeois Radicalism: Political Ideology in Late Eighteenth-Century England and America* (Ithaca: Cornell University Press, 1990), 20.

[43]   Paul Keen's analysis links the republican rhetoric with the formation of bourgeois individualism: "[I]t was precisely authors' immersion within the individualist ethos of commercial society that made classical republicanism attractive as a mediating language capable of establishing an important cultural role for authors: an identity-in-difference which situated authors both within and above the division of labour. To put it another way, the discourse of classical republicanism gained its value as a descriptive paradigm precisely because it did *not* accurately reflect the ethos of modern commercialism which necessarily characterized eighteenth-century literary production. It enabled authors to say something unique about themselves, to argue for a privileged discursive position by recuperating the possibility of disinterested commitment to the general good—a quality that was traditionally viewed as the sole prerogative of an elite community distinguished by landed wealth." *The Crisis of Literature in the 1790s: Print Culture and the Public Sphere* (New York: Cambridge University Press, 2006), 84.

language of radicalism until at least the 1832 Reform movement, faced a challenge from liberalist ideology, that Kramnick identifies as a "modern self-interested, competitive, individualistic ideology emphasizing private rights."[44]

Recasting the early nineteenth century in terms of the conflict between a residual republicanism and an emergent liberalism allows us to incorporate Gramsci's analysis into the central question: the formation of the working-class intellectual, rather than being entirely subsumed by the larger narrative of the political and cultural fallout with the bourgeois public sphere (glimpsed in Elliot's question), traffics with a related but different need in which we may glimpse the introjection of a "liberalist" ideology. While the worker's experience of political, cultural and economic exclusion radicalizes the intellectual production of the age in unprecedented ways, it is equally true that the public sphere, shaped as it was by intellectual activity, exerted a parallel pressure—a kind of 'epistemic violence'— on the creation of working-class identity. The following example of a plea made by a "Poor Student" to the readers of the *Gentleman's Magazine* in 1796 reveals the ways in which the republic of letters both empowers (as an equal interlocutor) and (we may say) interpellates the worker within a new intellectual identity:

> From a *boy* ... I have been particularly fond of *study*, and the love of books increases with increasing years. Unfortunately for me, my finances are too narrow to enable me to enjoy that learned leisure, which is peculiarly adapted to my inclinations ... With a mind not uncultivated, and inclination thus ardent in the pursuit of knowledge, I find myself ill-calculated to undertake any servile employment in order to live.[45]

On the one hand, there is the "accessibility, the social neutrality of reason, and the ever-expanding diffusion of knowledge,"[46] offered by new ethos; on the other, its utopian promise is circumscribed by class. The disadvantaged worker's desire to enter into that paradigm can only be enacted as a split in his identity that at once confirms and erases his status as a subaltern. For the worker, identity is produced through the discovery of intellectual capacities that, within a modality of bourgeois individualism, has to sublate a prior class identity. Predictably, Thomas Cooper himself becomes the site of this double narrative where the (re)structuring of the public sphere through the worker's agency is paralleled (or even cancelled) by the inscription of the worker's identity within the public sphere. Cooper's anxiety to conform to the intellectual culture of his times expresses itself as an endorsement of an Arnoldian vision of literature that contrasts with the earlier project of consolidating a working-class canon:

> I thought it possible that by the time I reached the age of twenty-four I might be able to master the elements of Latin, Greek, Hebrew, and French; might well get through Euclid, and through a course of algebra; might commit the entire

---

[44]   Kramnick, 35.

[45]   Quoted in Paul Keen, 76.

[46]   Paul Keen, 13.

'Paradise Lost,' and seven best plays of Shakespeare to memory; and might read a large and solid course of history, and of religious evidences; and be well acquainted also with the current literature of the day.[47]

Cooper's example is not unique: Henry Mayhew reports that in nineteenth century, the most popular books for working-class readers were *Rasselas, The Vicar of Wakefield, Peregrine Pickle, Tom Jones,* Goldsmith's histories, *The Sentimental Journey, Pilgrim's Progress, Robinson Crusoe, Philip Quarles, Telemachus, Gil Blas,* the letters of Junius, Shakespeare, Pope, James Thomson, William Cowper, Burns, Byron and Scott.[48] Jonathan Rose has focused much attention on what he calls "working-class cultural conservatism" that was so pervasive that even "[a]t the dawn of the twentieth century, when literary modernism was emerging, the self-educated working classes had only just mastered the great English classics."[49] In his *Intellectual Life of the British Working Class*[50] Rose inscribes the conservative taste of working class readership as corrective to (Marxist) conceptions of "class as economic in origin, exclusive in scope and conflictual in implication."[51] For Rose, the history of audiences generates an alternate historical methodology for evaluating working-class identity, away from a narrowly materialistic approach, while functioning as a corrective to cultural studies' narrowly textual interpretation of subaltern politics. James Raven reveals the details of this approach:

> The decoding of the reading experience, more textual creation than passive reception, embraces study of diverse reading sites, different performative modes (including individual or communal reading aloud), and multiple effects upon auditors and participants. Texts foster unintentional meanings, which are, in effect, codes of perception ordered and enacted by individual readers. Such a reading history or social history of the reader can tell us more about what a text is and what reading means as an historical force. It might suggest how particular readers read a text and become aware of belonging to a greater or particular audience, and one which might transcend such social classification as profession, gender and religion.[52]

To come back to the main argument: seen from the perspective of his investment in the public sphere, the working-class intellectual appears to be a liminal figure

---

[47]   Quoted in James Epstein, "Bred as a Mechanic," 64.

[48]   See Jonathan Rose, "A Conservative Canon: Cultural Lag in British Working-Class Reading Habits," *Libraries and Culture,* Vol. 33, No. 1 (Winter, 1998), 98–99.

[49]   Rose, "A Conservative Canon: Cultural Lag in British Working-Class Reading Habits," 100.

[50]   Jonathan Rose, *Intellectual Life of the British Working Class* (New Haven, CT: Yale University Press, 2001).

[51]   James Thompson, "After the Fall: Class and Political Language in Britain, 1780–1900," *The Historical Journal,* Vol. 39, No. 3 (September, 1996), 792.

[52]   James Raven, "New Reading Histories, Print Culture, and the Identification of Change: The Case of Eighteenth-Century England," *Social History,* Vol. 23, No. 3 (October, 1998), 270.

for whom intellect functions as, borrowing Gayatri Spivak's words, "the symbolic circuit of the mobilizing of subalternity into hegemony."[53] In this version of events, as Epstein says, "the act of writing itself ... constitute[s] a 'symbolic rupture,' empowering such plebeian intellectuals in the cause of liberty but simultaneously distancing them from the world of the artisan's workbench."[54] It is this aspect of the bourgeois public sphere that Nancy Fraser, following Marx through Foucault, associates with "political domination" in order to rewrite its legacy of the parity of common humanity. According to Fraser,

> [the] elaboration of a distinctive culture of civil society and of an associated public sphere was implicated in the process of bourgeois class formation; its practices and ethos were markers of 'distinction' in Pierre Bourdieu's sense, ways of defining the emergent elite, of setting it off from the older aristocratic elites it was intent upon displacing on the one hand and from the various popular and plebeian strata it aspired to rule on the other.[55]

The agonistic ambivalence of the bourgeois public sphere replicated itself in the split identity of the working-class intellectual who may be seen as a double agent of conflict and consent. Hegemony translates into the repeated stress laid on "discipline" and "reason" by leaders such as Thelwall, as can be glimpsed from this speech at Copenhagen-House in 1795:

> I will tell you, according to my judgment, what is the line of conduct by which we may obtain it [liberty]. It is not by tumult. It is not by violence. It is by reason; by turning our serious attention to facts and principles; by bold and determinate investigation, not to be checked by idle threats, nor turned aside by actual danger.[56]

The intellectual's fluctuation between middle-class values and working-class culture can be glimpsed in the social mobility of Francis Place. Apprenticed a tailor, Place rose from impoverishment to become a prominent leader within the

---

[53]   Gayatri Chakravarty Spivak, "Can the Subaltern Speak?" in *Marxism and the Interpretation of Culture*, eds Cary Nelson and Larry Grossberg (Chicago: University of Illinois Press, 1988), 271–313.

[54]   James Epstein, "Bred as a Mechanic," 69.

[55]   Nancy Fraser, p. 116–117. Zygmunt Bauman further links the hegemonic aspect of the bourgeois public sphere with the role of the intellectual: "At the time it entered the west European vocabulary, the concept of 'the intellectuals' drew its meaning from the collective memory of the Enlightenment era. It was in that era that the power/knowledge syndrome, a most conspicuous attribute of modernity, had been set. The syndrome was the joint product of two novel developments which took place at the beginning of the modern times: the emergence of a new type of state power with resources and the will necessary to shape and administer the social system according to a preconceived model of order; and the establishment of a relatively autonomous, self-managing discourse able to generate such a model complete with the practices its implementation required" (Bauman, 2).

[56]   Thelwall, 9.

LCS in the nineteenth century. Place's exposure to the world of letters resulted in a disavowal of working-class culture, and a vehement rejection of "taverns and tavern company," with the declaration, "I cannot drink, I cannot for any considerable time consent to converse with fools."[57] For Place, the London Corresponding Society was valuable only for its ability to inculcate middle-class values that Kramnick associates with "order, routine and subordination in factory, school, poorhouse, and prison,"[58] a locale where men were induced "to read instead of spending time at public houses ... [and] elevate them[selves] in their own opinion." [59] In his consensual role, the working-class intellectual appears analogous to the "disciplinarian capitalist" who, according to James Mill, "should be in loco parentis to the poor, guiding and restraining them like children." [60]

The contradictory roles of the intellectual leads R. Radhakrishnan to raise a question that underlies this project as a whole: "Situated as absences within a theoretical historiography not their own, these [subjugated] knowledges are faced with a problem at the moment of their insurrection. Where will they speak from: rupturally from within the hegemonic body or from a position "without" that is not complicitous with the mandates of the official body of knowledge?"[61] Historians have responded to this dilemma by shifting the narrative of the "making" of the working class away from a materialist analysis to a more discourse oriented one, an analytical mode that especially dominates discussions of Chartism. In the work of Gareth Stedman Jones, for example, "class" is a word that is "embedded in language ... and should be analyzed in its linguistic context."[62] Patrick Joyce's declaration, "the consciousness of a class need not be the consciousness of class"[63] also advocates a move away from economic determinants of class identity and towards a more amorphous sense of working-class self-representation. To borrow Marc Steinberg's appraisal of the postmodernist turn in the narrative of

---

[57] Quoted in E.P. Thompson, *Making of the English Working Class* (New York: Viking, 1964), 58.

[58] Kramnick, 81.

[59] Quoted in *Making*, 155. Iain McCalman has examined the methods and effects of Place's middle-class values by placing them within a parallel low-brow trajectory espoused by the Spencean circle towards the end of the eighteenth century. In this reading Place's emphasis on respectability and sobriety become markers for distinguishing him from the insurrectionary discourse of Thomas Evans and Spence, a demarcation that did much harm to the reputation of the Spenceans. *The Radical Underworld: Prophets, Revolutionaries, and Pornographers in London, 1795–1840* (Cambridge: Cambridge University Press, 1988).

[60] J.S. Mill, *Principles of Political Economy*, Book IV, Chapter 7 (New York: A.M. Kelley, 1965), 753.

[61] R. Radhakrishnan, "Towards an Effective Intellectual: Foucault or Gramsci?," in *Intellectuals: Aesthetics, Politics, Academics*, ed. Bruce Robbins (Minneapolis: University of Minnesota Press, c1990), 63.

[62] Gareth Stedman Jones, 7.

[63] Patrick Joyce, *Visions Of The People*, 15.

class identity, "[t]he postmodernists argue that meaning is created not in the crucible of experience, that struggle centres around the construction of mobile identities, not enduring motives predicated on shared material interests, and that the historical process itself is not so much a tale of collective human agency but of discursive formations."[64] But inscribing the worker entirely within a post-representationalist vocabulary overwrites the very real impact of working-class presence in the public sphere, a subject that has inspired a number of recent scholars to rewrite the legacy of the bourgeois public sphere. The Chartist moment is striking for a quality of immanence where labor activism on the streets is matched by a cultural narrative that, despite its many significant failings, in the words of Anne Janowitz, "offer[ed] conventions for group identity, and a social matrix within which people could discover themselves as belonging to an on-going set of traditions, goals, and expectations."[65] But even more interesting is the idea that through the combination of these two aspects that address the literature of politics and the politics of literature, rendered by recent historians as alternately complementary and contradictory, Chartist writers shape their own critical reception in history. In Paul Keen's analysis, like in many of the recent studies of eighteenth- and nineteenth-century print culture, the creation of working-class counterpublics suggests nothing less than the breakdown of Enlightenment logocentrism itself:

> [T]he democratization of reading did not just expand the reading public, it fractured it into multiple overlapping publics with competing priorities, points of consensus, and normative assumptions. Reason, far from operating as a consolidating dream of a discursive position beyond social difference ... had become an important site of contestation—'a dangerously unstable zone'—in itself.[66]

For Janowitz, the "communitarian" narrative generated by working-class intellectuals provides a crucial challenge to the more "individualist" lyric espoused by the Romantic artist in the early nineteenth century. Iain McCalman rewrites the entire political landscape of the late eighteenth century through his focus on the pornographers, prophets, and revolutionaries such as Thomas Spence, Robert Wedderburn, whose status as *lumpenproletariat* threatened the more respectable forms of radicalism espoused by the London Corresponding Society.

As the nineteenth century wore on, the earlier moment of synergy between the working class's need for reconstituting itself and the inauguration of the new intellectual tended toward a mutually critical framework. With the growing presence of the working classes in the public sphere, the intellectual's identity

---

[64] Marc W. Steinberg, "'A Way of Struggle': Reformations and Affirmations of E.P. Thompson's Class Analysis in the Light of Postmodern Theories of Language," *The British Journal of Sociology*, Vol. 48, No. 3 (September, 1997), 472.

[65] Anne Janowitz, *Lyric and Labor in the Romantic Tradition* (Cambridge: Cambridge University Press, 2005), 135.

[66] Keen, 140.

came to be measured in terms of his or her distance from that public sphere that validated his or her role as an "expert." Tennyson's "nausea" at the prospect that "his honest thoughts in type" may be smeared by the Chartist mechanic's "bloody thumb" forms the backdrop for a new intellectual identity in the middle of the nineteenth century that, Heyck says "reflected a desire by thinkers, and writers to separate themselves from the limitations imposed by the immediate desires and needs of the general public ... . to break away from a market relation with their publics in order to pursue some kind of self-validating scholarship or art."[67] Rose forges a more direct link between the aesthetic turn of the late nineteenth century and the presence of a working-class readership: "The intellectuals feared the masses not because they were illiterate but because, by the early twentieth century, they were becoming more literate, thanks to public education, adult education, scholarships, and cheap editions of great books. If more and more working people were reading the classics, if they were closing the cultural gap between themselves and the middle classes, how could intellectuals preserve their elite status as arbiters of taste and custodians of rare knowledge."[68] Twentieth-century intellectuals, often excoriated as "cultural elite," continue that symbiotic relationship between class (now caught in the figure of the ordinary man) and intellectual production. As Bruce Robbins laments, in the present times the intellectual is more often than not represented as

> an elite whose privileges are based not on a skill and accomplishments in the real world of production, but only on the acquisition of culture, which is to say on something unproductive, unreal, or at least unverifiable, a matter of minority taste and arbitrary fashion. Estranged from the solid values of ordinary people, therefore, while it is also neglectful of their economic needs, not to speak of the greater urgencies of the "disadvantaged," culture can only be intended to bolster the interests of the elite itself.[69]

In *The Holy Family* Marx discusses the experience of "human self-estrangement"— which we may translate into the figure of the intellectual—in ways that are central to both bourgeois and working-class subjects:

> The propertied class and the class of the proletariat present the same human self-estrangement. But the former class feels at ease and strengthened in this self-estrangement, it recognizes estrangement as its own power and has in it the semblance of a human existence. The class of the proletariat feels annihilated in estrangement; it sees in it its own powerlessness and the reality of an inhuman existence.[70]

---

[67]   Heyck, 182.

[68]   Jonathan Rose, "A Conservative Canon," 102.

[69]   Bruce Robbins, *Secular Vocations: Intellectuals, Professionalism, Culture* (London: Verso, 1993), 1–2.

[70]   Karl Marx, *The Holy Family*, trans. Richard Dixon and Clement Dutts, MECW, Vol. 4 (Moscow: Progress Publishers, 1975).

The experience of self-estrangement, reflected in the twin agons of middle-class culture—as a debilitating "alienation" *and* a morally permissible "disinterestedness"—becomes the central ingredient of the worker's identity, but only in its destructive capacity. The important question is, how can that estrangement present itself outside of narratives that convert it into "semblance of human existence?" For Bruce Robbins the answers lie not in "counterhegemonic" practices, but in "antihegemonic" ones. In Robbins' analysis, the intellectuals' "unique subject positions" do not depend upon "their critical mass or their growing significance to the prevailing social order." Rather, "the issue is whether they can represent themselves politically in a manner similar to the great social classes of the bourgeois epoch." The counterhegemonic intellectual is "the voice of the voiceless" crowd "which can insert itself into history only through the instrumentality of his voice." But it is antihegemonic intellectual who really subverts the Enlightenment, who "represents not a political class but a desire that languishes on the margins," and whose "transgression consists in suggesting an alternative moral order in which freedom is defined as much by the unfettered exercise of desire as by political rights." [71]

For the plebeian intellectuals of the eighteenth century—Duck, Yearsley and Burns—counterhegemonic struggles were largely defined by their quest for status within a highly exclusionary literary culture, even if it meant occupying the roles of a "traditional intellectual." The late eighteenth and nineteenth century essays respond to a distinct shift in working-class literature and politics with the strengthening of print culture and a corresponding radicalization of the worker's identity. The eighteenth-century binaries of traditional vs. organic, hegemonic vs. counterhegemonic are central here as well, but also, in response to the "dictatorship of the bourgeoisie," is the question of the antihegemonic intellectual. The evaluative standard is one based on Radhakrishnan's idea that the precondition of the intellectual's "solidarity with a revolutionary politics" is that "this intellectual allow him/herself to be represented and reparsed within the syntax of the emerging subaltern politics."[72] Aruna Krishnamurthy's discussion of John Thelwall establishes a homology between his radicalism and that of the London Corresponding Society. While Thelwall creates a blueprint for working-class identity by recasting the ignored, invisible and oppressed people of the late eighteenth century within the rational humanism of the Enlightenment, his middle-class orientation limits the scope of that working-class anti-authoritarianism. An in depth examination of Chartist literary culture and "radical expression" of the 1800s is provided by four essays. First, Rob Breton revisits Ebeneezer Elliot's linking of the politics and poetics by examining the impact of sensational literature upon the more overtly radical discourse of Chartism. While the use of melodramatic tactics as entertainment might be at odds with the serious business of creating working-class literature, for Breton it presents a healthy counter to

---

[71]   Bruce Robbins, *Intellectuals*, 11.
[72]   Radhakrishnan, 75.

the culture of intellectualism and education that threatened to dominate Chartist culture; in Breton's analysis populism *is* political. In Kathryn Prince's essay the problematic "cultural conservatism" of working-class readers is examined through the centrality of Shakespeare in Chartist magazines such as *The Black Dwarf*. But the presence of Shakespeare in the radical circuit, rather than indoctrinating the worker into elite aesthetic ideals, has the opposite effect of reinscribing his legacy within the demands—of both conflict and consent—that defined the Chartist movement. Sambudha Sen establishes a more direct but reverse link between radical and bourgeois aesthetics in mid-nineteenth century: in his analysis it is the radical caricaturists such as William Hone and George Cruickshank that shape the novelistic technique of middle-class writers such as Thackeray and Dickens, rather than the other way around. Sen examines the stylistic aura of the language of radicalism backwards to Paine and forward to Dickens; in Dickens's technique that combines the visual and the linguistic he locates the afterlife of radical expression that moved from militant artisanal politics to the drawing rooms of pro reform middle class-consumers. Richard Salmon provides another examination of the traffic between radical and middle-class narratives through an in-depth examination of Charles Kingsley's *Alton Locke* whose Chartist hero captures middle-class understandings and anxieties regarding the proliferation of radical culture. Salmon filters the image of the Chartist as an "unaccredited hero" through the well-established Carlylean paradigm of Robert Burns, the mid-Victorian *bildungsroman*, and the tradition of self-improvement that dominated the working-class canon, all of which exchange the radicalism implicit in being "unaccredited" with an emphasis on the conditions upon which he might become visible—the ideal of gaining credit in a market economy. The next two essays depart from the tradition of the counterhegemonic intellectual to shed light upon upwardly mobile working-class writers and intellectuals in the figures of Alexander Somerville and Michael Faraday, men who took advantage of the mid-nineteenth century culture of radical expression and self-improvement. Julie Codell's essay uses the figure of Somerville to depict the working-class intellectual as an ensemble of contrary aims and loyalties: Somerville disliked the Chartists, but was deeply sympathetic to the working classes, he was patriotic, but had a well-developed anti-authoritarian streak, he benefited from middle-class ideals of self-improvement but expressed a deep-seated ressentiment against the anti-Corn-law Cobden that distinguished him from the compliant attitude of Francis Place. Alice Jenkins describes an essay-circle of young London artisans who met monthly between July 1818 and December 1819 to read and criticize one another's literary productions, and analyzes in particular one of its member's—Michael Faraday's—impact on ideas of class and intellectual aspiration from Regency to High Victorian Britain. Inured into middle-class values of self-help, clearly aspiring class mobility, and inspired by the conservative Sandemanian Church, Faraday and his circle form an intriguing conformist counterpart to other artisanal groups of the early nineteenth century that met to debate Reform. What is interesting about the narratives generated by this group is that their middle-class ideals are not complemented by the formation of a "bourgeois" subject; rather than relying upon the individualism found in working-class autobiographies of the age, Faraday galvanizes an atavistic neo-classical lexicon in his writings. Finally, Ian Peddie's essay examines the bifurcation between working-class and middle-class cultures in his essay through the rise and fall of working-class narratives and artists in the music halls of Victorian England, which he depicts as a battleground for working-class resistance against middle-class cultural appropriation. Peddie shows how the "antithetical radicalism" of singers such as Ned Corvan and stock working-class figures such as the cockney costermonger were targeted by mid-Victorian capitalism and ended up staging its idioms of morality.

Works Cited

Bauman, Zygmunt. *Legislators and Interpreters: On Modernity, Post-Modernity and Intellectuals*. New York: Polity Press, 1987.

Boggs, Carl. *Intellectuals and the Crisis of Modernity.* SUNY Press, 1993.

Briggs, Asa. "Middle-Class Consciousness in English Politics, 1780–1846," *Past and Present*, No. 9 (April, 1956), 65–74.

Calhoun, Craig. *The Question of Class Struggle*. Oxford: Oxford University Press, 1982.

———. ed. *Habermas and the Public Sphere*. Cambridge, MA: MIT Press, c1992.

Chartier, Roger. *The Cultural Origins of the French Revolution.* Durham, NC: Duke University Press, 1991.

Christmas, William J. *The Lab'ring Muses Work, Writing, and the Social Order in English Plebeian Poetry, 1730–1830.* Newark and London: University of Delaware and Associated University Presses, 2001.

Duck, Stephen. "The Thresher's Labour," in *The Thresher's Labour by Stephen Duck and The Woman's Labour by Mary Collier*, eds E.P. Thompson and Maria Sugden. London: Merlin Press, 1989.

Epstein, James. "Bred as a Mechanic: Plebeian Intellectuals," in *Intellectuals and Public Life*: *Between Radicalism and Reform*, eds Leon Fink et al. Ithaca: Cornell University Press, 1996.

Fink, Leon, Stephen T. Leonard, and Donald M. Reid, eds. *Intellectuals and Public Life: Between Radicalism and Reform*. Ithaca: Cornell University Press, 1996.

Forster, John. *Class Struggle in the Industrial Revolution.* London, 1974.

Foucault, Michel. *Power/Knowledge: Selected Interviews and Other Writings, 1972–77*, ed. Colin Gordon. New York: Pantheon Books, c1980.

Fraser, Nancy. "Rethinking the Public Sphere: A Contribution to the Critique of Actually Existing Democracy," in *Habermas And The Public Sphere*, ed. Craig Calhoun. Cambridge, MA: MIT Press, c1992.

Goldgar, Ann. *Impolite Learning: Conduct and Community in the Republic of Letters, 1680–1750*. New Haven: Yale University Press, 1995.

Goodridge, John. *Rural Life in Eighteenth-Century English Poetry*. Cambridge University Press: Cambridge, 1996.

Goodwin, Albert. *The Friends of Liberty: The English Democratic Movement in the Age of the French Revolution.* Cambridge, MA: Harvard University Press, 1979.

Gramsci, Antonio. *Selections from Prison Notebooks*, eds and trans., Hoare and Smith. New York: International Publishers, 1978.

Heyck, T.J. "From Men of Letters to Intellectuals: The Transformation of Intellectual Life in Nineteenth-Century England," *The Journal of British Studies*, Vol. 20, No. 1 (Autumn, 1980), 158–183.

Hill, Bridget. *Women, Work, and Sexual Politics In Eighteenth-Century England.* Oxford: B. Blackwell, 1989.

Janowitz, Anne. *Lyric and Labor In The Romantic Tradition.* Cambridge: Cambridge University Press, 2005.

Keen, Paul. *The Crisis of Literature in the 1790s: Print Culture and the Public Sphere.* New York: Cambridge University Press, 2006.

Klancher, Jon. *The Making of English Reading Audiences, 1790–1832.* Madison, WI: University of Wisconsin Press, 1987.

Klaus, Gustav. *The Literature of Labour: Two Hundred Years of Working-Class Writing.* New York: St. Martin's Press, 1985.

Kramnick, Isaac. *Republicanism and Bourgeois Radicalism: Political Ideology in Late Eighteenth-Century England and America.* Ithaca: Cornell University Press, 1990.

Krishnamurthy, Aruna. "'Assailing the THING': Politics of Space in William Cobbett's *Rural Rides*," *Romantic Textualities*, No. 7 (December, 2001).

Landry, Donna. *The Muses of Resistance: Laboring-Class Women's Poetry In Britain, 1739–1796.* Cambridge: Cambridge University Press, 1990.

McCalman, Iain. *The Radical Underworld: Prophets, Revolutionaries, and Pornographers in London, 1795–1840.* Cambridge: Cambridge University Press, 1988.

McIntosh, Carey. *Common and Courtly Language: The Stylistics of Social Class in Eighteenth Century English Literature.* Philadelphia: University of Pennsylvania Press, 1986.

McKeon, Michael. *The Origins of the English Novel: 1600–1740.* Baltimore: Johns Hopkins University Press, 1987.

Marx, Karl. *The Holy Family*, trans. Richard Dixon and Clement Dutts, MECW, Vol. 4. Moscow: Progress Publishers, 1975.

Mill, J.S. *Principles of Political Economy.* New York: A.M. Kelley, 1965.

Perkin, Harold. *The Origin of Modern English Society 1780–1880.* London, 1969.

Radhakrishnan, R. "Towards an Effective Intellectual: Foucault or Gramsci?" in *Intellectuals: Aesthetics, Politics, Academics*, ed. Bruce Robbins. Minneapolis: University of Minnesota Press, c1990.

Raven, James. "New Reading Histories, Print Culture, and the Identification of Change: The Case of Eighteenth-Century England," *Social History*, Vol. 23, No. 3 (October, 1998), 268–287.

Robbins, Bruce. *Secular Vocations: Intellectuals, Professionalism, Culture*. London: Verso, 1993.

————. ed. *Intellectuals: Aesthetics, Politics, Academics*. Minneapolis: University of Minnesota Press, c1990.

Robbins, Caroline. *The Eighteenth-Century Commonwealthman*. Cambridge: Cambridge University Press, 1959.

Rose, Jonathan. "A Conservative Canon: Cultural Lag in British Working-Class Reading Habits," *Libraries and Culture*, Vol. 33, No. 1 (Winter, 1998), 47–70.

————. *The Intellectual Life of the British Working Classes*. New Haven and London: Yale University Press, 2001.

Southey, Robert. *The Lives and Works of the Uneducated Poets*, ed. J.S. Childers. London: n.p., 1925.

Spivak, Gayatri Chakravorty. "Can the Subaltern Speak?" in *Marxism and the Interpretation of Culture*, eds Cary Nelson and Larry Grossberg. Chicago: University of Illinois Press,

Stedman Jones, Gareth. *The Languages of Class*. Cambridge: Cambridge University Press, 1983, 1988.

Steinberg, Mark. W. "'A Way of Struggle:' Reformations and Affirmations of E.P. Thompson's Class Analysis in the Light of Postmodern Theories of Language," *The British Journal of Sociology*, Vol. 48, No. 3 (September, 1997): 471–492.

Thelwall, John. *The Politics of English Jacobinism: Writings of John Thelwall*, ed. Gergory Claeys. Pennsylvania State University Press, 1995.

Thompson, E.P. *Customs in Common*. London: Merlin Press, c1991.

————. *Making of the English Working Class*. New York: Viking, 1964.

Thompson, James. "After the Fall: Class and Political Language in Britain, 1780–1900," *The Historical Journal*, Vol. 39, No. 3 (September, 1996): 785–806.

Unwin, Raynor. *The Rural Muse: Studies in the Peasant Poetry of England*. London: Allen and Unwin, 1954.

Vicinus, Martha. *The Industrial Muse*. New York: Barnes and Noble, 1974.

Wright, D.G. *Popular Radicalism: The Working-Class Experience, 1780–1880*. London and New York: Longman, 1988.

Chapter 2
'From threshing Corn, he turns to thresh his Brains':
Stephen Duck as Laboring-Class Intellectual

William J. Christmas

The epithet "thresher-poet" has followed Stephen Duck from the fields of Wiltshire into the annals of modern criticism. The phrase represents a description, indeed an identification, Duck found difficult to overcome despite a public career that spanned twenty-five years and saw him advance to the position of Rector of Byfleet before his death in 1756. Duck wrote only one sustained poem about his experiences as a hired agricultural laborer—"The Thresher's Labour"—which was famously read at court in 1730 and helped launch Duck as a literary celebrity in London. This one poem has continued to define Duck's value to literary history. A brief foray into critical assessments of Duck shows that we have come full circle with regard to how we measure this value. Robert Southey saw fit to quote liberally from "The Thresher's Labour" in his 1831 essay, *The Lives and Works of the Uneducated Poets*, concluding that the poem was "the best specimen of…Duck's productions in verse" because of "the command of language and the skill in versification which it displays."[1] Almost a century later, Rose Mary Davis, Duck's most exhaustive biographer to date, called "The Thresher's Labour" "the best poem Duck ever wrote."[2] Both Southey and Davis value the autobiographical elements in the poem, but their assessments are based largely on formal or aesthetic considerations. Ironically, Duck probably owes the resurgence of critical interest in his work over the last thirty years to feminist critics championing Mary Collier, whose poem *The Woman's Labour* (1739) is addressed to Duck. Studying Collier's powerful proto-feminist response to Duck's denigration of female agricultural workers in "The Thresher's Labour" meant that Duck's poem, at least, was still required reading. Political or ideological readings of "The Thresher's Labour," however, have most recently given way to a return to formalism; essays focusing on the aesthetic and generic innovations of the poem have proliferated.[3] While these

---

[1] Robert Southey, *The Lives and Works of the Uneducated Poets* (1831), ed. J.S. Childers (London: Humphrey Milford, 1925), 105.

[2] Rose Mary Davis, *Stephen Duck, The Thresher-Poet*, University of Maine Studies, 2nd series, No. 8 (Orono, ME: University Press, 1926), 11.

[3] See Bridget Keegan, "Georgic Transformations and Stephen Duck's 'The Thresher's Labour,'" *Studies in English Literature 1500–1900*, Vol. 41, No. 3 (Summer, 2001),

arguments have contributed much to our understanding of the value of Duck's labor-poem, they also perpetuate the notion that "The Thresher's Labour" is the only "good" poem Duck wrote. The "thresher-poet" remains alive and well.

My intention here is not to undermine a critical tradition that values Duck for his labor-specific verse. For a variety of reasons—both aesthetic and ideological—I agree that "The Thresher's Labour" is very likely Duck's best poem. But what are the effects of such an assessment? One is the notion that Duck only achieved "authenticity" as a poet when he wrote about his class-specific labor experience, and that such authenticity should be valued above all other concerns. This view is grounded, of course, in an post-Romantic definition of what counts as true poetry, illustrated, for example, in E.P. Thompson's appraisal that Duck "recover[s] authenticity" in "The Thresher's Labour" only "when the details of habitual labour take us into places for which the polite culture provides little precedent" and that Duck's "feelings were far more directly engaged when [he] reflected on threshing."[4] Another effect is the privileging of a specific narrative of Duck's career that argues that Duck's coming to court, gaining the queen's patronage, and embarking on a course of standardized education forced him into writing blasé neo-classical verse and fawning panegyric that ruined his natural poetic powers and caused the depression that apparently led to his suicide. Not surprisingly, Thompson encapsulates this narrative in a single, dismissive sentence: "From the moment that he left the thresher's barn it was downhill all the way."[5]

I intend to challenge this narrative of deracination and corrupted authenticity by considering Duck within the transhistorical context of working-class intellectualism posed by this collection. As Thompson's own assessment of Duck's work above makes clear, when we trace the figure of the working-class intellectual from the early decades of the eighteenth century into the nineteenth, we are confronted with the problem of explaining the connection between a tradition of class-specific literary/intellectual production that is apparently quite different from that produced by urban artisans, for example, in the 1790s. Because the Thompsonian version of the working-class intellectual that emerged in the 1790s was given to more explicitly political, class-conscious, communitarian forms of expression, there has been a tendency to devalue, dismiss, or at best redefine those forms that came

---

545–562; James Mullholland, "'To Sing the Toils of Each Revolving Year': Song and Poetic Authority in Stephen Duck's 'The Thresher's Labour,'" *Studies in Eighteenth-Century Culture*, Vol. 33 (2004), 153–174; Peggy Thompson, "Duck, Collier, and the Ideology of Verse Forms," *Studies in English Literature 1500–1900*, Vol. 44, No. 3 (Summer, 2004), 505–523; and Steve Van-Hagen, "Literary Technique, the Aestheticization of Laboring Experience, and Generic Experimentation in Stephen Duck's *The Thresher's Labour*," *Criticism*, Vol. 47, No. 4 (Fall, 2005), 421–450.

    [4] E.P. Thompson, "Introduction," in *The Thresher's Labour by Stephen Duck/The Woman's Labour by Mary Collier: Two Eighteenth Century Poems*, eds E.P. Thompson and Marian Sugden (London: Merlin Press, 1989), i.

    [5] Ibid., vii.

before. To be sure, neither Duck nor the many laboring-class poets that followed him into print appear to offer much that measures up to Thompson's criteria. To the extent that this earlier tradition of laboring-class poets is different, I will use the descriptor "laboring-class intellectual" to mark that difference in Duck, especially with regard to the lack of overtly politicized, class-conscious discourse in his published work. Though perhaps tinged with anachronism (an issue I will address below), considering Duck within this context of laboring-class intellectualism allows for a reevaluation of his career achievement according to the cultural terms and standards embraced by Duck, his patrons, and even their enemies.

There can be no doubt that Duck himself was a willing participant in the fantastic changes that occurred in his life in the early 1730s. Freed from the drudgery of manual labor, under the tutelage of Dr. Alured Clarke and others at court, Duck read more widely, learned Latin, and essentially assimilated himself to literary Augustanism. Such cultural assimilation, I shall argue, is key to understanding Duck as a prototype for what, by the 1790s, can be described as the figure of the working-class intellectual. This argument revolves around a central paradox: that Duck's potential transgressiveness in this context is defined by his successful assimilation to the dominant literary and cultural forms of his day. Unlike the politically committed, class-conscious working-class literary intellectual of the 1790s and beyond, after "The Thresher's Labour," Duck largely eschewed references to his class origins and laboring experience in his poetry outside of the accepted registers of deference and humility. Duck's published work does not anticipate the communitarian radicalism of late-century labor movement leaders like Thomas Spence, or nineteenth-century Chartist poets like Gerald Massey. Simply put, Duck eludes such a ready-made framework for explaining his historical significance in this context. Duck represents instead a complex type: both an acknowledged "natural genius" and, by the late 1730s, a man of remarkable learning; both a poet who wrote competently in the regular forms of his day and one who was nevertheless remembered for his singular poem about his occupational past; both a laboring-class man who seems to have understood the ways in which his society exploited agricultural workers, and one whose primary goal appears to have been to assimilate into that dominant culture. Duck's assimilationist tendencies are readily seen in his court poems, religious verse, and Horatian imitations, a surprising number of which reveal a man of talent, intellect, guile, sense, and fortitude. It is precisely because these characteristics were featured publicly—on the national literary stage no less—for the first time in a man from the laboring classes that Duck can be seen as such a culturally disruptive and influential force. The unprecedented public transformation of class identity that Duck successfully negotiated in the mid-century period was both disruptive to the contemporary literary establishment and paved the way for later forms of working-class expression. In what follows, I offer an alternate narrative of Duck's career that suggests that he, and those responsible for his education and subsequent preferment, carved out cultural space for what we might now understand as an example of the laboring-class intellectual.

I

Raymond Williams points out that the use of "intellectual as a noun to indicate a particular kind of person doing a particular kind of work dates effectively from [the early nineteenth century], though there were some isolated earlier uses."[6] One obvious source for eighteenth-century usage is Samuel Johnson's *Dictionary*, which confirms Williams's historical claim but offers only editorial evidence for his appended qualifier. At mid-century, Johnson defines the noun "intellectual" as "intellect; understanding; mental powers or faculties," and comments "this is little in use."[7] If the definition Johnson provides for intellectual-as-noun is archaic, then what meaning is taking its place? Johnson's three illustrations for this entry all date from the Restoration period, and his editorializing is suggestive of an historical shift in meaning—from abstractions like "mental powers or faculties" to reference specific sorts of people doing a specific kind of work—germinating by the mid eighteenth century.

Two significant social-historical forces affecting this eventual shift in meaning of intellectual-as-noun include the rise of coffeehouse culture and the concomitant rise of print culture in the early eighteenth century. According to Lewis Coser and others, London coffeehouses fostered a new kind of "sociability and tolerance" among men that encouraged traffic in ideas.[8] Coser also elaborates a process of specialization taking place in this period as specific coffeehouses effectively became associated with specific groups of like-minded men. The further splintering of the coffeehouse crowd into clubs created "new divisions" that Coser contends were nevertheless marked by "lines of achievement and interest rather than rank."[9] While it is true that middle-class men like Pope or Swift could rub elbows with aristocrats like Bolingbroke or Harley in this club context, I suspect there was little room in these intellectual coteries for laboring-class members.[10] Indeed, the policing of the boundaries of inclusion in this new group of what we might call "public intellectuals," particularly by middle-class men-of-letters like Pope, Swift, and Johnson, for example, is much in evidence in the decades after Duck's court preferment, as we shall see below.

---

[6]   Raymond Williams, *Keywords: A Vocabulary of Culture and Society* (New York: Oxford University Press, 1976, expanded edition, 1983), 169.

[7]   Samuel Johnson, *A Dictionary of the English Language* (1755), facsimile reprint, 2 vols (Burnt Mill, Harlow, Essex: Longman Group, 1990), 1:np.

[8]   Lewis A. Coser, *Men of Ideas: A Sociologist's View* (New York: The Free Press, 1965), 21. For more recent accounts, see Markman Ellis, *The Coffee House: A Cultural History* (London: Weidenfeld & Nicholson, 2004), and Brian Cowan, *The Social Life of Coffee: The Emergence of the British Coffee House* (London and New Haven, CT: Yale University Press, 2006).

[9]   Coser, *Men of Ideas*, 24.

[10]   Though no club member, Duck was very likely a frequenter of coffee houses. See Jennifer Batt, "From the Field to the Coffeehouse: Changing Representations of Stephen Duck," *Criticism*, Vol. 47, No. 4 (Fall, 2005), 451–470.

In a characteristically thought-provoking essay on Swift, Edward Said extends Coser's observations on the historical formation of the intellectual in England by emphasizing the "spirited intellectual activity carried on in print during [this] period."[11] Borrowing language from Marx and Engels (*The German Ideology*) and the post-Marxist tradition, Said locates Swift within a matrix of later definitions of the intellectual, arguing that such a person "play[s] a crucial role in both the change and the preservation of civil society;" sees himself as a "champion of conscience and…an enemy of oppression;" and exercises his "intellectual capital," that is, his "rhetorical skill as a writer on the ideological field of battle."[12] Even through this fog of neo-Marxist lingo, one cannot fail to recognize the Swift of *The Drapier's Letters*, *Gulliver's Travels*, and a range of other Scriblerian-tinged work of the 1720s. Said also raises the Gramscian categories of the "traditional" and the "organic" intellectual, which have become particularly influential in recent work on early nineteenth-century working-class intellectuals.[13] In his *Prison Notebooks*, Gramsci distinguished the "organic" from the "traditional" intellectual by emphasizing both origin and function: such leaders were to emerge from the very groups or classes seeking socio-political change, and these leaders were to direct "the ideas and aspirations of the class to which they organically belong."[14] Except for a few passages in "The Thresher's Labour" where Duck appears to articulate the interests of his "class," or at least his group of oppressed (male) agricultural wage-laborers, this definition of the intellectual hardly applies, however much we might want it to.

If it is possible to invoke the category of the intellectual in the early to mid eighteenth century, as Coser, Said, and others have done despite the lack of a fully formed historical definition of the term, then the question becomes how to view Duck in this context. One might reasonably expect a particular kind of person in the first half of the eighteenth century—like a classically-educated Pope or a Trinity-trained Swift—to engage in mental labor, publish his work, and perhaps even develop a public career in this capacity. But this expectation does not hold equally for a thresher who happens to be able to read Milton and write verses. Elsewhere I have discussed the classist tendencies in this polite, gentleman-of-letters response to plebeian literary production in terms of its labor component,[15]

---

[11]   Edward Said, "Swift as Intellectual," in *The World, The Text, The Critic* (Cambridge, MA: Harvard University Press, 1983), 79.

[12]   Ibid., 80–81, 83.

[13]   See, for example, James Epstein, "'Bred as a Mechanic': Plebeian Intellectuals and Popular Politics in Early Nineteenth-Century England," in *Intellectuals and Public Life: Between Radicalism and Reform*, eds Leon Fink, Stephen T. Leonard, and Donald M. Reid (Ithaca and London: Cornell University Press, 1996).   •

[14]   Antonio Gramsci, *Selections from the Prison Notebooks of Antonio Gramsci*, eds and trans. Quintin Hoare and Geoffrey Nowell-Smith (New York: International Publishers, 1971), 3.

[15]   See William J. Christmas, *The Lab'ring Muses: Work, Writing, and the Social Order in English Plebeian Poetry, 1730–1830* (Newark and London: University of Delaware and Associated University Presses, 2001), esp. 20–22, 157–161.

but there is also an explicit intellectual component to these arguments that deserves elaboration here. A prominent *Grub Street Journal* leader, probably by Pope, that appeared early in 1731 criticizes the elevation of versifying laborers and tradesman from their proper stations by invoking the category of wit in relation to London geography: "Wit, which was thought to be setting in the west, is risen again in the east. A new theatre has been erected in Goodman's-fields: and the late extension of the Royal bounty to Stephen Duck has given birth to new Poets, in a corner of the town, the most remote from the sun-shine of the Court."[16] Once an east-ender, always an east-ender, or so the argument seems to go. Later in the century, Samuel Johnson described the trend of publishing untrained writers who had not devoted themselves to the life of the mind—be they nobles, peasants, soldiers, tradesmen or women—as an "intellectual malady" engulfing the land.[17] And, speaking of Duck in particular, Hannah More noted to her friend and fellow Bluestocking, Elizabeth Montagu, that "*Stephen* was an excellent Bard as a *Thrasher*, but as the Court Poet, and rival of Pope, detestable."[18] Not only does More's statement reify Duck as "thresher-poet," it also defines his new station in life in very particular terms. According to More, Duck has transgressed the bounds of acceptability for a rural natural poetic genius not because he writes, but because of *what* he writes. Embedded in the idea of Duck as "Court Poet, and rival of Pope" is an implicit critique of the sort of patronage Duck received, and the sort of poet he tried to become.

In certain respects, Duck's ambition was indeed to become the kind of poet Pope represented. Duck's only apparent contact with Pope's work before coming to court involved a short poem published in the *Spectator*, and the *Essay on Criticism*, which Joseph Spence records Duck having read, and Clarke advised him to memorize.[19] But once ensconced at Richmond, Duck would have had ample opportunity to digest what his new neighbor was publishing. The effects of that reading on Duck's own artistic choices will be the subject of some analysis below. What is germane here is the notion that Duck apparently rejected one version of the poet Pope represented—the witty, urbane, sometimes caustic satirist—in favor

---

[16]   *The Grub Street Journal*, No. 55, January 21, 1731 in *The Grub Street Journal*, 1730–33, ed. Bertrand A. Goldgar, 4 vols (London: Pickering & Chatto, 2002), 1:np. Further references to the *Grub Street Journal* are from this source.

[17]   *The Adventurer*, no. 115, 11 December 1753, in *The Yale Edition of the Works of Samuel Johnson*, ed. W.J. Bate (London and New Haven, CT: Yale University Press, 1963), 2, 458.

[18]   Hannah More to Elizabeth Montagu, 27 September [1784] in *The Female Spectator: English Women Writers Before 1800*, eds Mary R. Mahl and Helene Koon (Bloomington and London: Indiana University Press, 1977), 279.

[19]   From his interviews with Duck in September, 1730, Spence emphasizes that Duck had read "Pope's Essay only." See James M. Osborn, "Spence, Natural Genius, and Pope," *Philological Quarterly*, Vol. 45, No. 1 (January, 1966), 128. For Clarke's comment, see Katherine (Byerley) Thomson, *Memoirs of the Court and Times of King George the Second*, 2 vols (London: Henry Colburn, 1850), 1, 194.

of another: the learned, didactic arbiter of social values. In his *Essays Addressed to Several Persons*, for example, which began appearing in the early 1730s, Pope certainly took seriously the *ipso facto* role of poetry as public discourse, and his role as public persuader. In many ways, Duck's coming to court and his subsequent preferments were about preparing him for such a role too, though in the service of Hanoverian policies and values. In the period between 1731 and 1736 when Duck was revising his early pirated poems, including the popular "Thresher's Labour" and "Shunamite," and producing new ones for his subscription volume he was engaged in serious study of classical texts, supplementing his innate intellectual gifts to create the foundation he would need to lend authority to his public voice, one that was supposed to influence the formation of public opinion. It is in this process of cultural assimilation—and its subsequent poetic products—that we can locate a version of the early laboring-class intellectual.

II

When Duck arrived in London for an audience with the queen in early October 1730, his laboring life was forever altered by the terms of Caroline's patronage, the details of which, including Duck's annuity and new housing situation at Richmond, became the stuff of public knowledge thanks to a thriving partisan press and disreputable booksellers eager to cash in on Duck's success. Many assumed that Duck, the new literary sensation at court, was to replace Laurence Eusden as poet laureate. Swift certainly felt this way, writing to Gay in November that "the vogue of our few honest folks here is that Duck is absolutely to Succeed Eusden in the Lawrell."[20] Ad hominem attacks against Duck quickly became a staple of the anti-Walpole literature and opposition press of this period. Speculation about Duck's intellectual capacities was a prominent feature of this satiric literature. Swift's opening witticism in his epigram on Duck, probably written in late 1730 during the height of the laureate craze, is perhaps the best-known example of this trend:

> The thresher Duck could o'er the Q[ueen] prevail.
> The Proverb says; *No Fence against a Flayl*.
> From *threshing* Corn, he turns to *thresh* his Brains;
> For which Her *M[ajest]y* allows him *Grains*.[21]

For a fellow of Duck's class origins, corn threshing is fine—but brain threshing is another matter. The figure Swift creates in the third line by linking the most salient action verb of Duck's former workaday life to his "Brains" has the rhetorical effect of calling into question Duck's very capacity to perform his new labors well.

---

[20] Swift to Gay and the Duchess of Queensbury, 19 November 1730, in *The Correspondence of Alexander Pope, vol. III 1729–1735*, ed. George Sherburn (Oxford: Clarendon Press, 1956), 151.

[21] Jonathan Swift, "On Stephen Duck, the Thresher, and Favourite Poet, A Quibbling Epigram. Written in the Year 1730," in *Swift's Poems*, 2nd ed., ed. Harold Williams (Oxford: Oxford University Press, 1958), 521.

What I will call the "anti-intellectual" trope of this satiric response to Duck became de rigueur throughout the early 1730s. The *Grub Street Journal* was but one of many opposition papers that turned up the political pressure on Walpole's administration and the court during the laureate debate as references to Duck appear often in its pages in late 1730. The following epistle, for example, is explicitly addressed to Duck and ironically celebrates his threshing across class- and labor-specific boundaries:

> Thrice happy Duck! a milder fate
>> Thy genius does attend:
> Well hast thou thresh'd thy barns and brains,
>> To make a Queen thy friend![22]

Much of the satiric material published in the *Grub Street Journal* was reissued in other pamphlet-style publications, like *The Windsor Medley* (1731), which included an anonymous epigram arguing that Duck was born "Less fit to gather Bays than Corn;/Has thresh'd, and sweat, and threshes yet,/But ne'er thresh'd out one Grain of Wit."[23] Echoing Swift, James Miller (himself a sometimes contributor to the *Grub Street Journal*) took his shot at Duck in *Harlequin-Horace: or, The Art of Modern Poetry* (1731), an imitation of Horace's *Ars Poetica* with contemporary poets in mind:

> The *Sacred Nine* first gave th' uncommon luck,
> To charm the Royal Ear, to *Stephen Duck*;
> To sing the *Thresher's Labours*, and recite
> Things done by *Man of God* for *Shunamite*.
> Laborious *Duck*! Who with prodigious Pain,
> Hast thresh'd from thy course, tough, hard-yielding brain,
> A most abundant Crop of *golden* Grain.[24]

But the most hard-hitting example of this type of verbal abuse appeared in Thomas Cooke's *The Battle of the Poets; or, The Contention for the Laurel* (1731), an updating of his 1725 poem, *The Battel [sic]of the Poets: An Heroic Poem in Two Cantos*, for the playhouse. Cooke's satiric piece on the laureate issue first gained air as an addition to Henry Fielding's anti-Walpole play, *The Tragedy of Tragedies* at the Hay-Market Theatre on 30 November 1730.[25] The published text

---

[22]   *The Grub Street Journal*, No. 40, October 8, 1730.

[23]   *The Windsor Medley: Being a Choice Collection of Several Curious Pieces in Prose and Verse: That were a handed about in Manuscript and Print, During the Stay of the Court at Windsor-Castle last Summer. Most of them never before Printed* (London, 1731), 13.

[24]   [James Miller], *Harlequin-Horace: or, The Art of Modern Poetry* (London, 1731), 13.

[25]   For evidence of attribution and performance history, see Allardyce Nichol, *History of English Drama, 1660–1900*, 6 vols, Vol. 2 (Cambridge: Cambridge University Press, 1952–1959), 316.

indicates that Duck was satirized on the stage in the character of "Flail," who is the last of the candidates to be interviewed by the King's ministers:

> Lord Truetaste: Pray, my Lord, upon what Account is this Fellow introduced?
>
> Flail: Whoy, I'm but a West-country Thresher; but I heard Volk were making Varses vor a Place at Court, zo I come to zhow my Zel; for an Rhiming be all, I'ze rhime as thick as Hail, I warrant ye.
>
> Lord Grizzle: Have you ever been acquainted with Poetry?
>
> Flail: Ah!—Laud help your Head, read Poetry, quotha!—I've read *Patient Grizzle*, the *Babes i' the Wood*, *Chevy Chace*, and the *Dragon o' Wantley*.
>
> Noodle: You're learned.[26]

This is a more devastating portrait, not only of Duck—who appears as a rural clown whose reading extends no further than popular balladry—but of the pretensions to literary taste of the court during the Walpole years. The fact that poetry and party politics were deeply intertwined at this time has been well documented,[27] and there can be little doubt that the flaying of Duck's character in this context was always in the service of larger political and cultural arguments. The constant barrage against Duck's intellectual makeup and capacity for wit may even have had an effect on the outcome of the laureate race. Colley Cibber ultimately gained the post, perhaps as reward for his long-time Whig partisanship, and perhaps because he was perceived to have more wit, or at least the political savvy and skills necessary to handle the abuse which was sure to continue.[28] As a device of political rhetoric, the anti-intellectual trope associated so often with Duck in satiric writing of this period was effective, though the picture it created could not have been farther from the truth.

Duck's responses to this satiric abuse were few, and rarely public. He indulged in no witty verse exchanges in the 1730s, but he had not forgotten certain of his detractors a decade later. In 1741 Duck published a lengthy verse epistle addressed to "Laelius" (probably Spence) titled *Every Man in his Own Way*. Here Duck satirizes a range of gentlemanly characters who cannot find their bliss, and moralizes on his own personal happiness achieved through writing: "And shall

---

[26]   [Thomas Cooke], *The Battle of the Poets; or, The Contention for the Laurel... Written by Scriblerus Tertius* (London, 1731), 18–19.

[27]   See, for example, *Bertrand Goldgar, Walpole and the Wits: The Relation of Politics to Literature, 1722–1742* (Lincoln and London: University of Nebraska Press, 1976); and Christine Gerrard, *The Patriot Opposition to Walpole: Politics, Poetry, and National Myth, 1725–1742* (Oxford: Clarendon Press; New York: Oxford University Press, 1994).

[28]   These are the conclusions drawn by Daniel J. Ennis, "The Making of the Poet Laureate, 1730," *The Age of Johnson*, Vol. 11 (2000), 228–229.

not I indulge my harmless Pen?/And have my Way, as well as other Men?"[29] In this sense, the entire poem can be read as a response to the previous decade's worth of criticism Duck endured for turning poet—and one can certainly detect a vein of "authentic" feeling coming from Duck in defending his right to poetry. Though Duck did not like to write in the satiric mode, he shows himself capable in this piece, borrowing from Pope's *Of the Characters of Women: An Epistle to a Lady* (1735) the basic structure of a series of character-types all given Latinate names. None of these has been identified with any of Duck's contemporaries, and it is more than likely that Duck is not trying to satirize specific men. However, James Miller is singled out later in the poem in an author's note attached to the following lines:

> Thus He, who mimics POPE's immortal Pen,
> (Tho' awkwardly as Monkeys mimic Men)
> With Wicked Farce profanes the hallow'd Gown,
> And to expose our Folly, shews his own. (179)

Duck's note reads "See Harlequin Horace, p. 7 where the Author professes he has imitated the style of Mr. Pope." So it is that one imitator of Pope lashes another, as Miller comes off as a "Monkey" poet, aping Pope's *Dunciad* and blaspheming the Anglican clergy. Duck would take Holy Orders himself in 1746, and this further change in his life launched another round of satiric commentary in the periodical press. Again Duck remained publicly mute, but included the following lines in a letter to Spence in 1750 after gaining a chaplaincy from the king:

> You think it (Censor) mighty strange
>   That born a Country Clown,
> I should my first profession change,
>   And wear a Chaplain's gown!
> If Virtue honours the low Race
>   From which I was descended,
> If Vices your high birth disgrace,
>   Who should be most commended.[30]

Clearly there is more wit in the thresher-turned-poet than is usually accorded to him based merely on his published verse.

The portrait of Duck that emerges from surviving non-satiric evidence in fact reveals a man of striking sensibility and intellectual gifts. After his initial meeting with Duck at Winchester, Spence gushed to Pope that "one sees the Struggles of a

---

[29] *Every Man in his Own Way. An Epistle to a Friend*, in *Eighteenth-Century English Labouring-Class Poets, 1700–1740*, ed. William Christmas, 3 vols, gen. ed. John Goodridge, Vol. 1 (London: Pickering & Chatto, 2003), 179. Further references to this poem are from this edition.

[30] Duck to Spence, 5 December 1750, in Joseph Spence, *Anecdotes, Observations and Characters of Books and Men*, ed. Samuel Weller Singer (Carbondale, IL: Southern Illinois University Press, 1964), 258.

great Soul in him; much light he has, & much he wants: but there's so much more knowledge in the man than could be expected."[31] Of particular interest in Spence's notes from these interviews before Duck was sent to court, is his description of Duck's reactions to passages from Shakespeare read aloud:

> He trembled at ye Ghosts' Speech w[he]n I read it to him, & admired ye Speeches
> & turns in ye Mob ab[ou]t Caesar's body more (he said) than ever he had done.
> (His change of Countenance, & sharp look sometimes. Applause more strong in
> his face, than ever I saw it.)[32]

Spence's rendering of Duck's display of emotional susceptibility here works to establish Duck's intellectual and emotional capacities—most importantly the valued connection between them—against the contemporary template of sensibility and sentimentalism. In representing Duck's (apparently) innate ability to empathize with the distress of Shakespeare's characters and to exhibit his own exquisite feeling at specific speeches, Spence effectively uses the nascent cultural discourses of sensibility to raise his subject. Ultimately, these notes would be the source for Spence's pamphlet, *A Full and Authentick Account of Stephen Duck* (1731), designed to correct the misinformation about and caricatures of Duck that circulated during the laureate debate. Here, in more polished form, Duck is represented as "an extraordinary Man" blessed with literary talent both innate and cultivated.[33] In Spence's view, Duck is a sensitive reader, capable of observing "several particular Beauties" of *Paradise Lost*, "which it requires a nice and just Eye to discover," and a careful, self-reflexive writer, capable of discerning the strengths and faults of his own lines.[34]

Duck's trajectory to an ecclesiastical career essentially begins here, in mid-September of 1730, during this battery of interviews conducted by Spence and Clarke as to his character make-up and suitability for receiving the queen's benefactions. Spence records that Duck "thinks he c[oul]d learn Latin, & has a great desire to it," and Clarke is almost ready to turn teacher (against his occupational inclination) after the week is over:

> I have had so much entertainment in observing the quick relish he has of any sort
> of useful knowledge, that as little as I love teaching, I should think it the highest
> employment of my time to spend it in communicating all I could to a mind so
> well disposed to receive it.[35]

---

[31]   Osborn, "Spence, Natural Genius, and Pope," 126.

[32]   Ibid., 128.

[33]   Joseph Spence, *A Full and Authentick Account of Stephen Duck, The Wiltshire Poet* (London, 1731), 5.

[34]   Ibid., 11.

[35]   Osborn, "Spence, Natural Genius, and Pope," 128; Clarke to Mrs. Clayton, 19 September 1730, in Thomson, *Memoirs*, 190.

Clarke goes on in the same letter to advise Lady Sundon regarding Duck's reading list, suggesting that he avoid Swift, Montaigne, South, Cowley, and "the writers in the Dunciad Controversy" in favor of natural philosophy ("Burnet's Theory of the Earth, and Ray's Wisdom of God in the Creation") and a popularization of Cartesian metaphysics ("Dr. Clark's Rohoult").[36] Duck certainly would have had access to these titles in the queen's library at Richmond, and, by 1735, he was spending a lot of time there having been promoted to "Keeper of Merlin's Cave," the queen's name for her architectural extravagance. Duck had been originally pegged for the post of gardener, but he appears to have taken to his learning so well, this plan was abandoned and Duck was given the resources and a measure of independence to follow his Muse. Though Duck and his second wife, Sarah Bigg, apparently had some occupational duties at Merlin's Cave, primarily providing information and guided tours to visitors, Duck nevertheless had ample time to read, study Latin, and prepare his volume of poems for publication.[37] Both Clarke and Spence proved instrumental in promoting Duck to what he seems to have wanted most: to be steeped in Augustanism while serving both God and queen.

III

In his brief discussion of the late-century milkwoman poet, Ann Yearsley, as a "female plebeian intellectual," Jonathan Rose notes "she could only find her independent voice by mastering classical literature."[38] This is an important insight because it offers an alternative perspective for understanding the trend, observable in so many laboring-class poets of the eighteenth century, to engage in the imitation of various classical poetic kinds. A systematic study of such laboring-class imitations is beyond the scope of this essay, but I would like to focus on the concerted effort Duck made to imitate the Horatian ode for his 1736 authorized collection, *Poems on Several Occasions*. Davis has noted how much of the new material written for this volume reflected Duck's classical training since coming to court: nine of the new poems are based on Latin models.[39] Of these, three are titularly identified as imitations of specific Horatian odes.

---

36   Thomson, *Memoirs*, 191–192.

37   For a lively vignette of Duck and his wife serving in this capacity, see [Edmund Curll], *The Rarities of Richmond: Being Exact Descriptions of the Royal Hermitage and Merlin's Cave*, 2nd ed. (London, 1736), 6–11. Davis dismisses this description because of its obvious satiric content, but Curll's ironic jibing at Duck's poetic abilities does not detract from its biographical and historical value (*Stephen Duck*, 73–74). Duck corroborates this chance meeting with Curll in a letter to Spence dated October 29, 1735 (*Anecdotes, Observations and Characters of Books and Men*, 226).

38   Jonathan Rose, *The Intellectual Life of the British Working Classes* (London and New Haven, CT: Yale University Press, 2001), 19.

39   Davis, *Stephen Duck*, 161–162.

Duck probably first encountered the Horatian ode in his reading of the *Spectator* while still working as a thresher. Spence records that Duck mentioned, "with more regard than usual," "the *Justum & Tenacem* from *Horace*" from this source.[40] But, after coming to London and immersing himself in things literary, Duck was likely also influenced in his choice by Pope, whose own imitations of Horatian poetic forms began appearing in February 1733. Pope presents especially stiff competition, and Duck's apprehensiveness about his Horatian endeavors is recorded in his "Author's Apology," prefixed to the volume:

> I confess myself guilty of a great Presumption in publishing Imitations of HORACE, when many eminent Hands have done it much better before me: But when I was only endeavouring to understand him, I found it difficult to conquer a Temptation I had to imitate some of his Thoughts, which mightily pleas'd me. If I may be forgiven this Experiment, I promise to trouble the World with nothing of this Nature again, at least, till I may be able to do my Author more Justice.[41]

With characteristic humility and deference to other "eminent Hands," Duck attempts here to pass off his Horatian imitations as merely the stuff of school-boy exercise. To be sure, Duck is concerned, as he should be, about what his middle- and upper-class readers will think about his essentially presenting himself as one of them, having absorbed the lessons of Addisonian politeness and taking on one of the main authors from its reading list. However, I suspect Duck is calling his readers' attention to his Horatian poems because he is also quite invested in this poetical "Experiment." Reading these poems carefully against the originals shows that Duck, like Cowley, Rochester, Dryden, Pope and even Horace himself, was expressing himself through a specific poetic tradition. If at times Duck's imitations of Horace reveal infelicities that separate his efforts from his more well known forbears, they also show that Duck was engaged as a *poet* in the complexities of "free translation,"[42] and those Horatian "Thoughts" that "mightily pleas'd [him]" are carefully chosen and modernized into original verse.

The first of Duck's Horatian experiments to appear in *Poems on Several Occasions* is "An Imitation of the Tenth Ode of the Second Book of Horace," which showcases Duck trying out a variety of metrical forms and modernizing the didacticism of Horace's original. With regard to form, Duck renders Horace's six regular stanzas into three irregular ones that vary markedly in terms of length,

---

[40] Spence, *Full and Authentick Account*, 23. Horace's "Justum et Tenacem" is the third ode of Book III, and was reproduced as epigraph to essay no. 12 of the revived *Spectator*, dated February 12, 1715. See Batt, "From the Field to the Coffeehouse," 465n16.

[41] Stephen Duck, *Poems on Several Occasions* (London, 1736), viii.

[42] For a concise and useful discussion of the mid-seventeenth-century debates about "free translation" that eventually grew into the form of "Imitation" by the eighteenth century, see Frank Stack, *Pope and Horace: Studies in Imitation* (Cambridge: Cambridge University Press, 1985), esp. 19–21.

meter, and rhyme scheme. Duck's opening twenty-line stanza encapsulates the first three of Horace's, and is worth quoting in full to observe Duck's aesthetic choices:

> If we, my Lord, with easy Strife,
> Would pass this fickle Tide of Life;
> We must not always rashly sail
> With ev'ry light, inconstant Gale;
> Nor yet, at ev'ry Surge that roars,
> Too tim'rous, seek the craggy Shores.
> The Man who keeps the *Golden Mean*,
> Where raging Storms are seldom seen,
> Avoids the dang'rous Rocks and Pools,
> That fright the Wise, and swallow Fools:
> He's ne'er despis'd among the Crowd,
>   Nor envy'd in the Court;
> But steers between the Base and Proud,
>   To gain the peaceful Port.
> While lofty Spires and Cedars fall,
>   Storm-beaten, to the Plain,
> The lowly Shrub, and humble Wall,
>   Are Proof to Wind and Rain;
> And Lightnings guiltless o'er the Cottage fly,
> But smite th'ambitious Hills, that, tow'ring, threat the Sky.[43]

The metrical shifts in this stanza between octosyllabic couplets (ten lines), alternating tetrameter and trimeter (eight lines), and the irregular closing couplet that introduces the first line of pentameter, followed immediately by an Alexandrine, appear dizzying at first glance. Is Duck merely trying to dazzle his readers with this metrical variation, or is there reason behind his rhyming? To be sure, Duck is displaying a metrical complexity he had hitherto avoided in his best-known poems, which were all in heroic couplets. I would like to suggest that Duck's highly irregular meter in this poem is neither egotistical nor whimsical. When we recall that Horace's original ode is about keeping to "the *Golden Mean*," or middle path, and avoiding emotional extremes, we can glimpse Duck connecting the strong metrical shifts—between blocks of lines and even within the final couplet itself— to the poem's didactic message. As Duck puts the case in the second stanza: "With Times, our Tempers vary round,/Nothing immutable is found,/But all to Change inclin'd" (297). And so it is that the subsequent stanzas each retain the metrical elements noted in this first stanza, but in differing number and order.[44]

---

[43]   Duck, *Poems on Several Occasions*, 295–296. Further references to Duck's Horatian imitations are from this edition and will be given by page number only in the text.

[44]   See Davis, *Stephen Duck*, 162–163n75 for a full scansion of this poem. To take but one example, the second stanza embeds a pentameter line in its midst and does not include an Alexandrine, while the third stanza reintroduces the combination but embeds the Alexandrine and ends with a line of pentameter.

Of course, Duck is not *avoiding* extremes in his verse; he is *imaging* them vis à vis his use of metrical variation, effectively reinforcing the foundational image the entire poem turns upon: the proverbial "sea of life." This image is available in the opening stanza of Horace's original:

> Better will you live, O Licinius,
> not always urging yourself out upon the high seas,
> nor ever hugging the insidious shore
>   in fear of storms.[45]

Duck picks up on this conceit, but his imitation extends Horace's use of the image in important ways. Sticking close to his source, Duck stretches the image throughout his own first stanza, and returns to it, as does Horace, in his last. Duck's awareness of the centrality of this image is both evidenced in his diction ("Sea," "Calm," "Tempest," "steer," "Storms," " foamy Wave," "Gales," "Bark," "swelling Sails," and "Ship" all appear in the fifteen lines of his third stanza) and, significantly, in his use of metrical variation (298). In this respect, Duck's poem appears on the page, and reads, as a sea of irregular metrical patterns. If this aesthetic decision appears discordant with the poem's didactic argument, it nevertheless is in tune with its overarching metaphor. Hence, Duck is producing something more that mere "translation;" he is successfully engaging with that paradoxical eighteenth-century poetic form, the imaginative imitation.

Duck's "Tenth Ode" also includes a finely-turned compliment to Pope that both modernizes Horace's original, but also requires some knowledge of it to gain the full effect. Picking up on Horace's reference to Apollo—"Sometimes Apollo/ awakens the mute Muse with his harp," (72)—Duck closes his second stanza with the following lines:

> Tho' Pope with Illness oft complains,
> Pope is not always rack'd with Pains;
>   But, warm'd with Phoebus' Fire,
> Sometimes he wakes the sleeping String,
> Or bids the silent Muses sing,
>   And charms us with his Lyre. (297)

Duck's celebration of Pope not only lacks the obsequiousness that usually attends such compliments paid to established gentlemen-of-letters by aspiring plebeian poets, but it also gains force by linking Pope to Apollo. Pope must have appreciated the gesture, not only because it was something of a witty modernization of Horace's original text, but also because it came from a poet in the queen's employ who was more often given to Hanoverian panegyric than to celebrating critics of the crown and its political administration.

---

[45]   *The Complete Odes and Satires of Horace*, trans. Sidney Alexander (Princeton: Princeton University Press, 1999), 72. Further references to Horace's poems are from this edition and will be given by page number only in the text.

The second poem in Duck's Horatian series, "An Imitation of the Sixteenth Ode of the Second Book of Horace," is largely a stanza-by-stanza translation of Horace's original, modernized to fit Duck's historical moment, and, significantly, to reveal something of the poet's personal situation. For this, Duck chooses a homostrophic form based on the couplet, extending Horace's rough stanzaic divisions slightly from twelve to fourteen numbered stanzas. Each of Duck's quatrains includes three lines of tetrameter followed by a closing line of pentameter, rendered as two rhyming couplets per stanza. Whereas Horace's poetic sentences sometimes bleed from one stanza to the next, Duck's stanzas are always end-stopped. The metrical regularity of this imitation sharply contrasts with the previous poem in the series and, while this regularity appears to have little to do with meaning, it shows Duck working with an extended poetical palette in these poems.

In general, Duck makes apt decisions in his translation of this ode, which is concerned with the theme of attaining peace of mind through practicing restraint. Horace's dramatic opening—"O Peace! implores the mariner of the gods/when he is overtaken on the broad Aegean/by a black tempest" (81)—is rendered by Duck as follows:

> The trembling Merchant begs for Ease,
> When toss'd upon the foaming Seas;
> When frowning Clouds obscure the Skies,
> And dreadful Thunder roars, and Lightning flies. (299)

Duck's version is given dramatic immediacy not through the voice of the seaman, but rather through images of almost-personified nature: "frowning Clouds," roaring "Thunder," and flying "Lightning," the latter two offering sensory detail not available in the original. The poem will go on to argue that true peace cannot be purchased; hence, in specifying Horace's "mariner" as a "trembling Merchant," Duck also modernizes this thematic focus by invoking an image easily associated by his readers with the contemporary discourses of commercialism. It is an image he will build upon as subsequent references to the spoils of colonial trade ("Not all the Gems the *Indies* hold"), the frivolity of modern fashion ("Yards of Lace"), and the moralizing against "Luxury" ("I envy not the purple Dye,/Nor all thy gaudy Pomp of Luxury") all serve to unify the poem's argument around a particular set of images with a didactic function (300, 303, 304). Duck even shows himself capable of making his couplets sting, as in this stanza subtly skewering those who attempt to find peace by turning expatriate:

> Not those, who fly from Pole to Pole,
> Can fly the Cares, which rack the Soul;
> But, in remotest Regions, find,
> They leave their Country, not themselves, behind. (301)

Duck also reveals in this imitation that his intellectual pursuits at Merlin's Cave have extended beyond studying classical poetry. In the second stanza, Duck turns Horace's reference to the "fierce" "Tracians" who pray for "Peace" into a reference to "the proud *Iberians*" who likewise pray for "Ease" "[w]hen Martial

Engines round 'em play" (81; 300). Here Duck's alteration is not so much a modernization—Duck's Iberians were, like Horace's Tracians, also an ancient, people—as it is probably an attempt to marshal a more relevant allusion, and perhaps show off his learning in ancient history: the ancient Iberians were likely subdued by the Celts, a theory to which Duck appears to subscribe given his image of the Iberians' desire for peace under unknown attack. Horace's later references to the mythological figures of "Achilles," who suffered an "untimely death," and "Tithonus," who was granted immortality but not eternal youth and so suffered "protracted old age," are modernized by Duck, and the order reversed (82):

> Age, Wars, and Tumults, factious Hate,
> Made COTTINGTON desire his Fate;
> While tender SHEFFIELD meets his Doom
> Just in the Flow'r of Life, and youthful Bloom. (302–303)

Duck's note on Cottington, "See CLARENDON'S *History*," makes it possible to identify the reference as Francis Cottington (1579?–1652), an important political figure during the Civil War period whose support for the royalist cause led to his exile, conversion to Catholicism, and eventual death in Spain (302).[46] Duck's source, the earl of Clarendon's multi-volume *History of the Rebellion and Civil Wars in England* (1702–1704), shows that his studies have not been confined to the classics; he has been digesting modern as well as ancient history. He is apparently reading contemporary periodicals too: Sheffield is identified in another author's note as "Late Duke of *Buckingham*" and so must be the young Edmund Sheffield, 2nd Duke of Buckingham, who died in Rome in 1735 of consumption at age nineteen (303). An elaborate funeral procession took place in London on 31 December 1735, accounts of which were carried in periodicals like the *Gentleman's Magazine*.[47] It counts as a contemporary example of "untimely death," but Duck is reaching here: Sheffield was hardly on par with Achilles.

Finally, Duck uses Horace's turn toward the examination of his own life at the end of this ode to assert his own identity as a poet, always a potentially transgressive move by a laboring-class poet in this period. Horace's closing lines read:

> On me Fate, never false,
> a humble farm has conferred
> And the subtle inspiration of the Greek Muse
> And nothing but contempt for the malicious mob. (82)

Duck translates this as:

> I share some Sparks of PHOEBUS' Fire,
> To warm my Breast, if not inspire;
> Too little Wealth to make me proud,
> And Sense enough to scorn the envious Crowd.

---

[46]   See Fiona Pogson, "Francis Cottington (1579?–1652)" in the *Oxford Dictionary of National Biography*, online version.

[47]   See *The Gentleman's Magazine*, Vol. 6 (January 1736), 54.

It is perhaps the cover of imitation that allows Duck to assert his claim to poetic "Fire" (it's there in the original after all) more forcefully than he does, say, in the "Preface" noted above, but we should remember that Duck himself chose to imitate this particular poem. He avoids the ready-made connection between Horace's small farm in the Sabine hills and his own house in Richmond, preferring instead to keep the focus on poetry. The lines are further revealing in that one can feel the push beyond a merely private purpose of poetry ("to warm my Breast") to a potentially public one: to "inspire" or influence a readership. The closing line of the stanza also offers a high-minded answer, again channeled through Horace, to all those hacks who saw fit to take pot-shots at Duck after his coming to court. Here, then, Duck's assimilationist project in imitating the Horatian ode at once allows for a more authentic, even vaguely critical, laboring-class voice to be heard.

Duck's last poem in the series, "An Imitation of the Sixteenth Ode of the Third Book of Horace," is perhaps the most uninteresting of the three, but nevertheless, all of the elements I have been suggesting that raise Duck's imitations above mere hack work are evident. In a return to the irregular form, Duck constructs a lively admixture of classical allusion (he maintains Horace's opening moralizing tale of Danae and her father Acrisius), modern European history and politics (French involvement in the War of the Polish Succession is referenced), and personal reflection. Following Horace's lead in addressing this ode to his friend and patron, Maecenas, Duck dedicates his imitation to "the Reverend Mr. Stanley," one of his early Wiltshire patrons, most notably responsible for suggesting that Duck write about his agricultural labors (305). The didactic purpose of this poem—moralizing against the power of gold and arguing for contentment with one's lot in life—might easily be construed as conspicuous in the hands of a laboring-class writer like Duck. Therefore, the value of this piece appears more ideological than technical:

> O STANLEY, Honour of my Muse!
> I fear, and justly fear,
>   To steer the Course Ambition shews
> Or soar beyond my Sphere.
> He's poor, who always after Wealth aspires;
> He's rich, who always curbs his own Desires.
> I more admire an humble Seat,
>   Than all the Pomps, which vex the Great;
>   And from their gilded Roofs retire,
>   On *Isis'* Banks to tune my Lyre.
> In this Retreat I'm nobler bless'd,
>   Than CROESUS e're could be,
> Than if (like Misers) I possess'd
>   A *wealthy Poverty*. (308–309)

Duck's self-presentation here is clearly in deference to a rigidly classist society as he attempts to allay the fears of his social betters by noting that, although "Ambition" offers a path to "soar beyond [his] Sphere," he is nevertheless content with his "humble" station. Duck's closing analogy cinches the point: he is more "bless'd" merely writing poetry on the banks of the Nile (Thames!) than Croesus, the last Lydian king who had been miraculously redeemed by Apollo from the pyre. Duck not only puts his recent study of Herodotus to good use in this poem (the story of Croesus appears in Book 1 of the *History*), more importantly he also continues to define his identity as a laboring-class poet, asserting his right to poetry, to "tune [his] Lyre," as Horace had, in the service of the public good.

IV

Duck's literary career is more distinguished by his desire to assimilate to the themes and forms of Augustan poetics, as evidenced by his religious verse, the Latin imitations he published in 1736, and the several occasional poems thereafter, than by his one effort at writing about his agricultural working life. This has long been viewed as a bad thing by critics otherwise sympathetic to Duck's class origins and literary aspirations. Witness Raymond Williams who lamented Duck's transition "from a Wiltshire field to Richmond Park and Royal Gardens" in his influential study, *The Country and the City*: "Within a few years Duck was writing, with the worst of them, his imitations from the classics, elevated and hollowed to the shapes of that fashionable culture."[48] More recently, critics attuned to Duck's technical "competence" are nevertheless turned off by "the same self-effacing tone and small repertory of obsessions with the evil of avarice and ambition, and the valor of modesty, contentment, and gratitude" that characterize Duck's Latin imitations and other didactic verse.[49] To be sure, very little of this poetry from Duck would survive a line-by-line comparison to similar poems, freer translations one might say, produced by a Pope or a Johnson. However, if my analysis of Duck's three Horatian odes above is successful, it not only recovers something of Duck's personal intellectual development and technical skill as a poet, it also shows the degree to which, even by 1736, Duck was implicitly arguing for the laboring-class poet's right to a life of the mind and the public role of the poet. Of all the plebeian poets who published in the eighteenth century, Duck most fully achieved assimilating himself to this role, even if his laboring-class origins were never fully effaced on the public stage.

    Even after Caroline's death in 1737, Duck continued his social rise through the help of friends like Spence, but also because of his own merits and intellectual achievement. As Jeremy Gregory has shown, "the threshold standards for entry into the clerical profession" in the eighteenth century were "much higher than is

---

[48]   Raymond Williams, *The Country and the City* (New York: Oxford University Press, 1973), 90.

[49]   Paul Jacob, "Stephen Duck (1705?–1756)," in *Dictionary of Literary Biography*, Vol. 95, "Eighteenth-Century British Poets: First Series," ed. John Sitter (Detroit: Gale Research, 1990), 54.

usually assumed."[50] When he was ordained in 1746, Duck would likely have had to submit to an examination by the archbishop (or one of his examining chaplains) that, according to Anglican canons 33 and 34, required the applicant to "'be able to yield an account of his faith in Latin, according to the articles of religion,'" and to provide testimonials "'of good life and conversation, under the seal of some college in Cambridge or Oxford [...] or of three or four grave ministers.'"[51] A decree, from the Archbishop Sancroft, "that no-one should be ordained without being a university graduate" dates from the late seventeenth century.[52] Certainly Duck's case is evidence that some non-graduates got through the system anyway in this period, but it is testimony to Duck's extraordinary abilities as an autodidact, as much as to his influential friends, that he succeeded in his ordination. Initially, Duck probably acted as curate at Kew before his first preferment, to Chaplain of Ligonier's Dragoons, came from the king in 1750. He became preacher at Kew chapel the following year, and his final appointment, to Rector of Byfleet, Surrey, in December of 1751, can be attributed to Spence's influence with Henry Clinton, Earl of Lincoln, who was in control of the living. By all accounts, Duck availed himself well in his various ecclesiastical duties.[53]

Duck's final preferment to the ecclesiastical living in Spence's Surrey neighborhood likely provided Duck with a modicum of cultural authority that he could exploit in his verse, and that might protect him from potential critics. Duck's only published poem from this period is *Caesar's Camp: or St. George's Hill* (1755) in which he appears as "Reverend Mr. Duck, RECTOR of Byfleet" on the title page. This is a prospect poem, in the tradition of John Denham's *Cooper's Hill* (1655) and Pope's *Windsor Forest* (1713). Rose Mary Davis first singled out this poem for its potential influence on Thomas Gray, arguing that Duck's visionary sequence in the poem anticipated Gray's *The Bard* (1757) in significant ways.[54] And Paul Jacob has recently described *Caesar's Camp* as "Duck's patriotic masterpiece" which "blends Pindaric enthusiasm, local description, panegyric, and georgic prophesy in a way that redefines the poet as both medium and messenger of national spirit," though he ultimately reads the poem, contra Davis, as "a parodic antitype of *The Bard* through its unintended caricature of servile genius."[55] What interests me in Jacob's description is not the potential for controversy with regard to Duck's influence on Gray; rather, it is the clear sense that Duck has continued to refine his public

---

[50]   Jeremy Gregory, "Standards for Admission to the Ministry of the Church of England in the Eighteenth Century," *Dutch Review of Church History*, Vol. 83 (2003), 283–295; this passage, 284.

[51]   Quoted in ibid., 286.

[52]   Ibid., 288.

[53]   For the chronology of Duck's ecclesiastical preferments and accounts of his performance, see Davis, *Stephen Duck*, 99–106; J.L. Nevinson, "Stephen Duck at Kew," *Surrey Archaeological Collections*, Vol. 58 (1961), 104–107; and Leonard R. Stevens, *A Village of England: Byfleet*, 2nd ed. (London: Livrevin Ltd., 1972), 37–39.

[54]   Davis, *Stephen Duck*, 170–172.

[55]   Jacob, "Stephen Duck," 55.

role as poet through another distinct poetic tradition. For Duck, the view from St. George's hill is crowded with panegyric of a distinctly nationalistic kind in the form of topographical description ("Guilford's lovely plain"), architecture (Weston Hall, Hampton Court), and people (George, Spence, Lincoln, to name a few).[56] The *Monthly Review* provided only brief notice of the poem, however significant for the fact that the markers of Duck's former workaday life and plebeian status are conspicuously absent. The reviewer merely glosses over Duck's past—"The poetical talents of Mr. Stephen Duck are too well known to the public, to require our enlarging on this article"—and closes by paying sober compliment to Duck's efforts, noting that he has "enriched [his] subject with a sufficiency of invention and fancy."[57] We might, therefore, read in this account a measure of acceptance for the level of cultural assimilation Duck achieved by the 1750s. Though there would always be witty detractors, there were now, at least, independent voices publicly complimenting his verses, and implicitly sanctioning the intellectual and social transformation of a one-time agricultural wage laborer.

If, as I have argued, Duck was successful in transforming himself from corn to brain thresher—that is, from a culturally acceptable labor identification for a man of his class origins to a culturally transgressive one—he is the largely unacknowledged prototype of the English working-class intellectual. Duck's autodidacticism, literary/cultural assimilation, and subsequent social rise were all very public features of his existence either aped or desired by many laboring-class literary types that followed in his wake. The fact that the public poetic voice Duck developed out of his assimilation to literary Augustanism tended to be so mainstream is perhaps the reason that he has not been recognized for his pathbreaking in this context. Originality and independence are typically the bywords we associate with intellectualism and those individuals who make a difference in public life—not imitation and assimilation. But, in the end, it is the paradox of transgressive assimilation that defines Duck as an early example of the laboring-class intellectual.

Works Cited

Batt, Jennifer. "From the Field to the Coffeehouse: Changing Representations of Stephen Duck." *Criticism*, Vol. 47 (2005), 451–470.

Christmas, William J. *The Lab'ring Muses: Work, Writing, and the Social Order in English Plebeian Poetry, 1730–1830*. Newark and London: University of Delaware and Associated University Presses, 2001.

[Cooke, Thomas]. *The Battle of the Poets; or, The Contention for the Laurel... Written by Scriblerus Tertius*. London, 1731.

Coser, Lewis A. *Men of Ideas: A Sociologist's View*. New York: The Free Press, 1965.

---

[56]   Stephen Duck, *Caesar's Camp: or, St. George's Hill* (London, 1755), 4.

[57]   *Monthly Review* 12 (February, 1755), 159.

Cowan, Brian. *The Social Life of Coffee: The Emergence of the British Coffee House.* London and New Haven, CT: Yale University Press, 2006.

[Curll, Edmund]. *The Rarities of Richmond: Being Exact Descriptions of the Royal Hermitage and Merlin's Cave.* 2nd ed. London, 1736.

Davis, Rose Mary. *Stephen Duck, The Thresher-Poet.* University of Maine Studies. 2nd series, No. 8. Orono, ME: Maine University Press, 1926.

Duck, Stephen. *Caesar's Camp: or, St. George's Hill.* London, 1755.

———. *Every Man in his Own Way. An Epistle to a Friend (1741). Eighteenth-Century English Labouring-Class Poets, 1700–1740*, ed. William Christmas. London: Pickering & Chatto, 2003.

———. *Poems on Several Occasions.* London, 1736.

Ellis, Markman. *The Coffee House: A Cultural History.* London: Weidenfeld & Nicholson, 2004.

Ennis, Daniel J. "The Making of the Poet Laureate, 1730," *The Age of Johnson*, Vol. 11 (2000), 217–235.

Epstein, James. "'Bred as a Mechanic': Plebeian Intellectuals and Popular Politics in Early Nineteenth-Century England," in Leon Fink, et al., eds, *Intellectuals and Public Life: Between Radicalism and Reform.* Ithaca and London: Cornell University Press, 1996.

Gentleman's Magazine, Vol. 6 (1736), 54.

Gerrard, Christine. *The Patriot Opposition to Walpole: Politics, Poetry, and National Myth, 1725–1742.* Oxford: Clarendon Press and New York: Oxford University Press, 1994.

Goldgar, Bertrand. *Walpole and the Wits: The Relation of Politics to Literature, 1722–1742.* Lincoln and London: University of Nebraska Press, 1976.

———, ed. *The Grub Street Journal*, 1730–1733. 4 vols. London: Pickering & Chatto, 2002.

Gramsci, Antonio. *Selections from the Prison Notebooks of Antonio Gramsci*, eds and trans. Quintin Hoare and Geoffrey Nowell-Smith. New York: International Publishers, 1971.

Gregory, Jeremy. "Standards for Admission to the Ministry of the Church of England in the Eighteenth Century." *Dutch Review of Church History*, Vol. 83 (2003), 283–295.

Horace. *The Complete Odes and Satires of Horace*, trans. Sidney Alexander. Princeton: Princeton University Press, 1999.

Jacob, Paul. "Stephen Duck (1705?–1756)," in *Dictionary of Literary Biography*, Vol. 95, ed. John Sitter. Detroit: Gale Research, 1990.

Johnson, Samuel. *A Dictionary of the English Language* (1755). 2 vols. Burnt Mill, Harlow, Essex: Longman Group, 1990.

———. *The Yale Edition of the Works of Samuel Johnson*, Vol. 2., ed. W.J. Bate. London and New Haven, CT: Yale University Press, 1963.

Keegan, Bridget. "Georgic Transformations and Stephen Duck's 'The Thresher's Labour.'" *Studies in English Literature 1500–1900*, Vol. 41 (2001), 545–562.

Mahl, Mary and Helen Koon, eds. *The Female Spectator: English Women Writers Before 1800*. Bloomington and London: Indiana University Press, 1977.

[Miller, James]. *Harlequin-Horace: or, The Art of Modern Poetry*. London, 1731.

Monthly Review, Vol. 12 (1755), 159.

Mullholland, James. "'To Sing the Toils of Each Revolving Year': Song and Poetic Authority in Stephen Duck's 'The Thresher's Labour.'" *Studies in Eighteenth-Century Culture*, Vol. 33 (2004), 153–174.

Nevinson, J.L. "Stephen Duck at Kew." *Surrey Archaeological Collections*, Vol. 58 (1961), 104–107.

Nichol, Allardyce. *History of English Drama, 1660–1900*. 6 vols. Cambridge: Cambridge University Press, 1952–1959.

Osborn, James M. "Spence, Natural Genius, and Pope." *Philological Quarterly*, Vol. 45 (1966), 123–144.

Pogson, Fiona. "Francis Cottington (1579?–1652)." *Oxford Dictionary of National Biography*. Online. 1 Feb. 2006.

Pope, Alexander. *The Correspondence of Alexander Pope*, Vol. 3, ed. George Sherburn. Oxford: Clarendon Press, 1956.

Rose, Jonathan. *The Intellectual Life of the British Working Classes*. London and New Haven, CT: Yale University Press, 2001.

Said, Edward. *The World, The Text, The Critic*. Cambridge, MA: Harvard University Press, 1983.

Southey, Robert. *The Lives and Works of the Uneducated Poets* (1831), ed. J.S. Childers. London: Humphrey Milford, 1925.

Spence, Joseph. *Anecdotes, Observations and Characters of Books and Men*, ed. Samuel Weller Singer. Carbondale, IL: Southern Illinois University Press, 1964.

———. *A Full and Authentick Account of Stephen Duck, The Wiltshire Poet*. London, 1731.

Stack, Frank. *Pope and Horace: Studies in Imitation*. Cambridge: Cambridge University Press, 1985.

Stevens, Leonard R. *A Village of England: Byfleet*, 2nd ed. London: Livrevin Ltd., 1972.

Swift, Jonathan. *Swift's Poems*, ed. Harold Williams, 2nd ed., 2 vols. Oxford: Oxford University Press, 1958.

Thompson, E.P. "Introduction," in *The Thresher's Labour by Stephen Duck/The Woman's Labour by Mary Collier: Two Eighteenth Century Poems*, eds E.P. Thompson and Marian Sugden. London: Merlin Press, 1989, i–xiii.

Thompson, Peggy. "Duck, Collier, and the Ideology of Verse Forms." *Studies in English Literature 1500–1900*, Vol. 44 (2004), 505–523.

Thomson, Katherine (Byerley). *Memoirs of the Court and Times of King George the Second*. 2 vols. London: Henry Colburn, 1850.

Van-Hagen, Steve. "Literary Technique, the Aestheticization of Laboring Experience, and Generic Experimentation in Stephen Duck's *The Thresher's Labour*." *Criticism*, Vol. 47 (2005), 421–450.

Williams, Raymond. *The Country and the City*. New York: Oxford University Press, 1973.

———. *Keywords: A Vocabulary of Culture and Society*. Expanded ed. New York: Oxford University Press, 1983.

The Windsor Medley: Being a Choice Collection of several Curious Pieces in Prose and Verse: That were a handed about in Manuscript and Print, During the Stay of the Court at Windsor-Castle last Summer. Most of them never before Printed. London, 1731.

Chapter 3
Protest and Performance: Ann Yearsley's *Poems on Several Occasions*

Monica Smith Hart

For mine's a stubborn and a savage will;
No customs, manners, or soft arts I boast,
On my rough soul your nicest rules are lost;
Yet shall unpolish'd gratitude be mine.
—Ann Yearsley, "To Stella," in *Poems on Several Occasions*, 1785

Nil admirari should be the maxim with Reviewers: but when milkwomen write tragedies, is it possible to refrain from a little vulgar wonderment?
—*Monthly Review*, November, 1791

During her lifetime, reception of Ann Yearsley's poetry and prose was indeed tainted by what the *Monthly Review* in 1791 so pointedly called "vulgar wonderment," wonderment on the part of reviewers, publishers, and patrons alike, since her very existence as a literary woman simultaneously provoked amazement and derision. For "the Milkwoman of Bristol" to ascend from sure starvation in a barren, frozen cottage[1] to literary success as protégé of Hannah More and Elizabeth Montagu of the Bluestocking circle[2] and then to ownership of a circulating library seems even now to be an awe inspiring socio-economic climb.

---

[1]   Yearsley, her husband, their four children, and Ann's mother, Mrs. Cromartie, were left destitute and starving after the landlord confiscated the remaining livestock in partial compensation for back rent; the furniture and few other belongings had long since been sold or burned for fuel. John Yearsley, most likely an out-of- work agricultural laborer, was found "famished," and Mrs. Cromartie was discovered "bedridden in a corner on a heap of straw" by a local man, Mr. Vaughn. Through his assistance, Ann, John, and the children were saved from starvation, but despite his efforts, Mrs. Cromartie died of malnutrition soon after discovery. J.M.S. Tompkins, "The Bristol Milkwoman," *The Polite Marriage: Eighteenth-Century Essays* (Cambridge, 1938), 62.

[2]   Ann Yearsley sold milk to Hannah More's cook; through her servants, More learned of Yearsley's history and of her fondness for composing lyrical poetry. More offered to be Yearsley's patron after reading some of the poems, a gesture that, as Moira Ferguson notes, "assumed the milkwoman's unconditional gratitude and reflected a fashionable eighteenth-century welcome for 'untutored genius.'" Ferguson, *Eighteenth-Century Women Poets: Nation, Class, and Gender* (Albany, NY: State University of New York Press, 1995), 46.

Consequently, modern assessments of Yearsley's writings tend to concentrate on three areas: first, her relationship with More, particularly their disastrous quarrel and subsequent estrangement;[3] second, her self-conscious literary identifications; and third, the questions regarding her working-class origins and/or class status.[4] A kind of "vulgar wonderment" also shapes this current criticism, asking how in fact a milkwoman, a laborer with no formal education, no advantages, and no sense of literary history or heritage, becomes not only a published writer but also a respected one as well. And perhaps more important for late eighteenth-century and Romantic studies is the question of how she manages this outside of the patronage system.[5] As a result, the majority of recent scholarship addresses Yearsley's later volumes,[6] particularly *Poems on Various Subjects*, the collection of verse published immediately after her split with More.[7] In treating the larger issues at

---

[3]   For this particular item, see note 7 below.

[4]   See in particular Lucinda Cole and Richard G. Swartz, "'Why Should I Wish for Words?': Literacy, Articulation, and the Borders of Literary Culture," in *At the Limits of Romanticism: Essays in Cultural, Feminist, and Materialist Criticism*, eds Mary A. Favret and Nicola J. Watson (Indiana University Press, 1994), 143–169; Mary Waldron, "Ann Yearsley and the Clifton Records," *The Age of Johnson: A Scholarly Annual*, Vol. 3 (1990), 301–329; Mary Waldron, "'By No Means Milk and Water Matters,'" The Contribution to English Poetry of Ann Yearsley, Milkwoman of Clifton, 1753–1806," *Studies on Voltaire and the Eighteenth Century*, Vol. 34 (1992), 801–804; Mary Waldron, "'This Muse-Born Wonder:' The Occluded Voice of Ann Yearsley, Milkwoman and Poet of Clifton," in *Women's Poetry in the Enlightenment, The Making of a Canon, 1730–1820*, eds Isobel Armstrong and Virginia Blain (St. Martin's Press, 1999), 113–126; and Linda Zionkowski, "Strategies of Containment: Stephen Duck, Ann Yearsley, and the Problem of Polite Culture," *Eighteenth-Century Life*, Vol. 13, No. 3 (1989), 91–108.

[5]   For discussion of some of Yearsley's more vicious (and unpublished) attacks on the demands of the patron system, see Ferguson, "Ann Yearsley, the Unpublished Poems: Confrontation Unmediated, Empathy Undisguised," *Eighteenth Century*, 75–89.

[6]   One notable exception is Donna Landry who reads "Clifton Hill" and "To the Honourable H--E W--E, On Reading The Castle of Otranto. December 1784" as two of "the most ambitious and successful of Yearsley's early poems." *The Muses of Resistance: Laboring-Class Women's Poetry in Britain, 1739–1796* (Cambridge University Press, 1990), 144.

[7]   *Poems on Various Subjects* contains much of the controversial material on which critics have focused their studies, including Yearsley's "To the Noble and Generous Subscribers" introductory "Narrative" in which she addresses charges that she has "proved ungrateful to [her] patroness" (xv). Yearsley also attaches to *Poems on Various Subjects* a copy of the Deed of Trust which More convinced (some claim rushed) her to sign; the trust put control of all monies earned by Yearsley from sales of her poetry in the hands of More and her patron Elizabeth Montagu: "they, the said Hannah More, and Elizabeth Montagu, shall be at liberty to lay out, expend, apply, and dispose of, as well the principal sum, as the interest thereof, from time to time, in such way and manner as they shall think most for the benefit and advantage of her, the said Ann Yearsley, and her children" (xxviii). Yearsley appealed privately to More for her name to be added to the trust as "joint trustee" and for "the money to be equally divided according to the number of

stake in Yearsley's publication history and even her existence in publication at all, current criticism, with a few exceptions,[8] does not specifically address readings of Yearsley's poems from her first volume of verse, *Poems on Several Occasions*. The unstated consensus seems to be that since the extent of More's influence on the first volume cannot be known, it is better to leave the early poems alone. What close examination of this particular text reveals, however, bears on many of the issues and queries these commentaries have raised and for the most part left unanswered: What were Yearsley's political aims as a laboring-class poet? Which texts did Yearsley have access to? How did those readings affect her poetry? And how are we to read Yearsley as not only a laboring-class poet, but also as a laboring-class intellectual? *Poems on Several Occasions* reveals an important socio-political theme previously unacknowledged in Yearsley's work, one which in part answers these very questions: the development of human intellect and the realization of an individual's potential through education.

Poeta nascitur non fit

The recovery of eighteenth- and nineteenth-century laboring-class writers has largely focused on one of two figures: the poet who fits nicely into our already determined notions of who and what a particular group of writers are, solidifying our conception of movement or period (e.g. John Clare and canonical male Romantic poets), or the poet who falls outside the parameters of established norms, satisfying our need to challenge our own conceptions of aesthetics or literary history (e.g. didactic and political Chartist verse). Thus we have largely preferred a John Clare over a Robert Bloomfield, a Mary Leapor or Elizabeth Hands over an Ann Candler, and thus our critical preconceptions sometimes limit whom and what we are able to find. At first glance, Ann Yearsley, the "Milkwoman of Bristol," would not seem to be a poet whose current reception has suffered because of our biases. After all, she is becoming more regularly anthologized;[9] some of her works are available

---

her children, and subject to their demand on their arrival at the age of twenty-one years" with the stipulation that "Ann Yearsley, her present, or any future husband, [were] *never* to have the least demand on the principal sum, but wishes to receive the interest without controul" (xxx). More was outraged by Yearsley's requests and refused them all, so Yearsley went public. The squabbling, both in public print and private correspondence, has earned much critical attention, with the effect of obscuring much of Yearsley's poetry, particularly her early work. *Poems on Various Subjects* is available as part of the *Revolution and Romanticism, 1789–1834* facsimile reprint series, edited by Jonathon Wordsworth, and *The Rural Lyre; A Volume of Poems*, edited by Caroline Franklin, is available from Routledge. Ann Yearsley, *Poems on Various Subjects* (London: G.G.J. and J. Robinson, 1787).

[8]   See Landry, Cole, and Swartz.

[9]   While Yearsley's works have yet to be featured in the most canonical of undergraduate teaching tools, *The Norton Anthology of English Literature,* selections of her verse can be found in the following: Andrew Ashfield, ed., *Romantic Women Poets, 1770–1838* (Manchester University Press, 1995); Tim Burke, ed., *Eighteenth-Century*

as facsimiles; she has been the subject of a full-length critical biography;[10] and there is an ever growing body of critical analysis of her works. All in all, Yearsley has fared far better than most of her contemporaries. But because Yearsley's first volume, the 1785 *Poems on Several Occasions*, was shaped by the guiding vision of her patron Hannah More, many critics have viewed her later works as those ostensibly produced under less restrictive conditions, supposing that Yearsley had freed herself from the oppressive influence of a controlling editor.[11] The question of whether or not Yearsley was ever able to operate successfully as a poet outside of the patronage system, however, is hardly a settled one, as the writings of Moira Ferguson, Mary Waldron, and Frank Felsenstein have made plain.[12] More importantly, the very debate over whether or not Yearsley could survive without patronage betrays our own critical desires, motivations usefully critiqued by Waldron, Felsenstein, and Bridget Keegan: by and large, we want to prove that she did, and we want to believe that she could, for the alternative is blatantly unattractive. Yet unattractive though the workings of patronage may have been,

---

English Labouring-Class Poets, 1700–1800 (Pickering & Chatto, 2003); Paula Feldman, ed., *British Women Poets of the Romantic Era: An Anthology* (Johns Hopkins University Press, 1997); Margaret Randolph Higonnet, ed., *British Women Poets of the 19ᵗʰ Century* (Meridian, 1996); Jerome J. McGann, ed., *The New Oxford Book of Romantic Period Verse* (Oxford University Press, 1994); Anne K. Mellor and Richard E. Matlak, eds, *British Literature 1780–1830* (Harcourt Brace, 1996); and Duncan Wu, ed. *Romantic Women Poets: An Anthology* (Blackwell, 1997).

[10]   Mary Waldron, *Lactilla, Milkwoman of Clifton: The Writings of Ann Yearsley, 1753–1806* (University of Georgia Press, 1996).

[11]   In "Yearsley and the Clifton Records," for example, Waldron wishes to claim that "*Poems on Several Occasions* was compiled under the eye of Hannah More, and it is to be expected the *Poems on Various Subjects* will be freer in expressing Yearsley's real feelings" (317). In "Hannah More and Ann Yearsley: A Collaboration Across the Class Divide," Madeline Kahn provides a notable counter to this impulse by maintaining that attempting to divorce our readings of early verse from our knowledge, or lack thereof, about More's influence "obscures a larger truth by putting the two women poets into separate categories and opposing them" and assuming "that the fierce dispute that eventually ruptured Yearsley's relationship to More defines the entire relationship." "Hannah More and Ann Yearsley: A Collaboration Across the Class Divide," *Studies in Eighteenth-Century Culture*, Vol. 25 (1996), 203. While Kahn ultimately argues for a more sympathetic reading of More's interaction than I will in this essay, given the specific tradition of laboring-class literary patronage in which I place Yearsley, her point is an important one.

[12]   See in particular Ferguson, "The Unpublished Poems of Ann Yearsley," *Tulsa Studies in Women's Literature*, Vol. 12, No. 1 (1993), 13–46; Waldron, "A Different Kind of Patronage: Ann Yearsley's Later Friends," *The Age of Johnson: A Scholarly Annual*, Vol. 13 (2002), 283–335; "Ann Yearsley: The Bristol Manuscript Revisited," *Women's Writing*, Vol. 3, No. 1 (1996), 35–45; and Frank Felsenstein, "Ann Yearsley and the Politics of Patronage: Throp Archives I" and "Ann Yearsley and the Politics of Patronage: Throp Archives II," *Tulsa Studies in Women's Literature*, Vol. 21, No. 2 (2002), 347–392.

they were certainly a reality for laboring-class women writers of the eighteenth and nineteenth centuries in England.

Further complicating these issues of patronage and editorial presence is the uncertainty of Yearsley's educational background; how can we read her as an intellectual if overt performance as one in her poetry would have disqualified her from the only sources of patronage—and thus the only means of publication— open to a female laboring-class writer?[13] Pierre Bourdieu suggests that cultural and cultivated sensibilities derive from a specific cache of cultural capital provided by the individual's socio-economic placement and privilege.[14] And it is those writers and critics with access to this cultural capital who were in many significant ways controlling access to literacy and publication not only for one another but also— and particularly—for laboring-class writers. Entrance into the literary world was usually dependent upon access to a specific sort of education and training, entrance to Bourdieu's class of "intellectuals," a class to which Ann Yearsley did not belong. But this lack of formal educational and literary training does not work against Yearsley, but rather for her, nor does it render her incapable of intellectual work and engagement; quite the opposite. Instead the very thing that made her so attractive to her patron Hannah More was that she seemed to be the writer capable of proving *poeta nascitur non fit.*

"The ductile mind / Pliant as wax, shall wear the mould you give"

Yearsley was not alone in devoting her energies to grappling with the questions of education; those concerned with educational reform ranged from social reformers and clergy to publishers and philosophers to novelists and poets.[15] Her poetry

---

[13]   As Dustin Griffin reminds us, subscription was the method of publication for laboring-class writers, and patrons were the key to securing subscriptions. Additionally, women were denied access to most benefits of the patronage system: "a woman in the eighteenth century would not be named private secretary to a peer, or set up as a political journalist, or appointed to a church living." *Literary Patronage in England, 1650–1800* (Cambridge University Press, 1996), 189. Couple these with the eighteenth-century vogue for the "natural genius," the writer who demonstrates *poeta nascitur non fit*, that poets are born and not made, then a writer like Ann Yearsley had a fine and precarious line to walk: talented, but not too much so; conversant with some literary texts, but not too many; ambitious, but not overly.

[14]   Pierre Bordieu, *The Field of Cultural Production* (Columbia University Press, 1993).

[15]   For example, Adam Smith's *The Wealth of Nations* (1776), in which he advocated state education for working-classes; Robert Raikes, publisher, founder of Sunday school movement; Tom Paine, *Rights of Man* (1794), which held that education would promote political parity; Mary Wollstonecraft, *A Vindication of the Rights of Woman* (1792), in which she argues for female middle-class education; William Godwin, *An Enquiry Concerning Political Justice* (1793), advocated keeping education away from governmental control, but was in favor of an education that would help individuals reach their full promise;

demonstrates her acute understanding of how important it was to declare her own educational history and literary background through her verse, to establish both her poetic gifts and her intellectual accomplishments, particularly given the literary and social climate in which she wrote and published. Even before breaking with More, Yearsley seems to have been aware that "individual solutions to problems did not work; external aid mattered and had to be invoked, wherever possible."[16] In order to be taken seriously, Yearsley had to combat presumptions about the shortcomings of plebeian poets. But these presumptions cannot be dismissed as conventions, misunderstandings, or products of the late eighteenth-century British literary world, for they have not miraculously disappeared in the past two centuries. These suppositions endure in modern scholarship, and as a result, working-class poetry continues to struggle under the weight of some erroneous critical assumptions. A particularly precarious one holds that plebeian writings automatically enact either radical rebellion or absolute assimilation. In this scenario, either the poetry should be read as overt social commentary/criticism or regurgitated middle-class rhetoric. Yet Yearsley's poetry, particularly her early verse centering on education, complicates this premise in interesting ways. In "To Mr. R____, on his Benevolent Scheme for Rescuing Poor Children from Vice and Misery, By Promoting Sunday Schools,"[17] for instance, what at first glance appears to be an example of working-class interpretation of class roles, religious duty, and intellectual aims shaped by middle-class discourse instead reveals itself to be a subtle and sophisticated employment of that same discourse in critiquing the governing classes.

In their essay, "'Why Should I Wish for Words?:' Literacy, Articulation, and the Borders of Literary Culture," Lucinda Cole and Richard G. Swartz claim that in "championing the Sunday school movement [...] Yearsley neglects the quite different set of values embodied in her own relatively improvised and so typically laboring-class manner of acquiring literacy."[18] Additionally, they consider "To Mr. R____" as dismissive of "the existence of the kinds of private, unofficial schooling that were actively supported by a significant proportion of the laboring poor for whom Sunday schools represented either an unwelcome imposition from above or a failure in their own terms, since children frequently left them still unable to read."[19] Accordingly, Cole and Swartz's argument hinges on reading both the

---

Thomas Malthus, *Essay on Population* (1798), argued in favor of government sponsored education in order to reduce the strain of the populace on charity; William Wordsworth, who opposed a single governmental program of education because of the value of diversity in the English population, which he feared certain instructional systems might squash; Dr. Andrew Bell, *An Experiment in Education* (1797), the system that Wordsworth favored by 1815; Bell's system was based on the manufacturing model and allowed to educate large numbers of the population with very few available teachers.

[16]   Ferguson, *Eighteenth-Century*, 51.

[17]   Ann Yearsley, *Poems on Several Occasions* (T. Cadell, 1785), 47–59.

[18]   Cole and Swartz, 149.

[19]   Ibid. Cole and Swartz continue this line by maintaining that in Yearsley's case, however, to erase or obscure her early (unofficial) education serves an immediate purpose intimately connected to her poetic ambitions. In so doing, Yearsley is able to accept and promote a definition of herself as a poet who *intuitively* grasped the moral, aesthetic, and

poetic voice as humble, grateful, and sincere and Yearsley as a laboring-class mouthpiece for the middle classes. Given these assumptions, their analysis does not, indeed cannot, take into consideration the critique buried within the poem. Yet within their own argument Cole and Swartz present compelling evidence for just such a critique through their discussion of Yearsley's "claim[s] to inarticulation" which are "at odds with what her writing actually performs."[20] The speaker in "To Mr. R____" perfectly demonstrates this particular tension. Seemingly lamenting that "the flame / Which ever seeds [Mr. R's] servency of soul" will in all likelihood not "illumine" her soul (5–7), she continues for four additional lines in this self-deprecating vein:

> Ah no! on me 'twere lost;
> My faculties, my poverty of thought,
> Wou'd ever disappoint that grand design,
>   And render great commissions all abortive. (7–10)

Next, through an extended illustration of the tension between poetic protest and performance, Yearsley's speaker spends the next 165 lines contradicting that single statement.

The first two lines of the poem, "O, R____! my timid soul would fain aspire / To rapture such as thine," contain an interesting etymological puzzle: how to read the word "fain." Taken in the ordinary sense of "rather" or "happily," it would seem to indicate nothing more than the speaker's eagerness to emulate Robert Raikes, author of the letter published in *The Gentlemen's Magazine* that supposedly initiated the Sunday school movement.[21] But in the late eighteenth century, an additional meaning was in usage, one that was often found in combination with the infinitive (as we find in the first line of Yearsley's poem: "my timid soul would fain [to] aspire"). The *Oxford English Dictionary* alternately defines *fain* as "glad under the circumstances; glad or content to take a certain course in default of opportunity for anything better, or as the lesser of two evils."[22] Bearing this signification in mind, the speaker's praise becomes more reserved and

---

literary imperatives of middle-class culture—as, that is, a natural genius overcoming the disadvantages of her impoverished background—even while she represents herself as a milkmaid who, deficient in relation to these very systems of value, required the patronage of More and her friends (149). In other words, Yearsley had to take the stance and create the persona that she does in order to promote both her poetry and her poetics. Unfortunately, such a critical stance borders on criticizing Yearsley for subtlety and sophistication. Because she does not possess the characteristically aggressive rhetoric and stance of some of her working-class peers (Elizabeth Hands, Robert Burns, Janet Little, Elizabeth Bentley, William Lane, to name a few), it is indeed tempting to read her as either meekly acquiescent to middle-class hegemony or deliberately obscuring her background out of shame or desire for advancement. Both approaches predicate themselves on an idea of what Yearsley's poetry should be or might have been instead of what it is.

[20] Ibid, 151.
[21] Cole and Swartz, 164, fn.10.
[22] "Fain," *Oxford English Dictionary*, 1970 ed.

less resolute; if choosing between "poverty of thought" and opportunity offered under the guise of religious instruction, she will choose the latter of the two evils.

The governing classes are depicted as the "better souls, / Ye nobler few, who slumber in your race;" (34–35) they fail in their duty as governors of those less fortunate. They do not "lend [their] aid" to "save" a "fellow-spirit lost ... / swallow'd in the ever-yawning gulf that frights the mental eye" (37–39). They have allowed the laboring-classes to become lost not in a faith-less void, but rather in a place empty of mental, intellectual development. Subtly (or not so) threatening those in power with "O think! the coming hour will soon be yours" (42), the speaker asks if they will fail to "dip" in "heavenly tints" the "form which bears [their] Maker's image," if they will fail to "raise the new idea, lift it high" (42–46). She calls for a baptism in thought, one that bears the tint of salvation—mental liberation—through literacy. She baits the hook with the reminder that the "ductile mind / Pliant as wax, shall wear the mould you give (47–48)." Granted, given the (nonexistent) state of education for the working-classes in late eighteenth-century Britain, it would be easy to read this suggestion as Yearsley conforming to middle-class notions of class maintenance. Through her dealings with More, she came in direct contact with that sentiment in letters exchanged between the two and even in More's prefatory remarks to *Poems on Several Occasions*.[23] But another possibility exists: that Yearsley was reminding the ruling classes that they could "mold" minds if and only if those minds were susceptible to persuasion. Those who are illiterate and uneducated cannot be swayed by reason, even spiritual, Anglican-sanctioned reason. But if through the church the working classes gain access to literacy, church doctrine and its accompanying discourse of class maintenance can be reinforced and maintained. In "Ann Yearsley and the Clifton Records," Mary Waldron dismisses the poem's message as being "one of support for paternalism."[24] Undoubtedly this is the text's overt argument, but neither Waldron nor Cole and Swartz address Yearsley's cagily staged, implied platform for education. Just as women in the eighteenth century were not educated for fear of becoming unmarriageable,[25] the working classes were not educated for fear that they would become unmanageable.[26] Yearsley's enacted desire for paternalism

---

[23]   In "A Prefatory Letter to Mrs. Montagu," More notes that by securing publication for Yearsley, she does not wish to "place her in such a state of independence as might seduce her to devote her time to the idleness of Poetry. I hope she is convinced, that the making of verses is not the great business of human life; and that, as a wife and a mother, she has duties to fill, the smallest of which is of more value that the finest verses she can write .... . Pressing as her distresses are, if I did not think her heart was rightly turned, I should be afraid of proposing such a measure, lest it should unsettle the sobriety of her mind, and, by exciting her vanity, indispose her for the laborious employments of her humble condition" (xii-xiii). In private correspondence, More confided to Montagu that she was "*utterly* against" taking Yearsley out of her "station."

[24]   Waldron, Ann Yearsley and the Clifton Records, 316.

[25]   See Waldron, "'This Muse-Born Wonder,'" 115.

[26]   See More's comments in "A Prefatory Letter" for middle-class anxieties about working-class literacy and control (note 9 above). Also see Waldron, "'This Muse-Born Wonder,'" 115.

as one of the (un)educable masses allows her to play on middle-class desire for authority, thereby gaining a measure of control for the working classes. Through literacy, laboring-class readers and writers will be able to enter into discourse (as Yearsley does with *Poems on Several Occasions*) and reshape the very doctrine meant to control them.

"In youth the mind's best gifts most strongly shine"

Just as she transforms middle-class desire for her own purposes, so too does she transform canonical literature, simultaneously reminding readers of her own hard-won literary education. A close reading of "Thoughts on the Author's Own Death, Written When Very Young"[27] suggests Yearsley's clear familiarity with *Hamlet*— both storyline and particular moments, a familiarity not gained through listening to someone tell her the story, but rather only through reading the text herself. Reshaping Hamlet's scene with his father's ghost to fit her own distinct agenda in this poem, Yearsley explores the relationship between the supernatural and the terrestrial, allowing the two supposedly distinct spheres of existence (or the lack thereof) to become less rigidly demarcated as the verse progresses. Describing her goal as a sort of chase, "I'll the grim shade pursue, / And bring the distant terror to my view," (9–10) the speaker deliberately attempts to bring the horror of death within her line of sight. She seeks an embodiment of mortality in order to embrace it; she craves a joining of the intangible and the unseen with human vision and mind, i.e. the ability to "see"—both with the eye and mind—and through this "sight," ultimately conquer. Through her active pursuit of death, she will make it "familiar," and in becoming familiar, death will forfeit "half its power" (12). The speaker's absolute confidence in her ability to actively seek death in the name of knowledge without fearing that it (either her plan or death) will turn on her would seem to underscore the youthfulness, the naiveté, of the "Very Young" author. Her fearlessness comes, though, not from the brazen ignorance of youth, for underlying this pursuit of death lies the pursuit of truth. Yearsley's speaker gently rebukes her fears, first invoking "Peace then" for "ye passions of ungovern'd youth" and then reproaching them as "[f]oes to reflection [and] enemies to truth" (14).

The pursuit of truth in "Thoughts on the Author's Death" takes shape in the form of a literary allusion and may, in part, answer the question concerning the makeup of Yearsley's literary readings. In her "Prefatory Letter to Mrs. Montagu" appended to the beginning of Yearsley's first volume, More notes that among her other reading, Yearsley has read "a few of Shakespeare's Plays,"[28] although she does not specify which ones. "Thoughts on the Author's Own Death," however, contains multiple allusions to and parallels of *Hamlet*, indicating not only Yearsley's familiarity with the play, but also her willingness to manipulate story and form to her own purposes: she places herself in the position of Hamlet and re-stages the Hamlet-Ghost, child-parent encounter, although with profoundly different aims.

---

[27]   Yearsley, *Poems on Several Occasions*, 17–22.

[28]   More, xi.

Both Yearsley's speaker and Hamlet encounter spirits, address them, converse with them, and quit the meeting firmly determined to change subsequent behavior(s). The distinct parallels between the language in the two texts reveal Yearsley's ability to allude to traditional British literature while contemporizing the scene and character for her own purposes.

With a "pensive soul," Yearsley's speaker describes the "harsh scream of yon death-boding owl" (23–25), wondering if the owl possibly calls "some lingering, tardy ghost / To smell the world, ere the dread hour be lost / That parts the night from morn" (25–27). In *Hamlet* 1.5, the Ghost of Hamlet appears to his son and tells him that Claudius is the murderer, but he interrupts his telling with "But soft, methinks I scent the morning's air. / Brief let me be" (1.5.58–59), just as Yearsley's speaker suspects the owl may be warning a phantom to be aware of the changing night into day. She addresses the "restless souls" that walk the night-earth, imploring them to "[r]elax from [the] torture" of purgatory, the place wherein "earthly crimes" are "purge[d in] liquid fire" and "[i]n anguish plung'd, till ages shall expire" (29–30). Hamlet's father too describes the pains of purgatory: "Doomed for a certain term to walk the night, / and for the day confined to fast in fires / Till the foul crimes done in my days of nature / Are burnt and purged away" (1.5.10–13). And the tale of purgatory that that the Ghost would impart to Hamlet, if he were not "forbid / To tell the secrets of [his] prison-house" (1.5.14–15), would be so horrible that the "lightest word / Would harrow up thy soul, freeze thy young blood, / Make thy two eyes like stars start from their spheres" (1.5.15–17). Similarly, the ghost Yearsley's speaker encounters describes death for her own horrified listener: "The dying eyes fix'd on some darling friend, / While strong convulsions their wild orbs extend" before the "soul shoots forth, and groans a last adieu" (55–58).

Interestingly, even though the apparitions will speak to Hamlet and Yearsley's speaker, both ghosts maintain a certain distance in their storytelling, albeit for different reasons. Hamlet's father specifically states that he is forbidden to divulge purgatory's secrets, while Yearsley's ghost tells as much as it can, but stops short, realizing that it "dare[s]" to say "no more" (59). But while the Ghost of King Hamlet has a specific purpose in mind, that of urging his son toward revenge, Yearsley's ghost has a much different aim; where Shakespeare's Ghost seeks death, Yearsley's craves the preservation of life. Warning off the "too curious maid" (59), the apparition implores the speaker to "[s]eek not to pierce th' impenetrable shade / Which wraps futurity," for if she does she is "sure to die" (60–61). The future should not be investigated too arduously, for not only is it ultimately "impenetrable," such investigations are profoundly dangerous; Shakespeare's Ghost does not advise his son in the same way, and Hamlet dies. Yearsley's ghost proves cognizant of the relationship between the "curious eye" and "blank despair," whereas the Ghost in Hamlet is either unaware or unconcerned for the possible harm to his living son. And while the spirit enacts a silence in order to motivate Hamlet toward vengeance, Yearsley's ghost in contrast enacts silence in order to protect her listener. Despite these differences, Yearsley's speaker, like Hamlet, subsequently resigns herself to a life devoid of desire and delight—"Henceforth, vain Pleasure, I renounce thy joy, / Enchanting Fair, who tempst'st but to destroy" (69–70)—devoting herself instead to "redeem[ing] each mis-spent hour" (76). Her supernatural encounter leaves her dedicated to developing her intellect and reason, her manifest, human powers of understanding, during the time she has been given: "In youth the mind's best gifts most strongly shine, / Ah! let them not too suddenly decline!" (77–78). Ultimately, this evolution of mind will leave her better prepared to face the demise of the corporeal; she hope that in her "few remaining years," education will lead to enlightenment, causing the "grave to lose its sting" and her "soul to lose its fears" (80).

The speaker's final message of the verse resonates in interesting ways against the title of the poem. She vows in the last two stanzas to "renounce" the "joy" of "vain Pleasure" (69), for pleasure only "temp'st but to destroy" (70). Neither will she count herself among the "thoughtless maids who transient dreams pursue" (71), nor will she "share" her "soul in empty mirth ... / Or fondly relish pleasures ring'd with care" (74). Recognizing that it is in her youth that her "mind's best gifts most strongly shine" (77), she pleads with the "all merciful[,] omniscient Power" to "teach [her] to redeem each mis-spent hour" (75–76). The speaker does not plead for time to grow emotionally; instead, she appeals to God to give her time to develop her mind. Her intellect needs a "few remaining years," in which time the "grave shall lose its sting" and her "soul shall lose its fears" (80) through the mind's enlarged ability to cope with the complexities of the unknown, abstract mortality. Growth of the mind leads to expansion of the soul's capacity for understanding, not *vice versa*. But if this poem was written when "the Author" was "Very Young" as the title indicates, to what extent are the final conclusions of the speaker to be taken seriously? Had Yearsley intended the verse to be a treatise on death, afterlife, purgatory, indeed, even Christian views of death, why would she cast the verse in the voice of a "very young" and supposedly inexperienced, unsophisticated thinker and writer? Possibly to indicate that even the young are aware of the need for education, for literacy.[29]

---

[29] There seems to be another *Hamlet* connection in Yearsley's volume, although not as direct. From "Night. To Stella":

At this lone hour, when Nature silent lies,

    And Cynthia, solemn, aids the rising scene,

    Whilst Hydra-headed Care one moment sleeps,

    And listless, drops his galling chain to earth;

    O! let swift Fancy plume her ruffled wing,

    And seek the spot where sacred raptures rise;

    Where thy mild form, relax'd in guiltless sleep,

    Forgets to think, to feel; may dreams of bliss

    Lull thy soft sense, nor paint the scene of woe,

    I lately told ... . (1–10)

Lines 7–9 could be read as a reference to Hamlet's soliloquy in 3.1, particularly lines 66–67: "To die, to sleep. To sleep, perchance to dream." This desire for peaceful, dreamless, untroubled sleep, be that actual sleep, respite from care, or death itself, permeates Yearsley's volume. Additionally, Hamlet's soliloquy hinges on "Whether 'tis nobler in the mind to

"Else why this search—and where's the great success?"

Mary Waldron, one of the few critics to engage specifically with Yearsley's treatment of theology, argues that More had "ideas of her own about religion."[30] Yet her assertions regarding Yearsley's independent views toward traditional doctrine rest somewhat tenuously upon baptismal records for Yearsley's children. Of their six children, John and Ann baptized the first two immediately after birth; Waldron maintains that after the eldest son's death in 1779, Yearsley was unable to reconcile the loss of a child with Anglican Christianity,[31] and so she did not baptize her next three children. It is only when the sixth child, born 1784, is christened that the other three children[32] are baptized. Waldron reads this coincidence of date— 1784—and action (mass baptism) as More's influence (and possible demand) prior to the publication of *Poems on Several Occasions.*[33] Although a seductive theory, Waldron's argument regarding Yearsley's motives and More's persuasion rests on conjecture; reasonable though it may be, it cannot fully answer why Yearsley chose not baptize her children, or why she suddenly had a change of heart. She may have left clues, suggestions, even a partial explanation, however, in her verse, especially in "A Fragment."[34]

The poem begins with the Anglican Church and then proceeds from the enclosed, regimented discourse of both house of worship and organized religion to the freedom of the natural world and independent thought, paralleling the tension between regimented or undeveloped mind and actualized intellect in Yearsley's verse. If we read "A Fragment" as beginning within both the literal and

---

suffer / The slings and arrows of outrageous fortune, / Or to take arms against a sea of troubles, / And, by opposing, end them" (59–62) much in the same way a great portion of Yearsley's text(s) are devoted to wrestling with the same issue, i.e. how to reconcile in one's mind both outrageous fortunes and a sea of troubles.

[30]   In "'This Muse-born Wonder': the Occluded Voice of Ann Yearsley, Milkwoman and Poet of Clifton," Waldron confines the majority of her remarks to "Soliloquy" from *The Rural Lyre* and "On Jepthah's Vow" from *Poems on Various Subjects* (118–119). When addressing "To Mr. R____, on his Benevolent Scheme for Rescuing Poor Children from Vice and Misery, By Promoting Sunday Schools" from *Poems on Several Occasions*, she reads the poem as Yearsley's attempt at "destroying illusions about rural innocence" and does not address any of the overt or implied religious material (120). Curiously, Donna Landry's ground-breaking study, *The Muses of Resistance*, does not address the theological issues in Yearsley's poems either, ostensibly because they fall outside the parameters of her investigations.

[31]   See Waldron, "Ann Yearsley and the Clifton Records," 305.

[32]   From Waldron, "Ann Yearsley and the Clifton Records," 303–304: According to Clifton Parish records, the Yearsleys had six children: a boy (1775–1779), a girl (b. 1776), John (b. 1778), Charles (b. 1780), Ann Cromarty (b. 1782), and Jane Jones (b. 1784). It is at Jane's christening that John, Charles, and Ann Cromarty were also baptized.

[33]   See Mary Waldron, "Ann Yearsley and the Clifton Records": "Miss More may have known about, and even had a hand in the arrangements, for the baptisms. ... It may be that she and Mrs. Montagu wished to dissociate themselves from the Yearsleys' backsliding," 304.

[34]   Yearsley, *Poems on Several Occasions*, 37–42.

figurative confines of the Anglican Church, a sharp schism occurs only a few lines into the poem; the verse begins *in medias res*, "—My soul is out of tune" (1), and has the distinct feel of a soliloquy. Lines two through six, "no harmony reigns here, 'tis discord all: / Be dumb, sweet Choristers, I heed you not; / Then why thus swell your liquid throats, to cheer / A wretch undone, for ever lost to joy, / And mark'd for ruin," can be read as the speaker silently addressing her fellow Anglicans and simultaneously addressing the discordant rantings of her conflicted soul. The speaker moves from the inharmonious realm of the first five lines to a "leafy grove" in line six. "Indulgent bliss" (6) awaits the speaker there, in sharp contrast to the "Drear, joyless, vacant" (7) site of tradition. In this place, the speaker will be free to tend her "wasted soul / Disrob'd of all [its] bliss" (8–9). But just at the moment when Yearsley seems to have placed the poetic voice in a place of comfort and freedom, she undoes the very gift she gives: "here heave, my heart, / Here sigh my woes away; unheard the groan, / Unseen the falling tear; in this lone wild / No busy fool invades thy hoarded griefs, / And smiles in ignorance at what he feels not" (9–13). Though the speaker can unburden her heart, sigh, groan, and cry, all of these actions go "unseen" by the insensitive watcher, the "busy fool," yes, but also by the perceptive and potentially sympathetic one as well. If this scene is to be played, it must remain out of sight, an (un)scene.

Indeed, the speaker cautions herself to "indulge not" (14) in excess of feeling, for she is unsure to what extent these "Coherent sighs" (15) may be caught by the "list'ning winds" and "waft[ed] far away" (15). But though she is concerned about this excess of feeling, it is not just a fear that her "woes [will] be to the winds difus'd" (18) when they are "No longer [hers], once past the quiv'ring lip" and become like "flying atoms in the sightless air" (19–20). The greatest concern is that even if her woes leave her immediate consciousness and drift outward, uncontrolled and undirected, the chances of them reaching a receptive place are slim, for even though some "might descend on the gay, grinning herd / ... few, how few, wou'd reach the feeling mind" (21–22). The change the speaker seeks depends upon reaching not those who either think or feel, but those who have incorporated both intellect and emotion into a "feeling mind." The mind is capable of action, but reason and understanding alone are not enough; it is only through the combination and integration of sense and sensibility, intellect and emotion, that corrective action can be taken. Rationale untempered by pathos leads to a "reasoner" who "raves, / Lifts the hard eye, and with long-winded speech / And self-applauding dialect, condemns / My mind" (38–41)—the mind of the religious skeptic and the laboring-class poet—one topic that is never to be questioned and one writer who is to represent class issues and boundaries, not call into question the very foundations upon which that class structure rests. The generosity of the world is doubtful, and the motivations of the ruling class, those who "so frankly hold'st the embitter'd draught," (36) are questionable. To those who treat her as a beast of burden,[35] she offers her "surly thanks," (37) even though "few are due / Where little is bestow'd" (37–38).

---

[35]   From the *OED*: draught: "Something used in drawing or pulling, as harness for horses to draw with."

As in "Thoughts on the Author's Death," the speaker in "A Fragment" seeks "truth" as well, although in this instance it is not to squelch her fears, but instead to vent her rage against those who squander "truth" for their own aims while simultaneously blocking the speaker's attempts at individual exploration. She demands of the "studious sages" who "have trod the endless, endless whirl / Of measureless conjecture, still upheld / By brilliant Fancy's rapture- giving wing" (45–47) to show her the "fix'd abode," the "eternal home, beyond the grave" (56–57). She begs that they "deign to tell a fellow wretch" what the final "great result" of their searching is. She badgers—"Say, have you found it? can you teach the road / Which thither leads?" (61)—though ultimately she seems to have known the answer she sought all along. The speaker's tone is one of mockery: "Ah, no!" (62) she answers in reply to the question she poses. Despite the wise thinkers and studious sages who have grappled with the problem of religion and spirituality, none have found an acceptable, workable answer to the question, for "th' accounts brought home / Differ so far, millions of Heavens are formed" (62–63). Ultimately, the verse builds toward the speaker's statement of profound mistrust of theology, or "philosophy." Because religious doctrine is crafted by man, it is inherently flawed, since each

> vain philosopher, by pride misled,
> Presents you a futurity his own;
> by that secur'd, the self-sufficient sage,
> Indifferent, views the groupe of anxious souls
> Searching the path to rest; if they miss,
> He swears no other way can e'er be found,
>   and then consigns them o'er to endless woe. (64–70)

Though she knows that the answer does not lie with the thinkers she questions, she cannot abandon the search, for she is "Unwilling to be nothing" (59). Indeed, this unrelenting search for answers binds those "who so frankly hold'st the embittered draught" (36) and the speaker together, for she asks them if they "are not" as "[u]nwilling to be nothing" as she (59): "Else why this search—and where's the great success?" (60)

Yet it remains difficult to reconcile this seeming rejection of conventional doctrine and thought with the last stanza of the poem, particularly the last four and one-half lines:

> Oh! narrow notion of a God supreme!
> Oh! barbarous portrait of a God all love!
> I'll think no more. Ye deep-distracting doubts,
> Bewilder not my soul; for see, the page
> Of boundless Mercy, and of Christian Faith,
> Clears up the doubtful future; all is peace,
> Hope dawns, an earnest of the perfect day. (71–77)

If one were to make a case for editorial intervention into Yearsley's work, this verse would provide a perfect starting place. The last lines, from "Ye deep-distracting doubts" forward, are incongruent with the rest of the poem. The earlier argument reads as too sophisticated to be summed up and summarily dismissed in a few last lines of conventional Christian rhetoric. Maybe More added these lines or demanded that this sentiment be appended as part of "correction" of Yearsley's verse, or perhaps Yearsley acquiesced to overt or implied pressure from More. That Yearsley herself realized the potentially explosive tenor of the verse and tacked on the discordant but repentant ending is equally possible. Regardless, the tone of the rest of the verse leaves the sincerity of the last few lines in question. Linda Zionkowski notes that with "few exceptions, Yearsley's *Poems on Several Occasions* validates her patrons' attempts to mold her into their idea" of the laboring-class woman poet (101); she maintains that while Yearsley "occasionally asserts herself as independent of More's control [...], the poems in this collection, with their repeated themes of gratitude and awakened sensibility, assert that [she] welcomed More's influence over her work" (101). Careful examination of "A Fragment," however, complicates this reading of Yearsley's work, for regardless of the motivation for appending the last few lines to the verse, the bulk of the text undercuts the simplistic and quite possibly deliberately insincere ending.

Poems on Several Occasions is more than an interesting anecdote in Yearsley's career and more than a specimen of note in the history of literary patronage. The volume should be examined closely within the context of Yearsley's career as well that of laboring-class poetry from the late eighteenth century, for both the poet and the poetry challenge what it means to publish and produce within the confines of restricted literacy and access to publication for working-class writers. What modern criticism at times misinterprets as Yearsley's acquiescence to middle-class literary mores can be read instead as sophisticated manipulation of those same mores for her own purposes—one of which was to promote the cause of working-class education. In this sense, Yearsley can be placed not only in the company of successful plebeian poets, but also in the larger context of writers debating the need, value, and arrangement of formal education for anyone not included in the public school/private university system: writers and works such as Mary Wollstonecraft's *Vindication of the Rights of Woman* and *Maria*, Mary Shelley's *Mathilda* and *Frankenstein*, Joanna Baille's *A Series of Plays*, Anna Letitia Barbauld's *The British Novelists*, and Jane Austen's *Perusasion*. As Yearsley herself noted in her verse, hers was a "stubborn and a savage will," one not afraid of debate, comparison, or struggle; such a will could comfortably stand as a poetic voice in the company of Romantic women prose writers and dramatists as they together grapple with the same theme of educating the ineducable: the women and workers of late eighteenth-century England.

Works Cited

Bourdieu, Pierre. *The Field of Cultural Production*. New York: Columbia University Press, 1993.

Burke, Tim. "Ann Yearsley and the Distribution of Genius in Early Romantic Culture." in *Early Romantics: Perspectives in British Poetry from Pope to Wordsworth*, ed. Thomas Woodman. New York: St. Martin's Press, 1998, 215–230.

Burke, Tim, ed. "Introduction" to Poems by Ellen Taylor, the Irish Cottager. 1792, *Eighteenth-Century English Labouring-Class Poets: 1700–1800*, Vol. 3. London: Pickering & Chatto, 203, 255–256.

Candler, Ann. *Poetical Attempts, By Ann Candler, A Suffolk Cottager; with a Short Narrative of Her Life*. Ipswich: John Raw, 1803.

Christmas, William J. *The Lab'ring Muses: Work, Writing, and the Social Order in English Plebeian Poetry, 1730–1830*. Newark: University of Delaware Press, 2001.

Christmas, William, ed. "Advertisement" to *The Woman's Labour: An Epistle to Mr. Stephen Duck; in Answer to his late Poem, called The Thresher's Labour.* 1739. By Mary Collier. *Eighteenth-Century English Labouring-Class Poets: 1700–1800*, Vol. 1. London: Pickering & Chatto, 2003, 376.

Cole, Lucinda and Richard G. Swartz. "'Why Should I Wish for Words?': Literacy, Articulation, and the Borders of Literary Culture," in *At the Limits of Romanticism: Essays in Cultural, Feminist, and Materialist Criticism*, eds Mary A. Favret and Nicola J. Watson. Bloomington: Indiana University Press, 1994, 143–169.

Demers, Patricia. "'For Mine's a Stubborn and a Savage Will': 'Lactilla' (Ann Yearsley) and 'Stella' (Hannah More) Reconsidered," *Huntington Library Quarterly*, Vol. 56, No. 2 (1993), 135–150.

"Fain." *Oxford English Dictionary.* 1970.

Felsenstein, Frank. "Ann Yearsley and the Politics of Patronage: The Thorp Arch Archive: Part I," *Tulsa Studies in Women's Literature*, Vol. 21, No. 2 (2002), 347–392.

———. "Ann Yearsley and the Politics of Patronage: The Thorp Arch Archive: Part II," *Tulsa Studies in Women's Literature*, Vol. 22, No. 1 (2003), 13–56.

Ferguson, Moira. *Eighteenth-Century Women Poets: Nation, Class, and Gender*. Albany, NY: State University of New York Press, 1995.

———. "Resistance and Power in the Life and Writings of Ann Yearsley," *The Eighteenth Century: Theory and Interpretation*, Vol. 27, No. 3 (1986), 247–268.

———. "The Unpublished Poems of Ann Yearsley," *Tulsa Studies in Women's Literature*, Vol. 12, No. 1 (1993), 13–46.

Griffin, Dustin. *Literary Patronage in England, 1650–1800*. Cambridge: Cambridge University Press, 1996.

Kahn, Madeline. "Hannah More and Ann Yearsley: A Collaboration Across the Class Divide," *Studies in Eighteenth-Century Culture*, Vol. 25 (1996), 203–223.

Keegan, Bridget. "Lambs to the Slaughter: Leisure and Laboring-Class Poetry." *Romanticism on the Net*, Vol. 27 (2002), 77 pars, February 1, 2005. Available at <http://www.erudit.org/revue/ron/2002/v/n27/006562ar.html>

Kord, Susanne. *Women Peasant Poets in Eighteenth-Century England, Scotland, and Germany Milkmaids on Parnassus*. Rochester, NY: Camden House, 2003.

Klaus, H. Gustav. *Factory Girl: Ellen Johnston and Working-Class Poetry in Victorian Scotland*. Frankfurt: Peter Lang, 1998.

Landry, Donna. *The Muses of Resistance: Laboring-Class Women's Poetry in Britain, 1739–1796*. Cambridge: Cambridge University Press, 1990.

Mahl, Mary R. and Helen Koons, eds. *The Female Spectator: English Women Writers before 1800*. Bloomington: Indiana University Press, 1977.

Mellor, Anne. *Mothers of the Nation: Women's Political Writing in England, 1780–1830*. Bloomington, IN: Indiana University Press, 2000.

The Monthly Review; or, Literary Journal. London, 1749–1845.

More, Hannah. "A Prefatory Letter to Mrs. Montagu. By a Friend," in *Poems on Several Occasions* by Ann Yearsley, 1785. *Eighteenth-Century English Labouring-Class Poets: 1700 1800*, Vol. 3, ed. Tim Burke. London: Pickering & Chatto, 2003, 61–64.

Murphy, Paul Thomas. *Toward a Working-Class Canon: Literary Criticism in British Working-Class Periodicals, 1816–1858*. Columbus: Ohio State University Press, 1994.

Nardin, Jane. "Hannah More and the Problem of Poverty," *Texas Studies in Literature and Language*, Vol. 43, No. 3 (2001), 267–284.

"Preface" to *The Recommendation*, 1781, by Susannah Harrison, in *Eighteenth-Century English Labouring-Class Poets: 1700–1800*, Vol. 2, ed. Bridget Keegan. London: Pickering & Chatto, 2003. 377.

"Preface" to *Songs in the Night*, 1780, by Susannah Harrison, in *Eighteenth-Century English Labouring-Class Poets: 1700–1800*, Vol. 2, ed. Bridget Keegan. London: Pickering & Chatto, 2003, 376.

"To the Reader." *Poems on Several Occasions*, 1733, by Mary Masters, in *Eighteenth-Century English Labouring-Class Poets: 1700–1800*, Vol. 1, ed. William Christmas. London: Pickering & Chatto, 2003, 234.

"To the Reader." *Poems upon Several Occasions*, 1748, by Mary Leapor, in *Eighteenth-Century English Labouring-Class Poets: 1700–1800*, Vol. 2, ed. Bridget Keegan. London: Pickering & Chatto, 2003, 53–54.

Waldron, Mary. "Ann Yearsley and the Clifton Records," *The Age of Johnson: A Scholarly Annual*, Vol. 3 (1990), 301–329.

———. "Ann Yearsley: The Bristol Manuscript Revisited," *Women's Writing*, Vol. 3, No. 1 (1996), 35–45.

————.'"By No Means Milk and Water Matters': *The Contribution to English Poetry of Ann Yearsley, Milkwoman of Clifton,* 1753–1806," *Studies on Voltaire and the Eighteenth Century*, Vol. 34 (1992), 801–804.

————. "A Different Kind of Patronage: Ann Yearsley's Later Friends," *The Age of Johnson: A Scholarly Annual*, Vol. 13 (2002), 283–335.

————. *Lactilla, Milkwoman of Clifton: The Writings of Ann Yearsley, 1753–1806*. Athens, GA and London: University of Georgia Press, 1996.

————. "'This Muse-Born Wonder,' The Occluded Voice of Ann Yearsley, Milkwoman and Poet of Clifton," in *Women's Poetry in the Enlightenment, The Making of a Canon, 1730–1820*, eds Isobel Armstrong and Virginia Blain. New York: St. Martin's Press, 1999, 113–126.

Yearsley, Ann. *Poems on Several Occasions*. London: T. Cadell, 1785.

————. *Poems on Various Subjects*. London: G.G.J. and J. Robinson, 1787.

Zionkowski, Linda. "Strategies of Containment: Stephen Duck, Ann Yearsley, and the Problem of Polite Culture," *Eighteenth-Century Life*, Vol. 13, No. 3 (1989), 91–108.

Chapter 4
Hoddin' Grey an' A' That: Robert Burns's Head, Class Hybridity, and the Value of the Ploughman's Mantle[1]

Luke R.J. Maynard

There is no real need to begin with a plea for consideration of Robert Burns as a working-class poet rather than a poet of Scottish nationalism (the banner under which he is still most popularly read). These two dangerously definitive archetypal constructions are not mutually exclusive, and in any case, evaluations of Burns as a poet of the working classes have been made since the first publication of his poems and are clearly justified by the content of the poems themselves. Although criticism of working-class literature as its own independent discourse is still an emergent branch of current scholarship (in comparison to criticism of women's literature, postcolonial literature or even gay/lesbian literature), it is far from an embryonic or recently discovered approach to construct working-class literature in such categorical terms, especially where the poetry of Burns and other "working-class intellectuals" of the eighteenth century are concerned. On the contrary, Burns has been known and critiqued as a "Heaven-taught ploughman" since Henry Mackenzie first ascribed the fateful epithet to him in December of 1786.[2] In the tradition of Burns criticism, the archetype of the Heaven-taught ploughman, when applied to Burns, describes him fairly enough as a writer *from* the working classes, but also depicts him somewhat inappropriately as a writer *for* the working classes—that is, a champion of working-class laborers and their causes. Ironically, by making Burns the almost singular voice of an enormous Scottish working-class demographic, the earliest English middle-class biographers of Burns (both his supporters and his harshest critics) were ensuring that his voice of dissent was made loud enough, at least in England, to drown out the voices of the very people they believed him to represent. In England, Burns became a somewhat overwhelming figurehead of Scottish poetry, as Walter Scott had of Scottish prose; similarly, to the aristocracy

---

[1]   I would like to begin by extending heartfelt thanks to J. Davis Barnett who, at one time or another, donated a large number of extremely old and rare books of Burns criticism to the D.B. Weldon library at the University of Western Ontario. A study of these tomes was the cornerstone of this essay, and without his generosity such a project would not have been possible.

[2]   Kenneth Simpson, "Robert Burns: 'Heaven-taught plowman'?" in *Burns Now*, ed. Kenneth Simpson (Edinburgh: Canongate, 1994), 70.

of Scotland, Burns demonstrated a wisdom that was seen as quite uncommon in the "common" man, and so became an icon of sorts for the working class as well. In both cases Burns's work was judged the "best" example of literature from the marginalized groups he seemingly represented, and by narrowing their focus and admiration to such an elevated figure, the critics of his time could largely ignore the often more troubling or directly confrontational cries of dissent among other working-class Scottish writers, who in comparison to Burns remain less-known and less frequently studied even today.

Burns's recognition as a working-class intellectual follows on the heels of his status as an iconic working-class writer. There is a significant and prolonged tension between these two mantles, and the florid critical language of the period frequently fails to specify which of these it regards; but even in the earliest criticism, Burns's status as an "intellectual" is separate and distinct from ascribing to him a strictly poetic talent. Mackenzie's 1786 essay, from which the "Heaven-taught ploughman" coinage is often remembered at the expense of its other content, is one of the earliest and most significant responses to Burns, and already the distinction between his poetic and intellectual strengths is being made clear. Mackenzie defines the notion of "genius" in relation to Burns as "that supereminent reach of mind by which some men are distinguished,"[3] and in a review that is less glowing than its impact or importance might suggest, finds that Burns's famed poetic language is not an element of this genius, but a barrier to it:

> One bar, indeed, his birth and education have opposed to his fame, [is] the language in which most of his poems are written. Even in Scotland, the provincial dialect ... is read with a difficulty which greatly damps the pleasure of the reader; in England it cannot be read at all, without such a constant reference to a glossary, as nearly to destroy that pleasure.
>
> Some of his productions, however, especially those of the grave style, are almost English.[4]

Mackenzie does not exactly discount Burns's poetic talent, but nevertheless there is a divide evident in his essay between the inspired conceits of Burns's work and the medium in which these are delivered, suggesting that for Mackenzie, at least, the real strength of Burns's work was something closer to an intellectual sensibility than an æsthetic one.

If Mackenzie's review does not go far enough to establish Burns as a working-class intellectual, it is for two reasons: first, he clearly imposes an intended middle-class English audience on Burns, for whom the Ayrshire dialect is a difficulty.

---

    [3]   Henry Mackenzie, "Extraordinary Account of Robert Burns the Ayrshire Ploughman; with Extracts from his Poems," in *The British Essayists; with Prefaces Biographical, Historical, and Critical*, ed. Lionel Thomas Bergher, 45 vols, Vol. XXXVII (London: T. and J. Allman, 1823), 295.

    [4]   Ibid., 297.

Even if an "intended audience" could be established, Mackenzie fails to consider that the dialect might stand as an indicator of, and not a barrier to, the intended audience of the poetry. Second, and more central to this volume as a whole, is that the working-class intellectual, at least as defined in E.P. Thompson's *The Making of the English Working Class*, was simply not manifest in the critical mindset of the time. The mantle itself is widely seen as a product of the transformation of working-class identity that only begins to surface in the 1790s. In *Class, Ethnicity, and Social Inequality,* Christopher McAll has offered a useful summary of this transformation in relation to Thompson:

> From the Industrial Revolution onwards class is "present" in the evidence, in that groups organize themselves as classes as well as being the conceptual tool with which the historian attempts to understand society. Prior to that revolution groups organized and thought of themselves on other lines ... .On the one hand there are the vertical relationships of patronage that link place-seekers and place-bestowers, and the broader cultural hegemony of a paternalistic gentry that was accepted by the poor, but only at a price, and on the other the traditional culture of the poor themselves, from which the working-class identity of the nineteenth century was to emerge. Eighteenth-century society cannot, therefore, be characterized simply in terms of vertical relationships nor of straightforward class opposition but only in terms of the combination of vertical and horizontal alignments that were to begin to crystallize in the 1790s along the lines of what would become nineteenth-century class divisions.[5]

McAll's timeline of the emergence of working-class identity reveals much about the critical tension surrounding Burns's difficult status: as a working-class intellectual, Burns is often ascribed a social function that, sociologically speaking from McAll's or Thompson's perspectives, could not quite have existed during his own lifetime. The two remedies I have found for this paradox are imperfect and incomplete ones (there are, I hope, other and better remedies to come): the first is a concession that, in his lifetime, Burns was by necessity of this paradox an ambiguous and fluid figure, something *approaching* rather than exemplifying Thompson's modern definition of the working-class intellectual, within the confusion of a still-emergent understanding of class divisions and struggle. The second is a realization that Burns's identity as a working-class intellectual was still being developed well into the nineteenth century, that this identity may provide for a useful analysis of the posthumous social impact of his poetry in spite of amounting to an anachronistic retrospective superimposition of the identity on Burns, and that one result of Burns's early and central establishment in this working-class tradition has been a series of discursive ties between the developments of Burns scholarship and critical understandings of the working class, resulting in a fluid definition of Burns as a working-class intellectual that evolves in accordance with the needs and demands of the sociological window through which he is interrogated.

---

[5]   Christopher McAll, *Class, Ethnicity, and Social Inequality* (Montreal: McGill-Queen's University Press, 1992), 95–96.

The key point to distill from this is that Burns's identity as a working-class intellectual is fluid and evolutionary in nature; and that as an exemplar of the working-class intellectual paradigm, it may be valuable to observe aspects of the paradigm's development through a study of Burns's development within the role. There has never been a shortage of working-class criticism on Burns himself, but most of this criticism is generated through the window of its moment, the "current state" of working-class criticism at the time it is written. As a result, this work privileges the "end result" of the development of working-class criticism over the influence that early writings about his life and work have had on more current understandings of his public image and private beliefs. It is this early criticism to which I will now turn my focus, in the hope that it provides some insight into not only Burns's current identity as a working-class intellectual, but the process by which that identity has taken shape and the complications inherent in each stage of its development.

It is not surprising that Burns's identity within the paradigm of working-class intellectual has traditionally been ascribed to him by middle-class critics of the nineteenth century who were anything but "Heaven-taught": when Gabriel Setoun remarked in 1896 that the "bursts of bitterness which we find now and again in his poems ... are assuredly the natural outcome of these unsocial and laborious years,"[6] he not only dismissed Burns's disdain of the aristocracy as petty jealousy, but also assumed that every man who lived such a "wretched and leisureless existence,"[7] whatever aspect of Burns's life that may denote, would naturally hold the same opinion.

There are, of course, many old sources (some reliable, some dubious) that indicate Burns's feelings toward the class structure and his oppression under it: of those precious sources that come directly from the hand of Burns himself, there are not only his well-known poems, but also an uncommonly large collection of his surviving correspondence. In a letter to Margaret Chalmers dated November 21, 1787, Burns writes in good humor that

> Charlotte [Hamilton] and you are just two favourite resting places for my soul in her wanderings through the weary, thorny wilderness of this world. God knows, I am ill-fitted for the struggle: I glory in being a poet, and I want to be thought a wise man—I would fondly be generous, and I wish to be rich.[8]

When Burns's body was exhumed for what was at least the second time on March 31, 1834, letters such as this were taken (and, in my judgment, misappropriated) to reinforce the findings of the phrenological team that produced from Burns's skull an extensive study that, not surprisingly, made him out to be exactly the man that popular middle-class opinion had reported him to be: "[t]he bumps on

---

6   Gabriel Setoun, *Robert Burns* (Edinburgh: Oliphaunt Anderson & Ferrier, 1896), 20.
7   Ibid., 20.
8   Robert Burns, *The Prose Works of Robert Burns*, ed. Robert Chambers (Edinburgh: W.S. Orr & Co., 1839), 30.

the exhumed skull prove beyond doubt, says [phrenologist George] Combe, that Burns was a highly creative individual, possibly even a professional writer."[9] With regards to Burns's letter above, phrenologist Robert Cox declared that

> The indifference with respect to money, which Burns occasionally ascribes to himself, appears therefore to savour of affectation—a failing into which he was not unfrequently led by love of approbation and secretiveness. Indeed, in one of his letters to Miss Chalmers, he expressly intimates a wish to be rich.[10]

Notwithstanding the fact that phrenology has long since been dismissed as quackery, this study is fascinating in showing the elitism with which Burns was viewed by the middle class in the nineteenth century. Elsewhere in the grisly "The Cranium of Burns," we are told that

> [t]he combination of Acquisitiveness, Cautiousness, Love of Approbation, and Conscientiousness, is the source of his keen feelings with regard to pecuniary independence ... No phrenologist can look upon this head, and consider the circumstances in which Burns was placed, without vivid feelings of regret ... [i]f he had been placed from infancy in the higher ranks of life, liberally educated, and employed in pursuits corresponding to his powers, the inferior portion of his nature would have lost part of its energy, while his better qualities would have assumed a decided and permanent superiority.[11]

What is most striking about this conclusion, aside from its overt reliance on a suffocating intellectual snobbery for its understanding of æsthetic value, is that although class-based notions surrounding Burns (both his feelings toward the classes and the "regret," as the early critics describe it, of his working-class origins) are no longer derived from the shape of his cranium, some of these notions have remained fairly constant since that fateful April Fool's Eve when the skull was exhumed. The opinion that Burns's poverty somehow prevented

---

[9]   George Combe, quoted by Carol McGuirk in "Burns and Nostalgia," in *Burns Now*, ed. Kenneth Simpson (Edinburgh: Canongate, 1994), 53.

[10]   Robert Cox, quoted by William and Robert Chambers in "The Cranium of Burns," in *The Life of Robert Burns, with a Criticism on His Writings; by James Currie, M.D.*, eds William Chambers and Robert Chambers (Edinburgh: W.S. Orr & Co, 1838), 76. The awkward nouns used here, and in further quotations below, to describe mental qualities—affectation, love of approbation, secretiveness, and acquisitiveness—are among the typical jargon of a nineteenth-century phrenologist's vocabulary. For a deeper explanation of what exactly they signify, particularly as phrenologists Cox or Combe interpret the terms, it is best to refer to Combe's own extensive work, *A System of Phrenology* (5th ed. Revised, 2 vols, Edinburgh: MacLachlan & Stewart, 1853). While Combe's *System* is hardly an objective standard for phrenological study (indeed, it is arguable whether a single standard system ever existed), it does provide the best and most detailed account of the methodology Combe used when dealing with Burns.

[11]   Ibid., 76.

him from "reaching his full potential" is a classist claim that still rears its head (when it is not more subtly at work) in critical circles, even though there is little to suggest that Burns's poverty was a detriment to his poetry, aside from two relatively simple observations: first, that his long hours of work, ill health and premature death at thirty-seven no doubt lessened the sheer volume of poetry he might have produced; and second, that he went largely unrecognized as a serious poet by much of Victorian England, excluded from the canon on the merit of both his background and his use of a nationalist Scots dialect that was deemed by many to be "sub-standard."

Further, the Chambers brothers' seminal wish that Burns had been more "liberally educated" betrays a certain ignorance regarding the true extent of Burns's education, despite Sir Walter Scott's earlier acknowledgement that Burns "had an education not much worse than the sons of many gentlemen in Scotland."[12] Even in his little-known 1896 biography of Burns, in which a great amount of middle-class bias can still be found, Gabriel Setoun[13] acknowledges shrewdly that

> Burns is too often regarded merely as a *lusus naturæ*; a being gifted with song, and endowed by nature with understanding ... but there is more than mere natural genius in his writings. They are the work of a man of no mean education, and bear the stamp—however spontaneously his songs sing themselves in our ears—of culture and study.[14]

At the same time, Setoun's comment and similar arguments regarding the depth of Burns's literary background can be misleading unless they are tempered by an awareness of the limitations of such a solid education. Mary McKenney promotes such an awareness in "Class Attitudes & Professionalism" with the valuable claim that "education and a good job don't turn a black person white and they don't negate a white working-class person's background."[15] In short, Setoun does manage to assert though biographical evidence that Burns's working-class origins did not stand in the way of a strong education and literary upbringing; but conversely, an adherence to McKenney's view supports the argument that his strong education does little to undercut his "authenticity" as a working-class poet.

---

[12]   Walter Scott, quoted by Kenneth Simpson in "Robert Burns: 'Heaven-taught plowman'?" in *Burns Now* (Edinburgh: Canongate, 1994), 70.

[13]   Gabriel Setoun was the pen name of Thomas Nicoll Hepburn (1861–1930), a Scottish headmaster and sometime author of children's poems.

[14]   Gabriel Setoun, *Robert Burns* (Edinburgh: Oliphaunt Anderson & Ferrier, 1896), 13.

[15]   Mary McKenney, "Class Attitudes & Professionalism," in *Building Feminist Theory: Essays from Quest*, ed. Quest Book Committee (New York: Longman, 1981), 147. McKenney's essay sits at a crossroads of identity politics, and her statements about perceived class paradigms are interwoven with parallel systems of racial and gender identity. By implying a parallel here between the paradigm of class and that of race, McKenney raises an issue well beyond the scope of this study. Still, the problems raised where varying dimensions of identity and marginalization intersect are better acknowledged than excised, even if they cannot be immediately solved.

McKenney's critical roots in feminism, and the feminist critical vocabulary of her analysis, also lead to associations between the power structures of class theory and feminist theory, with the effect that the critical language of one can be applied (in a somewhat modified form) to fill gaps in the other. This is a particularly useful strategy when dealing with issues of "marginality" in working-class intellectual writing: where socioeconomic class, and the theory surrounding it, resist reduction to a simple binary of discursive marginality, a great deal of feminist criticism (especially criticism dating recent feminist and queer theory began to undercut the idea of a "natural" gender binary) sees in the discourse of gender an essential binary of the empowered and the marginalized. Where socioeconomic theory has typically shied away from the extreme simplification of the empowered/marginalized binary as a tool for examining complex class structures, it makes sense to consider such an approach when literary discussions surrounding working-class writers (Setoun's work is a fine early example) are often all too eager to reduce the class system to a definite binary of haves and have-nots. Such binaries of empowerment and marginality are the shorthand by which working-class writers are often discussed; and if there is a key to reconciling the complexity of social class with the simplicity of the power structure used to understand and mythologize it, that key lies in the appropriation of feminist theory, which has developed a sophistication and complexity even when dealing with the basic dichotomy of biologically male/female. Hélène Cixous's theories of *bisexuallisme*,[16] for instance, while essentially grounded in an understanding of gender, can be reapplied to define a sort of "biclassism" in the case of Burns and others; and through this association with Cixous, a borrowed argument emerges in which Burns's origins in the working class have no detrimental effect on the quality of his writing and in fact have much to contribute to his work by offering him a decentralized (and thus, a vastly expanded) perspective.

Within the structure of many (though not all) branches of feminism, the man/woman paradigm forcibly established by a patriarchal order closely mirrors the middle-class/working-class paradigm of late eighteenth–century literary theory, and incorporates many subtle nuances of power that are in play beyond the basic similarities and differences evident in a typical "binary of opposites." The famous argument of Cixous concerning the bisexualism of identity asserts that in a system that centralizes the masculine perspective, women have the benefit of access to both masculine and feminine perspectives in their thought and writing. Through the process of writing, Cixous can psychologically annex, so to speak, both the perspectives of Self and Other within the gender binary: "writing is woman's ... it means that woman admits there is an other ... Writing is the passageway,

---

[16]   The term *bisexualité* was used by Cixous herself; I use *bisexuellisme* here to mark the difference between the "bisexualism" of identity or of the self, of which she speaks, and the "bisexuality" of sexual orientation/preference, as the two are often confused and conflated by readers unfamiliar with Cixous and her theories. The French neologism, I think, makes for less frequent misreadings among readers of Cixous in translation.

the entrance, the exit, the dwelling place of the other in me."[17] The viewpoint to which Cixous is referring here in *Sorties* gained great popularity within the discourses of lesbian and feminist criticism in the mid-1980s; this viewpoint of bisexualism is, to use a Hegelian term, a synthesized hybrid of the centralized and marginalized viewpoints that is independent and able to critically examine both the centralized thesis and marginalized antithesis. Bonnie Zimmerman most clearly describes the value of such a "hybridized viewpoint" when she applies it to lesbian criticism, stating that "this perspective can be uniquely liberating and can provide new insights into life and literature because it assigns the lesbian a specific vantage point from which to criticize and analyze the politics, language and culture of patriarchy."[18]

This theory of the hybridized viewpoint is found in some form throughout feminist criticism at least as far back as Virginia Woolf. However, I believe that Zimmerman is one of the first writers to take this theory from the discourse of sexual identity and apply it to the discourse of sexual orientation: the very title of her essay, "What Has Never Been: An Overview of Lesbian Feminist Literary Criticism" (117),[19] illustrates the relative newness (I hesitate to use the word "novelty" for all its negative connotations) of lesbian criticism, as Zimmerman recognizes:

> In the 1970s, a generation of lesbian feminist literary critics came of age ... [b]eginning with nothing, as we thought, this generation quickly began to expand the limitations of literary scholarship by pointing to what had been for decades "unspeakable"—lesbian existence.[20]

There are some striking similarities between the emerging discourse of lesbian literary criticism in the 1970s and the discourse of working-class literary criticism at the turn of the twenty-first century: both discourses describe from an oppressed (but not *sup*pressed) point of view the workings of a social structure founded on a discourse of power and human inequality. On a general level, this is an important connection to make because it allows for the use of certain social and psychological theories to interrogate class values in ways that much traditional class criticism could not—Karl Marx and many of his successors, for example, construct the proletariat largely as a faceless mass of beings within an ingenious but ultimately limited economic model. While the Marxist model has its benefits, it typically ignores (and thus, through its enormous influence, also discourages) the application of theories of individual psychology and literature (especially where late

---

[17]   Hélène Cixous, "From 'Sorties'," in *A Critical and Cultural Theory Reader*, eds Anthony Easthope and Kate McGowan (Toronto: University of Toronto Press, 1992), 149.

[18]   Bonnie Zimmerman, "What Has Never Been: An Overview of Lesbian Feminist LiteraryCriticism," in *Feminisms: An Anthology of Literary Theory and Criticism*, eds Robyn R. Warhol and Diane Price Herndl (New Brunswick, NJ: Rutgers University Press, 1991), 117–118.

[19]   Ibid., 117.

[20]   Ibid., 117.

twentieth-century developments such as feminist and queer theory are concerned) specifically to the working classes. By making connections between lesbian and working-class discourses, though, it is possible to fill the holes that Marxist theory has left in the critical vocabulary of class (and especially working-class) studies: specifically, feminist and queer theory fills what might be called the "individuality gap" in Marxist theory, by emphasizing not only the political but the personal advantage to the position of subaltern, in which a working-class writer who has access to both the centralized and marginalized aspects of the class dichotomy is not only politically empowered by the possession of dialogic quality, but also empowered as an individual artist simply by virtue of having a broader palette of voices, understandings and discursive experiences. The working-class intellectual, overall, is often constructed by popular myth and serious criticism alike as a figure of heroic individuality; and it is the discursive hybridity available to the subaltern, identified (and best explored) in the writings of Cixous and others, that typically affords the working-class intellectual a unique significance and scope that intellectuals from the empowered centre of social class cannot hope to match.

With Burns in particular, whose greatness as a poet has long been attributed to his supposedly "rustic" origins, the understanding of the subaltern perspective through feminist criticism in the tradition of Cixous is one key to interrogating the origins and specific qualities of the long-standing myth of the "Heaven-taught ploughman." Returning at last to Burns, then, it is my hope to bring into the mix some recent theories of "lesbian feminist discursive hybridity," reconfigured as class hybridity, to unearth something of Burns that is of more lasting value than the dimensions of his skull: specifically, a more accurate picture of how the unique combination of Burns's background, education and personal experience influenced the treatment of class issues in his poetry, and how it contributed to the popular construction of him as a working-glass intellectual. First, it is important to acknowledge that if this hybridity manifests itself (as I think it does in several places) in Burns's poetry as a hybridity of working-class and middle-class assumptions and sentiments, this cannot be categorically condemned as a failure on Burns's part to accurately represent the working class (although we can admit the argument that a single "accurate" representation is impossible to achieve from only one tokenized representative of such a large demographic). What ultimately occurs in Burns's work, however, is the same sort of "psychological annexation" that occurs in the work of Cixous's marginalized writer: he enters the forum of Scottish nationalist poetry, which at the time was dominated by middle-class and aristocratic literary patriarchs such as James Boswell, armed with a broadened social and national perspective that comes, in part, from his origins in the marginalized working class. In "To a Mouse," Burns takes advantage of the middle-class georgic tradition, but offers the reader a pessimism that is too far removed from bourgeois pastoral sentiment to faithfully serve a middle-class agenda:

> But Mousie, thou art no thy lane,
> In proving foresight may be vain:
> The best-laid schemes o' mice an' men
> Gang aft agley,

An' lea'e us nought but grief an' pain
   For promis'd joy!
Still thou art blest, compared wi' me!
The present only toucheth thee:
But och! I backward cast my e'e,
   On prospects drear!
An' forward, tho' I canna see,
   I guess an' fear![21]

On the surface, the poem reads as a simple product of Burns's spontaneous cleverness, exercised as he turns up a mouse's den while ploughing a field. Immediately he finds a rapport with the "sleekit, cowrin, tim'rous beastie",[22] though there is a degree of envy at work in the narrator's tone, both for the mouse's inability to imagine an unhappy future, and perhaps for the mouse's (at least moral) claim to the ownership of the land as well: in late eighteenth-century Scotland, ploughmen such as the narrator typically served a laird or other wealthy landowner, and often had no claim to the land they tilled. There is a subtle indication here, though I think it would have been less subtle for a reader in Burns's situation, that even the tiny mouse, by building a home on the laird's land, has more claim to it than the ploughman himself: Burns's lifetime also saw the early years of the Highland Clearances, in which countless landowners drove tenants from their homes to clear the land for farming and raising cattle and sheep. By turning over the mouse's house with his farming tools, the ploughman, who by looking "backward" or "forward" can despair over his own recent or forthcoming eviction, assumes the role of oppressor in a parallel eviction of the mouse.

This understanding of the poem, and the skilled class hybridity in which it casts its narrator (since he is both the oppressed worker of the laird's land, and the powerful usurper of the mouse's) are frequently all but forgotten under the weight of the two Victorian counter-arguments to such an understanding: either that he was in fact a secretly "affected" writer by way of his gentleman's education, or that he embodied the "noble savage" archetype by generating poetry spontaneously, naturally, and without artifice.[23] The earliest Burns scholars were quite taken by what they might have called the "natural" sound of his prosody, and so suggested (erroneously, I think) that

> [Burns] was born a poet ... and to his native genius alone is owing the perpetuity of his fame ... When inspired to compose poetry, poetry came gushing up from the well of his human affections, and he had nothing more to do than to pour it like

---

[21]   Robert Burns, "To A Mouse," in *Poems and Songs of Robert Burns*, ed. James Barke (Glasgow: Collins, 1955), 112.

[22]   Ibid.

[23]   Renderings of Burns within the "noble savage" mold, and the corresponding denials of his "artifice," do flatter the lack of pretentiousness or bourgeois affectation in Burns's poems, but at the same time they sell short the degree of conscious thought and shrewd craftsmanship of his work—a tradeoff which seems more to Burns's detriment than to his advantage as a serious literary figure.

streams irrigating a meadow, in many a cheerful tide ... there is no delusion, no affectation, no exaggeration, no falsehood, in the spirit of Burns' [sic] poetry.[24]

While the fatalistic ending of "To a Mouse" is hardly the "cheerful tide" of which Wilson speaks, this passage stands as a fairly straightforward example of the myth that the poems simply leapt into Burns's head unbidden, immaculate, pre-rhymed and grammatically polished. This stands in opposition to Setoun's argument that Burns's poems "are the work of a man of no mean education, and bear the stamp—however spontaneously his songs sing themselves in our ears—of culture and study."[25] This argument is the one more often championed in more recent scholarship: Alan Bold, for instance, manages to resolve the tension between these early and conflicting understandings of Burns when he asserts that "early critics ... turn[ed] the well-educated son of a tenant-farmer into an ignorant ploughman. Yet they were not so much patronizing the poet ... Burns himself cultivated the ignorant-ploughman syndrome and the critics simply acquiesced."[26]

Even Bold's resolution of the "nature *versus* nurture" debate over Burns's poetic gifts, however, is still a dangerous one to buy into, as to talk about the poems themselves as products formed exclusively "of culture and study" is to discount the working-class experiences that motivated them. It is one thing to say that Burns was more capable than early critics initially thought of self-editing, revising, and deliberately fabricating both writing *personae* and textual situations. At the same time, however, no amount of "deliberate construction" on the part of Burns can fully supplant the grim reality of his working-class existence: while poems such as "To a Mouse" are in no case completely objective recollections of real events, it is equally wrong to suggest that such a poem could be produced from culture and study (or at least, institutional or classroom study) in a vacuum devoid of working-class experience.

To be fair, Burns may be held accountable for intentionally adopting the less-than-honest mask of the ignorant farmer, although this claim dramatically undercuts the popular insistence (which Bold is stating here ironically) that "[h]is poetry is full of eulogies to honesty. It is, to Burns, the virtue of virtues."[27] Bold evaluates his own claim for us, arguing that through this near-deifying elevation, "Burns, as the vernacular prophet of honesty, is transformed into Burns the patron saint of honesty. In fact he was martyred by his inability to live with this impossible, almost solipsistic, notion, for he was also obliged to live with other people and to be acceptable to them."[28]

---

[24] Wilson, quoted by James Marshall in *A Winter with Robert Burns* (Edinburgh: P. Brown, 1846), 10.

[25] Setoun, 13.

[26] Alan Bold, "Robert Burns: Superscot," in *The Art of Burns*, eds R.D.S. Jack and Andrew Noble (London: Vision, 1982), 220.

[27] Ibid., 216.

[28] Ibid., 216.

What comes out of this statement is that Burns lived among others, and wrote as much in their symbolic language as he did in his own. He can still be held responsible, perhaps, for adopting the ignorant-ploughman figure, but he cannot be too heavily blamed for his decision, as it was this very *persona* that allowed him to bridge the gap between his own working-class experiences and an audience who was, for the most part (at least where his patrons were concerned), far removed from such experience. The myth of the Heaven-taught ploughman, at its core, may even have been a deliberate (on Burns's part) georgic adaptation of the noble savage myth, a model that was immensely popular throughout the Enlightenment and probably well-known to him: the ideological, economic and even linguistic disadvantages of Daniel Defoe's Friday in his relationships with Robinson Crusoe would not have an especially foreign concept to Burns, who was criticized even by Scottish aristocrats for his adherence to a rural dialect that was sometimes perceived as humorous, sub-standard, or even anti-Imperialist.

Beyond the mere identification of Burns with the noble savage myth, however, lies the (even unconscious) familiarity of his aristocratic reader with this archetype. For this reason, the persona that Burns crafted within it may have operated as an effective "mythological shorthand" through which he could communicate to a wider audience at least some of the meaning that would have been otherwise indecipherable without some amount of first-hand working-class experience. In the dark conclusion of "To a Mouse" Burns imbues his narrator with an awareness of the future without foreknowledge of it, which itself has analogues in quintessential eighteenth-century Imperialist depictions of the noble savage as a (usually black, and always poor) male who is intelligent enough to intuit the inevitability of his own death without the "wisdom" or perspective provided by good Christian faith; and further, this similarity need not be Burns's intent (nor even an accident of which he is aware) for it to be effective in practice.

In many ways, Burns's narrator in this poem, and indeed in a great number of works, taps into the same basic attributes of the noble savage archetype that have been too often occupied by stereotyped minorities ever since Aristotle's claim that comedy represented men "of ... a lower type."[29] The narrator, within the discourse of class, even holds some parallels to figures within gender and racial discourses: As with the African-American blackface stereotype of the American Civil War-era minstrel shows, the tone of Burns's working-class narrator swings between a tragic humility and an almost carefree whimsy, which is better expressed here in the first stanzas of the poem:

> Wee, sleekit, cowrin, tim'rous beastie,
> O, what a panic's in thy breastie!
> Thou need na start awa sae hasty
>   Wi' bickering brattle!
> I wad be laith to rin an' chase thee,
>   Wi' murdering pattle![30]

---

[29]   Aristotle, *Poetics*, trans. S.H. Butcher (New York: Hill & Wang, 1991), 57.

[30]   Burns, "To a Mouse," 111.

Andrew Noble argues that Burns, like a great many post-sixteenth century Scottish poets, "is radically flawed by an inability to treat with imagination the fundamental areas of creative activity but to retreat into whimsical or comic fantasy,"[31] and there is no shortage of ammunition for this argument: in this stanza alone, the cutesy imagery of the "wee '... beastie" and the implied farce of Burns chasing the creature with his enormous plough (as if he found such merriment in driving the plough after years of tenant-farming toil) paint an almost slapstick picture of that is reinforced for "centralized" readers (that is, the colonial English or the Scottish aristocracy) by the language and prosody of Burns's trademark Ayrshire brogue, which was seen by many readers as an almost pidgin dialect language. It has been noted (and reinforced) by countless figures of literature and popular culture, ranging from author Jamie Stuart[32] to comedian Mike Myers, that most of the Scots dialect, by virtue of its difference from the King's English sounded "funny" both in the sense of strangeness or otherness and of humor—especially in a time when all dialects in relation to the King's English were seen as sub-standard, as evidenced by Currie's claim that

> James VI ... encouraged Latin or English only, both of which he prided himself on writing with purity ... Scotsmen of talents declined writing in their native language, which they knew was not acceptable to their learned and pedantic monarch.[33]

The humorous othering of Scottish dialects certainly predates not only the twentieth century, but Burns's time as well: the provincial Northernisms of the Reeve in Chaucer's *Canterbury Tales*, played for humor, demonstrate just how far back such linguistic conventions reach. In this light, there *is* a certain whimsy inherent in Burns's "To a Mouse," but I would follow Noble's claim only so far as to admit the presence of such whimsy: to call it a "radical flaw" of the work, I think, misses the point entirely. As Burns's narrator continues to observe the mouse whose home he has disturbed, his whimsy immediately fades into guilt in the second stanza:

> I'm truly sorry man's dominion
> Has broken Nature's social union
> An' justifies that ill opinion
>   Which makes thee startle
> At me, thy poor, earth-born companion
>   An' fellow mortal![34]

---

[31]   Andrew Noble, "Burns, Blake and the Romantic Revolt," in *The Art of Burns*, 210.

[32]   While Stuart lacks the universal renown of Myers, who has used a false Scottish accent in at least five popular films at the time of this publication (*So I Married an Axe Murderer*, both sequels to *Austin Powers*, and all three *Shrek* films), Stuart's anthology *A Glasgow Bible* (Edinburgh: St. Andrew Press, 1997) is not only the best piece of literary evidence to this claim, but also one of the most rewarding renderings of the Bible into a new vernacular since John Wyclif first took up his quill.

[33]   James Currie, *The Life of Robert Burns, with a Criticism on His Writings*, eds William Chambers and Robert Chambers (Edinburgh: W.S. Orr & Co., 1838), 59.

[34]   Burns, "To a Mouse," 111.

The sorrow of the poem is all the more poignant because it is delivered with gradually accumulating regret as the narrator realizes the full extent of what he has done, not only destroying the home of the poor beast (and unveiling the similarities between his eviction of the mouse and the Highland Clearances), but leaving her (and in the subtitle, he does identify the mouse as a "her") with no means to rebuild and start over so close to winter, with "naething, now, to big a new ane."[35]

It seems to me that Burns's use of the familiar second person is not looking forward to a Romantic poetic affectation,[36] but backward to the original usage of *thou*, which firmly places the narrator as a social superior to the mouse. In this manner, and by citing the power of "man's dominion" over the beast, Burns is quietly establishing a microcosm of the relationship between landowner and tenant, and more generally, between the middle and working classes. The narrator is a hybrid figure who, although working-class (and we see in him a growing awareness of his own socioeconomic situation, and its similarities to that of the mouse, over the course of the poem), embodies middle-class attitudes towards the mouse; and even when he takes pity on the mouse, it is exactly that—*pity*—which is problematic in itself. The initial "whimsy" of the poem, which Noble so savagely critiques, is reconstructed as ironic by the later stanzas. Burns's keen awareness of commonalties between men[37] of all classes, of which we have many examples in later poems and letters, allow him to translate the whimsy, flippant air, and general carelessness from his perception of the middle-class "cuif" onto his narrator in the first stanza. In the end, Burns ultimately allows the simple ploughman in "To a Mouse", himself a middle-class stereotype of the working-class georgic tenant, to function as a symbol of the middle class itself.

While "To A Mouse" is perhaps the clearest and most literal example of Burns's class hybridity at work, we can find repetitions of this same pattern throughout Burns's other poems. The georgic nature of the ploughman stereotype is addressed more indirectly in Burns's "Rusticity's Ungainly Form:"

> Rusticity's ungainly form
>   May cloud the highest mind;
> But when the heart is nobly warm,
>   The good excuse will find.[38]

---

[35]   Ibid.

[36]   The use of *thou* as familiar pronoun in reference to God, which appears by Burns's time in the King James Bible and other liturgical sources, may be responsible for the later use of *thou*, from Blake onward, as an elevated form of the modern singular *you* in later poetry, whether it be the product of a flawed understanding or deliberate misconstruction.

[37]   "Men" should be taken literally here, not as a biased synonym for "people." I am aware that it stands as a sometimes awkwardly gendered word in cases such as this, but where Burns is concerned, a great deal of his profound social awareness is limited to men. For a deeper discussion of Burns's understanding of gender, see Leith Davis, "Gender and the Nation in the Work of Robert Burns and Janet Little," *SEL*, Vol. 38, No. 4 (Autumn 1998), 621–45; and Kirsteen McCue, "Burns, Women and Song," in *Robert Burns and Cultural Authority*, ed. Robert Crawford (Iowa City, IA: University of Iowa Press, 1997), 40–57.

[38]   Burns, "Rusticity's Ungainly Form," in *Poems and Songs of Robert Burns*, 343.

When attempting to evaluate Burns independently of the middle-class conventions that have come to define him, it initially seems that there is no "rustic form" more ungainly when applied to Burns than that of the stereotypical ploughman of "To a Mouse". It is an ungainly model of Burns because it is at best a one-sided construction of him, and at worst a false one. Many critics, both early and recent, have now pointed out the inherent errors in the stereotype, although a good number of these still continue to make use of it. Further, it is ungainly because Burns himself was an active participant in its propagation; and frequently, as Alan Bold argues, this was as much for his own personal benefit as for the furthering of any textual "message":

> Burns first advertised himself as a rustic bard because he knew this was the image the back-to-nature eighteenth-century public wanted ... Burns *used* his humble birth to implant a sense of guilt in others who could expiate their sins by bestowing patronage on the unfortunate poet.[39]

In "Is There For Honest Poverty," Burns offers his most famous description of his "cuif" figure, the ignorant and laughably pretentious aristocrat, who buys into the "tinsel show" of the glamorous court and "struts, an' stares, an' a' that."[40] The "cuif" himself is a figure of whimsy, and it takes little more than a subtle translation and toning down of the figure's dandyisms to arrive at the ploughman narrator of "To A Mouse." This ploughman figure, however, is redeemed because he possesses the very same class awareness that Burns has cultivated through his class hybridity: although the narrator fills a middle-class role in the poem, he too is a "poor, earth-born companion" to the mouse—he too is a helpless subject of the working class whose fate is left to the whim or carelessness of "man's dominion." This awareness, coming out of the narrator's experience as both victor and victim of a class-based power structure, is the consciousness Burns wishes to cultivate in the middle class; effectively, it negates the pretentiousness of the narrator, which is much less pronounced here than in the "cuif" of "Is There For Honest Poverty." In "Mark Yonder Pomp," the foppish airs of the aristocrat are transferred from the individual to his environment with Burns's usual indignation:

> What are the showy treasures?
> What are the noisy pleasures?
> The gay, gaudy glare of vanity and art!
> The polish'd jewel's blaze
> May draw the wond'ring gaze,
> And courtly grandeur bright
> The fancy may delight,
> But never, never can come near the heart![41]

---

[39] Bold, 217.

[40] Burns, "Is There For Honest Poverty," in *Poems and Songs of Robert Burns*, 643.

[41] Burns, "Mark Yonder Pomp," in *Poems and Songs of Robert Burns*, 643–644.

From the juxtaposition of the foolish aristocrat to the vain and gaudy world of the wealthy comes a startling glimpse of the idea that Burns blames the milieu as much as the man. At his worst, the "cuif" is foolish, greedy, and led easily astray by his own ignorance; but the world he buys into, full of bright lights and sounds, is able to "draw the wond'ring gaze" and delight the fancy. The pomp of aristocracy is perhaps nothing more than an illusion, but Burns recognizes here that it is an illusion with great powers of seduction at its disposal.

Perhaps Burns himself was in part seduced by the illusion; perhaps he was only afraid of being seduced. It is dangerous to assume that Burns's private confession that "I wish to be rich"[42] signifies anything more for Burns than a desire to live comfortably without the thankless toil, poor health and premature death (and all the subsequent "involuntary resurrections" of his decomposed head) that were his ultimate fate. But Burns has also stated that

> [t]o crouch in the train of meer, stupid Wealth & Greatness, except where the commercial interests of worldly Prudence find their account in it, I hold to be Prostitution in any one that is not born a Slave.[43]

Here Burns reveals a willingness to serve nonsensical middle-class pretense when conditions of worldly prudence are met, and a keen awareness that despite his "humble" origins, Burns does not occupy the lowest space on the socioeconomic totem pole: that position is reserved for the victims of slavery, and while there remains insufficient evidence to confirm exactly how Burns felt about slavery, at least it is clear here that he was intensely conscious of it.

Even amidst the shrewdness of Burns and his deliberate manipulation of his own literary *persona* and public image, it would be a vicious mistake to suggest that Burns was in any way a sell-out, to the middle classes or to anyone else. Nevertheless, there remains the nagging question of *why* Burns became so renowned and so successful: he is among the most famous and celebrated Scottish poets who ever lived, and has come closer to entering the canon of English literature than Robert Fergusson, Edwin Muir, Robert Tannahill, James Boswell, or any of the others who have been elevated to such heroic heights as Scottish literary legends. In the end, Burns's handling of class is too complicated to offer a decisive judgment in this regard: claims that he catered to the poetic needs and desires of his readers from England and among the Scottish aristocracy fall flat in the shadow of just how subversive to these powers much of his work could be. It is not enough to say simply that Burns was just a very good poet; yet here is where criticism usually falls silent. There are a few varied (and sometimes contradictory) opinions on Burns when it comes to his life, his education, and his constructions of certain class and gender paradigms, but rare indeed are the occasions when any doubt in Burns's skill is intelligently voiced. Burns's appeal among Scottish poets

---

42   Burns, *The Prose Works of Robert Burns*, 30.
43   Burns, quoted in Thomas Crawford, *Boswell, Burns and the French Revolution* (Edinburgh: Saltire Society, 1990), 6.

of the eighteenth century is for the most part unmatched, and this appeal itself may spring from his position of hybridity. The earlier claim of class representation—that by being a poet *of* the working classes, Burns was in fact seen as a poet *for* the working classes—must be reconfigured, in light of the understanding of class hybridity that has now been assembled here. By operating from a hybridized viewpoint, isolated from the binaries of self and other, Burns is accurately able to write of both sides of the class binary—and in this way, can effectively write *for* both sides of the binary as well. The middle-class attributes of Burns's narrative *persona* lead to similarities (and more remarkably, to identification) between his working-class narrators and his aristocratic audience, and by obscuring the barriers between classes in this manner, he often seems able to use mechanisms of class hybridity to climb beyond the discourse of class altogether.

Burns cannot quite be called a poet of "universal" appeal—the controversy surrounding Burns's treatment of gender in particular underscores the fact that his writing does not touch all readers equally—but at the same time, the unifying properties of Burns's work that spring out of his class hybridity go far, especially given the age in which he lived, toward educating his readers as to what lies on the other side of the class barrier, and in some cases even toward breaking down the class barrier altogether. This is all the more remarkable when considered alongside the developmental timeline of working-class identity as provided by critics such as E.P. Thompson and Christopher McAll: both might argue that a unified social understanding of the working class as such does not exist in Burns's lifetime, and yet the poems of Burns show considerable evidence of such an understanding—perhaps anticipating the later large-scale development of a working-class identity, and perhaps even provoking it. In "Is There For Honest Poverty," Burns intimates an idealistic hope, extending far beyond his simple desire to be rich,

> [t]hat man to man the world o'er
> Shall brithers be for a' that.[44]

In the study of Burns as a working-class intellectual, it is this lofty goal that proves perhaps the last mystery. George Combe and Robert Cox's theories of phrenology were defunct long before Cixous's theories of the *bisexuelle* writer surfaced in any form that was applicable to Robert Burns; and it is impossible to say now (without a third unnecessary exhumation) whether the shape of Burns's skull might have indicated a tendency to transcend the boundaries of class using mechanisms of discursive hybridity. According to the Chambers brothers, however, the shape of Burns's skull did indicate a certain "Love of Approbation,"[45] and by this measure, if Burns could know that his parallel audiences were truly united as "brithers," if only in some small capacity by a shared appreciation of his work, perhaps it would not displease him.

---

[44]   Burns, "Is There For Honest Poverty," in *Poems and Songs of Robert Burns*, 643.
[45]   Chambers and Chambers, "The Cranium of Burns," 76.

Works Cited

Aristotle. *Poetics*, trans. S.H. Butcher. New York: Hill & Wang, 1991.

Bold, Alan. "Robert Burns: Superscot," in *The Art of Burns*, eds R.D.S. Jack and Andrew Noble. London: Vision, 1982, 215–238.

Burns, Robert. "Is There For Honest Poverty," in *Poems and Songs of Robert Burns*, ed. James Barke. Glasgow: Collins, 1955, 642–643.

———. "Mark Yonder Pomp," in *Poems and Songs of Robert Burns*, 343–344.

———. *The Prose Works of Robert Burns*, ed. Robert Chambers. Edinburgh: W.S. Orr & Co., 1839.

———. "Rusticity's Ungainly Form," in *Poems and Songs of Robert Burns*, 343–344.

———. "To a Mouse," in *Poems and Songs of Robert Burns*, 111–112.

Chambers, William, and Robert Chambers. "The Cranium of Burns," in *The Life of Robert Burns, with a Criticism on His Writings; by James Currie, M.D.*, eds William Chambers and Robert Chambers. Edinburgh: W.S. Orr & Co, 1838, 75–76.

Cixous, Hélène. "From 'Sorties'," in *A Critical and Cultural Theory Reader*, eds Anthony Easthope and Kate McGowan. Toronto: University of Toronto, 1992, 147–157.

Crawford, Thomas. *Boswell, Burns and the French Revolution*. Edinburgh: Saltire Society, 1990.

Currie, James. *The Life of Robert Burns, with a Criticism on His Writings*, eds. William Chambers and Robert Chambers. Edinburgh: W.S. Orr & Co., 1838.

McAll, Christopher. *Class, Ethnicity, and Social Inequality*. Montréal: McGill-Queen's University Press, 1992.

McGuirk, Carol. "Burns and Nostalgia," in *Burns Now*, ed. Kenneth Simpson. Edinburgh: Canongate, 1994, 31–69.

McKenney, Mary. "Class Attitudes & Professionalism," in *Building Feminist Theory: Essays from Quest*, ed. Quest Book Committee. New York: Longman, 1981, 139–148.

Mackenzie, Henry. "Extraordinary Account of Robert Burns the Ayrshire Ploughman; withExtracts from his Poems," in *The British Essayists; with Prefaces Biographical, Historical, and Critical*, ed. Lionel Thomas Bergher, 45 vols, Vol. XXXVII. London: T. and J. Allman, 1823, 295–302.

Marshall, James. *A Winter with Robert Burns*. Edinburgh: P. Brown, 1846.

Noble, Andrew. "Burns, Blake and the Romantic Revolt," *The Art of Burns*, 191–214.

Setoun, Gabriel. *Robert Burns*. Edinburgh: Oliphaunt Anderson & Ferrier, 1896.

Simpson, Kenneth. "Robert Burns: 'Heaven-taught plowman'?" *Burns Now*, 70–91.

Zimmerman, Bonnie. "What Has Never Been: An Overview Of Lesbian Feminist Literary Criticism," in *Feminisms: An Anthology Of Literary Theory And Criticism*, eds Robyn R. Warhol and Diane Price Herndl. New Brunswick, NJ: Rutgers University Press, 1991, 117–137.

Chapter 5

Coffeehouse vs. Alehouse: Notes on the Making of the Eighteenth-Century Working-Class Intellectual

Aruna Krishnamurthy

In the year 1800, W.H. Reid, a spy for the government of William Pitt, published a pamphlet entitled *The Rise and Dissolution of the Infidel Societies in the Metropolis* that identified three different groups that were influenced in the 1790s by the French Revolution. According to Reid, these groups "converged in popular debating clubs—some of an intellectual rationalist disposition, others of a more convivial type which met in alehouses to voice a mélange of blasphemy, millenarianism and sedition, and to plot insurrection in secret."[1] One of these groups was comprised of those who championed a spirit of anti-authoritarianism within the public sphere, men such as William Godwin and the Deist Richard Price, labeled by Reid as "infidels, or political freethinkers, dedicated to moral and intellectual subversion."[2] At the other end of the spectrum was a more impoverished group of men, made of "an 'auxiliary' force of lower-class religious enthusiasts with a passion to overthrow the established order."[3] This amorphous set was represented by Thomas Spence, Thomas Evans, and their circle of prophets, revolutionaries and pornographers that Iain MacCalman has identified as the "radical underworld" of the 1790s. But the group that most caught the ire of the Pitt ministry, and faced the maximum degree of censorship and surveillance was "the mainly artisan proponents of French Jacobin-republicanism." This group was comprised of men such as Thomas Hardy and John Thelwall—artisans by birth and occupation, autodidacts who spearheaded the first working-class organization, the London Corresponding Society (LCS).

While Reid's exaggerated fear of sedition and anarchy reflects his position as a government informer, there were other descriptions in the early nineteenth century that viewed the last decade of the eighteenth century in a more positive way. William Hazlitt remembers the 1790s as a time when "our young gownsmen

---

[1] Quoted in Iain MacCalman, *Radical Underworld: Prophets, Revolutionaries, and Pornographers in London, 1795–1840* (Cambridge: Cambridge University Press, 1988), 1.

[2] Ibid., 2.

[3] Ibid., 2.

of the greatest expectation and promise, versed in classic lore, steeped in dialectics, armed at all points for the foe, well read, well nurtured, well provided for, left the University and the prospect of lawn sleeves, tearing asunder the shackles of the free-born spirit and the cobwebs of school-divinity, to throw themselves at the feet of the new Gamaliel, and learn wisdom from [Godwin]."[4] In our time, the 1790s provides the backdrop against which E.P. Thompson and other labor historians have charted the formation of an English working-class identity. What I attempt to do in this essay is to filter the radical culture of 1790s England through the figure of the working-class intellectual. Despite their cultural and class distance, all three radical groups identified by Reid are implicated in the categories of "working class" and "intellectual" in some way. The literary output of Thelwall, Godwin, and Spence was equally popular with a laboring audience, and the three groups cultivated close links with one another. Thelwall was Godwin's close friend and follower, and Spence and Thelwall, as members of the London Corresponding Society knew each other quite well. While each of these figures offers interesting possibilities as a working-class intellectual, my main interest is in Thelwall, the figure in between the more highbrow Godwin and the more proletarian Spence. Indeed, it is Thelwall's very in-between-ness that interests me, which I place reflexively within another trajectory—the formation of working-class identity—in the eighteenth century. I suggest that Thelwall's role as an intermediary between polite and popular culture, or between coffeehouse civility and alehouse hostility, is homologous to the in-between-ness of working-class organizations such as the LCS that sought to reconstitute the workers within the eighteenth century "republic of letters," but could only do so by distancing them from an earlier type of "pre-capitalist" identity based on rough folk culture. E.P. Thompson views this plebeian culture as a traditional site of resistance to the hegemony of paternalism; folk songs and satirical ballads such as "Brave Dudley Boys" allow a glimpse into that radicalism:

> We bin marchin' up and deown
>> Wo boys, wo
>> Fur to pull the housen deown
>> And its O the brave Doodley boys
>> Wo boys, Wo
>> It bin the brave Doodley boys, Wo!
> Some goten sticks, some gotten steavs
>> Wo boys, Wo
>> Fur to beat all rogues and kne-avs ...[5]

Quite different from the intellectual's mediating role, the crowd deploys a vigorous, self-activating culture of the people seen in the figures of the "brave Doodley boys," who threaten to "pull the housen deown" and "beat up all rogues and kne-avs."

---

[4]   William Hazlitt, *The Spirit of the Age; Or, Contemporary Portraits* (London: G. Richards, 1904), 25.

[5]   Quoted in E.P. Thompson, *Customs in Common* (London: Merlin Press, c1991), 65.

Where the intellectual was a solitary artist working within the signifying economy of the republic of letters, the crowd, defined by the shared experience of labor and folk culture's "rough music" constituted a threat to official descriptions of reality. In displacing this tradition of radicalism, the process of formation of the working-class intellectual in the eighteenth century can be seen as the pre-history of modernity where a rebellious plebeian culture is made to undergo a process of "rationalization" instituted through the process of wage-labor (which initiated a shift from task-orientation to timed labor), finally to emerge as the crowd of alienated monads in Manchester, who, in the words of Friedrich Engels, "rush past each other as if they had nothing in common, nothing to do with one another."[6] I suggest that the emergence of the intellectual is paralleled by the effacement of the revolutionary crowd of popular morality. It is this double legacy—the growth of the intellectual accompanied by the loss of a revolutionary crowd—that is concretized in the experience of modernity.

In *The Structural Transformation of the Public Sphere*, Jurgen Habermas investigates the rise of the "public sphere" as the agency and product of Europe's transition from a 'traditional' society organized around feudal hierarchies, to a bourgeois ethos that stressed individual autonomy and confidence in man's rational capacities.[7] The "bourgeois public sphere," a "child of the eighteenth century,"[8] signified a radical break from the social and cultural forms of expression of courtly society in foregrounding a universalist lexicon of 'liberty' and 'principles.' The key aspects of the new public sphere, egalitarianism and inclusiveness, hinged on the rise of a discourse oriented society, explained by Habermas as follows:

> First, they preserved a kind of social intercourse that, far from presupposing the equality of status, disregarded status altogether. The parity on whose basis alone the authority of the better argument could assert itself against that of social hierarchy ... [was] the parity of "common humanity" ... Secondly, discussion within such a public presupposed the problematization of areas that until then had not been questioned ... The private people for whom the cultural product became available as a commodity profaned it inasmuch as they had to determine

---

[6]   Friedrich Engels, *The Condition of the Working Class of England*, trans. Florence Kelley-Wishnewetsky (Oxford: Oxford University Press, 1993), 37. Also see my "'More Than Abstract Knowledge:' Friedrich Engels in Industrial Manchester," *Journal of Victorian Literature and Culture*, Vol. 28, No. 2 (2000), 427–448, which analyzes Engels as a working-class intellectual faced with the task of organizing the "alienated monads" of an industrialized Manchester into a revolutionary vanguard of Socialist revolution. I explore Engels' narrative as an intersection of various sub-plots hidden under the abstract method of Enlightenment discourse. Engels' transgressive desire to break away from his middle-class ethos finds voice in the apocalyptic vision of a classless society, thus relocating intellectual production within an interpretive web of lived spaces.

[7]   Jurgen Habermas, *The Structural Transformation of the Public Sphere: An Enquiry Into A Category of Bourgeois Society*, trans. Thomas Burger and Frederick Lawrence (Cambridge, MA: MIT Press, 1989).

[8]   Habermas, *Structural Transformation*, xviii.

its meaning on their own (by way of rational communication with one another), verbalise it, and thus state explicitly what precisely in its implicitness for so long could assert its authority ... Thirdly, the same process that converted culture into a commodity ... established the public as in principle inclusive.[9]

The analytic thrust of the republic of letters that energized the Thomas Paine-Edmund Burke debate on the French Revolution also trickles down into the lives of men "whose practice it is to go to a public house from the workshops after the labour of the day, to have their supper, and then regale themselves with a pint or pot of beer, and smoak thier pipes, and convers about the news of the day--the hardness of the times—the dearness of provisions" and, importantly, "directs thier conversation a little farther by inquiring into the *cause* of all those calamities of which they complain ... ."[10] E.P. Thompson rightly identifies the rise of working-class consciousness in England in the aftermath of the French Revolution by looking at the examples of London Corresponding Society (LCS), the first organization that made an attempt to reformulate working-class identity, and its most prominent leader, 'Citizen' John Thelwall, orator and writer, who from his median position between intellectual and proletarian worlds attempts to inscribe the disadvantaged worker within a civic identity based on "sentiments of humanity" and "pure emanations of expanded benevolence."[11] While evaluating the achievements of working-class organizations such as the London Corresponding Society, Thompson celebrates its ability to 'make' itself by utilizing the tenets of the bourgeois public sphere:

> Even the brief description of its first meetings ... indicate that a new kind of organization had come into being—features which helps define (in the context of 1790–1850) the nature of a "working-class organization." There is the working man as Secretary. There is the low weekly subscription. There is the intermingling of economic and political themes—"the hardness of the times" and Parliamentary Reform. There is the function of the meeting, both as social occasion and as a center for political activity. There is the realistic attention to procedural formalities. Above all, there is the determination to propagate opinions and to organize the converted, embodied in the leading rule:" That the number of our Members be unlimited."[12]

LCS's critical reception in history has typically followed the blueprint laid out by Thompson, as an agency that radicalized the worker through facilitating his entry

---

⁹   Ibid., 36–38.

¹⁰   Thomas Hardy, "Thomas Hardy's Account of the Origin of the London Corresponding Society (1799)," in *Selections From the Papers of the London Corresponding Society 1792–1799*, ed. Mary Thale (Cambridge: Cambridge University Press, 1983), 8. Hereafter, materials from the papers will be referred to as "*Selections*."

¹¹   John Thelwall, "Selections from *The Tribune*," in *The Politics of English Jacobinism: Writings of John Thelwall*, ed. Gregory Claeys (University Park: Pennsylvania State University Press, 1995), 85. Material from *The Tribune* will be referred to as "*Tribune*" hereafter.

¹²   E.P. Thompson, *Making of the English Working Class* (New York: Viking, 1964), 21.

into the public sphere, and simultaneously effected a radicalization of the polite republic of letters. This is the first step in the putative journey of the working classes from the "class-in-itself" to the "class-for-itself" stage.[13] But I would like to view LCS's legacy through a different lens by suggesting that in the very delineation of the LCS as a place for working-class resistance, Thompson's narrative emphasizes (and indirectly approves of) the tenets of the bourgeois public sphere. While the LCS signified a radicalization of middle-class Reform societies such as the SCI and Friends of the People that furnished it with a vocabulary and a modus operandi for working-class self-representation, paradoxically, its identity depended upon its ability to imitate the public sphere's cultural imaginary, as seen from Thompson's quote above. To push this analysis further, it can asserted that the LCS has a double function of both challenging *and* representing the bourgeois public sphere and that this ambivalence in the form and function of the LCS may, in fact, constitute a prototype for working-class identity as it emerged from England's transition from an "ideology of leisure" to "an ideology of labor"[14] in the eighteenth century.

The significance of the transformation in the worker's identity can be delineated by examining earlier forms of class resistance, such as the rebellious "pre-industrial crowd"[15] that was marked by contradictory objectives and spontaneous modes of action such as rioting. The radicalism of the crowd that served as "public opinion poll"[16] often took shape around the ideals of the 'free-born Briton' and his "natural rights." For George Rudê the mob's adoption of a political idiom suggests a degree of political consciousness, despite evidence of the mob's pragmatic motivations of hunger, prices and wages, and its deference to the political ambitions and authority of John Wilkes or Lord George Gordon. While connecting the riots of 1768–69

---

[13]   Edward Andrew describes this process as follows: "As a class against aristocracy, but not yet "for itself"—still dependent upon political and cultural forms of the aristocracy—the bourgeoisie, constantly changing its character and composition, rose to political and social dominance. By analogy, as a class against capital but not yet "for itself"—still dependent upon the political and cultural forms of the bourgeoisie—the working class, constantly changing its character and composition, organized and disorganized on sectoral, regional, ethnic and sexual lines, will have to engage in a prolonged struggle for social and political dominance." "Class in Itself and Class against Capital: Karl Marx and His Classifiers," *Canadian Journal of Political Science*, Vol. 16, No. 3 (September, 1983), 584.

[14]   Isaac Kramnick identifies classical republicanism as "ideology of leisure" and bourgeois republicanism or liberalism as "ideology of work." *Republicanism and Bourgeois Radicalism: Political Ideology in Late Eighteenth-Century England and America* (Ithaca: Cornell University Press, 1990), 1–2.

[15]   George Rudê's term for distinguishing the dominant form of rebellious activity of eighteenth century crowd from later culture of industrial protest. *Paris and London in the Eighteenth Century: Studies in Popular Protest* (New York: Viking, 1971).

[16]   Ian Gilmour points out that mob rioting performed the function of a "public opinion poll" in the absence of any other kind of forum to inform the authorities about public reactions to particular laws and bills. *Riot, Risings and Revolution: Governance and Violence in Eighteenth-Century England* (London: Pimlico, 1993), 337.

with concurrent industrial disputes of weavers and coal-heavers, Rudê examines the Wilkes affair from multiple registers that coalesced in the persona of Wilkes, whose appeal to the "meanest mechanic, the poorest peasant and day labourer"[17] was compounded by a significant middle-class interest in his political career. The composition of the mob was not limited to the lower classes but also included "gentlemen" and "well-dressed persons."[18] Not only the fact that Wilkes drew "support from a substantial section of the merchants and property owners in the City of London ... and financial support and sympathy ... [from] prosperous citizens in London, Westminster and Southwark,"[19] but, more importantly, the nature of his relationship with his plebeian following, problematizes the link between the leader and the working-class crowd. "Do you suppose," it is said Wilkes asked his opponent, while watching the cheering throngs on the hustings, "that there are more fools or rogues in that assembly?"[20] While Wilkes' distance from his constituency of mechanics and laborers casts a shadow of duplicity upon his function as leader that is further confirmed by his active role in the suppression of mobs during Gordon riots in 1780, the political expression of the protest is worth considering. Rudê places the contradictory elements of "Wilkes and Liberty!" in a trajectory where the event "marks an important stage in the political education of the 'middling' and common people of Britain; yet it marked but the early beginnings of a radical movement with a stable popular base ... [which] revived and bore richer fruits in the 1790s ..."[21] The rallying of the masses around the symbol of "No. 45"[22] captures this idea well. "No. 45" functioned as a signifier of the power of lower orders. Marking up of private spaces of authority and exclusion—both, at the level of the body politic/city and the body—underscores the way in which "No. 45" operated within a 'sub-political' tradition of "customary consciousness,"[23] outside of its immediate

---

[17]   Wilkes's reference to the working classes is quoted in E.P. Thompson's *Making of the English Working Class* (New York: Pantheon), 83.

[18]   Ibid., 262.

[19]   Ibid., 257–258.

[20]   Mentioned in Thompson, *Making*, 70.

[21]   Rude, 267.

[22]   "No. 45" referred to *North Briton*'s 45th issue of April 1763 in which Wilkes had implied that "if George III was he not a liar was the puppet of lying ministers." Quoted in Gilmour, 305.

[23]   E.P. Thompson's term for describing the making of the English working classes, is an important category for this study. Against a strictly structural (Althusserian) model, Thompson explains that "the conservative [plebeian] culture of the plebs as often as not resists, in the name of custom, those economic rationalizations and innovations (such as enclosure, work-discipline, unregulated "free" markets in grain) which rulers, dealers, or employers seek to impose. Innovation is more evident at the top of society than below, but since this innovation is not some normless and neutral technological/sociological process ("modernization", "rationalization") but is the innovation of capitalist process, it is most often experienced by the plebs in the form of exploitation, of the expropriation of customary use-rights, or the violent disruption of valued patterns of work and leisure.

context of politicking and journalism. Viewed in this context, the slogan of "No. 45" (along with others such as "No Popery!" and "Church and King!") became a tool for exacting social revenge, as seen from this experience of Justice Richard Capel, who was sent to disperse the mob at Bermondsey Street:

> Accordingly he went to the said House with an Officer and a Body of Light Guards, and found there a great number of Persons assembled in a riotous manner. He then and there exhorted them to disperse and told them the Danger of their Behaviour. Then one John Percival took him by the collar and said 'Damn you, I'll mark you;' and accordingly he did mark him with large figures No. 45 on the cape of his great coat.[24]

Another relevant point about these political riots was their display of two different models of leadership, as is seen in this image of a London mob comprising of

> parades of itinerant bands, marching (or running) through Shoreditch, the City of London, Westminster or Southwark, gathering fresh forces on the way ... . Frequently they were 'captained' by men whose personality, speech, dress or momentary assumption of authority marked them out as leaders: such 'captains,' sometimes described by eyewitnesses as 'carrying a drawn sword' or 'riding on a horse,' were Tom the Barber ...William Pateman, a journeyman wheelwright ... and Thomas Taplin, a coach-master ... . They may, too, have passed on to their followers the slogans of the day, whose chanting in unison both terrified 'respectable' onlookers and served so effectively to rally supporters—such slogans as 'Down with the Irish!' (1736), 'Wilkes and Liberty!' (1768) and 'No Popery!' (1780).[25]

The mob organized itself around a parliamentary turf of the gentleman, such as John Wilkes, who held an iconic appeal for the common man, and while taking up the cause of the gentleman, the mob placed itself under a temporary and arbitrary leadership of a Thomas Taplin or a William Pateman, who spontaneously arose from the crowd for the practical task of directing it towards some immediate objective, and disappeared into it upon its completion. Where the gentleman initiated some abstract ideal ("Liberty," "No Popery!," "Church and King!"), the 'captain' was responsible giving it the concrete shape of destruction of property.

The LCS gained ascendancy by challenging both these aspects of radical action as it consciously distanced itself from the influence of the gentleman as well as the mob. A pamphlet published in 1795, written "expressly for the Members of the London Corresponding Society," cautions the readers against the two extremes

---

Hence the plebeian culture is rebellious, but rebellious in defense of custom ... But when people search for legitimations for protest, they often turn back to the paternalist regulations of a more authoritarian society, and select from among these those parts most calculated to defend their present interests." *Customs in Common*, 9–10.

[24] Rude, 236.

[25] Ibid., 295.

of "tyranny" and "slavery" that readers must abjure.[26] Where tyranny obstructed the march of reason and benevolence under the sway of arbitrary authority, slavery signified the danger of "pristine ignorance" becoming a tool of political faction. In the formulation of a new radical identity, questions of rights and liberties of the 'free-born Briton' were severed from determinations of property and class, and relocated within a universalistic notion of virtue. Emphatically separating itself from a *sansculotte* identity in a resolution on 6 June 1793, by declaring that "[r]epublicanism forms no part of this Society's principles," the LCS saw itself more in the role of "corresponding ... to collect the opinion and sense of the nation."[27] This central function was to be motivated by the ideal of dispelling the "gross ignorance and prejudice of the bulk of the nation and instill into ... minds [of the lower classes] by means of press a sense of their own rights as freemen, and of their duty to themselves, and their posterity, as good citizens, and heridatory guardians of the liberties transmitted to them by their forefathers." [28]A quick look at the crowd action of the LCS emphasizes the shift in the political identity of its members, especially in this description of an LCS street rally that celebrated the acquittal of its leaders in the treason trials of 1794:

> After welcoming them with acclamations of heart-felt joy, by repeated huzzahs, they ... conducted [the leaders] to a public-house, where, after passing an hour in mutual congratulations and welcome ... the glorious sight began. In a few seconds the darkness of the night was illumined by the bright blaze of over 200 flambeaus and torches, and the order of procession began as follows: first—A beautiful silk flag, on which was inscribed in large letters—THE LIBERTY OF THE PRESS ... then came the coach drawn, not by horses, but by an immense crowd ... in regular

---

[26]   Edward Henry Iliff, "A Summary of the Duties of Citizenship! Written expressly for the Members of the London Corresponding Society; including Observations on the Contemptuous Neglect of the Secretary of State, with regard to their late Address to the King!" (London, 1795). There was a clear disavowal of any long-term connections with men of position, especially if they were involved in active politics. Thomas Hardy's objection to a proposal for appointing Lord Daer as chairman is "upon this ground that it would still appear to be a party business and might prevent the people exerting themselves in their own cause and depend implicitly (as formerly) upon the mere ipse dixit of some Noble Man or great Man without the least trouble of examining themselves ..." (Hardy 8). He further recalls that the LCS was "so scrupulous about the admission of any of those of the higher ranks that when any of them offered to pay more than we usually demanded on the admission of a new member We would not receive it but told them that we had money sufficient for all necessary purposes Viz. for printing, postage of Letters, and stationary" (8). The disengagement of leadership from status is further reflected in the position occupied by the eminent intellectual-cum-politician Rev. John Horne Tooke, who was incarcerated and tried for treason along with Thelwall and Hardy in 1794. Unlike Wilkes, Horne Tooke's role was more that of a mentor, whose contribution was proofreading and embellishing the Society's pamphlets and notices.

[27]   Thelwall, *Tribune*, 71.

[28]   Selections, 6–7.

order ... [O]n the top of the coach was an emblematical transparent painting, supported by two patriotic twine behind which were two large flambeaus. In the front of the painting was a figure of the Goddess of Liberty. In her right hand she held a medallion of THOMAS ERSKINE [who was the lawyer for the defendants] resting on an altar, on the base of which was inscribed this motto REFORMATION TO THE WORLD. The background represented the SUN, rising with redoubled splendour out of a dark cloud; emblematical of the People rising from the black shades of ignorance, superstition and oppression ... . The procession thus arranged, moved slowly through all the principal streets ... amidst the joyful shouts of thousands, and the roaring of cannon, which at particular stated intervals rended the air and pierced even to the skies ...[29]

Rather than the untutored symbol of "No. 45," the Enlightenment symbols of the rising sun, and the goddess of liberty allows for a self-reflexive location of working-class identity within an unfolding dialectic of history, as "people rising from the black shades of ignorance, superstition and oppression."[30] It is important to note that in a society polarized along the lines of Burkean conservatism and Paineite radicalism, where a nervous administration was heavy handed towards its critics, Jacobin organizations such as the LCS were forced to disavow violence, an agenda that seems to have inspired the above commentary. Nevertheless, the contrast between an LCS political demonstration and the earlier example of crowd action, which seamlessly combined the personal with the political, "bread" and the English Constitution, indicates a significant paradigm shift that freed the lower classes from political opportunists, but simultaneously distanced them from their past tradition of collective action. The rise of the artisan-intellectual leader in the radical circuit of the 1790s is the cultural fallout of this larger transformation of working-class identity, where Thelwall's self-fashioning based itself on a ressentiment with a past shaped by Tom the Barber and John Wilkes. In comparing himself with the iconic hero of popular morality, Wat Tyler, Thelwall says,

When Wat Tyler, and his insurgents, oppressed by the hardships brought upon them by mad and frantic crusades for the subjugation of France, spread terror to the very recesses of the court; were these insurgents men of enquiry? Were they men who had been in the habit of political association? Were they members of *Corresponding Societies*, or did they attend *Lectures in Beaufort Buildings*? No, neither lectures in Beaufort Buildings, not London Corresponding Societies then existed. Political associations were then unknown; and the men who committed the violence had never heard of meetings for the discussion of political principles.[31]

---

[29] Extract of a letter from Sheffield, dated December 22nd 1794, Francis Place Collection (London: British Library).

[30] James Chandler's links Romanticism with the idea of history consciousness in a similar self-reflexive way. *England in 1819: The Politics of Literary Culture and the Case of Romantic Historicism.* Chicago: University of Chicago Press, 1998.

[31] Thelwall, *The Tribune*, 322.

Thelwall's speeches were instrumental in directing his constituency away from earlier modes of public action and collective empowerment towards a new model focused around a new leadership defined by intellectual and oratorical skills. The heroic ideal of resistance was located in the moral agency of the individual, to be measured by his ability to conform to the ideals of the public sphere:

> I wish I knew how to give you a Spartan determination of soul, together with the benevolence and philanthropy with which a few speculative philosophers of the present day have endeavoured to inspire mankind. I would make you as hard as rocks, against the assaults of corruption, prejudice and oppression ... But, at the same time I would fill your souls with a deflation of every thing like violence, rancour, and cruelty. O that I could make you feel the true determination of generous valour, and that you might be as wise and benevolent as you were determined and resolute! [32]

The shift from a spontaneous praxis of the crowd to an informed agitation based on the "virtuous principle of liberty"[33] inaugurated a new structure of relationship between members of a collective. As Habermas says, "people were to be brought up to the level of culture; culture was not lowered to that of the masses."[34] The spatial arrangement of this form of radicalism was designed to reflect a predilection towards rational thought rather than spontaneous action. During mass rallies and meetings, the field was organized around a focal point of the tribune erected a few feet above the ground level, from where the citizen-leader would exhort the masses to exercise their rational faculties. The democratic ideal of the LCS was also reflected in the everyday affairs of the Society. A proposal was raised in August 1793 for the abolition of all titles in favor of adopting "citizen" as a mode of address within the LCS. The adoption of the 'citizen' identity meant the dissolution of hierarchical structures within the Society, where the same individual could occupy two opposite roles between two successive meetings:

> In each of the divisions it was agreed to appoint a Chairman every meeting night, by acclamation or a Show of hands—on the next meeting night the Chairman was to descend to become door keeper in rotation. It was not deemed any degradation to the man who filled that high and elevated Station of *president*, to stoop to take upon him the *lowest office* in Society, *door-keeper*, when it was for the express purpose of promoting, and securing happiness, order, and Tranquillity in the Society.[35]

Class distinctions were also erased in a democratic process whereby "[e]very three Months new Officers were elected by ballot or the old ones rechosen if they

---

[32]   John Thelwall, *The Tribune*, 151.

[33]   Thelwall, *The Tribune*, 73.

[34]   Jurgen Habermas, *Toward a Rational Society; Student Protest, Science, and Politics*, trans. Jeremy J. Shapiro (Boston: Beacon Press, 1970).

[35]   Selections, 9.

found it convenient—There was a uniform rule by which all Members were admitted high and low rich and poor."[36] In all this, the LCS, as a gatherer of 'public opinion' replicates the egalitarianism that is the founding principle of bourgeois society where self-interest is made to co-exist with common weal, with the submission of both to the rule of common law. LCS's idealization of self-improvement and discipline directly aligns it with the cultural imperatives of the bourgeois public sphere, which as Foucault says, "discovered the liberties, also invented the disciplines."[37] Foucault's analysis of the arrestment and regulation of radical culture and the eighteenth century "floating population" within the modalities of discipline and knowledge has a great deal of relevance for understanding the double effect of the LCS as both an agency of interpellation as well as a junction point of liberation. According to Foucault:

> [Discipline] clears up confusion; it dissipates compact groupings of individuals wandering about the country in unpredictable ways; it establishes calculated distributions. It must also master all the forces that are formed from the very constitution of an organized multiplicity; it must neutralize the effects of counterpower that spring from them and which form a resistance to the power that wishes to dominate it: agitations, revolts, spontaneous organizations, coalitions—anything that may establish horizontal conjunctions. ... Lastly, the disciplines have to bring into play the power relations, not above but inside the very texture of the multiplicity, as discreetly as possible, as well articulated on the other functions of these multiplicities and also in the least expensive way possible: to this correspond anonymous instruments of power, coextensive with the multiplicity they regiment, such as hierarchical surveillance, continuous registration, perpetual assessment and classification. In short, to substitute for a power that is manifested through the brilliance of those who exercise it, a power that insidiously objectifies those on whom it is applied; to form a body of knowledge about these individuals, rather than to deploy the ostentatious signs of sovereignty.[38]

Middle-class ideologues of the eighteenth century institutionalized the ideal of discipline into a coercive pogrom that sought to convert the lower classes into a stable base of laboring population to serve the Industrial revolution. Reacting, no doubt, to the excesses of "Wilkes and Liberty" riots, Jonas Hanway, Esq., while advocating religion through the "habit of sober discipline" in "*reading* and *thinking*"[39] to mechanicks and apprentices, suggests that

---

[36] Ibid.

[37] Michel Foucault, *Discipline and Punish: The Birth of the Prison*, trans. Alan Sheridan (New York: Vintage Books, 1995), 211.

[38] Foucault, *Discipline and Punish*, 208–209.

[39] Jonas Hanway, Esq., "Observations on the Causes of the Dissoluteness which Reigns among the Lower Classes of the People; the propensity of some to larceny: and the danger of gaming, concubinage, and an excessive fondness for amusement in high life, &c. ... in three letters to a governor of Bridewell" (London, 1772), 15.

[i]f the infant parish poor were sent to remoter parts of the country, than is now practiced ... the children preserved might become the more beneficial to the community: The price which is now paid for nursing them, would certainly make it the interest of nurses, in the country, to preserve them. ... In such case the advantage might be considerable; for all *foundlings, illegitimates, orphans*, or others not demanded by their parents, might in due time be placed out to husbandry and manufactory, on the spot where they are bred: and this would be attended with another happy consequence; for the children of the poor of these cities, not depending on parish charity, might then fill up the vacant offices in the drudgery of life, in these great cities.[40]

Hanway called for institutionalizing of discipline, where "parish officers [were to be] vested with the power to encourage industry, in order to prevent parishioners from becoming paupers, [following which] they might keep them out of the paths which lead so directly to the gallows."[41] It was further demanded that working-class spaces of leisure and amusement be made subservient to the values of industry and deference by converting alehouses (that functioned as urban centers of rebellion) into Sunday Schools. In 1787 "Clericus" makes a suggestion to coffee-house readers that

it is worth while that millions be saved *certainly* from temporal, and *probably* from endless ruin: if it is worth while, I say, to contribute to the preventing these dire evils,—not only gin shops, night-cellars, and all such engines of debauchery, should be utterly abolished, but the number of our ale-houses throughout the kingdom should be abridged, and the irregularities of such as are suffered, should be carefully restrained. For it is fact, beyond all doubt, that public-houses, unrestrained, are a great source of the above specified mischiefs to thousands and ten thousands in lower life. [42]

These examples remind us that while the objective of setting up a working-class corresponding society in the image of the SCI and other more gentlemanly organizations is one part of the story, equally important is the reverse effect of its membership that resituated the public sphere ideal of disinterested intellectual activity within the charged ethos of the popular sphere. When viewed against such draconian attitudes towards the lower classes, the mass gatherings and rallies of the LCS, with its many intrepid leaders who braved England's reign of anti-Jacobin terror indisputably point to the monumental achievements of the LCS as a junction point. Working-class locales such as Copenhagen Fields and alehouses were converted into sites of resistance where thousands of people gathered to hear

---

40   Ibid., 19.

41   Ibid., 42.

42   [Pseudonym] Clericus, "A Principal Cause of the Miseries of the Poor, and of their Great expence to the Public Shewn: in hopes of getting these evils in some measure obviated, and so rendering the poor more happy in themselves, and less burdensome to the community," (London: n.p., 1787), 18.

the 'seditious' rhetoric of universal rights, and often to witness repressive actions of the government first hand.[43] In his analysis of the making of English reading audiences, Jon Klancher points out that while "[e]ighteenth-century journals had organized English audiences by forming the reading habit ... after 1790 that habit became the scene of a cultural struggle demanding a new mental map of the complex public and its textual desires, a new way to organize audiences according to their ideological dispositions."[44] In contrast with the mass writer's public,

> the radical audience was a *focused* gathering. Between the eighteenth-century "crowd" and the radical writer's "audience" intervened another collective form, that of radical "meeting," whether the formal meetings of London Corresponding Society in 1792, the Hampden Clubs of 1817, or the open-air meetings attended by thousands of artisans.[45]

LCS brought about a dialogic interaction between the speaker and his audience, unleashing civic discourse into the sphere of popular opinion and giving it, in the words of Bakhtin, "an orientation towards an answer."[46] Not only does the forum of public speaking indicate a formal shift from the *salon* tradition of the SCI (whose members were men with property and education) and the Philomathean Society (with its purely intellectual orientation), but it also allows a redefinition of republican ideals through the interactive process of public address. Hardy's account of LCS's first open-air meeting reveals the heteroglossic reception of 'liberty' and its apostle, Paine:

---

[43]   In one of the meetings in 1797 LCS leaders Ferguson, Tuckey and Galloway were arrested after the magistrate read out the Riot Act. Interestingly, the report on this event in two different newspapers *The Times* (anti-Jacobin) and *The Morning Chronicle* (pro-Jacobin) shows the deep involvement of the Press in fashioning popular opinion. While *The Times* reported that "The meeting consequently broke up, and the wise interference and timely activity of the Magistracy completely succeeded in preserving the maintenance of the public peace, and in preventing the mischiefs that were likely to have arisen from an assembly whose political sentiments would, if unrestricted, lead to the most dangerous innovations, and the subversion of every civil and religious blessing," *The Morning Chronicle* focused upon the violence of the authorities by emphasizing that "When they left the office [after arrest and bail] [the leaders] were drawn to their homes by the populace. Mr. Ferguson received a hurt in the eye by the Constable who took him into custody having struck him with is staff." LCS's official report too focused upon the self-discipline of the audience: "We are at a loss justly to delineate the cool and collected Courage, with which the People acted on that Day (*in despite of ministerial threats, and military parade*) we feel ourselves incapable of doing them that justice which their conduct merits; though we admire their courage, we cannot *less* respect their strict observance of Peace and good Order." *Place Collection* (London: British Library).

[44]   Jon Klancher, *The Making of English Reading Audiences, 1790–1832* (Madison, WI: University of Wisconsin Press, 1987), 20.

[45]   Ibid.

[46]   Mikhail Bakhtin, *The Dialogic Imagination* (University of Texas Press: 1982), 280.

> That being the first General Meeting of the Society that was held in the open air
> it caused a great stir in London ... many curious and laughable observations were
> made by the bystanders some saying that "Tom Paine was come to plant the tree
> of liberty" and other that the French Jacobines were come—and others that the
> London Corresponding Society were met to lower the price of provisions—God
> bless them says some of the women and poor working people—success to them
> said others ...[47]

The response of the onlookers, their "curious and laughable observations," refer
to a low-brow world of literal comprehension (Paine planting the tree of liberty)
that marks the entry of that discourse into an uncircumscribed and dialectical field
of mutual redefinition. Even the weekly meetings of the LCS in predominantly
working-class areas such as Spitalfields and Bethnal Green display a sense of
multivocality, where, as Joseph Goulding complained, "[a]lmost everybody
Speaks, and there is allways a very great noise, till the Delegate gets up—People
generally grow very outrageous and wont wait, then the Delegate gets up and
trys to soften them ..."[48] Most importantly, radical culture of the early 1800s that
appropriated the Reform agenda of the bourgeois public sphere, in its very failure
to secure reform for its constituency revealed the limits of universalist coffeehouse
vocabulary. The worker could be integrated within the coffeehouse identity only
as a privatized property owner, which meant (especially within an emergent
industrial-capitalist society) the selling of his or her own body in the form of wage
labor. In 1808, a Select Committee of Parliament situated the idiom of liberty
within a laissez-faire model, and rejected a minimum wage stipulation for workers
by arguing that "no interference of the Legislature with the Freedom of Trade, or
with the perfect Liberty of every individual to dispose of his time and his labour
in the way and on terms which he may judge most conducive to his own interests,
can take place, without violating general Principles of the first Importance to the
property and happiness of the community."[49]

By locating the intellectual within a history of the working classes, and the
history of the working class within an intellectual tradition, I want to show how the
working-class intellectual both reflects and shapes that larger transition of identity in
which the LCS occupies a middle ground. John Thelwall is an appropriate figure for
that role as his intellectual output includes explicitly political speeches delivered to
mass audiences, as well as a more literary type of writing such as *The Peripatetic*[50]
and other semi-Romantic poetry. The narrative space of *The Peripatetic* allows us
to understand the ways in eighteenth-century lexicon of classical republicanism
effects a rapprochement between self-expression and political expression, but

---

[47]   Quoted in *Selections*, 87.

[48]   Quoted in *Selections*, 14.

[49]   Quoted in Francis Hearn, *Domination, Legitimation, and Resistance: the
Incorporation of the Nineteenth-Century English Working Class* (Westport: Greenwood
Press, 1978), 82.

[50]   John Thelwall, *The Peripatetic*, ed. and intro. Judith Thompson (Detroit: Wayne
State University Press, c2001).

also the points at which they separate out from each other. The John Thelwall I draw upon here is not so much the friend of the Romantic poets Wordsworth and Coleridge,[51] but more a writer who places himself within the eighteenth-century literary tradition of Johnson and Sterne. First, a brief biographical sketch, and a description of Thelwall's links with the working classes are in order. A London silk-mercer's son, whose family fell into poverty after his father's death, Thelwall, like so many reformers of the period, was largely self-educated. Though Thelwall apprenticed in tailoring and law, his literary and political interests shaped by the 1790s culture of enquiry turned into him into a radical and intellectual. During the early 1790s Thelwall became increasingly active in the debating and reform societies, and by 1793, when he was 29, he had risen to become a prominent lecturer and a leading theorist of the LCS. LCS and its culture of debates and argumentation offered Thelwall an attractive space for combining his desire for edification and ambition for eminence. Thelwall presents himself as a man who, "without patronage and without pecuniary assistance ... devoted the whole powers of his mind to the asserting the rights of his fellow-countrymen, by those unanswerable arguments, which being communicated by one intellectual friend of freedom to another, and ... being diligently promulgated through the various ranks of society, from the highest to the lowest, [made] the tyrannical and oppressive government of the day tremble in its strongholds."[52] Like many other reformers of the late eighteenth century, Thelwall paid a heavy price for taking up the cause of the working classes. Historian Gregory Claeys, allows us a glimpse into the kind of repression Thelwall faced throughout his career:

> With the *Tribune* halted, and his lecturing prospects reduced to a nil in London, Thelwall now set out for the provinces ... to rally support and recoup some of his losses ... In at least four towns, Thelwall was physically attacked, usually with the connivance of local authorities. At Yarmouth ... a crowd of some ninety persons rioted on his arrival, and a large group of sailors ... assisted by several clergymen, seemed bent on carrying him off into forced naval service ... Here Thelwall rescued himself only by putting a pistol to the head of his most resolute pursuer and exclaiming, "Offer the least violence, and you're a dead man!" But the books on which he was to lecture ... were either torn to pieces or carried off as trophies. At Lynn, loyalists smashed the windows of his hall and threw brickbats and stones at his audience. Riots provoked by soldiers also led to the gutting of two public houses when Thelwall returned to Norwich to lecture ... In the Midlands, at Derby, on 23 March 1797, he faced an angry loyalist mob with a pistol in his hand, declaring that he "would shoot any person who molested him," and again escaped without injury.[53]

---

[51] Look at E.P. Thompson's analysis of that link in his *Romantics: England in a Revolutionary Age* (New York: New Press, c1997) and also Nicholas Roe, *Wordsworth and Coleridge: The Radical Years* (Oxford: Oxford University Press, 1988).

[52] Mrs. Thelwall, *Life of Thelwall by his Widow*, Vol. 1 (London: John Macrone, St. James's Square, 1837), 41.

[53] Claeys, xxx–xxxi.

It doesn't come as a surprise to find Thelwall declaring in 1798: "Let me be part farmer and fisherman. But no more politics—no more politics in this bad world!"[54]

As a prime advocate for the transformation of "an Ignoran[t] and Barbari[c] crowd that acted under the influence of turbulent passions"[55] Thelwall's lectures often exhorted his working-class audience to display "the energy of the mind, not the energies of the dagger—the logic of assassination."[56] Thelwall's mission of reinstating the worker within the republic of letters is accompanied by a subversive reinterpretation of it. Against Godwin's model of change that disavowed public action and stressed the "uncontrolled exercise of private judgment," Thelwall celebrated an "unrestrained intercourse with a bold, resolute, bustling, and disputatious race of men" in order to counter the "solitary abstraction" of the philosopher. He further emphasizes that the meaning of liberty "must be fought among thronged and promiscuous audiences, in theatres and halls of assembly." [57] Thelwall's success in transforming both, the public sphere idiom as well as working-class identity leads scholars Judith Thomson and Michael Scrivener[58] to argue for Thelwall's significance within the literary and cultural milieu of the eighteenth century. Against Hazlitt's censure that Thelwall was the "flattest writer [he] had ever read ... tame and trite and tedious,"[59] Judith Thompson stresses Thelwall's radical oratory and his multi-generic identity as a poet, novelist, journalist, editor, political theorist and student of medicine and law that together suggest "an enfranchisement of literature analogous to the political enfranchisement sought by members of reform societies."[60] Seen from this perspective, Thelwall's first popular fictional work, *The Peripatetic*, a quasi-novelistic medley of prose and verse, literature and journalism, politics and sentiment, satire and effusion, oratory and anecdote, occupies a unique discursive space within the eighteenth-century literary tradition, where the demand for a democratization of society is paralleled by a text based upon a principle of inclusion and open-endedness. Thelwall himself hints at such a reading when he claims in the Preface that his work was unprecedented in uniting "the different advantages of the novel, the sentimental journal, and the miscellaneous collection essays and political effusions."[61] Added to this multigeneric work is the "subject of our political abuses," geared at awakening "the tender sympathies of the reader's soul."[62]

---

[54]   Quoted in E.P. Thompson, *The Romantics*, 168.

[55]   Thelwall, *Tribune*, 316.

[56]   Ibid., 73.

[57]   John Thelwall, *SOBER REFLECTIONS on the seditious and inflammatory letter of the right hon. Edmund Burke, to a noble lord, addressed to the serious considerations of his fellow citizens* (London: printed for H.D. Symonds, 1796), 93–94.

[58]   Michael Scrivener, *Seditious Allegories: John Thelwall & Jacobin Writing* (University Park: Pennsylvania State University Press, c2001).

[59]   Quoted in *The Romantics*, 160.

[60]   Judith Thompson, 11.

[61]   Thelwall, *Peripatetic*, 72.

[62]   Ibid., 73.

The main action of *The Peripatetic* is presented through the reflections and impressions of its narrator, Sylvanus Theophrastus, who is joined by his friends Ambulator (a philosophe-intellectual type) and Belmour (a sentimental hero looking for his lost love, Sophia) in his perambulations in the suburbs of London. Thelwall uses the narrative structure of Laurence Sterne's *Sentimental Journey,* published in 1769, to create a digressive storyline shaped by an eccentric narrator's wanderings through various parts of the country. Into this travelogue Thelwall injects a radical agenda that converts many of his encounters into a political statement against the loss of freedom under an oppressive government. The "Bird Catchers" episode stands out most in this regard, where Sylvanus invokes the reader's "powers of sympathy" to draw attention to the plight of a lark, captured by the "rude hands of unfeeling clowns, and consigned ... to all the woes of cruel slavery; to taste the joys of liberty no more; to mourn, perhaps, his little widowed mate ... his callow, chirping young, who, robbed of the support derived from his provident assistance, may probably expire with lingering famine in the deserted nest."[63] The significance of this rather excessive sentimental outpouring lies in the connection Thelwall draws between the lark and other oppressed members of eighteenth-century society. The lark's situation is paralleled by a human example later in the novel, where a young, impoverished mother lies languishing in her nest after her husband has been kidnapped by press gangs and sent to war. Further, by linking the lark's captivity with that of the African who has been forced to leave his bride and his native land to toil in sugar plantations, the narrator exhorts a nation of unthinking consumers who

> Heedless of groans, of anguish, of chains,
> Of stripes inflicted, and tormenting pains,
>   At morn, at eve, [their] sweeten'd beverage sup,
>   Nor see the blood of thousands in the cup. [64]

By giving a central role to marginal figures such as the unemployed haymaker, or the sailor who returns from war to find that he has no material prospects, Thelwall "novelizes" familiar coffeehouse idioms. For instance, in his description of Bermondsey, a suburb of London, Sylvanus draws on the "travel writing" genre, but stresses the locale's ugliness, thus challenging the picturesque misrepresentations of guidebooks. The "mechanics and labourers" who live in "miserable shelters" in Bermondsey are represented in a satirical pastoral that critiques not only elite genres such as the picturesque that "have forbidden a tongue to the attachment or the necessities of the poor,"[65] but also the profit-oriented system of enclosure that forced peasants into crowded, unhealthy cities and suburban slums.

The Bermondsey episode concludes by privileging "the humble thatch," "the rustic wicket," "ruddy infants and the honest husbandsman" over the picturesque

---

[63]   Ibid., 90.
[64]   Ibid., 91.
[65]   Ibid., 135.

but artificial Attic temple, "the laboured stream" and the "decorating statue."[66] *The Peripatetic*'s adaptation of the open-ended form of the novel to with the experiences of an oppressed class allows the text to function as a "junction point" where varieties of literary traditions meet and clash within its discursive space and receive a working-class orientation through Thelwall's familiarity with and sympathy for the impoverished worker. Judith Thompson's suggestion that Thelwall invades and opens up Burke's intellectual property for "general distribution," while displaying both his mastery and mockery of its codes and conventions, celebrates this happy confluence of form and function in the figure of the working-class intellectual.

But alongside the idea of a junction point, I would like to view the text from a perspective that emphasizes strategies of containment as well as challenge. In this alternate reading of *The Peripatetic*, Thelwall's vacillation between the desire for, in Antonio Gramsci's words, a "practical transformation of the real world" (through a Reformist agenda) and a language "inherited from the past and uncritically absorbed"[67] (i.e. the convention of writing that dominated the 1790s literary scene) is dramatized in the narrator's fluctuation between alehouse and coffeehouse identities. As a spokesman for the working classes, Thelwall challenges middle-class conventions and its neglect of the working classes, but as an intellectual who identifies with the literary lineage of Sterne, Pope and Johnson (and beyond that Socrates, Virgil and Horace) he struggles to contain that critique within familiar idioms and stock representations of the working classes. The model for Sylvanus Theophrastus, as his Hellenic name suggests, is reminiscent of the Whiggish "independent commonwealthman" figure of the eighteenth century such as "Cato" to whom, "the Authority of Names is nothing" and who "judges all men by their Actions and Behaviour."[68] As an inheritor of eighteenth-century neo-classicism, Sylvanus measures contemporary ills against the ideal of ancient Greek society (an idea familiar to coffeehouse readers). What is interesting is Thelwall's slippage in the following instance that suggests the complications of being both Cato and a working-class spokesman at the same time. While lamenting the condition of modern education by comparing it against the "attic-columned school" of ancient times, Sylvanus complains that "the instruction of our early and invaluable years [are] carelessly resigned to pedants, sycophants, and drivellers, who, if once mankind should be emancipated from all distinctions, between those which intellect creates, would sink into the humble ranks of labourers and mechanics."[69] In this example, labourers and mechanics (and indeed the humble ranks of society) lose their radical signification of the Bermondsey episode, and function as representatives of working-class ignorance, a common stereotype of the eighteenth century.

---

[66]   Ibid., 137–138.

[67]   Antonio Gramsci, *Selections from Prison Notebooks*, ed. and trans. Hoare and Smith (New York: International Publishers, 1978), 333.

[68]   Caroline Robbins, *The Eighteenth-Century Commonwealthman* (Cambridge: Cambridge University Press, 1959), 120.

[69]   Thelwall, *Peripatetic*, 80.

Along with the rational bent of the Cato-type, Sylvanus also imbibes the characteristics of the eighteenth-century man of sentiment, who, according to *The Prompter*'s definition of 1735, "is not satisfied with good-natured actions alone, but feels the misery of others with inward pain."[70] The sentimental novel in the eighteenth century has been identified by John Mullan as a peculiarly middle-class space that reflected "an anxiety about the sociability of individuals" in an increasingly polite and commercial society.[71] Feelings or sentiment function as a mediator between the private act of reading and a public expression of sympathy for, and connection, with the larger community. Novels such as Sterne's *Sentimental Journey* on which *The Peripatetic* romanticize the possibility of human communication and fellow feeling that transcends class differences. But the episode in which Sylvanus converses with an old sailor shows how his intellectual distance from the lower classes overdetermines his attempt at meaningful communication. When the sailor confidently labels Sylvanus a tradesman, he evokes an irritated response from the latter (perhaps Thelwall was reminded of his familial link with trade), who feels that he is expected to "measure his lordship for his birthday honours."[72] Sylvanus's or Thelwall's discomfort with the class he was born into is also emphasized in "A Childish Retrospect," an episode closely modeled on Thelwall's own childhood experiences. In this episode, the narrator dramatizes his distance from the company of his relatives, who are described as "sagacious, sobersided mortals, whose animadversions are generally confined to a few hums and has about the decay of trade and the balance of power, and that useful kind of knowledge which is collected in the confines of the countinghouse."[73] The child steals away to enjoy the kind of communion with nature made famous by the Romantic poet a few years later. When Sylvanus emphatically informs the sailor about his mistake, he fears that "the false estimate of my importance might prevent that freedom of conversation from which alone the human heart can be revealed."[74] After these hurdles when they do manage to converse, Sylvanus is disappointed to discover that the sailor is a victim of "unlettered prejudices" and therefore unsympathetic towards reformist causes.[75] The sailor episode dramatizes Thelwall's desire for companionship with and distance from the lower classes and highlights a larger problem of a gap between the eighteenth-century working-class intellectual and his constituency. In 1795, when Thelwall goes on tour on foot to record firsthand the condition of the poor from village to village (rather like Theophrastus Sylvanus), his find that his "Every question was repelled by some sly

---

[70]   Quoted in R.S. Crane, "Suggestions Towards a Genealogy of the Man of Feeling," *ELH*, Vol. 1 (1934), 219–220.

[71]   John Mullan, "Sentimental Novels," *The Cambridge Companion to the Eighteenth-Century Novel*, ed. John Richetti (Cambridge University Press, 1996).

[72]   Thelwall, *Peripatetic*, 73.

[73]   Ibid., 111.

[74]   Ibid., 97.

[75]   Ibid., 99.

rub, or sagacious hint." Eventually he meets a laborer who was "inquisitive, shrewd, and communicative," but turns out to be "too full of liquor and *temporary politics*, to furnish any information on the subject of *political economy*."[76] In contrast with this instance of failed communication, the sense of communion between Thelwall and his intellectual friends Wordsworth and Coleridge is unmistakable. Writing to his wife in 1797 about his visit to Stowey where Wordsworth and Coleridge resided, Thelwall says: "We have been having a delightful ramble today among the plantations of a wild romantic dell ... There have we sometimes sitting on a tree—sometimes wading deep through the stream and again stretched on some mossy stone, a literary and political triumvirate passed sentence on the productions and characters of the age."[77]

The Peripatetic abounds in the twin elements of sentimental fiction: characters calculated to excite the leisurely reader's sympathy, such as the honest haymaker turned beggar, or the poor old man doomed to wander in vain for employment, men and women who suffer but do not speak directly to the reader. Instead, they make room for a demonstration of benevolence and philanthropy on the part of the narrator, whose hand, "sympathizing with the feelings of his heart, waited not for the cold approbation of Reason, but went immediately and instinctively to his pocket."[78] But there are other figures in the novel that exist outside pale of humanitarian appeal and civic society and present a challenge to the narrator. In one of the episodes Sylvanus encounters some gypsies in the countryside. The gypsies, with their "dark eyes, olive skin and peculiar cast of features"[79] take on an interesting significance in the novel. Against the narrator's self-conscious role of the wanderer-intellectual, the gypsies embody a permanently peripatetic identity. As a "race of wanderers"[80] they present a model of open-endedness, unlike the rational and sentimental locus (linked with the Enlightenment) of Sylvanus's carefully constructed wanderings. Furthermore, where other members of society, privileged or poverty-stricken, allow themselves to be categorized as the narrator's objects of scorn or sympathy, the gypsies, by being simultaneously innocent and indolent, escape the net of such classifications. As an impoverished group of beggars that

---

[76]   Quoted in *The Romantics*, 167–168. This idea is, of course, not confined to the eighteenth century intellectual. Not only the nineteenth century leader—Francis Burdett, Hunt and Cobbett (examined in E.P. Thompson's *Making* as "demagogues and martyrs"), but as Shlomo Avineri points out, even Marx's and Engels' attitudes too reveal a similar "disdain, if not outright contempt, for those leaders of the movement who were themselves of working class origin: especially, so far as Marx is concerned, a certain intellectual *hauteur* is clearly visible in his comments ... The Marx-Engels correspondence abounds in numerous allusions to the workers' intellectual limitations, stupidity, and narrow-mindedness." "Marx and the Intellectuals," *Journal of the History of Ideas*, Vol. 28, No. 2 (April–June, 1967), 275.

[77]   Quoted in E.P. Thompson, "Hunting the Jacobin Fox," *Past and Present*, No. 142 (February, 1994), 107.

[78]   Thelwall, *Peripatetic*, 87.

[79]   Ibid., 84.

[80]   Ibid.

resisted respectable labor, the gypsies challenge the haymaker's privileged status of justifiable and respectable beggary. Described as a timeless community untouched by historical processes, the gypsies are simultaneously figures of ruination, as well as members of an alternate organic community, "averse alike to the restraints of civilization and labour, and attached to no community but their own."[81]

This representation is significant when we consider Marx's description of a revolutionary working-class community. In the "Introduction *to The Critique of Hegel's Philosophy of Right*," Marx describes the proletariat as "a class with radical chains, a class of civil society which is not of civil society ... [a class] which does not stand in any one-sided antithesis to the consequences, but in all-round antithesis to the premises of statehood, [a class] which is the complete loss of man and hence can only win itself through the complete re-winning of man."[82] In one sense, the working-class intellectual represents this radical possibility, where though educated in the idioms of civil society, by challenging its exclusion of the worker, he is also, in an important sense, not of civil society. In another, slightly different sense, Marx's definition suggests that the proletariat, as a class both within and without civil society can achieve its radical role only by transcending the history of its birth. Only by dissolving its own identity as it were, can it "proclaim the secret of its own existence." In his essay, "Marx and Heterogeneity: Thinking the Lumpenproletariat,"[83] Peter Stallybrass uses the example of a "picturesque" painting to understand the ways in which the mid-nineteenth century bourgeois spectators confront a similar "sense of unfixing before a nameless thing."[84] In the painting, *Train Up a Child in the Way He Should Go; and When He Is Old He Will Not Depart from It*, a child and two well-dressed women encounter three lascars; the child is offering a coin to one of them, and the women's gaze is fixed on the child's. The figures are depicted in a romantic landscape, trees on either side, an impressive craglike ruin, shadowed down the middle, in the background. For Stallybrass, "[w]hat is most striking about the reception of the work is the way in which critics oscillated between interpreting it as a heroic portrayal of the absorption of the poor into the theater of bourgeois generosity, as an exotic depiction of the Other, or as an alarming juxtaposition of black and white, male and female, lumpen and well-to-do."[85] As the *Literary Gazette* observed, "We cannot read the lesson; whether to inculcate charity, or what? The meaning escapes our penetration."[86] In a move similar to the one attempted by my reading of the limits of

---

[81] Ibid., 95.

[82] Karl Marx, "Introduction to A Contribution to the Critique of Hegel's Philosophy of Right," in *History and Class: Essential Readings in Theory and Interpretation*, ed. R.S. Neale (Oxford: Basil Blackwell, 1983), 34.

[83] Peter Stallybrass, "Marx and Heterogeneity: Thinking the Lumpenproletariat," in *Representations*, No. 31, Special Issue: The Margins of Identity in Nineteenth-Century England (Summer, 1990), 69–95.

[84] Ibid., 70.

[85] Ibid., 75.

[86] Ibid., 78.

Thelwall's radicalism, Stallybrass traces the homogenizing gaze of the bourgeois spectator into Marx's *Eighteenth Brumaire*, where the unsettling presence of the *lumpenproletariat* threatens the project of narrativizing the revolutionary character of the proletariat. Marx describes the *lumpenproletariat* as follows:

> the lumpenproletariat ... in all big towns forms a mass sharply differentiated from the industrial proletariat, a recruiting ground for thieves and criminals of all kinds, living on the crumbs of society, people without a definite trade, vagabonds ... varying according to the degree of civilization of the nation to which they belong, but never renouncing their *lazzaroni* character."[87]

When Sylvanus comes upon the gypsies in the woods, he encounters a class that in its very unclassifiability, exists outside the idioms of civil society, and in that sense represents the radical possibilities of the working-class intellectual and his constituency. But Sylvanus, coming face to face with the dissolution of his own identity in theirs, turns towards the very conventions he has defined himself against. Though they are "infidels" and "sanscullotes," Sylvanus values the gypsies for their role within picturesque art as "an embellishment of rural scenery." He ruminates that "if these idle wanderers were exterminated, the landscape painter would be robbed of one of his most agreeable sources of embellishment, and the poet of an object well calculated to give variety to his descriptions."[88]

Works Cited

Andrew, Edward. "Class in Itself and Class against Capital: Karl Marx and His Classifiers," *Canadian Journal of Political Science*, Vol. 16, No. 3 (September, 1983), 577–584.

Avineri, Schlomo. "Marx and the Intellectuals," *Journal of the History of Ideas*, Vol. 28, No. 2 (April–June, 1967), 269–278.

Bakhtin, Mikhail. *The Dialogic Imagination*, trans. Caryl Emerson and Michael Holquist. University of Texas Press, 1982.

Chandler, James. *England in 1819*: *The Politics Of Literary Culture And The Case Of Romantic Historicism.* Chicago: University of Chicago Press, 1998.

Claeys, Gregory, ed. *The Politics of English Jacobinism: Writings of John Thelwall.* University Park: Pennsylvania State University Press, 1995.

Clericus, "A Principal Cause Of The Miseries Of The Poor, And Of Their Great Expence To The Public Shewn: In Hopes Of Getting These Evils In Some Measure Obviated, And So Rendering The Poor More Happy In Themselves, And Less Burdensome To The Community." London: n.p., 1787.

Crane, R.S. "Suggestions Towards a Genealogy of the Man of Feeling," *ELH*, Vol. 1 (1934), 205–230.

---

[87]   Quoted in Stallybrass, 84.
[88]   Thelwall, *Peripatetic*, 96.

Engels, Friedrich. *The Condition of the Working Class of England*, trans. Florence Kelley-Wishnewetsky. Oxford: Oxford University Press, 1993.

Extract of a letter from Sheffield, dated December 22nd 1794, Francis Place Collection. London: British Library.

Foucault, Michel. *Discipline and Punish: The Birth Of The Prison*, trans. Alan Sheridan. New York: Vintage Books, 1995.

Gilmour, Ian. *Riot, Risings and Revolution: Governance and Violence in Eighteenth-Century England*. London: Pimlico, 1993.

Gramsci, Antonio. *Selections from Prison Notebooks*, eds and trans. Hoare and Smith. New York: International Publishers, 1978.

Habermas, Jurgen. *The Structural Transformation of the Public Sphere: An Enquiry into a Category of Bourgeois Society*, trans. Thomas Burger and Frederick Lawrence. Cambridge, MA: MIT Press, 1989.

———. *Toward A Rational Society; Student Protest, Science, and Politics*, trans. Jeremy J. Shapiro. Boston: Beacon Press, 1970.

Hanway, Jonas. "Observations On The Causes Of The Dissoluteness Which Reigns Among The Lower Classes Of The People; The Propensity Of Some To Larceny: And The Danger Of Gaming, Concubinage, And An Excessive Fondness For Amusement In High Life, &C. in Three Letters To A Governor Of Bridewell." London: n.p., 1772.

Hazlitt, William. *The Spirit of the Age; Or, Contemporary Portraits*. London: G. Richards, 1904.

Hearn, Francis. *Domination, Legitimation, and Resistance: the Incorporation of the Nineteenth-Century English Working Class*. Westport: Greenwood Press, 1978.

Iliff, Edward Henry. "A Summary of the Duties of Citizenship! Written expressly for the Members of the London Corresponding Society; including Observations on the Contemptuous Neglect of the Secretary of State, with regard to their late Address to the King!" London: n.p., 1795.

Klancher, Jon. *The Making of English Reading Audiences, 1790–1832*. Madison, WI: University of Wisconsin Press, 1987.

Kramnick, Isaac. *Republicanism and Bourgeois Radicalism: Political Ideology in Late Eighteenth-Century England and America*. Ithaca: Cornell University Press, 1990.

Krishnamurthy, Aruna. "'More than Abstract Knowledge:' Friedrich Engels in Industrial Manchester," *Journal of Victorian Literature and Culture*, Vol. 28, No. 2 (2000), 427–448.

McCalman, Iain. *Radical Underworld: Prophets, Revolutionaries, and Pornographers in London, 1795–1840*. Cambridge: Cambridge University Press, 1988.

Marx, Karl. "Introduction to A Contribution to the Critique of Hegel's Philosophy of Right," in *History and Class: Essential Readings in Theory and Interpretation*, ed. R.S. Neale (Oxford: Basil Blackwell, 1983).

Mrs. Thelwall, *Life of Thelwall by his Widow*, Vol. 1. London: John Macrone, St. James's Square, 1837.

Mullan, John. "Sentimental Novels," in *The Cambridge Companion to the Eighteenth-Century Novel*, ed. John Richetti. Cambridge University Press, 1996.

Robbins, Caroline. *The Eighteenth-Century Commonwealthman*. Cambridge: Cambridge University Press, 1959.

Roe, Nicholas. *Wordsworth and Coleridge: The Radical Years*. Oxford: Oxford University Press, 1988.

Rudê, George. *Paris and London in the Eighteenth Century: Studies in Popular Protest*. New York: Viking, 1971.

Scrivener, Michael. *Seditious Allegories: John Thelwall & Jacobin Writing*. University Park: Pennsylvania State University Press, c2001.

Stallybrass, Peter. "Marx and Heterogeneity: Thinking the Lumpenproletariat," in *Representations*, No. 31, Special Issue: The Margins of Identity in Nineteenth-Century England, 69–95.

Thale, Mary, ed. *Selections from the Papers of the London Corresponding Society 1792–1799*. Cambridge: Cambridge University Press, 1983.

Thelwall, John. "SOBER REFLECTIONS On The Seditious And Inflammatory Letter Of The Right Hon. Edmund Burke, To A Noble Lord, Addressed To The Serious Considerations Of His Fellow Citizens." London: H.D. Symonds, 1796.

———. *The Peripatetic*, ed. and intro. Judith Thompson. Detroit: Wayne State University Press, c2001.

Thompson, E.P. *Customs in Common*. London: Merlin Press, c1991.

———. "Hunting the Jacobin Fox," *Past and Present*, No. 142 (February, 1994), 94–140.

———. *Making of the English Working Class*. New York: Viking, 1964.

———. *Romantics: England in a Revolutionary Age*. New York: New Press, c1997 .

Thompson, Judith. "Introduction," *The Peripatetic*. Detroit: Wayne State University Press, c2001.

Chapter 6
Genre in the Chartist Periodical

Rob Breton

> As we are convinced that all which elevates the feelings or heightens the aspirations, can but strengthen the political power of a people, we have placed poetry and romance side by side with politics and history.
>
> —"Preface" to the *Labourer; A Monthly Magazine of Politics, Literature, Poetry* (December 1847)

The geneses of Chartist aesthetics have been critically documented by Dorothy Thompson, Martha Vicinus, Louis James (in a roundabout way), and more recently by Patricia Anderson, Paul Thomas Murphy, and Ian Haywood, though I am not sure if any of them set out specifically to do so. Discussing the origins of Chartist writing, scholars have tended to place emphasis on grand historical narratives—such as an emerging political and economic class-consciousness—or on somewhat schematic ones—such as the stamp tax and subsequent "unstamped wars." The development of a Chartist language has also been seen through its literary history: an inheritance from oral traditions, broadsides, ballads, and various forms of street literature; the influence of the Romantics and classical poetry; or a legacy of political discourses ranging from Thomas Paine and the famous radical voices of the eighteenth century to nameless weavers and guildsmen. Two obvious observations might be made at this point: Chartist writing was built up from a number of factors, and that it was itself mixed and mottled.

From these observations I intend to draw a less safe conclusion about the fairly elusive (mixed and mottled) languages of Chartism. Chartist intellectuals turned to and borrowed from "sensational" working-class styles in order to differentiate themselves from the dominant middle-class rhetoric of the day and to confirm a distinctive working-class genre. In *Melodramatic Tactics: Theatricalized Dissent in the English Marketplace, 1800–1885*, Elaine Hadley argues that melodrama can imply an active, emotional, and participatory spectator. Hadley looks mostly at nineteenth-century drama, but the idea of a "melodramatic tactic" that asserts the public's "right to political participation"[1] can also be applied to a Chartist aesthetic, especially when the language of melodrama is punctuated by other more explicitly political discourses. I want to suggest that the addition of fictional devices to an essentially intellectual form had this effect but may also have been a symbolic gesture made by Chartist intellectuals—many of whom were outsiders

---

[1] Elaine Hadley, *Melodramatic Tactics: Theatricalized Dissent in the English Marketplace, 1800–1885* (Stanford: Stanford University Press, 1995), 57.

to the class they sought to empower—to the traditions of working-class writing. With the clash of popular, simplifying genres and intellectualizing or politicizing ones came a specific aesthetic amenable and familiar to working classes. Chartist leaders such as Feargus O'Connor, Thomas Martin Wheeler, and Thomas Cooper acquiesced to popular forms because doing so was inherently democratic and thus in keeping with their political objectives. Undoubtedly, they also wanted to sell magazines. But another benefit of mixing the often-dry discourses of Chartist politics (the endless reports on conventions, for example) with Manichean and deliberately visual ones, with fiction and fictional devices, is that this hybridity of the political and popular is continuous with earlier working-class expressions in England.

Initially, a number of Chartist publishers were against infusing their periodicals with fiction, understanding that novelistic discourses of sensation and sentiment mystify real social relations. The *Labourer* declared in December 1847 that it "had one great goal before our eyes – the redemption of the Working classes from their thraldom" to romance, and that though it saw the necessity of including poetry and romance, fiction was to be "subservient" to politics and history. At stake, however, as periodicals made themselves marketable to working-class tastes, was not simply the size of the readership or a perceived loss of integrity. Chartists feared that without fictional interventions into political genres they could never establish a concrete, living identification with working people. As Sally Ledger says,

> In the case of the Chartist writers, the turn to the writing of populist serial fiction was thoroughly instrumental in political terms. While far from immune to commercial pressures – the appeal of serialized fiction to a wide readership was doubtless one of the main reasons for Chartists' adoption of this mode of literary production – the Chartist writers were determined at the same time to use popular fiction as part of their political armory in an attempt to forge a collective class identity among the lower-class readers of Chartist newspapers.[2]

Announcing the value of hybridity and working-class print culture, and agreeing to modify the image of the Chartist and working-class intellectual accordingly, Chartists imply that the development of working-class consciousness and the movement towards a higher level of its intellectualism have to happen on working-class terms.

The idea that intellectual and political independence hinges upon maintaining aesthetic tastes and a cultural identity would also have greatly satisfied the autodidact ideologies of the working-class and Chartist intelligentsia. Choosing to leaven political discourses with fiction and miscellany and refashioning the image of the Chartist and working-class intellectual elite goes beyond establishing identification for it also underlines the importance of resisting ideologies that are imposed from above. There are Protestant overtones here, but as Jonathan Rose says, "there is

---

² Sally Ledger, "Chartist Aesthetics in the Mid Nineteenth Century: Ernest Jones, a Novelist of the People," *Nineteenth-Century Literature*, Vol. 57, No. 1 (2002), 36.

nothing distinctly 'bourgeois' in [the] desire for intellectual freedom".[3] Without doubt, some Chartist intellectuals wanted to adjust and to some extent even reconstruct the understood working-class aesthetic. Thomas Cooper's call for "a literature of our own" is the most famous of many such calls, all of which imply that working people did not have their own literature, or in fact a class consciousness. But we need not infer that Chartist intellectuals were attempting to reconstitute the cultural preferences of the working classes; rather, we might see Cooper *et al* as insisting that exciting or nostalgic narrative forms be used to good purpose. Instead of a generic story of injustice, write the story of the injustice faced by the poor and make an explicit political point dominate. In the anonymously written "A Simple Story," first appearing in the *English Chartist Circular* (1841–43), a story which is in fact half essay and half melodrama, the author implores readers for a class-based literature extolling "the virtues of the poor."[4] He or she then proceeds to share one of these potential stories, about a boy who goes starving so that his family can eat. It is a maudlin, sentimental story cut by a political purpose: "Should any of the readers of the CIRCULAR desire to know where poor Joe now is ... we regret to add that he died about three years after the incident occurred ... from a want of nourishment, the condition of too many of the working classes."[5] Such a story makes clear to readers that Chartism is essentially a bread-and-butter movement, not an abstract one, and that emotional content does not run counter to political rationality.

If the cultural identity of working people was to be respected, what of the identity and self-imaging of the working-class intellectual? Would adapting the public voice of the Chartist radical to storytelling modes compromise the goals of Chartism? The Charter, after all, implied that working people had the readiness, seriousness, and sophistication to use the vote wisely. Any sense of transgressing vanguard and armchair politics might be soured by a sense of "selling out," de-intellectualizing themselves and readers, and undermining their political credibility. But Chartist and working-class intellectuals did not generally see themselves as caught between these two positions, or between the two discourses of politics and fiction. Iain McCalman demonstrates in *Radical Underworld* that tracing "the lives and careers of individual members [of a politicized working class] reveals a long and intricate overlap between the allegedly separate spheres of 'respectability' and 'roughness.'"[6] Late in his life Thomas Cooper could lament that working men "had no longer the old seriousness of mind, the energy in the pursuit of knowledge,

---

[3]   Jonathan Rose, *The Intellectual Life of the British Working Classes* (New Haven: Yale University Press, 2002), 13.

[4]   Ian Haywood, ed., "A Simple Story," in *The Literature of Struggle: An Anthology of Chartist Fiction* (Aldershot: Scolar Press, 1995), 41.

[5]   Ibid., 45.

[6]   Iain McCalman, *Radical Underworld: Prophets, Revolutionaries and Pornographers in London, 1795–1840* (Cambridge: Cambridge University Press, 1988), 3.

the earnestness which had marked such men in his younger days."[7] This is after publishing numerous stories and novels that foreground the simple pleasures of the working-class idyll. The transition to the hybrid discourses of working people was easy and smooth for the intellectual class because, as it turned out, the fictional discourses only enhanced the political ones, radicalizing the political and social identity of the intellectual class. Embracing the enticements of narrative form, their political discourse becomes increasingly combative and rhetorical, while what had been compartmentalized as the stuff of fiction—relationships, betrayals, the ups and downs of life—was politicized, and seen as part and parcel of a same class struggle that had too often been reduced to the fight for the franchise. By absorbing the language of the fiction writer, working-class intellectuals became more fiercely polemical; by absorbing the aura of the fiction writer, they became more ideological, seeing things wholly.

If Chartists expected a measure of reciprocity by accepting fictional languages, in the form of working people accepting political writing, they could only have hoped for a change in emphasis. It is not as if before Chartism working-class writing was void of political content. Chartist intellectuals augmented their writing with fictional forms, but the result was the adoption of a various working-class aesthetic, not simply a sensationalized one. Most of the urban publications written by or for the working classes before or published alongside the rise of the Chartist periodical combined various genres and levels of discourse in a way that was striking even for newspapers, a medium based on variety to begin with. Not only were complex poems placed besides sentimentalizing fables, but also the languages of the diametric, of simple good versus pure evil, found their way into and continuously fused with social commentary. If there is such a thing as late eighteenth-century and early nineteenth-century working-class writing, it is inclusive and eclectic, both "serious" and "entertaining." Looking at the growth of a class-based literature in the nineteenth century, Martha Vicinus argues, "variety grew out of many long-developing political and social movements."[8] Certainly, working people's tastes before and after 1836—the year often given as the first of a properly Chartist literature—were not uniform: as a group and as individuals they consumed the racy and the religious, the lyrical and the sensational. As is now well documented, working people read Shakespeare and romances, Byron and murder stories, apparently without creating categories of high and low. That there was a market for diversity or that diversity satisfies different tastes and therefore increases the market is very much a factor in the development of a hybrid writing style and print culture designed to appeal to all working people and to get them excited by the prospect of enfranchisement. In the context of an emerging democratic movement, inclusive and popular writing are appropriate discourses; popular appeal has a corresponding political position.

---

[7]   G.D.H. Cole, *Chartist Portraits* (New York: Macmillan, 1965), 216.

[8]   Martha Vicinus, *The Industrial Muse: A Study of Nineteenth Century British Working-Class Literature* (London: Croom Helm, 1974), 94.

The first important printed material to manifest and take advantage of a working-class market for diversity was the broadside. The political content of broadsides was undeveloped and non-analytical, though discourses of protest and indignation had a place. Broadsides were dominated by royal gossip or outlandishly patriotic reports on the exploits of the British army. As Vicinus explains,

> The great bulk of broadsides were about romance, sensation and topical events, but they also included local commentaries, trade songs and political statements, making them one of the most complete sources for studying the development of working-class culture ... In time working-class culture came to encompass not only ballads, but also poetry, essays, fiction and autobiographies.[9]

Diversity is not a unique feature of the broadside, but the dialectical conflation of generic opposites would become the aesthetic litmus test to signal class allegiance, and a deliberate technique of Chartists and Chartist sympathizers in their attempts to appeal to mass audiences.

When mass-produced, serialized, illustrated newspapers replaced street literature in the 1830s the market for a broad spectrum of material only increased. Patricia Anderson demonstrates the multifarious nature of working people's taste by pointing out that from the 1830s to 1845 the *Penny Magazine* (1832–45) went from achieving a circulation of 200,000 to having sales of only 40,000 because it had not responded to the demand for a new discourse, fiction, when fiction began to be mixed into other periodicals.[10] The *Penny Magazine* had achieved its level of success by being inclusive, carrying sober educational material, classical poetry, and gentle humor. It had declined in popularity because it didn't respond to the growing demand for even more variety. That relatively well-educated editors wanted to attract readers who had various levels of education and literacy might also account for the trend towards more and more diversity. The 1830s saw working people participate in a number of educational movements; they were to organize libraries and discussion groups, such as the Mechanics' Institutes. Ulrich Schwab speaks of a "demand for serious reading material among the workers."[11] However, the rising literacy rates and plebeian autodidacticism of the 1830s did not mean that all working people were ready to abandon the less elevated languages of street literature as clearly is demonstrated by the emerging successes of John Cleave, G.W.M. Reynolds, and Edward Lloyd. The result was a wide range of discourses in periodicals produced for working people in the early 1800s: moralistic and emotionally charged ballads, fables, and tales; literary criticism and appreciation; gruesome crime reporting; didactic proverbs; satires and comedic dialogues; various forms of poetry; and class-oriented, political tirades

---

[9]   Ibid., 13.

[10]   Patricia Anderson, *The Printed Image and the Transformation of Popular Culture*, 1790–1860 (Oxford: Clarendon Press, 1991), 181.

[11]   Ulrich Schwab, *The Poetry of the Chartist Movement: A Literary and Historical Study* (Dordrecht: Kluwer Academic Publishers, 1987), 27.

and analyses. The inclusion of so many generic types running parallel to each other made the melding of generic types inevitable; the conflation of affective and analytical discourses or of simplifying and edifying material would seem natural to working-class audiences.

A number of specific events also contributed to the infusion of emotional discourses into intellectualizing and politicizing genres, leading to an identifiable style that eventually would be picked up by the Chartist press. The most important of these was the Stamp Tax of 1815. With the Stamp Tax, any periodical containing straightforward "news" of any sort was taxed fourpence. The stamp duty was eventually reduced to one penny in 1836, which was thought to be enough to preclude the proliferation of class-based readers, but not prohibit middle-class publishers from expanding their industry. The Whig government had hoped to stem the production of low-priced, political newspapers. But as Louis James has noted, their repressive measures only managed to radicalize the press, who referred to the levy as a "Tax on Knowledge."[12] The tax had another unintended effect. The radical presses that wanted to avoid the stamp but did not want to produce illegal material had to bury news items in other discourses. William Cobbett was the first to evade the tax this way. His *Political Register* (1802–1835) did not report on events, and thus did not require the stamp; rather, it *commented* on the news. Editorials, opinion pieces, and rants would convey current events. The unstamped radical weeklies that followed Cobbett's strategy—*Sherwin's Political Register* (1817–19) or the *Cap of Liberty* (1818–19)—continued to bury news items in political editorials, but also included fiction and miscellaneous material more common to the broadside than Cobbett's *Register*. Later periodicals such as *Cleave's Weekly Police Gazette* (1834–36) continued to convey news through expressions and styles not commonly associated with reporting. Cleave was able to appeal to a readership that was already accustomed to crossing between genres. When the Chartist press became established by the late 1830s, the *Police Gazette* transformed into *Cleave's Penny Gazette of Variety and Amusement* (1839–44), a portmanteau paper that advocated for Chartism but maintained the lighter languages of the entertainments. In this period Cleave also produced the *English Chartist Circular*, a political journal that was nonetheless to serialize fiction.

The "unstamped press" defied the publications laws altogether. The *Poor Man's Guardian* (1831–35) is generally considered to be the most important of the 550-plus unstamped papers printed between 1830 and 1836. Henry Hetherington, its publisher, was a signatory of the People's Charter. With Cleave he helped form the London Working Man's Association. But he also published the *Twopenny Dispatch, and People's Police Register* (1834–36), which followed the hybridized style of Cleave's publications, and promised "a repository of all the gems and treasures, and fun and frolic and 'news and occurrences' of the week. It shall abound in Police Intelligence, in Murders, Rapes, Suicides, Burnings, Maimings,

---

[12]   Louis James, *Fiction for the Working Man, 1830–1850* (London: Oxford University Press, 1963), 13.

Theatricals, Races, Pugilism, and all manner of moving 'accidents by flood and field.' In short, it will be stuffed with every sort of devilment that will make it sell."[13] Hetherington meant to finance the *Guardian* with the scandal-driven *Dispatch*, but the separation of popular taste and politics was never absolute for Hetherington in either the *Dispatch* or the *Guardian*, as it never was for Cleave in his publications. Both Hetherington and Cleave incorporated the popular into their political sermons by conveying injustice through the language of the scandal; conversely, they would deride the lifestyles of the nonworking classes in their "popular" productions. Hetherington simultaneously intellectualizes and dramatizes in the following article from the *Guardian*:

> At the point where the franchise is withheld injustice begins; when the demand for Universal Suffrage becomes general, and not till then, the whole country will be united; – then indeed the term *classes* will merge into some comprehensive appellation, and no bloodshed will ensue, for the claims of united millions will be irresistible. (3 December 1831)

In his very important book on the radical elements in popular working-class periodicals, *The Revolution in Popular Literature*, Ian Haywood argues that, "the real significance of the unstamped press was its embracing of popular, often sensational forms of reading pleasure which enhanced rather than diminished its radical appeal. It was this legacy which proved so influential for the Chartist press of the 1840s."[14]

Knowing that workers shared their reading material by reading it out loud, in part to offset costs and in part for the benefit of the non-literate (which had the added symbolic benefit of democratizing papers that would otherwise create divisive lines between the literate and non-literate), also meant that oratorical devices would be popular in many of the publications popping up in the 1830s. Dorothy Thompson argues that Feargus O'Connor, who initiated the *Northern Star* (1837–52), wrote his *Letters* in the tradition of Cobbett, where analysis and emotional appeals were not treated as rhetorically opposite, but were fused together in order to make for effective and affective public reading.[15] The following example from an 1847 *Northern Star* demonstrates that O'Connor was in fact writing in a number of performative traditions, fictional as well as oral, in order to establish reader identification and a sense of 'being there' with his audience:

> I tell you, that, sooner or later, thin gaunt men, dying of famine, pestilence, and hunger, must have been the result of the usurpations of a bloated aristocracy – an overpaid staff of Ministerial menials – a well-fed standing army – a gorged

---

[13]   Mitchell Stephens, *A History of News: From the Drum to the Satellite* (New York: Viking, 1988), 204.

[14]   Ian Haywood, *The Revolution in Popular Literature: Print, Politics and the People, 1790–1860* (Cambridge: Cambridge University Press, 2004), 6.

[15]   Dorothy Thompson, *The Chartists* (London: Temple Smith, 1984), 52.

church, over-paid officials, and pensioned paupers; of the absorption of the honey
of the factory bee, by the drone who owns the key; of a useless police, only
rendered necessary to reconcile men to their degradation, of over grown bankers,
merchants, and traders, speculating upon the blood, the misfortunes, and the
distresses of their country; and above all, that such must be the result so long as
the rich oppressor monopolizes all power over the poor oppressed. (23 January)

Another reason Chartists embraced the hybrid political-popular forms of
broadsides, the radical stamped press, and the unstamped press was that middle-
class publications, and especially the 'respectable presses' targeting working-class
readers, were vehemently opposed to them. Charles Knight, editor of the *Penny
Magazine*, rejected the "coarse" pleasures of the average reader, and was hostile
not only to the politics of Chartism and its sympathizers, but also to the way in
which radical and popular presses were fusing. In the "Preface" to the first volume
of the *Penny Magazine*, Knight told his readers what not to expect: "There have
been no excitements for the lovers of the marvellous—no tattle or abuse for the
gratification of a diseased taste for personality—and, above all, no party politics"
(31 March 1832). After the circulation of the magazine dropped from 200,000 to
40,000, Knight occasionally did include short stories. However, he was always
an outspoken opponent of any publication that could be said to be pandering to
the sensational tastes of the British public, and he understood radical politics as a
particularly dangerous species of sensationalism. As a leader of the Society for the
Diffusion of Useful Knowledge (SDUK), Knight would bewail that the "blithe-
looking father in his Sunday coat, and happy mother in her smartest bonnet" didn't
have leisure activities open to them: "no national gallery, no museum in South
Kensington."[16] He wrote a play which he submitted to Drury Lane and did as
much as anyone to popularize Shakespeare. But his genuine efforts to reach and
"improve" the "popular mind" were vitiated by the accompanying argument that
the political evolution of the working classes must be put into the hands of the
nonworking classes. Rejecting sensationalism meant accepting the political status
quo: allowing choices or tastes to be determined by others. For Chartists, accepting
sensationalism meant rejecting the political status quo.[17]

The market for improving material among the working classes was nevertheless
substantial. Reynolds and Lloyd, both of whom were pro-Chartist, also promised
their readerships opportunities to better themselves by offering exposure to

---

[16]   Charles Knight, *Passages of a Working Life*, 3 vols, Vol. 2 (London: Bradbury &
Evans, 1864–65), 26.

[17]   The Society for the Promotion of Christian Knowledge (SPCK) also set out to
improve the aesthetic standard of working people, though from a Christian point of view.
It published *Saturday Magazine* (1832–44). Interestingly, the *Evangelical Penny Magazine*
(1832) entered the market for affordable improvement periodicals at the same time as the
Penny and *Saturday* magazines, but only produced ten numbers. Its failure was likely due
to a policy to offer working-class readers only a monolithic, unitary alternative discourse of
Methodism to a working-class taste for hybridity.

"great works of art." But the nature of the educative and improvement material differed in Reynolds's and Lloyd's papers, where it was unabashedly combined with sensational stories. The refusal of Knight to accept the interplay of popular and improving material would allow the Chartist press, through embracing fictional devices and eventually fiction, to demonstrate that its attempts to inform and improve working people were different from *other* middle-class efforts to do the same (again, many in the Chartist press were from the middle class). In *The Old Printer and the Modern Press* (1854) Knight wrote, "The object of the general diffusion of knowledge is not to make men discontented with their lot ... but to give the means of content to those who, for the most part, must necessarily remain in that station which requires great self-denial and great endurance."[18] Bronterre O'Brien, a one-time editor of the *Northern Star*, wrote in the *Destructive* (1832–33), an unstamped newspaper, "the only knowledge which is of service to the working people is that which makes them more dissatisfied, and makes them worse slaves" (7 June 1834). Ernest Jones added in the *People's Paper* (1852–58), "A People's Education is safe only in a People's own hands" (3 July 1852). One contributor to the *Poor Man's Guardian* implicitly comments on the nature of middle-class educational drives by signing his or her poem as "One of the Know-Nothings." The poem itself would not be to Knight's liking. It is political, demotic, diametric, self-informed, and sarcastic:

> Wages should form the price of goods;
> Yes, wages should be all.
> Then we who work to make the goods,
> Should *justly have them all*;
> But if their price be made of rent,
> Tithes, taxes, profits all,
> Then we who work to make the goods
> Shall have – *just none at all*. (7 January 1832)

The Chartist press would see generic fusion—the integration of affective and analytical discourses—as a formal device to align their movement with working-class culture, as distinct from working-class social concerns and politics. Conceding to the infusion of popular expressions and fiction was a way to demonstrate that they were joining a culture and not attempting to convert it. In doing so, Chartists also sought to solidify a working-class aesthetic that was independent of middle-class evaluations. The debate over enfranchisement was often reduced to a cultural question, with nonworking classes maintaining that the disenfranchised had to be raised to a certain level of aesthetic rationality before they would demonstrate the maturity to choose England's leaders. Accordingly, emotional responses to affective art were thought to show that lower classes with the vote would only be swayed by rhetoric, which would result in the election of demagogues or quacks. Weaning readers from sensational discourses

---

[18]   Charles Knight, *The Old Printer and the Modern Press* (London: John Murray, 1854), 307.

(and radical politics) was considered due preparation for the franchise.[19] Many Chartists were suspicious of the idea that aesthetic assimilation was a necessary precondition for structural change, mainly because the *political* values and tastes of the classes were not the same. Self-consciously rhetorical, popular discourses could thus be used to express a rejection of the liberalisms which argued that "the march of the intellect" would reveal to the lower classes common interests, both aesthetic and political, between all the classes.[20] Chartist fiction often insists on the intellectual abilities of common working people. In "A Simple Story," for example, the author points out the need to publicize "a correct and more extensive knowledge of their intellectual attainments."[21] Melodramatic, affective, good versus evil language was also political in itself because middle-class voices were attempting to appeal to the working class by promising a glimpse into the *vita contemplativa*. The styles appropriated by the Chartist press promised something else. Embracing a hybrid of affective devices and intellectual or educative material—of melodrama and affairs of state, of topical and classical poetry—is political when, in 1833, W.A. Roebuck introduced the Education Bill on the grounds that, "as mere matter of police, the education of the people ought to be considered as a part of the duties of the government."[22]

Chartism appropriated the dichotomizing, sensationalizing language of working-class newspapers because the diametric trope of us versus them and good versus evil might generate partisanship, emotion, and action, but also because by doing so the Chartist press could show that it shared with the working classes its *langue* or ideologeme.[23] It is important to recognize that the first wave of Chartists was rarely from the working classes. John Charlton calls Chartism "a working-class movement with middle-class adherents."[24] The first Chartists were in fact often "petite bourgeoisie" shopkeepers and small businessmen, some of whom were former workers who had done well for themselves and scraped onto the electoral

---

[19]   Consider for example the quip attributed to both Robert Lowe and Benjamin Disraeli, "We must educate our masters."

[20]   Like Knight, John Cassell ran papers focused on the intellectual and cultural advancement of working people. A member of the National Temperance Society, Cassell conceived *Cassell's Illustrated Family Paper* (1853–1932) and the *Popular Educator* (1852–55) "to give the labourer a healthy publication" and to counteract the sensationalism of the radical presses. Haywood explores the irony of Cassell's papers—periodicals that were so antagonistic towards the language of the popular press that they used its own Manichean rhetoric of good versus evil to disparage it. Cassell only shifted the terms of good and evil: for Cassell, good was arguing for "common interests" and denying the good and evil, us and them attitude of his rivals.

[21]   Haywood, "A Simple Story," 42.

[22]   Anne Digby and Peter Searby, *Children, School and Society in Nineteenth-Century England* (London: Macmillan Press, 1981), 25.

[23]   Fredric Jameson defines the ideologeme as "the smallest intelligible unit of the essentially antagonistic discourses of social classes" (76).

[24]   John Charlton, *The Chartists: The First National Workers' Movement* (London: Pluto Press, 1997), 64.

register after 1832. David Vincent argues that early Chartist writing reflects a "sort of working-class intelligentsia."[25] For financial, political, and cultural reasons, however, their publications could not sustain a corresponding level of discourse. To attract readers from a range of working classes and to appear in the tradition of working-class publications, their journalistic and "serious" discourses had to be diversified, breaking down and bringing together generic opposites into an inclusive and pluralizing form. This style would also be active when Chartists began to write fiction, itself an indication that Chartism recognized that "serious" discourses could be complemented by popular ones. The stories that resulted confirmed a working-class aesthetic where directly political and expository writing is freely mixed with sensational devices, such as melodramatic plotting.

The most successful and renowned Chartist paper was the *Northern Star*. Feargus O'Connor, an estate owner and landlord, though a reformist landlord, began the *Star* in 1837 as a stamped paper and by the spring of 1839 it was selling over 48,000 copies a week. Since it was read aloud like many other nineteenth-century periodicals, no one knows the number of people it actually reached. In it notices and reports on local meetings, demonstrations, and radical initiatives were given prominence, the best real estate on the page. But it also included poetry from readers and the established Romantic poets (both the non-political, nature poetry and the idealistic poetry of freedom and democracy). In addition there were literature reviews, missing persons notices, financial columns, dramatized accounts of working-class suffering, and occasionally graphic descriptions of murders and beatings. It also reproduced the techniques of the popular press by including many woodcuts and steel-engraved portraits. A main feature of the *Star* and in fact of most Chartist periodicals was correspondence columns, which mostly responded to legal questions but would also respond to matters of etiquette. Anne Humphreys points out that the legal discourses are "the stuff of 'fiction,' particularly melodrama: blocked desire, frustrated love, wills and inheritances, questions of deportment and the law."[26] However, by no means was the *Star* "sensationalist." James Epstein says that it "was a serious political journal written by highly skilled journalists. On occasion the education of many an artisan or factory hand must have been taxed in reading its pages."[27] Yet the journalism of O'Connor and the *Star* in general—journalism being its pronounced feature[28]—was often infused with the more consumable languages of the scandal (of outrage

---

[25]   David Vincent, *Bread, Knowledge, and Freedom: A Study of Nineteenth Century Working-Class Autobiography* (London: Methuen, 1981), 51.

[26]   Anne Humphreys, "Popular Narrative and Periodical Discourse in *Reynolds's Weekly Newspapers*," in *Investigating Victorian Journalism*, eds Laurel Brake, Aled Jones, and Lionell Madden (Basington: Macmillan, 1990), 39–40.

[27]   James Epstein, *The Lion of Freedom: Feargus O'Connor and the Chartist Movement 1832–1842* (London: Croom Helm, 1982), 69.

[28]   The *Star* brought attention to the fact that it was a stamped paper relaying news. The cover page of its first volume directly alluded to its newspaper status: "Reader – Behold that little red spot, in the corner of my newspaper. That is the Stamp; the Whig *beauty* spot; your *plague* spot" (18 November 1837).

and indignation). Looking at the way in which "the *Star*'s success was dependent on the wide support of the working class," Epstein also says "there was always an appeal to a vague brand of popular democratic control."[29] O'Connor directly emphasized this aspect of democratic control in his own columns ("The *Star* is mine and the People's, and only ours" [*Northern Star*, 18 January, 1845]) and indirectly conveyed it by the popular languages he and his staff adopted: Chartist intellectuals don't always sound like Chartist intellectuals.

For the most part, reporters and editors for the *Star* attempted to include into their journalistic writing a sense of tension and immediacy. Reporting on a Chartist meeting but also arguing that no man without the vote should be compelled to military service, a writer for the *Star* mixes tenses, blends voices, and combines genres:

> An overflowing and most enthusiastic public meeting was held at the City Chartist Hall ... In moving the adoption of the resolution, he [the speaker, Thomas Martin Wheeler] said, it was an approved maxim "That taxation without representation was tyranny, and ought to be resisted." If this be true, by what stronger name shall we designate the compelling of the unenfranchised to serve in the militia – (hear, hear) – in an ensanguined livery? and where was the man that would not blush, aye, even deeper than the scarlet coat he would be compelled to wear, to be placed in such a disgraceful predicament? (Loud cheers.) There was no necessity for going to war with America about the Oregon territory. If land was wanted, there was plenty to be had at home. (Great cheering.) At any rate, he was resolved not to be a militiaman; and if the giving vent to that assertion was treason, "he was a traitor, aye, and prouder still to be surrounded by so many hundreds of such "traitors.'" (Tremendous cheering). (24 January 1846)

The past is conflated with the present; Wheeler's voice is conflated with the reporter's (Wheeler himself?); the impulse to dramatize is conflated with the one to intellectualize; and a report on a meeting is conflated with a fiery editorial rant.

Sales of the *Star*, however, declined yearly from 1839 to 1846, largely because it began to "pull away from the more popular, less self-conscious elements which had formed an important part of the movement and of the *Star*'s public in the early days"[30] (Thompson 53). Anderson points out that it developed "a highly particularized focus" (181) and thus grew limited in its appeal. In 1841 Plymouth Chartists complained that there was not enough reporting on London's murders. By 1844 the *Star* had moved from Leeds to London, changing its title to the *Northern Star and National Trades Journal*. It began to incorporate more news about trade-union activity, narrowing its focus even more. O'Connor had appointed George Julian Harney as editor of the newspaper in 1845. Harney subsequently turned his attention to an abstract internationalist theme. O'Connor would later accuse Harney of reaching out to "Socialists first and Chartists second" and eventually pressure Harney into resigning his editorship, though there were other reasons for

---

29   Epstein, *Lion*, 83.
30   Thompson, *Chartists*, 53.

their divergence as well. O'Connor rejected Harney's specialized focus because it was cut off from immediate working-class issues, and working-class tastes. In 1846, competing against Harney's new papers and still fighting slumping sales, he argued,

> That Chartism which has fustian jackets, blistered hands and unshorn chins as its emblems, has been denounced by those who would make it a thing of refinement and respectability, while we repeat the fact to our readers that Chartism means poverty – and poverty is a consequence of class legislation; the legitimate deduction from which is, that before poverty ceases class legislation must be destroyed. (1 August 1846)

Refinement and respectability are not the interests of the true Chartist press and working-class intellectual. Legitimacy and a corresponding share of the marketplace could only be won by sharing the social attitudes and concerns of workers, and the language that conveys it.

The most drastic measure the *Star* took to appeal to a wider audience was to publish fiction. In 1843 an anonymous commentator in the *Star* wrote, "We think novel reading, at the best, only an indifferent substitute for a worse occupation of time. But we are not ignorant of the fact that however we may moralize, many hundreds of new-born intellects of modern improvement and enlightenment look out for novels with avidity." Yet it did not publish a major piece of fiction, Thomas Martin Wheeler's *Sunshine and Shadow*, until 1849, serializing the novel in 37 parts. By 1849, sales of the *Star* were under 10,000 a week; more importantly, Chartism itself was in decline. Wheeler's novel, in fact, is in part an overview of Chartism's decline, part a clarification of current Chartist positions and policies, and part entertainment. The tendency of the novel to abruptly cross generic lines reproduces the format of the periodical in which it appeared, and also the popular periodical of variety with which the *Star* wanted to share an audience. In the novel, Wheeler, now a veteran of Chartism, directly and explicitly calls out for a working-class literature of its own: "The fiction department of literature has hitherto been neglected by the scribes of our body, and the opponents of our principles have been allowed to wield the power of imagination over the youth of our party, without any effort on our part to occupy this wide and fruitful plain."[31] *Sunshine and Shadow* is a political melodrama that infuses intellectualizing genres into a sensational form, telling the story of working-class autodidacticism while describing shipwrecks and relying on miraculous coincidences. In parts it is didactic, in other parts romantic. The story is a *bildungsroman*, a narrative of ups and downs, with a social counterpart, Chartism and its ups and downs. Accordingly, it includes a number of opposite themes: self-reliance and determinism, enthusiasm and disillusionment, idealism and reality frequently cross paths in it and the tension between them is never entirely resolved. The narrative follows Arthur Morton, an apprentice to a printer, as he experiences a series of emotional and cerebral victories (sunshine) followed by crushing social

---

[31]   Thomas Martin Wheeler, *Sunshine and Shadow* in *Chartist Fiction*, ed. Ian Haywood (Aldershot: Ashgate, 1999), 72.

defeats (shadows). His independently achieved intellectual development is in contrast to his social stagnation and the moral depravity of the well-to-do Walter North, the story's ostensible villain. *Sunshine and Shadow* dramatizes the rise of and obstacles to working-class intellectualism, blurring as it does so the generic lines between affective and analytical writing.

If it is true that content searches out and determines its own form, then Chartist literature, with the specific content of its own interests and experiences, would have its own form. If it is true, for example, that Chartist fiction uniquely introduces decentered values (collective versus individual action, public versus private space, physically effete heroes), as Ian Haywood argues[32], then it ought to carry signs of that decentering in its formal properties, such as dialectical devices, structures, and discourses. This is what we see in *Sunshine and Shadow*: it is not a novel that privileges any given genre. And yet there is a center of sorts to the story, oppositions. Ultimately the story contrasts a good Chartist and an evil class structure, repeating the dominant rhetorical feature of Chartist non-fiction and the strategy of dichotomizing social opposites and sensationalizing political content that was inherited from working-class and radical periodicals. Identifying both the diametric and melodramatic structure of Chartist prose writing, Elaine Hadley reports on an editorialist from *The Northern Star* who in 1839

> wrote melodramatically in what would now be labelled simplistic polar oppositions but which should be seen instead as historical artefacts from a society of relative moral and social consensus: 'The character of the people is unchanged – they are the same simple, peaceful, and confiding people that they ever were; and the character of the Whigs is unchanged – they are the same selfish, grasping subtle, cowardly political gourmands that they always were.'[33]

The "melodramatic mode" here creates a sense of unresolved tension, the function of affective writing having nothing to do with resolving tension. We should not hesitate to label the structure of Chartist writing as revolving around "simplistic polar oppositions." In 1840, the editors of the Scottish *Chartist Circular* (1839–41) explicitly identify this as a Chartist strategy: "The virtues of the masses ought to be sought out and extolled; the iniquities of the titled honestly exposed and condemned."[34] Chartist fiction, and especially *Sunshine and Shadow*, continued to emphasize that political writing could contract into an expression of a simple conflict. But the "simplistic" and melodramatic in no way suggests an apostasy of intellectual and educative goals. Wheeler does not approach the dual pressures to intellectualize and dramatize as a contradiction because it was not a contradiction in the tradition in which he was writing.

Discussing the rise of mass-produced sensational writing, *Reynolds's Miscellany* for example, Steve Devereux suggests that,

---

[32]   Ian Haywood, *Working-Class Fiction from Chartism to Trainspotting* (Plymouth: Northcote House, 1997), 23.

[33]   Hadley, *Melodramatic*, 110.

[34]   Haywood, *Revolution*, 139.

Chartism was the first mass political movement to find itself in competition with this new popular culture, the growth of which coincides with the movement's decline. It is perhaps not so surprising after all that those Chartists who were seeking to revive the movement should attempt to do so, in part, by writing radical popular fiction.[35]

But the argument that the Chartist presses "sold out" to popular appetites is predicated on the idea that the popular or that which pleases the populace ipso facto cannot be radical, an assumption that for democracy-touting Chartists of the 1840s would be tantamount to defeatism.[36] The instruments of romance do not need to be contrary to the aims of history, if readers are challenged by romance to view their interests as diametrically opposed to others. We must also remember that the style Chartists turned towards was not apolitical, or merely sensational romance. The pre-history of the Chartist press is not only scandal and sensation; it is the use of the languages of scandal and sensation in all contexts, including political ones. Vicinus also argues that, "Chartists began writing novels based on popular fiction when the movement began to falter politically."[37] But there is another way of approaching the adoption of fiction by the Chartist press. By including affective discourses—and arguably no other mode of writing can be as affective as fiction—Chartists continued the tradition of early working-class writing and allowed themselves to confirm their cultural alignment to working people, differentiating themselves all the while from the established presses of the middle class.[38]

The reason Chartists gave for including fiction, however, was often expressed in terms of a logic or symbolism that was more idealistic than *real*-political. In a letter addressed "To the Young Men of the Working Classes" Thomas Cooper writes,

> It now becomes a matter of the highest necessity, that you all join hands and head to create a literature of your own. Your own prose, your own poetry ... would put you all more fully in possession of each other's thoughts and thus give you a higher respect for each other, and a clearer perception of what you can do when united.[39]

---

[35] Steve Devereux, "Chartism and Popular Fiction," in *Writing and Radicalism*, ed. John Lucas (London: Longman, 1996), 134.

[36] The fact that both *Reynolds's Miscellany* (1846–69) and *Reynolds's Political Instructor* (1849–50) were advertised in the *Northern Star* suggests that O'Connor did not think his paper was in direct competition with the popular press.

[37] Vicinus, *Muse*, 114.

[38] Patrick Joyce is clearly correct to point out that working-class audiences did not monopolize the desire for melodrama. However, middle-class efforts to improve both working-class aesthetic and political tastes were diligently pursued by the presses of the SDUK and its successors up to the Second Reform Bill. These were the presses most directly in competition – at least ideologically – with the Chartist press.

[39] Vicinus, *Muse*, 108.

Cooper was the undisputed "poet laureate" of the Chartists.[40] Famously self-taught, he documents his influences in his autobiography: from *Paradise Lost* and *Hamlet* to *Life of Johnson* and *Life of Schiller*. He brought himself to study Church history, the poetry of Byron and Scott, Gibbon's *Decline and Fall of the Roman Empire*, and so on. Though garnering approving recognition from the middle class, *The Purgatory of Suicides*, which he wrote in jail between 1843 and 1845 after voting for a general strike at the Manchester Conference of 1842, was justly critiqued in Chartist and radical presses. Cooper was accused of deliberately writing verse that the group of people he explicitly said he wanted to reach would not relate to or understand. Vicinus argues that he was trying to impress his "betters."[41] The main function of the *Purgatory* does seem to be to display Cooper's learning and his comfort with middle-class aesthetics:

> Poet of Paradise, – whose glory illumed
> My path of youthful penury, till grew
> The desert to a garden, and Life bloomed
> With hope and joy, 'midst suffering, – honour due
> I cannot render thee; but reverence true
> This heart shall give thee, till it reach the verge
> Where human splendours lose their lustrous hue;
> And, when, in death, mortal joys all merge
> Thy grand and gorgeous music, Milton, be my dirge!

But Cooper's short stories, many of which were first published in Chartist periodicals, are simple fables written in the tradition of the broadside. Taking his own advice in the letter "To the Young Men of the Working Classes" he uses "plain words" and avoids an "inflation of expression." Perhaps the shift from verse to prose fiction occasioned a different style, but the shift is nonetheless pronounced. The stories collected in *Wise Saws and Modern Instances* (1845) include some of the high-mindedness of the *Purgatory*, but they also include simple, Manichean plotting and make direct social and political statements. In "The Lad Who Felt like a Fish out of Water," simplicity itself is valued in contradistinction to the pretensions for intellectual sophistication by the middle classes. The story, however, is a self-improvement story, demonstrating the means to self-guided working-class cultural elevation. Diggory Lawson, the "lad," is the naturally gifted son

---

[40]   Ernest Jones came later to Chartism than did Cooper and Wheeler, joining the movement in 1846 and rising to prominence only in the midst of its demise, in 1848, when he became the new undisputed Chartist "poet laureate." Like O'Connor he was not of the working class, but born wealthy. His "conversion" to Chartism was heralded in the *Northern Star*, and he became its literary editor from 1846 to 1848. Throughout his career he had to show that he was sufficiently of the working class, not simply in support of it. He did this in part by bringing together radical politics and sensation: "I do not see why Truth should always be dressed in stern and repulsive garb. The more attractive you make her, the more easily she will progress" (quoted in Vicinus, 114).

[41]   Ibid., 98.

of a poor, loving lace-weaver. He educates himself by watching his artisan father dabble in miscellaneous self-improving pursuits and by enjoying nature, which he explores with a "noble" yet "somewhat romantic" interest. Learning his father's trade and spending his leisure hours learning the art of literature, he was "happy enough, and was likely to make a happy and useful man."[42] But when his father becomes involved in "bobbin-net" speculation, the Lawsons decide to make Dig a gentleman. He is sent on embarrassing excursions to learn the respectable artifices of the bourgeoisie. Cooper has great fun distinguishing between the languages of the classes: Dig speaks plain English while his social opposites mostly try to impress each other with the latest expression. Confronted with "the infinite deal of nothings," the intellectually superior Dig, who would be happy to give his opinion on Socrates or Napoleon (being an autodidact like Cooper himself), is tongue-tied.[43] Diggory, of course, is the 'fish out of water,' unable to comprehend and accept the moral value of a certain Mrs. Strutabout's table etiquette. Not focused on the urban proletariat or a Chartist consciousness, the story nonetheless underlines unmistakable class antagonisms. Finally, in a sudden twist, Diggory's father returns to "associating with plain, sensible men, and cultivating knowledge in his leisure hours" and Diggory follows him in his trade, "happier every day" and content to be a "plain speaker."[44] The message of intellectual self-development is still prominent, but it is combined with diametric plotting and a plain, "non-intellectualizing," and distinguishable working-class language.

The titles of his periodicals from the early 1840s to the early 1850s also suggest that Cooper was learning to embrace "plain speaking" for cultural and ultimately political purposes: the *Midlands Counties Illuminator* (1841), the *Chartist Rushlight* (1841), the *Commonwealthsman or Chartist Advocate* (1842), the *Plain Speaker* (1849), and *Cooper's Journal: or unfettered Thinker and Plain Speaker for Truth, Freedom and Progress* (1850). Cooper, a Chartist intellectual, sought to articulate working-class culture and simultaneously appeal to it by moving away from middle-class discourses and adapting to a tradition of working-class expression that sullies generic purity, simplifies conflicts while promoting the idea of an independently reached working-class political consciousness, and organizes its political content through melodramatic devices. Cooper unapologetically combines sentiment and politics. He represents working-class culture so that it too includes intellectualizing and dramatizing voices. "Merrie England – No More" (1845), a story about the disenfranchised that illustrates a great deal of working-class pathos, as young men are forced into military service, ends with a direct statement about working-class knowledge: "let it be understood that ... whoever enters Leicester, or any other of the populous starving hives of England, must expect to find the deepest subjects of theology, and government,

---

[42] Thomas Cooper, "The Lad who Felt like a Fish out of Water," in *Wise Saws and Modern Instances* (London: Jeremiah How, 1845), 63.

[43] Ibid., 66–67.

[44] Ibid., 83.

and political economy, taken up with a subtlety that would often puzzle a graduate of Oxford or Cambridge."[45]

Cooper's and Wheeler's representation of intellectualizing working classes may have been more prescriptive than descriptive. But the fact that they maintained melodramatic modes in their writing as they promoted the idea of a working-class intellectualism suggests that they did not find sensationalism and intellectualism to be at odds with each other. It also suggests that Chartists sought to promote working-class political interests—confirming the idea that the working class had the political sophistication to use the vote wisely—by showing an allegiance to working-class cultural tastes, which were understood by both middle and working classes to be dramatically different from each other. If we feel compelled to judge Chartism harshly for conceding to sensation, we must then accept that Chartist writing and its working-class audiences were mutually defining. Describing the evolution of radical presses Louis James says there "had never been a sharp division between political and literary publications."[46] So if Chartist writing was consequent of a long eighteenth century—if it was the language of a nonworking-class radical literary tradition conveyed by a nonworking-class group of reformers—it was something else as well.

Works Cited

Anderson, Patricia. *The Printed Image and the Transformation of Popular Culture, 1790–1860.* Oxford: Clarendon Press, 1991.

Charlton, John. *The Chartists: The First National Workers' Movement.* London: Pluto Press, 1997.

Cole, G.D.H. *Chartist Portraits.* New York: Macmillan, 1965.

Cooper, Thomas. "The Lad who Felt like a Fish out of Water," in *Wise Saws and Modern Instances.* London: Jeremiah How, 1845, 42–59.

———. "'Merrie England'—No More," in *The Literature of Struggle: An Anthology of Chartist Fiction*, ed. Ian Haywood. Aldershot: Scolar Press, 1995, 53–9.

———. *The Purgatory of Suicides, a Prison-Rhyme: in Ten Books.* London: J. How, 1845.

Devereux, Steve. "Chartism and Popular Fiction," in *Writing and Radicalism*, ed. John Lucas. London: Longman, 1996, 128–49.

Digby, Anne and Peter Searby. *Children, School and Society in Nineteenth-Century England.* London: Macmillan Press, 1981.

Epstein, James. *The Lion of Freedom: Feargus O'Connor and the Chartist Movement, 1832–1842.* London: Croom Helm, 1982.

Hadley, Elaine. *Melodramatic Tactics: Theatricalized Dissent in the English Marketplace, 1800–1885.* Stanford: Stanford University Press. 1995.

---

[45]   "'Merrie England' – No More," in *The Literature of Struggle: An Anthology of Chartist Fiction*, ed. Ian Haywood (Aldershot: Scolar Press, 1995), 58.

[46]   James, *Fiction*, 26.

Haywood, Ian. *The Revolution in Popular Literature: Print, Politics and the People, 1790–1860*. Cambridge: Cambridge University Press, 2004.

———. *Working-Class Fiction from Chartism to Trainspotting*. Plymouth: Northcote House, 1997.

———, ed. "A Simple Story," *The Literature of Struggle: An Anthology of Chartist Fiction*. Aldershot: Scolar Press, 1995, 41–45.

Humphreys, Anne. "Popular Narrative and Periodical Discourse in Reynolds's Weekly Newspapers," *Investigating Victorian Journalism*, eds Laurel Brake, Aled Jones, and Lionell Madden. Basington: Macmillan, 1990, 33–47.

James, Louis. *Fiction for the Working Man, 1830–1850*. London: Oxford University Press, 1963.

Jameson, Fredric. *The Political Unconscious: Narrative as a Symbolic Act*. Ithaca: Cornell University Press, 1981.

Joyce, Patrick. "The Constitution and Narrative Structure of Victorian Politics," in *Re-reading the Constitution: New Narratives in the Political History of England's Long Nineteenth Century*, ed. James Vernon. Cambridge: Cambridge University Press, 1996, 179–203.

Knight, Charles. *The Old Printer and the Modern Press*. London: John Murray, 1854.

———. *Passages of a Working Life, 3 vols*. London: Bradbury & Evans, 1864–65.

Ledger, Sally. "Chartist Aesthetics in the Mid Nineteenth Century: Ernest Jones, a Novelist of the People," *Nineteenth-Century Literature*, Vol. 57, No. 1 (2002), 31–63.

McCalman, Iain. *Radical Underworld: Prophets, Revolutionaries and Pornographers in London, 1795–1840*. Cambridge: Cambridge University Press, 1988.

Rose, Jonathan. *The Intellectual Life of the British Working Classes*. New Haven: Yale University Press, 2002.

Schwab, Ulrike. *The Poetry of the Chartist Movement: A Literary and Historical Study*. Dordrecht: Kluwer Academic Publishers, 1987.

Stephens, Mitchell. *A History of News: From the Drum to the Satellite*. New York: Viking, 1988.

Taylor, Miles. *Ernest Jones, Chartism, and the Romance of Politics*, 1819–1869. Oxford: Oxford University Press, 2003.

Thompson, Dorothy. *The Chartists*. London: Temple Smith, 1984.

Vicinus, Martha. 1974. *The Industrial Muse: A Study of Nineteenth Century British Working-Class Literature*. London: Croom Helm, 1974.

Vincent, David. *Bread, Knowledge and Freedom: A Study of Nineteenth Century Working-Class Autobiography*. London: Methuen, 1981.

Wheeler, Thomas Martin. *Sunshine and Shadow*. In *Chartist Fiction*, ed. Ian Haywood. Aldershot: Ashgate, 1999, 65–193.

Chapter 7
Shakespeare in the Early Working-Class Press[1]

Kathryn Prince

What use was Shakespeare to the nineteenth-century working-class intellectual? For every autodidact who discovered in Shakespeare's works a source of instruction and delight, it seems, some more pragmatic relative or colleague rushed in to interrupt the reading experience with the dour observation that Shakespeare would never put bread on the table.[2] These experiences, part of the current critical discourse via a small number of published autobiographies, are both reflected in and belied by the wider debate about Shakespeare's relevance that took place in the periodicals published for the nineteenth century's rather larger population of working-class magazine readers. In periodicals for working-class readers, Shakespeare was sometimes presented simply as a source of pleasure, but more often as a model for the ambitious working-class intellectual, a representative of that class who had risen through the ranks simply by virtue of his own intellectual prowess and hard work. He was also presented as a political radical, the source of endless inflammatory quotations devoid of context, or sometimes as a dangerous establishment figure whose words and works resulted in the perpetuation of an unjust class system. Whether Shakespeare might be considered a working-class intellectual himself, and whether his works might be relevant to contemporary working-class issues, were topics that recurred with surprising frequency in magazines that might be expected to pay more attention to putting bread on the table than placing the plays of a long-dead author in workers' hands. This debate about Shakespeare's relevance in the nineteenth century, fundamental to the establishment of a working-class literary canon, focused on the extent to which an established figure of the national canon might resonate with working-class readers.

Periodicals were the most significant means by which knowledge of Shakespeare was disseminated to the nineteenth-century working-class reader, at least until 1870 when some of Shakespeare's plays became an official part of the state school curriculum. The circulation of periodicals below the middle class had at first been limited by technological and demographic factors, but in the early

[1]   A version of this article is included in my book *Shakespeare in the Victorian Periodicals* (Routledge, 2008); it appears here with the publisher's permission.

[2]   Andrew Murphy's invaluable work on Shakespeare in nineteenth-century working-class autobiographies, the topic of his forthcoming book, is previewed in his article "Shakespeare Among the Workers," *Shakespeare Survey*, Vol. 58 (2005), 107–117.

nineteenth century periodicals became for the first time financially and intellectually accessible to the working-class reader. The nineteenth-century magazine trade benefited from reduced government taxation and new technologies that together made magazines less expensive to produce and thus to purchase, while burgeoning literacy rates achieved through programs like the Sunday school movement created a new market for inexpensive reading material. Beginning with the radical political magazines in the early decades of the nineteenth century and continuing with the "useful knowledge" magazines of the 1830s and onward, publishers sought to provide working-class readers with the information they required to educate and empower themselves.

While radical magazine publishers and conservative charitable associations defined their educational enterprises rather differently, both were engaged in the process of educating, rather than merely entertaining, their readers. In the periodicals created to fill the market gap that literacy programs had created among working-class readers ill-served by periodicals intended for their social "betters," Shakespeare was treated as a hotly-contested piece of cultural property, employed both to reinforce nineteenth-century England's threatened class hierarchy and to empower politically disenfranchised workers. Since the French revolution, a dominant tendency in English Shakespeare criticism had been to quarantine his works from the contemporary political fray by placing them in a remote, historicized past through antiquarian and philological investigations. Working-class treatments of Shakespeare operate against this dominant mode, introducing his plays into debates about class relations in nineteenth-century Britain. Shakespeare's ideological usefulness is responsible for his popularization among working-class periodical readers. Far more frequently than the chance encounters with Shakespeare recorded in the published autobiographies, Shakespeare's appearances in the periodicals disseminated knowledge about the playwright and his works as they related to the topical issues addressed elsewhere in the same periodicals. In contrast to the more ephemeral encounters with Shakespeare experienced in the nineteenth-century theatre or lecture hall, difficult to recuperate unless the impressions they left were recorded in these autobiographies or in letters or journals, the periodical evidence remains largely intact and thus available for critical analysis. This evidence suggests that Shakespeare was sometimes employed as an instrument of enculturation, but also that dissenting voices used the periodicals to construct alternative ways of understanding Shakespeare and, in so doing, alternative ways of articulating their own place within the hierarchies of their culture. For purposes often acutely contemporary, Shakespeare was rehabilitated into a working-class hero, a proto-Chartist, and, contradictorily, an exemplar of the solidly middle-class values to which some magazines hoped working-class readers could be to taught to aspire.

Shakespeare's talent for placing rousing, dramatic speeches into the mouths of his characters made his plays a tempting and rewarding source of radical political rhetoric. Among the earliest examples, the political reformer William Cobbett's *Political Register* stands out both for its frequent recourse to Shakespeare and for its unusually virulent attack against Shakespeare's relevance to the working classes.

In an article not about literature but rather about the lack of nutrition in potatoes,[3] Cobbett likened a taste for this "worse than useless root" to the British fondness for Shakespeare. This analogy between an element in the everyday lives of his readers, potatoes, and the more abstract concept of the fashion for Shakespeare is typical of Cobbett's technique, well suited to readers more familiar with potatoes than with Shakespeare.[4] The attack's sincerity is undermined, however, when the article is situated within the magazine's overall treatment of Shakespeare. By drawing attention to the lack of mental nutrition in Shakespeare's plays and their reliance on what he dismissed as "bombast and puns and smut," Cobbett was being less than ingenuous. His own reliance on the "bombast" of Shakespeare's history plays for rhetorical purposes is evident in nearly every issue of his magazine. Cobbett's biographer, George Spater, notes that among a rich repertory of authors from whom Cobbett regularly drew quotations and analogies, he quoted Shakespeare far more often than any other author.[5]

In this, Cobbett was a man of his time. Quotations from Shakespeare were remarkably prevalent in the early radical periodicals. In Thomas Jonathan Wooler's successful *Black Dwarf,* for instance, Shakespeare was frequently employed to further the objective proclaimed in the magazine's prospectus, to "hold up a glass, in which no honest man need be ashamed to look, and every fool and knave may readily trace his resemblance."[6] Wooler was especially well qualified to represent radical Shakespeare; just prior to launching the *Black Dwarf* in 1817 he had published the theatrical periodical *The Stage* (1814–16), and two political articles published in early issues of the *Black Dwarf* led to his arrest for seditious libel. Wooler was both a committed radical willing to put his ideas in print and a believer in the power of the stage to further those ideas. As part of its ongoing mission to expose "political delinquency" and "spiritual imposition,"[7] and as a reflection of that confluence of the radical and the theatrical, Wooler's *Black Dwarf* frequently printed quotations from Shakespeare, often as the epigram to the lead article. In these cases, while the author is identified, the quotation is never attributed to a character or situated within a particular play, with the result that it serves Wooler's rhetorical purpose all the more precisely. Only in a few instances is the comparison rendered in more explicit terms, becoming an epic simile rather than an isolated quotation. For instance, Shakespeare's *Richard III* is invoked in an open letter from the *Black Dwarf* to Sir Francis Burdett calling on

---

[3] *Political Register*, 18 November 1815, 194.

[4] E.P. Thompson notes in his influential *The Making of the English Working Class* that Cobbett frequently employed "the homely, practical analogy, most commonly taken from rural life" to draw in his readers. *The Making of the English Working Class* (Harmondsworth: Penguin, 1968), 824.

[5] George Spater, *William Cobbett: The Poor Man's Friend*, 2 vols (Cambridge: Cambridge University Press, 1982), 1:18, 538.

[6] *Black Dwarf* 1.1, 22 January 1817, 1.

[7] *Black Dwarf* 1.1, 22 January 1817, 1.

the baronet to rebuke the principles of his protégé, John Hobhouse. After quoting from an objectionable speech in which Hobhouse expresses anti-radical views on parliamentary reform, Wooler inserts four lines from Shakespeare's *Richard III* to imply that like Richard, Hobhouse was a villain masquerading as a friend of the people.[8] In the same vein, an article on the death of George III and the ascent of his son to the throne seizes the opportunity to demand justice for radicals who had been injured or killed when the government responded with violence to a political gathering, an event known to posterity as the Peterloo Massacre. The *Black Dwarf* recommended that George IV take Shakespeare's Henry V as a model. Just as Henry "when he ascended the throne, parted with all the associates who had disgraced him," so George IV should dismiss the advisors who served him during his Regency, notably Sidmouth, Castlereagh, and Canning, blamed by the radicals for that bloody attack on the crowd assembled to hear Henry Hunt speak of parliamentary reform.[9] The analogy depends not on readers' familiarity with Shakespeare's plays, but simply on their recognition of his status within working-class culture. The *Black Dwarf* frequently relied on that elevated status in its column "The Blackneb," a selection of quotations from various authors intended to convey the sense that current political events represented a continuation of an age-old struggle for liberty and justice that had frequent recourse to Shakespeare.

Another of the *Black Dwarf*'s significant contributions to working-class Shakespeare reception is evident in the magazine's theatrical reviews, where Shakespeare's radical potential is explored. In a review of an otherwise unremarkable production of *Othello*, the magazine begins to consider what that radical potential might entail:

> DRURY LANE. – *Othello* – We sometimes go to the theatre, and sit there with the utmost astonishment, in the indifference we see around us. The stage has many charms. We can see there what we might in vain hope to find in the common walks of human life. We sometimes catch the living spark of freedom, and think we breathe in ancient Greece, or god-like Rome; or sit over the better remembrance of English liberty, or glory. We see the native dignity of man, unawed by rank, or title, boldly indulging the noblest feelings of humanity. What an invaluable school would the stage be, if it were quite unfettered. What a powerful engine to correct the abuses, and lash the follies of the times. But we turn with some regret from the consideration of what it might be. We must be content to take it at present as it is.[10]

Where that review accepts the stage "as it is," the magazine soon had occasion to draw attention to a fully realized intersection between drama and politics in a production of *Richard III*. The review, with the headline "Horrid Sedition at Covent Garden Theatre," suggests that audience members laughed during a production of

---

[8]   *Black Dwarf* 3.7, 17 February 1819, 97–102.

[9]   *Black Dwarf* 4.4, 2 February 1820, 109–116.

[10]   *Black Dwarf* 1.5, 26 February 1817, 78.

Richard III because they recognized a parallel between Shakespeare's Lord Mayor and the current occupant of that position. According to the review, the actor:

> made the Mayor of the tragedy as servile, officious, and contemptible, as Shakespear ever imagined, or modern times beheld. The real Mayor's reign approaches its close; let him not leave office without avenging his dignity, and asserting his exclusive right to be ridiculous in the robes of the annual magistracy.[11]

Covent Garden, along with Drury Lane, the Haymarket, and a host of more popularly-oriented theatres in working-class neighbourhoods, played a significant role in promoting Shakespeare to a popular audience.[12] Reviews in the working-class press gave actual and prospective spectators a political context for such Shakespeare productions, encouraging them to find topical applications that could yield "seditious" interpretations whether or not these were intended by the producers. Working-class periodicals gave their readers the ability to interpret Shakespeare's plays against the grain, finding their own radical politics and contemporary concerns reflected and thus crafting an alternative to the conservative responses to Shakespeare that are now more familiar to modern critics through such studies as Adrian Poole's *Shakespeare and the Victorians.*

The satirical radical periodical *Figaro in London* likewise recognized the connection between the theatre and what it dubbed "state theatricals." On the front page of one issue, *Figaro in London* depicted King George as a "royal puppet" in a production of *Othello* in which the king's puppet is manipulated by Lord Brougham, in the role of Iago, to the detriment of Desdemona, standing for Hibernia. Here, the details of Shakespeare's plot are less relevant than the circumstances of this production, as a puppet show. *Othello* had by this time become so prevalent in amateur and popular productions that Iago was probably familiar as a manipulative villain, but even without that context the parody is comprehensible because, as the accompanying text explains, the puppet's strings

> are held in the hands of persons, who amuse themselves by pulling first one and then the other as it may serve their temporary purposes. The funny little figure wriggles about first to one side and then the other just as it strikes the whim of those in whose hands he happens to be, and he is forced when acted on by them to play whatever antics they may deem desirable. One jerk may make the little fellow extend his hand in an attitude of friendship, while the next moment he may be made grotesquely to throw up his foot, as if he would kick down the very thing to which he had the moment before offered his hand, and this he wriggles about in every sense of the word the mere *puppet* of those who possess the power to play upon him.[13]

---

[11]   *Black Dwarf* 3.43, 27 October 1819, 706–707.

[12]   On London's popular theatre culture, see Jane Moody's *Illegitimate Theatre in London, 1770–1840* (Cambridge: Cambridge University Press, 2000).

[13]   *Figaro in London* 65, 2 March 1833, 1.

Figaro in London was an astute judge of Shakespeare's potential appeal to its readers, providing just enough context to make its caricatures effective among readers who required something like an editor's note to lay the groundwork for the joke. Like the *Black Dwarf, Figaro in London* mitigated the potential obstacle of readers' lack of familiarity with Shakespeare simply by summarizing the salient elements from his plays, explaining the joke. At the same time that *Figaro in London* was adopting this approach, conservative magazines were attempting to provide their readers with the cultural knowledge that might render such explanations unnecessary.

Beginning in 1832, conservative magazines began to offer working-class readers a rudimentary cultural literacy that would enable them to take part in the intellectual life of the nation. Shakespeare, the author who had already been identified as the epitome of English achievement,[14] was a necessary component of that curriculum. For the conservative periodicals, Shakespeare furnished readers with a model of appropriate, or perhaps aspirational, behavior, a working-class boy who had risen through the ranks by virtue of diligence, talent, and often such characteristically Victorian attributes as good manners and kindness to his mother. Because of his treatment as an exemplary Englishman in the conservative magazines, Shakespeare's views on a variety of matters including politics became significant. *Chambers' Edinburgh Magazine,* responding to a general tendency in its radical competitors to pillage Shakespeare's sources for incendiary quotations often attributed simply to Shakespeare rather than to his characters, quite rightly emphasized that "[i]n none of the persons of his dramas is anything of their author to be seen. Every one speaks and acts for himself, and as he ought to speak and act."[15] The *Chambers'* reader who wanted to know what Shakespeare really thought was directed instead to the sonnets, "a private means of disburthening the poet's mind of the sweet and bitter fancies which occurred to it."[16] Shakespeare is here detected "unbosoming himself of the mild complainings to which his situation and circumstances gave rise," and confessing the "melancholy which secretly preyed"[17] upon him as he ascended the social ladder. It would be tempting to conclude from the sonnets' very infrequent appearance in *Chambers'* and other overtly Christian magazines, despite their avowed biographical interest, that these

---

[14]   See Michael Dobson's *The Making of the National Poet* (Oxford: Clarendon, 1992) on the rise of Shakespeare during the eighteenth century.

[15]   *Chambers' Edinburgh Journal* 5.247, 22 October 1836, 309–310; quotation, 309. In addition to the biographical interest discernable in articles such as "The Will of Shakspeare" (10.472, 13 February 1841, 30), "Was Shakspeare Ever in Scotland" (4.181, 18 July 1835, 199), and "Did Shakspeare Visit Scotland?" (new series 1.17, 27 April 1844, 257–60), the magazine published several articles devoted to a more comprehensive biography: "Biographic Sketch" (5.247, 22 October 1836, 309–310), "Facts and Traditions Concerning Shakspeare" (new series 2.50, 14 December 1844, 369–373), and "Who Wrote Shakspeare" (New Series 17.449, 7 August 1852, 87–89).

[16]   *Chambers' Edinburgh Journal* 5.247, 22 October 1836, 309.

[17]   Ibid.

magazines were among the first to suspect the possible homoeroticism now thought to be discernible in the sonnets. It is more likely, however, that the sonnets were simply unsuited to the synopsis treatment usually accorded to Shakespeare's plays. Literary analysis was never a characteristic feature of the working-class press, whether radical or conservative, with the exception of the short-lived periodical with that explicit objective, the *Literary Test*.

The *Literary Test* intervened into the debate about Shakespeare's relevance at a time when his biography was already being found tremendously useful for conservative ends and his works were being ransacked in support of radical politics. While conservative magazines consistently depicted Shakespeare as an exemplary Englishman and an important item on the cultural literacy curriculum, radical magazines published from within the working class at this time can be characterized by their willingness to question all received ideas, including ideas regarding canonical literature and the biographies of so-called "great men." Readers of radical magazines were encouraged to use their own experiences as a frame of reference for their reading instead of laboring to acquire the trappings of a middle-class or upper-class education. Literature that failed to resonate with the realities of working-class life was simply expunged from this emerging alternative canon. Shakespeare, already occupying a lofty position in the established canon of the higher classes, was among the figures whose value to the working class was called into question. The *Literary Test* fired the opening salvo.

For the *Literary Test,* Shakespeare like any other literary figure had the potential to help or hinder the working-class cause, but when he was assessed according to this magazine's methods he emerged as a dismal failure. The inaugural issue of the magazine had explained that the "aim of all writers" should be "to instruct and to improve, by light and interesting means, the condition of their fellow creatures: – no one should take up the pen of authorship who has not such an object in view."[18] Shakespeare, already an established figure in the literary canon and sometimes an instrument of cultural hegemony, was an appropriate test case for this approach. While his skill as a writer was undisputed, his value to the working classes was, the magazine concluded, negligible:

> I at once admit that *Shakspeare's* powers of language and delineations are stupendous, and his poetry exquisite; but I have yet to ascertain whether all these advantages have been employed for a good object; or whether, instead of applying them to the furtherance of knowledge and increase of happiness, he has not somewhat preferred the advancement of his own individual interest, and tended to the perpetuation of ignorance and wretched inequality, by truckling to the vicious and distempered opinions of those who benefited by their continuance. That the state of things, however he intended, has not been much improved by his endeavours is very clear, and surely by such extraordinary powers as he possessed, any difficulty would have been surmountable. It is true that he lived in times even more despotic than the present; still, to a genius like his, the task

---

[18]   *Literary Test* 1, 1 January 1832, 2.

would have been easy to bring, without offending, the king into contact with the beggar – the rich with the poor – and to assist the latter with such powerful arguments as would compel the most violent of tyrants to own how unjust the dreadful disparity of their relative situations.

But, instead of doing this, he has drawn his scenes among kings and nobles, and taught mankind little more than that princes are but men, and prone to all the faults and weaknesses of mortality; – occasionally, however, contenting himself by saying a kind sentence or two in favor of the unfortunate – and those too so admirably and effectively that I can the less excuse his omission to say more. *Shakspeare* in fact only studied the amusement of the aristocracy of his day, who were yet more difficult to please than the "society" of the present; – if, indeed, he was not of himself rather inclined to agree with his betters, – or else, how could a mind of his substantial superiority have delighted so much in the pageantry of kings "and the pomp and circumstance of glorious war?"[19]

Ironically, while Shakespeare critics of the eighteenth and early nineteenth centuries had been largely preoccupied with defending Shakespeare from French criticism that he had breached the rules of decorum by mingling kings and clowns, the *Literary Test*'s main objection appears to be that he did not mingle them enough. While the *Literary Test* folded shortly after its attack on Shakespeare, the views it expressed resurfaced periodically, most famously in Ernest Crosby's 1903 book *Shakespeare's Attitude Toward the Working Classes*. The book provides examples of Shakespeare's shortcomings but adds little to the *Literary Test*'s argument, and probably would have been forgotten entirely if not for its foreword by Leo Tolstoy, which in turn gained something of an afterlife in George Orwell's reply.[20] The unwarranted longevity of Crosby's book, used to characterize late-Victorian views on Shakespeare and the working classes when it represents instead a more enduring minority opinion, is one reason a thorough investigation of periodical sources is so important.

Another advantage to placing works such as Crosby's in this context is that in contrast to the *Literary Test,* which like Crosby found little usefulness in Shakespeare's works, the majority of magazines with a similar political perspective were more enthusiastic. In *The National, a Library for the People,* for instance, Shakespeare's legacy was treated more positively. Like its more successful rivals *Figaro in London* and the *Northern Star, The National* combined cultural and political concerns, presenting them in a manner designed to appeal to working-class readers. With objectives very similar to those expressed by the editor of the *Literary Test, The National* came to a quite different conclusion about Shakespeare's relevance to the working classes. In its article "The Life of Shakspere," Shakespeare is depicted as a compatriot, a man who had risen from obscure beginnings and who had never abandoned his solidarity with the

---

[19]   *Literary Test* 3, 14 January 1832, 48.

[20]   "Lear, Tolstoy, and the Fool," reprinted in *The Collected Essays, Journalism, and Letters of George Orwell*, eds Sonia Orwell and Ian Angus (New York: Harcourt Brace Jovanovich, 1968) and frequently anthologized.

people of his own class. In its analysis of Shakespeare's value, *The National* uses Shakespeare's biography to mock the gentrifying tendencies of more highbrow publications, dismissing the usual claims about the "undoubted gentility" of Shakespeare's mother with the parenthetical comment "as if it were a matter of vital importance to the fame of the great dramatist!"[21] Shakespeare's significance lies in his ready identification as one of "the people," and the highlights of his biography are his working-class father and his first menial theatrical employment minding the horses of theatregoers, not his well-born mother and the investment of his theatrical proceeds in both a substantial property in Stratford-on-Avon and a coat of arms.

The National considered Shakespeare's biography a worthwhile topic because, as it explained in its first issue, this periodical envisaged the "pursuit of knowledge" as an inherently laudable and lofty goal. For *The National,* the "equal rights of all, the greatest happiness of the greatest number, and the never-ceasing improvement of humanity," a broadly utilitarian agenda, could be achieved by levelling the educational playing field so that the "grandest and profoundest thoughts of our master intellects," the "thoughts and opinions of the noblest spirits of the world, more especially those of our own country" might be rendered financially and intellectually accessible to everyone.[22] Information about Shakespeare was deemed essential to this enterprise not only because Shakespeare could serve as a model of the self-made man, the general consensus of the conservative periodicals, but also because the thoughts embodied in his plays and poems could elevate readers. By moving beyond biography to an analysis of the intellectual nourishment available in Shakespeare's plays and a recommendation that readers seek out this nourishment for themselves, *The National* furthered working-class Shakespeare reception.

Other magazines contributed more palpably to a discernible working-class tradition of Shakespeare reception by publishing criticism that made an overt connection between his plays and contemporary politics. The *Political Mirror*, for instance, found Shakespeare relevant to the working classes on explicitly political grounds, publishing a series on his works in 1837. In the first instalment, the series suggested that Shakespeare's plays remained politically relevant:

> In the pages of Shakespeare, may be traced not only the operation of those social relations which have, from the earliest periods, connected, or disjoined human beings – but a most faithful picture of those political relations, also, which human beings have always borne and still bear, to each other. In history, there is nothing new. All is re-production. Names may change – but the political principles and passions which now agitate the world, have agitated the world since the commencement of time.
>
> In England, we are in the habit of dividing politicians into Tories, Whigs, Radicals, and pretend Radicals. All these varieties may be found in Shakespeare – although the specimens are not so ticketed and labelled.[23]

---

21 *The National* 1, 1839, 277.
22 *The National* 1, 1839, 3.
23 *Political Mirror*, 19 August 1837, 12.

To demonstrate its theory that Shakespeare was relevant to working-class readers because his plays could help them to understand contemporary politics, in several subsequent issues the *Political Mirror* used *Julius Caesar*[24] and *Coriolanus*[25] to discuss contemporary political debates such as parliamentary representation and the mutual obligations of the social classes. While these politicized uses of Shakespeare did little to illuminate either play, they did succeed in disproving the *Literary Test*'s case against him. Shakespeare was indeed relevant to the working classes, as readers of the even more radical *Northern Star* would discover in the subsequent decade.

The *Northern Star,* the chief Chartist publication until it folded in 1852, regularly employed Shakespeare in the service of political ideals. Like the *Political Mirror,* the *Northern Star* frequently invoked Shakespeare's plays as analogies to contemporary events, quoting couplets from the plays to bolster its arguments and even running a five-part series, "Chartism from Shakespeare," in which lengthy quotations selected chiefly from the history and Roman plays reflect radical views on current events reported elsewhere in the magazine.[26] Initially, Shakespeare had been included in a feature called "Chartism from the Poets," alongside Milton and Thomson, but the *Northern Star* quickly realized that his plays offered the richest vein of apposite commentary and began to include a wide variety of quotations drawn exclusively from his works. Passages reflecting on the reciprocal duties of king and subject (from *Henry V* and *Henry VI*), justifying rebellion (*Henry IV, Julius Caesar, Coriolanus*) or lamenting the dismal state of the nation (*Richard II, King John*) are especially prevalent in these selections. The *Northern Star*'s approach to these quotations suggests that they are being employed as rhetoric, not as references intended to remind the reader of the plays from which they are drawn. "How poor an instrument / May do a noble deed! he brings me liberty," (mis)quoted from *Antony and Cleopatra* when the doomed Egyptian queen praises the lowly man who has delivered her a poisonous asp, is probably meant to encourage political radicalism, not to inspire readers to commit suicide. "The better part of valour is discretion" achieves its inspirational tone only if the reader fails to identify the speaker, the buffoon Falstaff, and the context, justifying his decision to "counterfeit dying" to avoid fighting and then to pretend that he has slain the noble Hotspur in battle with an eye to claiming a reward for such a valorous deed.[27]

Most references to Shakespeare in Victorian high culture depend on the reader's familiarity with the plays for their resonance, but in the "Chartism from Shakespeare" feature Shakespeare was useful for rhetorical purposes only if readers

---

[24]   *Political Mirror*, 19 August 1837, 12–15; 26 August 1837, 23–26; 2 September 1837, 42–43.

[25]   *Political Mirror*, 16 September 1837, 70.

[26]   *Northern Star*, 25 April 1840, 7; 2 May 1840, 7; 9 May 1840, 7; 23 May, 1840, 7; and 6 June 1840, 7.

[27]   *Northern Star*, 2 May 1840, 7.

refrained from connecting the quotations with their Shakespearean contexts. This would situate the *Northern Star* alongside earlier radical publications and suggest that like them the *Northern Star* promoted ransacking Shakespeare's plays, not reading them. That continuity is belied by the magazine's review of the *Pictorial Penny Shakespeare,* Charles Knight's important popular edition:

> The Englishman who has not read SHAKESPEARE may doubt his nationality; he is, at best, but half an Englishman, when ignorant of the works of his greatest countryman: and yet, to how many millions has SHAKESPEARE been but little, if anything, more than a mere name. It is painful to reflect that thousands, nay, millions have lived and died, and never known him, who, 'though dead yet speaketh,' and speaketh those words which, of mightier import than the words of priests or prophets, never fail to elevate the minds and purify the hearts of those who willingly list to them.[28]

In the *Northern Star*'s formulation, Shakespeare was an instrument for transforming working-class readers into full citizens, and given the magazine's radical agenda we need not assume that this citizenship was limited to a simple participation in the national culture that already revered Shakespeare as the epitome of Englishness. Citizenship in the *Northern Star* has connotations of equal rights, not just equal access to great thoughts, and in contrast to the fairly innocuous educational plan advocated by the *National* the education in Shakespeare provided by the *Northern Star* embodied more radical possibilities. Given the resistance and, at times, the outright hostility to Shakespeare evident in some of the other radical publications, the *Northern Star*'s attitude towards Shakespeare is striking in its confidence that his works remained relevant both as rhetoric and as intellectual preparation for societal change. In the magazine's review of the *Pictorial Penny Shakespeare*, as in its regular literary features like "Chartism from Shakespeare," the *Northern Star* taught its readers to find more than political propaganda in their reading. Shakespeare was not valuable merely for anticipating the political developments of the nineteenth century or for furnishing writers with apt quotations, as some other radical magazines suggested. Though the *Northern Star* might quibble elsewhere in its pages about just whose minds required elevating or hearts purifying, in this review the magazine expanded the breadth of Shakespeare's role for radical readers by encouraging them to turn from the magazine to Shakespeare's works, increasingly available in affordable editions like the *Pictorial Penny Shakespeare.*[29]

Radical periodicals like the *Northern Star* taught their readers to interpret Shakespeare radically, using his history and Roman plays in particular as sources of political commentary. These same plays would later figure on the national compulsory curriculum after 1870 as sources of conservative speeches glorifying patriotism and imperialism. In the meantime, the treatment Shakespeare was

---

[28] *Northern Star*, 29 November 1845, 3.

[29] On nineteenth-century editions for working-class readers, see chapter eight of Andrew Murphy's *Shakespeare in Print: A History and Chronology of Shakespeare Publishing* (Cambridge: Cambridge University Press, 2003).

accorded in the working-class periodicals had important repercussions in Shakespeare reception more widely, giving Shakespeare contemporary relevance and highlighting the political aspects of his life and works not otherwise widely noted in the criticism of the day. While it is true that Shakespeare was sometimes also used as a representative of an elite culture to which working-class readers should be convinced or coerced to aspire, that tells only part of the story. In the magazines published with less conservative ideals in mind, Shakespeare's life and works, stripped of their middle-class pretensions, helped working-class readers to resist that hegemony and to imagine alternatives to their continued subordination. Shakespeare may be less familiar as a working class hero than as the iconic playwright of the upper classes, but, as the nineteenth-century working-class periodicals discovered, Shakespeare need not be accepted merely according to the terms on which he is habitually offered. By finding innovative uses for Shakespeare's life and works, these periodicals expanded Shakespeare's status as the national poet to include political values that challenged class hierarchy, and that made him an important component of the emerging working-class canon.

Works Cited

Altick, Richard. *The English Common Reader: A Social History of the Mass Reading Public*, 1800–1900. Chicago: University of Chicago Press, 1957.

Anderson, Patricia. *The Printed Image and the Transformation of Popular Culture*, 1790–1860. Oxford: Clarendon, 1991.

Baer, Marc. *Theatre and Disorder in Late Georgian London*. Oxford: Clarendon, 1992.

Bailey, Peter. *Popular Culture and Performance in the Victorian City*. Cambridge: Cambridge University Press, 1998.

Barker, Clive. "The Chartists, Theatre, Reform and Research," *Theatre Quarterly*, Vol. 1 (1971), 3–10.

———. "A Theatre for the People," in *Nineteenth-Century British Theatre*, eds Kenneth Richards and Peter Thomson. London: Methuen, 1971, 3–24.

Bate, Jonathan, ed. *The Romantics on Shakespeare*. Harmondsworth: Penguin, 1992.

———. *Shakespearean Constitutions: Politics, Theatre, Criticism, 1730–1830*. Oxford: Oxford University Press, 1989.

Birrell, T.A. "The Political Register: Cobbett and English Literature," *English Studies*, Vol. 45 (1964), 214–219.

Booth, Michael. "East End and West End: Class and Audience in Victorian London," *Theatre Research International*, Vol. 2, No. 2 (February, 1977), 98–103.

Brantlinger, Patrick. *Bread and Circuses: Theories of Mass Culture as Social Decay*. Ithaca: Cornell University Press, 1983.

———. *The Reading Lesson: The Threat of Mass Literacy in Nineteenth-Century British Fiction*. Bloomington: Indiana University Press, 1998.

Brougham, Henry Peter. *The Life and Times of Henry Lord Brougham*, 3 vols. Edinburgh: William Blackwood and Sons, 1871.

Chambers, William. *Memoir of Robert Chambers, with Autobiographical Reminiscences of William Chambers*. New York: Scribner's, 1872.

Cole, G.D.H. *Chartist Portraits*. London: Macmillan, 1965.

Crosby, Ernest. *Shakespeare's Attitude Toward the Working Classes*. Syracuse: Mason Press, 1903.

Curran, James. "The Press as an Agency of Social Control: An Historical Perspective," in *Newspaper History: From the Seventeenth Century to the Present Day*, eds George Boyce, James Curran, and Pauline Wingate. London: Constable, 1978.

Davis, Jim and Victor Emeljanow, eds. *Reflecting the Audience: London Theatregoing, 1840–1880*. Iowa City: University of Iowa Press, 2001.

Dobson, Michael. *The Making of the National Poet: Shakespeare, Adaptation, and Authorship, 1660–1769*. Oxford: Clarendon, 1992.

Foulkes, Richard. *Performing Shakespeare in the Age of Empire*. Cambridge: Cambridge University Press, 2002.

———, ed. *Shakespeare and the Victorian Stage*. Cambridge: Cambridge University Press, 1986.

Hancher, Michael. "From Street Ballad to Penny Magazine: 'March of Intellect' in the Butchering Line'," in *Nineteenth-Century Media and the Construction of Identities*, eds Laurel Brake, Bill Bell, and David Finkelstein. Basingstoke: Palgrave, 2000, 93–103.

Harrison, Royden, Gillian B. Woolven, and Robert Duncan. *Warwick Guide to British Labour Periodicals, 1790–1970*. Atlantic Highlands, NJ: Humanities Press, 1977.

Hollis, Patricia. *The Pauper Press: A Study in Working-Class Radicalism of the 1830s*. Oxford: Oxford University Press, 1970.

Hurt, J.S. *Elementary Schooling and the Working Classes, 1860–1918*. London: Routledge, 1979.

James, Louis. *Fiction for the Working Man, 1830–1850: A Study of the Literature Produced for the Working Classes in Early Victorian Urban England*. London: Oxford University Press, 1963.

———. "The Trouble With Betsy: Periodicals and the Common Reader in Mid-nineteenth-century England," in *The Victorian Periodical Press: Samplings and Soundings*, eds Joanne Shattock and Michael Wolff. Toronto: University of Toronto Press, 1982, 349–366.

Klancher, Jon P. *The Making of English Reading Audiences, 1790–1832*. Madison: University of Wisconsin Press, 1987.

Knight, Charles. *Passages in a Working Life*, 3 vols. Shannon: Irish University Press, 1971 (1864).

Koss, Stephen. *The Rise and Fall of the Political Press in Britain: The Nineteenth Century*. London: Hamish Hamilton, 1981.

Maidment, Brian E. "'Penny' Wise, 'Penny' Foolish? Popular Periodicals and the 'March of Intellect' in the 1820s and 1830s," in *Nineteenth-Century Media and the Construction of Identities*, eds Laurel Brake, Bill Bell, and David Finkelstein. Basingstoke: Palgrave, 2000, 104–121.

Marshall, Gail and Adrian Poole, eds. *Victorian Shakespeares. Volume One: Theatre, Drama and Performance*. Basingstoke: Palgrave Macmillan, 2004.

———. *Victorian Shakespeares. Volume Two: Literature and Culture*. Basingstoke: Palgrave Macmillan, 2004.

Mitch, David F. *The Rise of Popular Literacy in Victorian England: The Influence of Private Choice and Public Policy*. Philadelphia: University of Pennsylvania Press, 1992.

Moody, Jane. *Illegitimate Theatre in London, 1770–1840*. Cambridge: Cambridge University Press, 2000.

Murphy, Andrew. "Shakespeare Among the Workers," *Shakespeare Survey*, Vol. 58 (2005), 107–117.

———. "Shakespeare Goes to School: Educational Stationers," *Analytical and Enumerative Bibliography*, n.s.12 (2001), 241–263.

———. *Shakespeare in Print: A History and Chronology of Shakespeare Publishing*. Cambridge: Cambridge University Press, 2003.

Murphy, Paul Thomas. *Toward a Working-Class Canon: Literary Criticism in British Working-Class Periodicals, 1816–1858*. Columbus: Ohio State University Press, 1994.

Paz, D.G. *The Politics of Working-Class Education in Britain, 1830–50*. Manchester: Manchester University Press, 1980.

Poole, Adrian. *Shakespeare and the Victorians*. London: Arden, 2004.

Roach, John. *Public Examinations in England, 1850–1900*. Cambridge: Cambridge University Press, 1971.

Rose, Jonathan. *The Intellectual Life of the British Working Classes*. New Haven: Yale University Press, 2001.

Salmon, Edward. *Shakespeare and Democracy*. New York: Haskell House, 1973 (1916).

Schoch, Richard W. *Shakespeare's Victorian Stage: Performing History in the Theatre of Charles Kean*. Cambridge: Cambridge University Press, 1998.

Smith, Harold. *The Society for the Diffusion of Useful Knowledge, 1826–1846: A Social and Bibliographical Evaluation*. Halifax: Dalhousie Occasional Papers No. 8, 1972.

Spater, George. *William Cobbett: The Poor Man's Friend*, 2 vols. Cambridge: Cambridge University Press, 1982.

Taylor, Gary. *Reinventing Shakespeare: A Cultural History from the Restoration to the Present*. London: Vintage, 1989.

Thompson, E.P. *The Making of the English Working Class*. Harmondsworth: Penguin, 1968.

Vincent, David. *Literacy and Popular Culture: England, 1750–1914*. Cambridge: Cambridge University Press, 1989.

Webb, R.K. *The British Working-Class Reader: Literacy and Social Tension*. London: George Allen and Unwin, 1955.

Chapter 8
Radical Satire and Respectability: Comic Imagination in Hone, Jerrold, and Dickens

Sambudha Sen

In a letter to Mrs. Brookfield, just before he left *Punch*, Thackeray declared that he was resigning because he found it impossible to "pull in the same boat" with a "savage little Robespierre" like Douglas Jerrold.[1] This outburst does of course tell us a great deal about Thackeray's political position. But it also points towards something that is more interesting from the point of view of this collection: the aesthetic conflict between Thackeray's middle-class sensibility and what James Epstein has called "radical expression."[2] The language of radicalism (of which Jerrold was a late practitioner) had remained an important presence in the world of nineteenth century print culture ever since Paine, Cobbett, Hone, Cruickshank and the rest had begun using popular satiric modes to represent the processes and people associated with power from a radical, plebeian view point. By the 1830s, radical expressive modes were circulating freely in the market for print entertainment, attracting the attention of middle-class consumers of satiric print entertainment and even of what the *Westminster Review* called "the novel reading public." The barely concealed disgust with which the *Westminster Review* responded to this discursive intrusion from below suggests the consolidation of a middle-class position against the aesthetic value of "radical expression." The journal followed Thackeray in constituting the radical mode as a strident and crude, indeed, as something that threatened to pervert "the novel from a form of art to a platform for argument and discussion."[3] In this essay I hope to show that radical expressive modes, contrary to the assertions of Thackeray and the *Westminster Review,* offered the novel ways of representing the elite and their discourses that were different from but not less interesting than the methods of the more properly literary, realistic forms of novel writing. I hope to show, moreover, that the radical expression that Thackeray wished to eject out of the serious business of novel writing were to lead

---

[1] Quoted in M.H. Spielman, *The History of "Punch"* (Cassell: New York, 1895), 323.

[2] James Epstein, *Radical Expression: Political Language, Ritual and Symbol in England 1790–1850* (Oxford: Oxford University Press, 1994), 4.

[3] Unsigned, "Modern Novelists: Charles Dickens," *Westminster Review*, Vol. 26 (October, 1864), 417.

a productive life in Dickens's novels, to generate effects that have too often been attributed solely to Dickens's unique comic imagination.[4]

One of the paradoxes of Thackeray's career was that he was adept in producing squibs, parodies and visual caricatures—that is, the kind of politically charged, satiric entertainment that threatened, as the *Westminster Review* suggested, to vitiate the properly literary novel. When Thackeray first joined *Punch,* the journal had been dominated by Jerrold and it had sought to sustain within an expanding print market the sort of radical political satire that had gained such popularity through the late eighteenth and early nineteenth centuries. In these circumstances Thackeray himself had little option but to provide for the magazine the parodies and caricatures that fed the "the quickening and widening of interest in public matters and public men, brought about by the agitation which had preceded the passing of the Reform Bill of 1832 and continued after its enactment."[5] Yet, although Thackeray publicly defended his early political satire as a legitimate means of earning his livelihood, he also remarked, often and anxiously, in his letters to his mother and to his closest friends that the satiric journalism that he was producing was very far from being "literature." [6]

For Thackeray the limitations of journalistic sarcasm were evident above all in its representation of the elite. In fact, one way in which we might chart more precisely Thackeray's responses to this problem is by focusing on the silences as well as the emphases that underlie the two long essays he wrote on artists whose work not only overlapped with Thackeray's early career but who represented the elite from the differing social standpoints which Thackeray associated with journalism, on the one hand, and literature on the other. In the first of these—a two part essay on Cruickshank—Thackeray creates around the figure of the illustrator

---

[4]   Sally Ledger's essay "From Queen Caroline to Lady Dedlock: Dickens and the Popular Radical Imagination" which is part of her recent book *Dickens and the Popular Radical Imagination* (Cambridge: Cambridge University Press, 2007) makes a strong case for Dickens's indebtedness to William Hone. Ledger's emphasis, in the section that she devotes to Dickens's later fiction, is on the continuities, in terms of thematic preoccupations as well as political attitudes, between the works of William Hone and those of Dickens. For example, she shows that *Bleak House* follows the lead of pamphlets like "The Political House that Jack Built" or the "Political Showman at Home" in relentlessly lampooning parliament and corrupt government ministers as well as organized religion. My concern is not with Dickens's opposition to this or that institution, but with the *expressive resources* that Dickens absorbed from the language of radicalism. See Sally Ledger, "From Queen Caroline to Lady Dedlock: Dickens and the Popular Radical Imagination," *Victorian Literature and Culture*, Vol. 32 (2004), 575–600.

[5]   Walter Jerrold, *Douglas Jerrold and "Punch"* (London: Macmillan and Co., 1910), 4.

[6]   There are numerous occasions where Thackeray makes this complaint. For an extended example, see his letter to Edward Fitzgerald, 7 October 1836, in *The Letters and Private Papers of William Makepeace Thackeray*, ed. Gordon N.Ray, Vol. 1 (Oxford: Oxford University Press, 1945), 322–323.

a powerful sense of nostalgia for a much loved world full of fantastic prints and illustrations that Thackeray's aging generation was losing. In this way Thackeray touches on the transforming effects of time—a problem that he was to explore with great sophistication in his fiction—but he also commits himself to a certain sympathy for even the kind of political caricature that had seemed to embarrass him in his letters to friends such as Edward Fitzgerald.

In fact Thackeray's well known description of Cruickshank's caricatures, as they were displayed in the print shops at Sweeting's Alley and Fleet Street, is so sympathetic that it has been quoted by radical historians as a historically accurate account of the milieu in which political prints of the early nineteenth century were produced and disseminated.[7] It seems to me, however, that Thackeray's representation seeks to smoothen and render as easily negotiable the disjunction between the upper-class readers for whom he was writing and the plebeian milieu for which Cruickshank produced his political caricatures. More specifically, in Thackeray's nostalgic recollection of what he projects as a lost world, the militant artisanal communities that gathered around the works of Cruickshank and Hone become "grinning, good natured mechanics" and Cruickshank's brutal caricatures of the most powerful politicians of the Regency, "merry harmless sprites."[8] This means that Thackeray's representation erases not only the confrontationist context in which Cruickshank's political prints were produced, but also the representational modes by which this confrontation with the political elite was expressed.

If Thackeray felt it necessary to evade any analysis of what seems to me to be a central feature of Cruickshank's political caricature—their propensity to represent the political elite from the point of view of the excluded—it was because he believed that Cruickshank's social location made it impossible for him to produce artistically viable images of the upper classes. Indeed in a second essay on his colleague John Leech, Thackeray sharply criticizes Gilray and, by implication, the brutal caricatural technique which Cruickshank was to bring into the domain of radical journalism precisely on the grounds that the "garret - - - or a tavern parlour" could never emerge as valid observation points for the representation of "public characters." On the other hand, as a "social painter" who belonged to "the world which he depict[ed] and native to the manners which he portray[ed]," Leech was properly positioned to delineate realistically the details of what Thackeray, addressing his upper- and middle-class readers, describes as "your house and mine."[9]

Thackeray's privileging of Leech over Gilray, and by extension over Cruickshank, is important for my purposes because it has implications for the

---

[7]   E.P. Thompson, *The Making of the English Working Class* (Harmondsworth: Penguin, 1980), 810.

[8]   W.M.Thackeray, "George Cruickshank" in *Ballads, Critical Reviews, Tales* (London: Smith Elder and Co., 1907), 287–288.

[9]   W.M. Thackeray, "Pictures of Life and Character" in *Ballads, Critical Reviews, Tales*, 488–489.

distinction that Thackeray made between journalism and literature, and looks forward ultimately to Thackeray's own movement away from "magazinery" to what he saw as the more properly literary vocation of novel writing. More specifically, Thackeray's comments on Leech, taken in conjunction with his increasingly contemptuous attitude towards the sort of radical satire that appeared in the early numbers of *Punch*,[10] may be seen as part of an ongoing polemic where Thackeray pits a novelistic aesthetic based on closely observed, realistic delineations of the social and political elite against a popular tradition of political representation that developed continuously from Paine to Jerrold, and that was predicated on, as Thackeray sarcastically remarked, looking "up at the rich and the great with a fierce, a sarcastic aspect, and a threatening posture."[11]

The language of radical satire, which Thackeray believed to be incapable of producing that nuanced realism that he associated with "literature," was an integral aspect of Dickens's staple writing. Indeed, in an article entitled "Modern Novelists: Charles Dickens," the *Westminster Review* argued that Dickens's authorial tone was inextricably bound up with those high pitched political debates of the reform years which, as I have tried to show, had sustained Jerrold's strident sarcasm as well, and "Modern Novelists" concluded with a suggestion which Thackeray would presumably endorse: that by seeking to cater to the tastes of the over politicized masses Dickens had demonstrated that he was not interested in "the novel ... [as] a work of art."

The Westminster Review's comments are useful because they situate Dickens's early career in the lower rungs of the market for print entertainment and, in this sense, gesture towards an objective discursive source for some effects in Dickens's novels that have all too often been attributed to his unique comic imagination. However, the *Westminster Review*'s condescension towards those forms of novel writing that do not qualify as "work[s] of art" obstructs what might, in my opinion, have been a more productive analysis of the relationship between the Dickensian novel and what the review vaguely describes as a "highly popular treatment of politics."[12] I will try, later in this essay, to unravel the precise strands from radical print culture that get "reactivated"[13] in the fiction of Dickens. I want just now to focus on what I think was an uninterrupted process of displacements and reactivations by which radical expressive modes got uprooted from the mobilizing texts that had originally sustained them, but continued to lead an active, if reified, existence in the entertainment-oriented Dickensian novel.

It is necessary to delineate the precise circuits through which discursive strategies first articulated in the works of Hone or Cobbett found their way into

---

[10]   See Spielman, *History of "Punch,"* 322–324.

[11]   Ibid. 421.

[12]   Unsigned, "Modern Novelists: Charles Dickens," *Westminster Review*, Vol. 26 (October, 1864), 417.

[13]   I use "reactivation" in Walter Benjamin's sense. See Walter Benjamin, "The Work of Art in the Age of Mechanical Reproduction" in *Illuminations* (New York: Schocken Books, 1975), 220–221.

the internal economy of the Dickensian novel because, surprisingly, the large and extremely rich body of work that has grown around radical print culture in recent years[14] does not really concern itself with the ways in which radical expression intertwined with certain popular forms that developed in the market for print entertainment after the radical journalistic tradition itself began to disintegrate during the 1830s. This afterlife of radical representational energies was, in my opinion, possible because of what Iain McCalman has called "the Rabelaisian"[15] strands that co existed within radical journalism with the more austere, rationalist pamphlets of Paine and Carlile. It was the sheer exuberance that radical satire acquired, especially in the immediate aftermath of Caroline's trial, the "delight" rather than the "solemnity," as E.P. Thompson put it in *The Making of the English Working Class*, with which Cruickshank, Hone, Davison and the rest baited authority that made the language of subversion also entertaining and therefore saleable. A very good example of a mobilizing text that might, at the same time, be seen as a landmark in literary entertainment was William Hone's "The Political House that Jack Built." "The Political House" was very much an exercise in political mobilization, provoked as it was by the Peterloo massacre. On the other hand, it was also cast as a parodic political squib—a form "long established among news vendors and patterers, and practiced in more sophisticated forms by men of all political parties from Wilkes to the writers of Anti-Jacobin"[16]—and it combined colloquialisms, parodic reaccentuations and the familiar rhythms of nursery rhymes to achieve a tone which, in its irreverence to the processes of power, would continue to resonate through many years, and in very different political situations, through the pages of *Punch* and indeed through novels like *Little Dorrit* and *Bleak House*. Moreover, "The Political House" was, in a very basic sense, co-produced by Cruickshank, and the combination of Cruickshank's etchings and Hone's letterpress not only inaugurated a format that would dominate the market for print entertainment through the next thirty years, it also set into motion an interactive relationship between visual and linguistic satire—a process that was, as I will try to show, to affect the Dickens's method in significant ways. Above all, "The Political House" did not just anticipate a recipe for a best seller; it turned out itself to be an instant bestseller. First published in 1820, "The Political House" sold 100,000 copies even at the relatively high price of one shilling.

The very high sales achieved by a radical pamphlet such as "The Political House" suggest that the demarcation made by one of the greatest historians of the popular press between "the journalism of a community or a movement" and

---

[14]   See Kevin Gilmartin, *Print Politics: The Press and Radical Opposition in Early Nineteenth Century England* (Cambridge: Cambridge University Press, 1996); James Epstein, *Radical Expression*; Marcus Wood, *Radical Satire and Print Culture 1790–1822* (Oxford: Oxford University Press, 1994); Iain McCalman, *Radical Underworld: Prophets, Revolutionaries and Pornographers in London 1795–1840* (Cambridge: Cambridge University Press, 1988); and Olivia Smith, *The Politics of Language 1791–1819* (Oxford: Oxford University Press, 1984).

[15]   McCalman, *Radical Underworld*, 173.

[16]   E.P. Thompson, *The Making of the English Working Class*, 793, 792.

"market journalism" based on more efficient production and distribution and incomparably higher levels of capitalization[17] was, in fact, never absolute. It is true, of course, that the commercial press irrevocably broke up the community of radical readers in the process of creating a larger, more diffuse, entertainment-seeking audience and indeed, as will become apparent at many points in this essay, the movement of radical satire from the mobilizing pamphlet to the Dickensian novel also implied the uprooting of this satire from real political struggles. On the other hand, it is equally true that radical journalism contributed very significantly to the shaping of the nineteenth-century market for print entertainment. Indeed, the radical journalists themselves often emphasized this. Thus, Hone himself was to claim that the illustrated pamphlets that he produced during the 20s had "created a new era in the history of publication:"

> By showing what engraving on wood could effect in a popular way, and exciting a taste for art in the more humble ranks of life, they created a new era in the history of publication - - - They are parents to the present cheap literature, which extends to a sale of at least four hundred thousand copies every week - - - Besides this - - - my little pieces acquainted every rank of society, in the most remote corner of the British dominions, with the powers of Mr. George Cruickshank, whose genius had been wasted on mere caricature till it was embodied in my ideas and feelings.[18]

Hone's anxious egoism is characteristic of many plebeian writers seeking to assert to a hostile middle-class audience their contribution to the making of culture and it should not blind us to the substantive point that he was making: that he and other radical journalists (whom Hone characteristically does not acknowledge) had generated formats, expressive resources, modes of articulation which, once they began circulating in the print market, would attract large sections of pro reform middle-class readers. In other words, Hone seems to be reflecting, from the hind sight of a decade, on the history of displacements and reactivations by which forms such as radical political caricature would move from militant artisanal politics to the drawing rooms of pro reform middle-class consumers. What Hone does not comment on in this passage is that radical expression in the 30s and 40s would inevitably have to contend with the demands of respectability. In fact, this tension between radicalism and respectability is visible across an entire sequence of works—from the journals produced by those radical writers who survived the 30s[19] through to the early numbers of *Punch*.

---

[17]   Raymond Williams, "Radical and\or Respectable," in *The Press We Deserve*, ed. Richard Boston (London: Routledge and Kegan Paul, 1970), 21.

[18]   Wood, *Radical Satire*, 269.

[19]   For instance, Richard Carlile whose early work as a editor and publisher represented the hard-line, austere, rationalist strand within radical journalism, found himself forced to move, by the thirties, to the sort of entertainment-oriented pro-reform political satire that would attract not just the older plebian audience that had grown around radical

Many writers have, of course, drawn attention to the tension between radicalism and respectability that runs through the early numbers of *Punch*, but in most accounts this tension is articulated as a prolonged conflict between Douglas Jerrold, on the one hand, and Thackeray and others, on the other hand. Although I, too, will discuss the importance of Jerrold's work as an interface between the radical pamphlets and Dickens's novels, I want at the moment to draw attention away from Jerrold's individual influence on *Punch* and to argue that *Punch*'s radical orientation can also be related to certain preexisting traditions of representation or, to adapt Roger Chartier's more precise formulation, to a "pre knowledge" that readers of *Punch* would have of certain conventions through which political satire was most effectively articulated. In "Texts, Printings and Readings" Chartier argues "people read books with previously gained knowledge that was easily evoked in the act of reading. This knowledge was gained from the recurrence of coded forms, from the repetition of themes, and from the books' images ... . This 'preknowledge,' as it were, was mobilized to produce comprehension not necessarily in conformity with that desired by the producer of the text or the maker of the text ..."[20]

There can be no doubt that many *Punch* readers had "pre knowledge" of some of the magazine's most characteristic devices and that the most recent sources of this were the radical newspapers and magazines. Hone's pamphlets, which had continued to circulate in their original forms as well as variations throughout the twenties and thirties, had generated many conventions of representation that were to remain part of the standard repertoire of political satirists throughout the first half of the nineteenth century. Clearly, therefore, *Punch* was depending on the "comprehension" that radical representational conventions would produce among its readers, when it deployed the nursery rhyme as a vehicle for political satire, or used the idea of the "political house" or the political menagerie as sites from which it could launch its satiric commentaries on politics and politicians.[21] On the other hand, however, *Punch* was also refashioning these radical tropes so that they would not offend the sensibilities of the increasing number of middle-class readers that the magazine was gathering around itself. For example, *Punch* followed the parodies of Hone in using the nursery rhyme form as the vehicle

---

newspapers, but middle class readers as well. In fact in his *Humorous Sketches*—a journal that he ran with some degree of commercial success between 1833 and 1836—Carlile had already begun the process of relocating radical expression within the moral universe of respectability that Dickens was to complete. Remarkably, when Chapman and Hall sought to repeat the commercial success *of Humorous Sketches*, they hired not only Carlile's illustrator Robert Seymour, but also a young and relatively unknown Dickens as a junior collaborator. See Louis James, *Fiction for the Working Man 1830–1850* (Harmondsworth: Penguin, 1073), 27–29.

[20]   Roger Chartier, "Texts, Printing, Readings," in *The New Cultural History*, ed. Lynn Hunt (Berkeley: University of California Press, 1989), 165.

[21]   See Richard Altick, *Punch: The Lively Youth of a British Institution 1841–51* (Columbus: Ohio State University Press, 1997), esp. 94–96.

for its anti- aristocratic satire in a series that it devised for Queen Victoria's children. On the other hand, it was also careful not to disturb the unimpeachable respectability of the royal nursery, so that this respectability may be deployed to contain any excess in tone or content that might offend middle-class tastes. This maneuver by which *Punch* sought both to exploit the expressive possibilities of radical satire, and at the same time to contain these possibilities, is evident again in the way that it deals with a second radical trope—the political menagerie. Here again *Punch* was following the lead of a pamphlet by Cruickshank and Hone in its use of zoomorphism as a means of political demystification.[22] Significantly, however, the element that disappears when we move from the woodcuts of "The Political Showman" to those of *Punch* is the violence that Baudelaire associated with early English caricature.[23] Thus unlike Cruickshank's deeply disconcerting representations of the Lord Chancellor as a crocodile, the Duke of Wellington as a scorpion, and the king himself as a water scorpion, the creatures who inhabit an etching like Doyle's "The Opening of Parliamentary Pie" have the bodies of birds, but faces that are untouched by the venomous distortions of caricaturists.

The respectabilizing trajectory that diffused the more brutal effects of radical satire for the increasing number of middle-class readers that *Punch* was beginning to attract, would alter the basic character of the magazine after the forties—shifting its focus from the political to social. Moreover, as I have already tried to show, Thackeray rode this trajectory; his movement from the caricatures and parodies that he half reluctantly produced for the early numbers of *Punch* to the more nuanced realism of *The Book of Snobs* looked forward to a novelistic aesthetic that would be fundamentally hostile to the methods of the radical publicists. On the other hand, Dickens himself did not personally produce graphic caricatures or political doggerel, nor was he ever a full time employee of *Punch*. Nevertheless, I want to argue that the Dickensian novel was deeply implicated in the process out of which *Punch* had emerged: the redeployment of radical expressive sources for the production of a certain kind of political satire that would cater not only to a radical artisanal community but to the middle classes as well. This should alert us to the restrictive influence that the deepening commitment to respectability would exercise on Dickens's political satire. But it should also enable us to think of the early numbers of *Punch*, and especially the work of Douglas Jerrold, as the conduit through which certain strands of radical expression found a continuing, if reified, existence in the novels of Dickens. It is on these strands that I will now focus.

The first and most basic of these strands would be what Gareth Stedman Jones called "the language of radicalism" and later Kevin Gilmartin called "a style of political opposition."[24]As we might expect, one important strategic orientation of

---

[22]   See *Punch* August 21, 1841, 62, and Altick, *Punch*, 135.

[23]   See Charles Baudelaire, "Some Foreign Caricaturists," in *Selected Writings on Art and Artists*, trans. E.P. Charvet (Cambridge: Cambridge University Press, 1972), 233–234.

[24]   Gareth Stedman Jones, *Languages of Class: Studies in English Working Class History* (Cambridge: Cambridge University Press, 1983), 104; and Kevin Gilmartin, *Print Politics*, 1.

the radical "style" would be to constitute as a community all those who were debarred from the processes of an unreformed parliament. Thus Paine often used the "present tense and the pronoun 'we'" to underline the experience of political exclusion that he shared with his readers and, in this way, to generate, as Olivia Smith has argued, "the illusion that he and [they] share the activity of constructing an argument."[25] For Paine, as for the other radical journalists, the discursive "we" was always part of a larger political process; Paine's books were read and discussed in taverns, debating clubs and mass meetings; they inspired political activism and invited prosecution. In contrast, Jerrold made his name writing for a magazine whose commercial success was based on its ability, on the one hand, to avoid anything that might attract legal or punitive action and, on the other, to sustain the interest of a large, subscribing readership. Therefore Jerrold's propensity to position himself among the plebeians while commenting sarcastically on, for example, the Duke of Wellington's moral exhortations to the poor[26] would suggest, not just the greater rights of expression that the radical journalists had fought for and won, or the state's increasing capacity to accommodate dissent, but also that the radical division between "us" and "them" could now be used freely in relation to the large, politically diffuse, socially disparate reading audience that *Punch* was gathering around itself.

We might then argue that although Jerrold's essays seem, in terms of their tone and orientation, to belong to the great radical pamphlets of the 20s, in fact, they operated within the economy of print entertainment: their significance lay not so much in their continuing ability to sustain radical movements, as in their role in redistributing radical expressive energies within the many popular forms that emerged out of the print market of the early nineteenth century. In his sense, Jerrold—as so many of his contemporaries realized—had more in common with Dickens than with Cobbett or Wooler[27] and indeed it is possible to see in Dickens's habitual use of "us" as a novelistic site capable of sustaining the point of view of the excluded, the completion of process by which the language of radicalism transformed itself from an instrument of political mobilization to a powerful expressive resource within the Victorian period's dominant form of print entertainment—the novel itself:

> There was a dinner party given in the Harley Street establishment, while Little Dorrit was stitching at her father's new shirts by his side that night; and there were magnates from the Court and magnates from the Lords, magnates from the Bench and magnates from the Bar, Bishop magnates Treasury magnates - - - - all the magnates who keep us going and sometimes trip us up.[28]

---

[25] Olivia Smith, *Politics of Language*, 53.

[26] See *Punch* August 21, 1841, 102.

[27] The comparison between Jerrold and Dickens was, in Philip Collins's words, a "critical commonplace of the period." See Philip Collins, ed. *Dickens: The Critical Heritage* (New Delhi: Vikas, 1971), 271. Collins's anthology contains many nineteenth-century essays that make this comparison.

[28] Charles Dickens, *Little Dorrit* (Harmondsworth: Penguin, 1976), 294.

Unlike the journalism even of someone like Jerrold who directed his attack against a specific, real life, political adversary the subjects of Dickens's discourse—the people to which it refers—have become fictional "nobodies,"[29] mere simulacra who would, at best, absorb and diffuse the antagonism that Dickens's readers might have felt towards real life politicians and bureaucrats. However, the movement from Paine's "we" to Dickens's "us" suggests not just dissipation but continuity as well, not just the fictionalization of politics, but also the politicization of fiction. In this sense, it seems to me, important to pick up, in Dickens's "us" "the stylistic aura" [30] of "the language of radicalism," to be alert to the effects that the discursive strategies of the radical style were to have on Dickens's representation of those great objects of the radical discourse—the processes and people associated with power.

As something committed to articulating the point of view of the "non-refined and politically concerned"[31] reading audience that came into its own in the immediate aftermath of the French Revolution, radical journalism was directed above all at the discourses of power: it sought to cut through the symbolism that consecrated these discourses with, as James Epstein said of Paine's writing, "an irreverence that proved fundamental to the development of popular radical language".[32] However, from its very inception the radical demystificatory project had found itself implicated in a major, but in my opinion, productive tension: that between the suspicion about the mystifying functions of icons, emblems and metaphors and the riot of figures, analogies and metaphors into which the radical discourse itself so often burst.

The suspicion that icons and emblems, metaphors and figures were vehicles of mystification was of course integral to English dissident thought since at least the beginnings of Protestantism, and it may be said to be the very heart of Tom Paine's *The Rights of Man*—the document that, in a very real sense, inaugurated the radical journalistic tradition. Paine recognized immediately that Burke's representation of the French Revolution achieved its most far reaching effects through what W.T.J. Mitchell was later to call its rhetorical "extremism and excess."[33] Against Burke's "pathless wilderness of rhapsodies," Paine generates a discourse based on "facts," "principles" and "data" within which signifier would always be accountable to

---

[29]   On the fictional "nobody," see Catherine Gallagher, *Nobody's Story: The Vanishing Acts of Women Writers in the Market Place 1670–1820* (Berkeley: University of California Press, 1994), and Catherine Gallagher and Stephen Greenblatt, *Practicing New Historicism* (Chicago: University of Chicago Press, 2000).

[30]   On the "stylistic aura," see Mikhail Bakhtin, *Speech Genres and Other Late Essays*, trans. Vern W. McGee, eds Caryl Emerson and Michael Holquist (Austin: University of Texas Press, 1986), esp. 87–88.

[31]   Olivia Smith, *Politics of Language*, ix.

[32]   Epstein, *Radical Expression*, 5.

[33]   W.T.J. Mitchell, *Iconology: Image, Text,, Ideology* (Chicago: Chicago University Press, 1986), 143.

the signified, and the metaphor would be exposed as a "fraud" that enveloped its object in a mist of illusory connotations:

> But, after all, what is the metaphor called a Crown, or rather what is Monarchy? - - - Does the virtue consist in the metaphor ,or in the man? Does the goldsmith that makes the crown, make the virtue also? Doth it operate like Fortunatus's wishing-cap, or the Harlequin's wooden sword ? Doth it make a man a conjuror?[34]

Paine's deep suspicion of symbolic consecration as a means of sustaining "Mystery," "craft," "fiction," "superstition" and ultimately "the puppet show of state and aristocracy,"[35] was to remain a very powerful strand in radical thinking until as late as Dickens's condemnation of the ceremonial unfolding of Chancery practice as "barbarous usages that the world has passed by."[36] Yet it is also true that many radical writers habitually deployed metaphors to counter symbolic consecration; they complicated Paine's dream of a transparent language where the signifier would be completely accountable to the signified by engaging in what E.P.Thompson calls "the contest for symbolic authority,"[37] symbolically—not just by stripping the consecrated object of its mystifying imagery, but by associating it with a new set of images, refiguring it as degraded or ridiculous.

As we might expect, the counter-imagistic allegorical techniques that developed within radical journalism enjoyed a particularly rich afterlife in the pages of *Punch*—a journal which sought to meet the contemporary interest in pro-reform politics not with hard, taxable news, but with the sort of satiric improvisations around current affairs that was to become increasingly identified with the figure of Jerrold. A typical improvisation of this kind, that appeared in an early edition of *Punch*, finds in the Harlequin's ability to transform the throne into a wooden chair the basis for a story about the Woky Poky Indians who burnt their Blue monkey god once "some thieves (republicans) despoiled" it of its consecrating ornaments.[38]

Jerrold's parable resonates at many levels against the extract from *The Rights of Man* that I quoted earlier. Both are centrally concerned with reducing to their basic material status the consecrating symbols that legitimize the arbitrary exercise of power. Moreover, both use the fantastic powers that the harlequin enjoys on stage to describe the transformations that metaphors are capable of bringing about in the commoner's perception of the unfolding of state power. For Paine, however, the (thankfully unrealizable) powers of the harlequin's bat has the potential to

---

[34] Thomas Paine, *The Rights of Man, The Selected Works of Tom Paine*, ed. Howard Fast (New York: Random House, 1945), 118.

[35] Ibid. 166, 113.

[36] Unsigned, "Things that Cannot be Done," *Household Words*, 8 October 1853.

[37] E.P. Thompson, *Customs in Common: Studies in Traditional Popular Culture* (New York: The New Press, 1993), 74.

[38] See Walter Jerrold, *Douglas Jerrold*, 8.

raise dangerous illusions; like the metaphor, it is capable of overlaying the metal headgear that the goldsmith designs for the king with a bogus "virtue" that it does not in itself have. On the other hand, in Jerrold's essay the transformatory power of the harlequin's bat (and of the metaphor) destroys the majestic aura of the throne by refiguring it as a wooden armchair. Indeed, like the pantomime itself, Jerrold's technique *thrives* on transformations. Thus Jerrold not only weaves around the object of demystification a range of counter images, he also rewrites the sanctifying protocols that surround the king (the blue monkey god) as an extended comic ritual that ends in an act of radical desacralization.

Jerrold's counter emblematic technique exemplifies the ways in which the visual strands within radical print culture influenced the *language* of radicalism and I hope, later in this essay, to explore in greater detail the implications of this process. Just now I want to relate Jerrold's allegorical improvisation to certain populist strands within the radical style. These strands drew their expressive energies not only from the colloquialisms, exaggerations, hyperboles, integral (as Bakhtin has shown) to popular speech, but also from the innumerable parodies that proliferated in the world of popular culture and that travestied every authoritative discourse from the bible to court proceedings.[39] Therefore, like Jerrold's counter imagistic allegory, the populist styles within radicalism sought, most often, to appropriate and degrade the adversary's discourse. A very good example of this kind of writing would be the following (fairly typical) polemic that Cobbett unleashes against Malthus:

> The laws of nature [are] written in our passions, desires and propensities - - - Yes, say you: but nature has *other laws*, and amongst these are, that man shall live by *food,* and that if he cannot obtain food, he shall *starve* Agreed, and if there be a man in England who cannot find, *in the whole country* - - -[a] shop, house, mill, barn - - - sufficient [food] to keep him alive; *then* I allow, that the laws of nature condemn him to die. "Oh!" you will, with Parsonlike bawl, exclaim, "but he must not commit *robbery* or *larceny*!" Robbery or larceny! What do you mean by that? Does the law of nature say anything about robbery or larceny? - - - So you will quit the law of nature now will you?[40]

The aggression that underlies Cobbett's tone is closely related to his embattled situation within an increasingly repressive state. But, it seems to me, that Cobbett's aggression also expresses a more enduring aspect of the radical style: its propensity to confront what Raymond Williams has called "the composed, quiet, and connected prose of the formally educated traditions,"[41] and especially the monopoly that this prose exercised in the articulation of public matters. Put another way, Cobbett is attacking not just Malthus's arguments but also those

---

[39]   See Mikhail Bakhtin, *Rabelais and his World*, trans. Helene Iswolsky (Bloomington: Indiana University Press, 1984), 187–90; and Marcus Wood, *Radical Satire*, 144.

[40]   Quoted in James Sambrook, *William Cobbett* (London: Routledge, 1973), 107–108.

[41]   Raymond Williams, *Writing in Society* (London: Verso, 1983), 89.

taken for granted, apparently neutral features of the educated style that, in fact, function as instruments of domination. Moreover, in seeking to destabilize the formal elegance of Malthus's prose, its rhetorically constructed illusion of logic, the truth effects that it achieves by the selective deployment of formal knowledge, Cobbett depends not on the Painite ideal of a clear, unencumbered prose style that would sustain the reasonable argument, but rather on an elaborate linguistic process of quoting, rewriting and parodying. Thus Cobbett generates a whole hybrid style within which Malthus's ideas—ripped out of the authorizing context of the scholarly treatise—are rearticulated in colloquial language, and the dignifying inflections of Malthus's official mode of address entangled in a tone of absolute contempt—reduced to a "Parsonlike bawl."

The techniques of satiric overwriting that Cobbett perfected are very important for my purposes because these techniques would feed the demand for the anti-establishment political entertainment that continued into the forties even after the confrontationist context in which Cobbett wrote had disappeared. Moreover, the proliferation within the print market of expressive techniques that could sustain the radical rewriting of the discourses of power implied that these were available to novelists such as Thackeray and Dickens who began their careers in the lower rungs of the market for print entertainment.

Thackeray, as I have already tried to show, depended a great deal on radical expressive resources for the many anti-aristocratic and anti-monarchial squibs, caricatures, and parodies that he contributed to *Punch*. However, it was precisely the problem of representing the world of the elite that set off in Thackeray's mind the very sharp distinction he was to make between "magazinery" and the novel as a form of "art." More specifically, Thackeray's properly literary representations of elite discourses were based on the orchestration of details that he felt could be available to only those with direct access to the world of the upper classes and they aimed, above all, at seamlessly integrating these discourses into the ebb and flow of the "real." In sharp contrast, Dickens self-consciously defamiliarized the language of power, represented it not as it really was but as it appeared to those excluded from its processes. Thus Dickens sought through a whole process of rewriting—through repetition, magnification, exaggeration, parody—to expose and also to ridicule the ways in which the languages of power drew upon their internal resources, on the socially sophisticated nuance, or on the rhetoric of formality, to constitute themselves into those "practical metalanguage[s]" which, as Bourdieu argues, disguise semantic arbitrariness beneath an awe inspiring formal rigor.[42] I have tried to show elsewhere[43] how the popular novelistic aesthetic that Dickens fabricated involved absorbing and redeploying, within the expressive system of the novel, those radical techniques of rewriting that Thackeray dismissed as

---

[42]   See Pierre Bourdieu, *Language and Symbolic Power*, trans. Raymond Adamson and Mathew Adamson (Cambridge: The Polity Press, 1991), 85.

[43]   Sambudha Sen, "*Bleak House* and *Little Dorrit*: The Radical Heritage," *ELH*, Vol. 65, No. 4 (Winter, 1998), 945–970.

modes appropriate for journalistic satire rather than "literature" and how these transformed the literary representation of those classic objects of radical satire— the upper-class deployment of language as a marker of status or class and the ceremonial discourses that came out of such institutions of the state as the law court or the parliament.

I have been focusing so far on the ways in which radical journalists used language to subvert a range of elite discourses. I want now to turn to the very strong visual component within radical journalism to track not just its independent engagements with the processes and persons associated with power but also the ways in which many of its most characteristic effects are absorbed into language. Radical publicists were, by no means, the first or the only ones to use cartoons and caricatures as a means of political mobilization. On the contrary, it was Gilray's horrific images of the French Revolution that both laid out the expressive parameters within which graphic satire was to develop and marked the entry of caricature as a hugely effective force in an expanding public sphere. At the same time, however, it should not be hard to recognize the natural affinity that would underlie the relationship between a discourse committed to destroying the mystique that adhered both to the state's dignitaries as well as its consecrating symbolism and a mode of graphic expression that was fundamentally satiric and demystificatory in its orientation. In these circumstances, it is not surprising at all that through the first two decades of the nineteenth century, radical publicists often thought of caricature as, in the words of one of their most powerful adversaries, "a deadly weapon."[44] Thus in a print entitled "Coriolanus Addressing the Plebeians," Cruiskshank shows King George as Coriolanus, seemingly standing firm against Cobbett, Carlile, Hunt, Wooler and the rest. But among these radical plebeians, two figures stand out. One is, in Jonathan Bate's summary, "William Hone holding two clubs, one marked 'PARODY' and the other 'MAN IN THE MOON-HOUSE THAT JACK BUILT', and the other is George Cruickshank holding a folio marked 'Caricature.'"[45]

The confrontation that Cruickshank was dramatizing should be taken seriously. A few years before the publication of "Coriolanus," Cruickshank had demonstrated for a very large, largely plebeian audience how opposition to an act or policy of the government could be inscribed in the images of state dignitaries. Thus in a devastating sequence of caricatures that he produced for Hone's pamphlets Cruickshank expressed the popular anger with the Peterloo massacre and with the king's marital behavior, by portraying King George himself, as a "dandy of sixty"—grossly overdressed, overweight, ridiculous in his attempts to appear young, and later in E.P. Thompson's words, "blind drunk in his throne surrounded by broken bottles in front of a screen decorated with satyrs and large breasted trollops."[46] Moreover, Cruickshank's "Coriolanus" is concerned with

---

[44]   Sidmouth quoted in McCalman, *Radical Underworld*, 176.

[45]   Jonathan Bate, *Shakespearean Constitutions: Politics, Theatre, Criticism 1730–1830* (Oxford: the Clarendon Press, 1989), 102.

[46]   Thompson, *Making of the English Working Class*, 810.

more than caricature's innate capacity to degrade its subject, or the increasingly public nature of the discursive space within which it was now operating. It is also a self-conscious celebration of the collaboration between caricature and the *language* of radicalism.

As it happens, Hone, whose satiric fabrications in language are in "Coriolanus" shown to complement Cruickshank's caricatures, commented at length in a later work on the relationship between the caricaturist's unalterable lines and the more abstract conjurations of language. Referring to "sketch" of a parish beadle that he has just delineated in prose, Hone acknowledges that the beadle's "corporeal lineaments are 'borrowed' (with permission) from a new caricature, if it be given so low a name " by one of the authors of "Odes and Addresses to Great." Interestingly, however, Hone's interest in this particular caricature seems inseparable from its movement away both from the definitiveness which, as W.T.J Mitchell has shown, was associated in Romantic theories of representation with the visual arts, and from the easily recognizable subjects of political caricature. Dissociated from the particularizing compulsions (and energies) of an existence in the theatre of real life, Hone's caricature exemplifies a mode of satiric articulation that is "broad and comprehensive," being directed not at a person but at a "class." We might argue indeed that Hone's "universal parish beadle" hovers on the edge of what Catherine Gallagher has called "the figure's alluring fictionality which stimulates our desire to witness palpable human fabrications 'appear as independent beings endowed with life.'"[47] Hone himself thinks of his beadle not as mere "caricatura" but rather as "a graphic satire of character" [48]—an imaginary entity which, freed from the fixity of the line drawing as well as the stable referents of real life, strives for those more speculative, abstract effects of literature.

Hone's collaborations with visual caricature—from the improvisations in language with which he complemented Cruickshank's devastating portraits of King George during 1820–21 to the caricature that he raised in his *Everlasting Calendar of Popular Entertainments* (1827) to a "graphic satire of character"—mark in an unexpectedly clear fashion the process by which the radical caricaturist's capacity to inscribe popular resentments in very physical image of a state official or dignitary passed into language and remained a potential expressive resource even in discourses that were generated not by the pressures of active real life politics but by the demand for satiric entertaining fiction.

As young entrants to the print market of the 1830s, Thackeray and Dickens inevitably encountered linguistic representations of such targets of radical caricature as the beadle, bureaucrat, or the member of Parliament, but they related to these in very different ways. As we might expect, Thackeray's relationship to

---

[47]   Catherine Gallagher and Stephen Greenblatt, *Practicing New Historicism*, 169.

[48]   William Hone, *The Every-Day Book; or, Everlasting Calendar of Popular Amusements Sports, Past Times, Ceremonies, Manners, Customs and Events* in 2 vols, Vol. 2 (London: Hunt and Clarke, 1827), 130. On Romantic theories of art, see W.T.J. Mitchell, *Picture Theory* (Chicago: Chicago University Press, 1994), esp. 116–120.

the demystifying techniques of radical portraiture was far more paradoxical than that of Dickens: he produced graphic caricatures of monarchs that seem almost like continuations of Cruickshank's portraits, but his novelistic "ethics" were also predicated on replacing the mobilizing, communitarian orientation of radical portraiture with the psychological complexity, the dense internal detailing, in short the "depth" of the "lifelike" character. Thus, as in so much of his other magazine work, Thackeray found himself pushed by the demands for anti-establishment satire in the print market of the 30s into producing a print like "Rex, Ludovicus, Ludovicus Rex" where the king, stripped of his royal regalia, is imaged as a balding, spindly-legged, pot-bellied, physically pathetic specimen of humanity. On the other hand, the movement from "Rex" to say the younger Sir Pitt Crawley in *Vanity Fair* is precisely a movement away from a mode of articulation that focuses skeptically on those external signs by which state officials legitimize their power, to a method that seeks to unravel a sharply individualized consciousness across time and in relation to that taken for granted, almost unnoticeable orchestration of details that would in fact be available only to those with access to the internal world of an aristocratic Whig politician.

Unlike Thackeray, Dickens was never a practicing cartoonist, but if Thackeray sought to keep out representational techniques of radical caricature from the literary "art" of novel writing, Dickens fabricated a novelistic aesthetic that drew its expressive energies from such popular forms as the radical caricature. Dickens's relationship with the tradition of radical portraiture was extremely close: a proximity that is best symbolized by the figure of Cruickshank, the trajectory of whose career connects as diverse texts as "The Political House" and *Sketches by Boz*. It is true, of course,[49] that by the time that Cruickshank began working on *Sketches by Boz,* he had moved away from his radical past and that the political cartoon was itself becoming dissociated from a "community or a movement" and moving increasingly into the market for print entertainment. But *Sketches by Boz* also testifies to the expressive energy of radical techniques even after these techniques had experienced a double displacement: on the one hand from the pictorial to the linguistic and on the other from the arena of active politics to that of the entertainment-oriented Dickensian text. For example the following "sketch" of a "doctor of civil law" uses the symbolic expression of language to generate precisely those visual details of dress and body that would go into the making of what Hone called "a graphic satire of character:"

> There was one individual who amused us mightily. This was one of bewigged gentlemen in red robes, who was straddling before the fire in the centre of the Court, in the attitude of a brazen Colossus, to the complete exclusion of everybody else. He had gathered his robes behind, in much the same manner as a slovenly woman would her petticoats on a very dirty day, in order that he might feel the full warmth of the fire ... . We shall never be able to lay any credit as a physiognomist again, for, after a careful scrutiny of this gentleman's

---

49   "'*Bleak House* and *Little Dorrit:*' The Radical Heritage."

countenance, we had come to the conclusion that it bespoke of nothing but conceit and silliness, when our friend with the silver staff whispered in our ear that he was no other than a doctor of civil law, and heaven knows what besides.[50]

For me the interesting thing about this passage is the way in which the caricaturist's naiveté—his ignorance of what any insider would know—itself becomes the basis of demystification. More specifically, the caricaturist's failure to recognize the official status of his subject is, in an important sense, a willed failure, predicated on the privileging the equalizing, if uninformed, point of view of the outsider over the hierarchizing operations of officialdom; the one sided skepticism of the political caricaturist over the rounded unraveling of consciousness characteristic of the more properly literary forms of novel writing. In this sense, this early sketch might help us to understand the whole sequence of caricaturized figures—from Bumble to Tite Barnacle—who appear in Dickens's fiction, not as failed attempts at realistic characterization or even as the products of Dickens's unique comic genius but rather as displacements within a certain form of entertainment-oriented fictionalizing, of a strand of radical satire oriented towards building around its irreverent representations of those who wielded political power, a community of the excluded.

In their confrontation with the persons and processes associated with state power, the radical caricaturists deployed not only the disfiguring techniques that I have been discussing but also that profusion of allegorical detail which, as Baudelaire suggested, was integral to the work of the English caricaturists.[51] The "art of the rebus and of the primitive ideographic script"[52] had, of course, always found expression in the insignia of the aristocracy and in the emblems of the state but it had also developed, through the early modern period, as a burlesque of official heraldry. Moreover, although the radical discourse itself sustained a considerable iconography which served as a target for conservative satirists, a great deal of its expressive energies was generated by the recognition that emblems, insignia, and symbols were never merely "the trimmings of political culture, but often went to the heart of what was ultimately at issue: how power at all levels of the state and civil society was to be defined and exercised."[53]

Radical publicists disrupted the state's consecrating symbols in many ways: from burlesquing the general's cocked hat or the judge's wig in their caricatures of these dignitaries of the state to generating full-blown counter emblematic reworkings of official protocols. For me the important thing is to locate traces of the counter-emblematic techniques of radical satire in the *language* of popular radicalism after this had moved from the mobilizing texts of the 1820s to the

---

[50] Charles Dickens, *Sketches by Boz* (Oxford: Oxford University Press, 1997), 87–88.

[51] See Baudelaire, *Selected Writings on Art*, esp. 231.

[52] E.H. Gombrich, *Meditations on a Hobbyhorse and Other Essays on the Theory of Art* (London: Phaidon Press, 1963), 122.

[53] Epstein, *Radical Expression*, 71.

print market of the 1830s. At this level, too, the work of Douglas Jerrold proves to be invaluable. Thus, an essay like "The Order of Poverty" not only addresses itself directly to the problem of what it sees as the arbitrary consecrating function of heraldry, it also self consciously reactivates, within the symbolic system of language, some of graphic satire's most effective modes of demystification.

One obvious example of such reactivation is Jerrold's use of juxtaposition as a means of demystification. Thus Jerrold habitually uses the synchronic possibilities of pictorial representation to generate disconcerting juxtapositions: for example, to set off against the prestige that a royal decoration confers, the actual achievements of those who receive such decorations. Moreover, the metonymic extensions through which counter emblematic graphic satire attains its most characteristic effects are not only replicated, but in fact find freer, if more diffused, expression in Jerrold's prose. Liberated completely from the boundedness of the physical image, and from even the minimal commitment to visible similarity as the basis of association, Jerrold can find in the radical indeterminacy of the linguistic signifier the means of effecting drastic and unexpected transformations on the object of his satire. Thus, it is not the visible imagery of the "Order of the Thistle" but its very antiquity that serves as the basis of Jerrold's destabilizing counter discourse.If the "order of the Thistle" is very old, it can by a metonymic extension be said to be as "old as asses" and then be made to sustain the full blown counter image of an asinine "nobility" that "browses" on thistles. This kind of radical refiguring of traditional imagery generates unlimited expressive possibilities in Jerrold's prose: the idea of the "order" itself proliferates into many parodic orders—for example, the Order of the Golden Calf whose knights have discarded armor and helmet for "the magic mail of impenetrable Bank-paper."[54] Again, since the counter-emblematic imagery that Jerrold fabricates in language exploits, but is no longer tied to the synchronicity of the picture frame, they become capable of sustaining not just a wider range of comic improvisations, but also sequence, and ultimately—as Jerrold's parable of the Woky Poky Indians testifies—narrative itself.

The transposition of emblematic satire into language, the possibility of generating within the spatially unconstrained novel form a narrative based on the metonymic extensions of visual caricature, all this had important implications for the popular novelistic aesthetic that Dickens was developing. Thus in contrast to *Vanity Fair* or *Pendennis* where, as Thackeray said, a coat had to be a "coat, and a poker a poker and - - - nothing else according to my ethics,"[55] and where the incessantly circulating emblems, insignias and crests remain immutable signs of power and of wealth, Dickens's basic representational strategy in *Bleak House*, for example, is to seize upon a ceremonial emblem or motif associated with Chancery practice, wrench it out of its context and recombine it with ideas or images that suggest the primitive shapelessness or the gothic cruelty of the dark ages. I have

---

[54]   Walter Jerrold, *The Essays of Douglas Jerrold* (London: J.M. Dent, 1903), 156, 159.
[55]   Gordon N. Ray, Vol. ii, 772.

tried to show in another essay[56] that the reactivization in *Bleak House* of the expressive resources of emblematic satire opened up enormous possibilities for the novel form itself: generating within it not just the counter-discourse of radical caricature but also a narrative energized by graphic satire's metonymic extensions. It was this new narrative energy that was to climax with the single most inventive episode in *Bleak House*: the symbolic death of Krook—the grotesque mirror image of the Lord Chancellor himself—by spontaneous combustion.

Did the alienated unfolding of radical expression within the Dickensian novel have any effect at all on the political or even literary establishment of the 1850s? At one level, of course, novels like *Bleak House* or *Little Dorrit* could hardly be said to have threatened the mid-Victorian establishment in the way that the radical newspapers and journals did in the early nineteenth century. Unlike Hone or Cobbett who always faced the risk of prosecution because their work exerted serious pressure on a state that was both vulnerable and oppressive, Dickens wrote well within the bounds of what the far more self-confident state of the fifties considered acceptable. Moreover, unlike Hone or Cobbett who wrote primarily to sustain real political struggles, Dickens saw "radical expression" as one among the many modes that made up the entertainment-oriented expressive economy of his novels. I want to argue, however, that the mid-Victorian establishment did not treat Dickens's caricaturization of high government officials, his satiric reprocessing of parliamentary debates and his propensity to turn the novel itself into a forum for discussing topical problems, merely as entertainment.

The anxiety that Dickens's later novels, especially, aroused in the mid-Victorian elite is, in my opinion, closely tied up with Dickens's status as the great popular novelist of the period. This was partly because of the conviction—widespread in the highbrow quarterly press—that the later Dickens's popularity had increasingly consolidated around the indiscriminate monthly part buying audience. As Edward Whipple argued, Dickens's criticism of the largest institutions of the state had resulted in his losing his educated readers. These readers, Whipple, asserted, had enjoyed Dickens's "humour and pathos," but had become irritated with his intrusions into "matters relating to social and economical science with which he was imperfectly acquainted." On the other hand, as Walter Bagehot argued in an influential piece first published in the *National Review*, Dickens's populism had enabled him to consolidate his hold over the indiscriminating masses that cared only for its "own multifareous, industrial, fig selling world."[57]

Bagehot thought of Dickens's lowbrow readers not as a politically active group, but as more or less passive consumers of literary entertainment. Still, in an age when periodicals, magazines, and part issues were emerging as major forms of entertainment, and when leisure itself was, in Peter Bailey's words, "a new, relatively uncharted area in the lifespace"[58] of the urban masses, the reading habits

---

[56] "*Bleak House* and *Little Dorrit*: The Radical Heritage."

[57] Walter Bagehot, "Charles Dickens", *The National Review*, Vol. vii (October, 1858), 458.

[58] Peter Bailey, "'A Mingled Mass of Perfectly Legitimate Pleasures:' The Victorian Middle Class and the Problem of Leisure," *Victorian Studies*, Vol. 21 (Autumn, 1977), 13.

of large groups of people were bound to have some political significance. It was this changing sociology of leisure that made the novel and especially the Dickensian popular novel such a potentially harmful public influence for a man like James Fitzjames Stephen who might otherwise never have condescended to write about as lowbrow a novelist as "Boz." Writing in 1855, Stephen argued that while the popularity of outdoor sports and even of the theatre and of spectacles had declined, "the habit of reading novels [had] become universal." This meant for Stephen that a "very considerable" number of "young people" took from novels "nearly all their notions of life." Stephen thought, therefore, that Dickens was behaving completely irresponsibly when he sent to his innumerable readers the message that "their Legislature is a stupid and inefficient debating club, their courts of law foul haunts of chicanery, pedantry and fraud, and their system of administration an odious compound of stupidity and corruption." To be sure, Dickens's writing did not deserve to be taken any more seriously than the antics of a clown, but it is in the very process of citing the crude origins of Dickens's art that Stephen betrays his deepest anxieties:

> Who, it may be asked takes Mr. Dickens seriously? Is it not as foolish to estimate his melodramatic and sentimental stock-in-trade seriously as it would be to undertake the refutation of the jokes of the clown in a Christmas pantomime? No doubt this would be true enough if the world were composed entirely or principally of men of sense and cultivation. To such persons Mr Dickens is nothing more than any other public performer – enjoying an extravagantly high reputation --- But the vast majority of mankind, unfortunately, think little, and cultivate themselves still less --- and to these classes such writers as Dickens are something more than amusement.[59]

What makes Stephen's critique significant is his fear that ideas about politics, society, language and novel writing that had germinated in the lower depths of popular culture were now entering the public realm of letters so assiduously cultivated by the journals for which Stephen wrote and by their eighteenth-century predecessors, and competing with these for the forming of public opinion. In an unsigned article that Philip Collins attributes to Stephen, Stephen picks that pivotal figure in the radical journalistic tradition—William Cobbett himself—as the person most responsible for diffusing the bourgeois public sphere and making possible the emergence of Dickens as the central writer in a vastly expanded world of letters. Stephen argued that as the writer who first demonstrated that it was possible to bypass sustained formal education, to write entirely "by the light of nature" and to convey opinions about public matters in the most emphatic language to a large, often subliterate audience, Cobbett began a process that Dickens would internalize for the novel:

---

[59]   James Fitzjames Stephen, "The Relation of the Novel to Life" (1855) reprinted in Edwin Eigner and George J. Worth, *Victorian Criticism of the Novel* (Cambridge: Cambridge University Press, 1985), 94; and James Fitzjames Stephen, "Mr. Dickens as Politician," *Saturday Review*, Vol.III (January 3, 1857), 8.

Though no two persons could resemble each other less in terms of character, the position of Mr. Dickens with respect to fiction is precisely analogous to that of Cobbett with respect to political discussion. The object of the arguments of the one was to drive his opinion into the dullest understanding – the object of the narrative of the other is to paint a picture that will catch the eye of the most ignorant and the least attentive observer. Mr.Dickens's writings are the apotheosis of what has been called newspaper English. He makes points everywhere --- . [60]

Like Thackeray and the anonymous author of " Modern Novelists" Stephen was profoundly hostile to the coming together of the novel and ""newspaper English."[61] But for me the significant thing about this passage is Stephen's articulation, from the point of view of the mid-Victorian establishment, of the process that I have been trying to outline in this essay: that despite many displacements— from its roots in a radical artisanal community to one strand among many within literary commodities consumed by a large, socially diverse audience; from the revolutionary political climate of the late eighteenth and early nineteenth centuries to the stability and prosperity of the mid-Victorian era—the language of radicalism not only survived (in the Dickensian novel), but also continued , in indirect ways , to influence public opinion. In this sense, Stephen's comments constitute a fitting concluding statement for this essay.

Works Cited

Altick, Richard. *Punch: The Lively Youth of a British Institution 1841–51.* Columbus: Ohio State University Press, 1997.

Bakhtin, Mikhail. *Rabelais and his World*, trans. Helene Iswolsky. Bloomington: Indiana University Press, 1984.

---

[60] From an unsigned review of the Library edition of the *Works* which Philip Collins extracts and attributes "almost certainly" to Stephen. See Philip Collins, ed. *Dickens: The Critical Heritage* (New Delhi: Vikas,1980), 385.

[61] Stephen responded to Dickens's politicization of the novel by developing in a fairly sustained manner a theory with which Thackeray would almost certainly agree and which was to cast a very long shadow over subsequent debates about what constituted the "legitimate province" of the novel. Thus Stephen sought to pin the novel down to the subjectivity of an individual destiny and to those "ordinary domestic relations" within which such subjectivity could be constituted. In these circumstances it is not surprising that Stephen should argue that "using the novel to ventilate opinions" was to step outside its "legitimate province." These and similar ideas, scattered through the many articles on the novel that James published in the *Saturday Review* and the *Edinburg Review* between 1855 and 1858, suggest that the emphasis on "character" and on familiar domestic experiences that were to become key components of what was later to be designated the "realistic" aesthetic, developed in the course of the polemics that the quarterlies spearheaded against not only "idealism" and "sensationalism" but also against the radical heritage of the popular Dickensian novel. The phrases quoted from James appear in "The Relation of the Novel to Life," 95. The License of Modern Novelists," 25; "The Relation of the Novel," 113.

————. *Speech Genres and Other Late Essays*, trans.Vern W. Mcgee, eds Caryl Emerson and Michael Holquist. Austin: University of Texas Press, 1986.

Bate, Jonathan. *Shakespearean Constitutions: Politics, Theatre, Criticism 1730–1830*. Oxford: Clarendon Press, 1989.

Baudelaire, Charles. "Some Foreign Caricaturists," in *Selected Writings on Art and Artists*, trans. E.P. Charvet. Cambridge: Cambridge University Press, 1972.

Benjamin, Walter. "The Work of Art in the Age of Mechanical Reproduction," in *Illuminations*. New York: Schocken Books, 1975.

Bourdieu, Pierre. *Language and Symbolic Power*, trans. Raymond and Mathew Adamson. Cambridge: Polity Press, 1991.

Chartier, Roger. "Texts, Printing, Readings," in *The New Cultural History*, ed. Lynn Hunt. Berkeley: University of California Press, 1989.

Collins, Phillip. Ed. *Dickens: The Critical Heritage*. New Delhi: Vikas, 1971.

Dickens, Charles. *Little Dorrit*. Harmondsworth: Penguin, 1976.

————. *Sketches by Boz*. Oxford: Oxford University Press, 1997.

Epstein, James. *Radical Expression: Political Language, Ritual and Symbol in England 1790–1850*. Oxford: Oxford University Press, 1994.

Gallagher, Catherine. *Nobody's Story: The Vanishing Acts of Women Writers in the Market place 1670–1820*. Berkeley:University of California Press,1994.

Gallagher, Catherine and Stephen Greenblatt, Eds. *Practicing New Historicism*. Chicago: University of Chicago Press, 2000.

Gilmartin, Kevin. *Print Politics: The Press and Radical Opposition in Early Nineteenth Century England* (Cambridge: Cambridge University Press), 1996.

Gombrich, E.H. *Meditations on A Hobbyhorse and Other Essays on the Theory of Art*. London: Phaidon Press, 1963.

Hone, William. *The Every-Day Book; or, Everlasting Calendar of Popular Amusements Sports, Past times, Ceremonies, Manners, Customs and Events*. 2 vols. London: Hunt and Clarke, 1827.

James, Louis. *Fiction for the Working Man 1830–1850*. Harmondsworth: Penguin, 1973.

Jerrold, Walter. *Douglas Jerrold and "Punch."* London: Macmillan and Co., 1910.

————. *The Essays of Douglas Jerrold*. London: J.M. Dent, 1903.

Jones, Gareth Stedman. *Languages of Class: Studies in English Working Class History*. Cambridge: Cambridge University Press, 1983.

Ledger, Sally. "From Queen Caroline to Lady Dedlock: Dickens and the Popular Radical Imagination," *Victorian Literature and Culture*, Vol. 32 (2004), 575–600.

————. *Dickens and the Popular Radical Imagination*. Cambridge: Cambridge University Press, 2007.

McCalman, Iain. *Radical Underworld: Prophets, Revolutionaries and Pornographers in London 1795–1840*. Cambridge: Cambridge University Press, 1988.

Mitchell, W.T.J. *Iconology: Image, Text , Ideology.* Chicago: Chicago University Press, 1986.

———. *Picture Theory.* Chicago: Chicago University Press, 1994.

Paine, Thomas. "The Rights of Man." *The Selected Works of Tom Paine,* ed. Howard Fast. New York: Random House, 1945.

Ray, Gordon N., ed. *The Letters and Private Papers of William Makepeace Thackeray.* Oxford: Oxford University Press, 1945.

Sambrook, James. *William Cobbett.* London: Routledge, 1973.

Smith, Olivia. *The Politics of Language 1791–1819.* Oxford: Oxford University Press, 1984.

Spielman, M.H. *The History of "Punch."* Cassell: New York, 1895.

Stephen, James Fitzjames. "Mr. Dickens as Politician," *Saturday Review,* Vol.III, Jan. 3, 1857.

———. "The Relation of the Novel to Life," in *Victorian Criticism of the Novel,* eds Edwin Eigner and George J. Worth. Cambridge: Cambridge University Press, 1985.

Thackeray, W.M. "George Cruickshank," in *Ballads, Critical Reviews, Tales.* London: Smith Elder and Co., 1907.

———. "Pictures of Life and Character," in *Ballads, Critical Reviews, Tales.*

Thompson, E.P. *Customs in Common: Studies in Traditional Popular Culture.* New York: The New Press, 1993.

———. *The Making of the English Working Class.* Harmondsworth: Penguin, 1980.

Unsigned, "Modern Novelists: Charles Dickens," *Westminster Review,* Vol. 26. October, 1864.

Unsigned, "Things that Cannot be Done," *Household Words,* 8 October 1853.

Williams, Raymond. "Radical and\or Respectable" in *The Press We Deserve,* ed. Richard Boston (London: Routledge and Kegan Paul, 1970.

———. *Writing in Society.* London: Verso, 1983.

Wood, Marcus. *Radical Satire and Print Culture: 1790–1822.* Oxford: Oxford University Press, 1994.

Chapter 9
"The Unaccredited Hero":
Alton Locke, Thomas Carlyle,
and the Formation of the
Working-Class Intellectual

Richard Salmon

This essay examines the formation of the working-class intellectual as a distinctive modern cultural figure within the work of two influential middle-class writers of the mid-nineteenth-century, Charles Kingsley and Thomas Carlyle. In Kingsley's celebrated novel, *Alton Locke, Tailor and Poet: An Autobiography*, first published anonymously in 1850, can be found one of the earliest fictional representations of a self-consciously defined working-class "hero." Written not long after the political crisis of 1848, when Kingsley, under the persona of "Parson Lot," had played a prominent part in seeking to negotiate the demands of Chartism, and to defuse its revolutionary potential, *Alton Locke* comprises a sympathetic first-person narrative account of the life of a self-educated artisan-poet, whose involvement in working-class Radical politics of the 1840s leads to a crisis of personal and cultural identity ending ultimately in his tragic demise.[1] Kingsley's fictional account of the career of Alton Locke was based partly on both direct and indirect familiarity with the lives of recent and contemporary working-class poets, many of whom had begun to compose their own autobiographies over the preceding two decades. *Alton Locke* was, in this sense, a conscious simulation of a textual object which had already begun to proliferate in authentic form by the 1840s: the narrative of working-class self-development, which existed in both specifically literary and broader cultural terms. Just as significantly, however, Kingsley's fabricated working-class autobiography also draws on an extensive knowledge of the writings of Carlyle, a biographer and critic whose immense cultural authority was by the middle of the century already secure, although he had himself risen from constricted origins in rural peasant society.[2]

It was through Carlyle that Kingsley encountered a model of the working-class writer couched specifically within a discourse of the heroic. One of the centerpieces

---

[1] For a biographical account of Kingsley's political activities during the period 1848–1850, see Brenda Colloms, *Charles Kingsley: The Lion of Eversley* (London: Constable, 1975), 88–139.

[2] On Carlyle's family background and early education, see Fred Kaplan, *Thomas Carlyle: A Biography* (Cambridge: Cambridge University Press, 1983), 17–43.

of Carlyle's well-known lecture "The Hero as Man of Letters," from the series *On Heroes, Hero-Worship and the Heroic in History* (1840), was his brief biographical account of Robert Burns, a figure for whom Carlyle held an abiding and ambivalent fascination, attributable in part to their shared cultural provenance. In turn, Kingsley placed Burns at the head of the modern "school" of self-taught poets in an essay published contemporaneously with *Alton Locke*, and manifestly influenced by Carlyle's analysis of Burns's cultural significance.[3] Carlyle's instrumental role in the development of the Burnsian myth was thus mirrored by Kingsley's role in the popularization of a certain tenor of working-class poetic biography. Independently of this development, moreover, it was through Carlyle's mediation that Kingsley acquired a new narrative form with which to chart the mental life of the working-class intellectual: a paradigm of individual "development" and "self-formation" derived from the German concept of *Bildung*. Stemming from Carlyle's 1824 translation of Goethe's *Wilhelm Meister*, the novelistic genre of the *Bildungsroman* had become a prolific medium of literary self-inscription by the date of Kingsley's text.[4] By reading *Alton Locke* primarily through its engagement with the cultural and philosophical legacy of Carlylean theory, then, this essay considers the historical formation of the figure of the working-class intellectual in a double and reflexive sense. It is the formation of the very idea of self-formation which constitutes one of the principal contributions to working-class intellectual culture of both writers, and it is with the fraught ideological articulation of this idea that the following discussion is largely concerned.

I

Returning from his first Chartist meeting, an event marking his initiation into the world of organized working-class politics, the eponymous hero and narrator of *Alton Locke* expresses surprise at "hear[ing] men of my own class—and lower still, perhaps, some of them- speak with fluency and eloquence," and wonders whence they can have acquired "[s]uch a fund of information - such excellent English."[5] Alton's companion, the more experienced and committed Chartist Crossthwaite, is quick to instruct him:

---

3   See Thomas Carlyle, "The Hero as Man of Letters" in *On Heroes, Hero-Worship and the Heroic in History*, ed. Carl Niemeyer (Lincoln/London: University of Nebraska Press, 1966), 188–195; and [Charles Kingsley], "Burns and His School" *North British Review*, XVI no. XXXI (November, 1851), 149–183.

4   See Thomas Carlyle, *Wilhelm Meister's Apprenticeship and Travels*. Translated from the German of Goethe, 2 vols (London: Chapman and Hall, 1899).

5   See Charles Kingsley, *Alton Locke, Tailor and Poet: An Autobiography*, ed. Elizabeth A. Cripps (Oxford and New York: Oxford University Press, 1983), 108. All subsequent references to this edition (based on the first published edition of 1850) will occur parenthetically in the main text.

From the God who knows nothing about ranks. They're the unknown great – the unaccredited heroes, as Master Thomas Carlyle would say, whom the flunkeys aloft have not acknowledged yet – though they'll be forced to, some day, with a vengeance.

Crossthwaite's rejoinder is intended, perhaps, to carry the force of a resounding statement of the obvious: since the capacity for "greatness" is not conditioned by "rank," the intellectual acquirements of the working-class speakers derive merely from the same—albeit transcendental—source as those belonging to any other class. Yet the remark also provides us with an explanation of the sense of wonder which it seeks to dispel. It is not inappropriate that Alton should experience such a revelation, though it may be implausible for a man of his status, for, in Crossthwaite's assessment, the working-class intellectual is defined precisely by his lack of cultural visibility, materializing only in figures of the "*un*known great" or "*un*accredited heroes." To middle-class readers, for whom Alton functions as a conduit in the above passage, the surprise can be presumed genuine.[6]

Crossthwaite's appeal to the authority of "Master Thomas Carlyle" is not the only occasion on which the novel seeks to link self-educated workers to the figure of the *hero*, central to the work of the most influential cultural critic of the mid-nineteenth century. In fact, exactly the same phrase—"unaccredited heroes"—is invoked on three separate occasions within the text: once to describe the collective character of the Chartist, as above, and twice in singular reference to Alton himself. Alton's initiation into the organized culture of working-class Radicalism is thus also a moment of self-identification, in which the representative status of Kingsley's hero is implicitly acknowledged. Significantly, the phrase is first employed by the Scottish bookseller, Sandy Mackaye, a character with a penchant for quoting Carlyle who is often assumed to be modeled directly upon him.[7] Referring to Alton's as yet unproven literary talent, Mackaye advises him: "Ye're an unaccreedited hero, the noo, as Thomas Carlyle has it. 'But gin ye do weel by yoursel,' saith the Psalmist, 'ye'll find a' men speak well o' ye'—if ye gang their gate'" (66). Here, too, the qualifier "unaccre[e]dited" designates a capacity for heroism hitherto unrecognized and thus outside the sphere of public representation. At this point in his narrative, Alton's social invisibility is, in part, attributable to the stage of development which his talent has attained *en route* to its eventual recognition. Yet this process is rendered conditional upon the working-class poet's accommodation to the heteronomous demands of a middle-class audience ("if ye gang their gate"), a warning which ominously prefigures Alton's future direction. The word "unaccredited," then, hints not only at the problem of visual recognition within

---

[6]   The interpellation of middle-class readers within scenes of working-class life was a common strategy of the early-Victorian "Condition of England" novel: on this point, see Regenia Gagnier, *Subjectivities: A History of Self-Representation in Britain, 1832–1920* (New York and Oxford: Oxford University Press, 1991), 114.

[7]   The more obvious points of resemblance are outlined in Cripps's "Introduction" to the Oxford University Press edition of *Alton Locke*, xvi–xvii.

the field of cultural representation for working-class intellectuals, but also, more literally, at the difficulty of acquiring the necessary social accreditation in order to become representable. This interpretation is supported by the ensuing paragraphs in which Alton receives qualified support for his intellectual development from his "Mammonite" uncle: "if you are inclined to help to raise the family name—not that I think much of book writers myself—poor starving devils, half of them—but still people do talk about them—and a man might get a snug thing as newspaper editor, with interest; or clerk to something or other—always some new company in the wind now—and I should have no objection, if you seemed likely to do us *credit*, to speak a word for you" (66–67; my emphasis). Alton's literary career is thus deemed worthy of assistance on the understanding that the process of becoming visible—the concession that writers are often "talk[ed] about"—may become a means of acquiring social "credit" for himself and his family. To achieve this goal, however, Alton must submit his intellectual development to a crudely economic reading of the metaphor of accreditation: though his uncle declares that "without capital ... brains [are] a curse," he implies that intellect itself may be exploited as a form of cultural capital, and so indirectly provide a means of social advancement. This, indeed, is the strategy self-consciously pursued by Alton's cousin George, a Cambridge undergraduate who views cultural acquirements as a transparent tool of class mobility and so reflects cynically upon Alton's high-minded appreciation of poetry and art. George Locke is Alton's exact figural antithesis, an embodiment of intellectual accreditation derived not only from his explicit association with institutional pedagogy, but also from his success in ensuring that no aspects of his cultural attainment should be beyond immediate visual recognition.

Fittingly, then, the third instance of the term "unaccredited hero" occurs, later in the narrative, when Alton characterizes his cousin's response to his own incipient social elevation through the patronage of Dean Winnstay:

> I had evidently risen immensely in his eyes; and I could not help applying, in my heart, to him, Mr. Carlyle's dictum about the valet species – how they never honour the unaccredited hero, having no eye to find him out till properly accredited, and countersigned, and accoutred with full uniform and diploma by that great God, Public Opinion. I saw through the motive of his new-fledged respect for me – and yet I encouraged it; for it flattered my vanity. (154)

Although Alton can now recognize the corrupt worldliness of those who fail to perceive heroism in its "unaccredited" forms, he himself no longer lives up to the nobility of the heroic type identified by his two mentors, and encountered paradigmatically in the meeting of Chartist intellectuals. Once more, this passage conceives of the process of cultural accreditation through the language of economic transaction, in which the intellectual capital of the poet-hero is re-imagined as a note of financial credit, legitimately "countersigned." More overtly, it draws upon a metaphor of clothing central to the Carlylean discourse of heroism and hero-worship from the conception of *Sartor Resartus* (1833–34) onwards, which is, of course, literalized in the very title of Kingsley's novel. Alton's allusion to

"Carlyle's dictum about the valet species" refers both to the idea that cultural accreditation functions in the manner of an approved code of dress, a clothing of the heroic figure in conventional symbolic forms, and to the wry suggestion that those who participate most intimately in the act of constructing this spectacle are often least impressed by the result. In fact, "No man is a Hero to his valet-de-chambre" is a dictum attributed to the French historian, Jules Michelet, and frequently cited by Carlyle, usually in ironic contexts.[8] For Carlyle, the proximity of the valet to his master figures the climate of skepticism towards the possibility of heroism in modern "democratic" society; yet, rather than endorsing this skeptical perspective as a liberating demystification of the hero's social construction, he associates it with worldly cynicism of the kind exemplified by Alton's cousin. Similarly, in Kingsley's text, the "valet species" apparently refers to all those who are incapable of recognizing heroism beyond the conventional "accoutrements" of social status—the sham-heroic figure presented in Carlyle's "The Hero as Man of Letters" as "advanc[ing] in royal stage-trappings, with measured step, trains borne behind him, trumpets sounding before him."[9]

We can thus trace in Kingsley's figure of the "unaccredited hero" both a transparent and a precise conceptual borrowing from the discourse of Carlyle. The distinction between a type of intellectual heroism which is seen or unseen, authorized or unauthorized, could, for instance, be traced to Carlyle's essay "Goethe's Works" (1832)—to take one of several possible illustrations—in which he seeks to distinguish between the "Great Man" and the "Noted Man" as worthy and unworthy objects of hero-worship. In the modern world, according to Carlyle, a proliferation of "Noted Men," attributed both to the democratization of fame ensuing from Revolutionary upheaval and to the development of print media through which that fame is disseminated, makes it increasingly difficult to recognize the "Great Men" with whom they are often mistaken. Greatness is popularly confused with visibility (the medium of "universal daylight"), Carlyle suggests, in what amounts to an early, and prescient, critique of the culture of celebrity. Though it is possible for the "Great Man" and the "Noted Man" to coincide, as in the case of Napoleon, Carlyle is often led to locate greatness in that which resists visual exhibition, or, in alternative sensory mode, in a 'silence' which refuses all speech.[10] In his 1838 essay "Sir Walter Scott," Carlyle wrote:

> It is one of the comfortablest truths that great men abound, though in the unknown state. Nay, as above hinted, our greatest, being also by nature our *quietest*, are perhaps those that remain unknown.[11] [original emphasis]

---

[8]   The version of the dictum quoted here is taken from "The Hero as Man of Letters" in *On Heroes, Hero-Worship and the Heroic in History*, 183. Similar examples, however, may be found in essays on Burns (1828) and Schiller (1831): see Thomas Carlyle, *Critical and Miscellaneous Essays*, 5 vols (London: Chapman and Hall, 1899), [I], 259; and [II], 167.

[9]   See Carlyle, *On Heroes, Hero-Worship and The Heroic in History*, 183.

[10]   See Thomas Carlyle, "Goethe's Works" in *Critical and Miscellaneous Essays* [II], 394–399.

[11]   Thomas Carlyle, 'Sir Walter Scott" in *Critical and Miscellaneous Essays* [IV], 49.

Here, by way of reaction to Scott, who ranks firmly in the category of "notable,"[12] Carlyle privileges the anonymity of the "unknown great," even reducing this phrase to something approaching tautology: if greatness does not consist of visibility or noise, perhaps invisibility and silence are greatness "by nature." Unlike Kingsley's Crossthwaite, Carlyle does not specifically define the collective ranks of the unknown great in terms of social class, but he opens up the category of the "Great Man" with such breadth that it could clearly encompass the figure of the working-class intellectual as represented in *Alton Locke*. Moreover, Carlyle invokes Thomas Gray's famous elegiac figure of the "mute Milton" to emblematize this negative ratio of true greatness: a figure which resonates strongly with the politics of social obscurity.[13]

Yet in both of these essays Carlyle problematizes any celebration of the unknown great as a type of heroism unassimilated to the degraded materiality of visual representation. He is aware of the epistemological difficulties posed by a doctrine of hero-worship which becomes incapable of perceiving its legitimate objects, almost by definition. Carlyle's response to this dilemma is to propose that all practices of hero-worship, however iconoclastic in conception, necessarily attain some form of visual embodiment - are directed towards some kind of "idol," a word which he defines through its Greek etymology [*eidolon*] as meaning "vision," "clear symbol," or "a thing seen." "All worship whatsoever," he declares in "The Hero as Priest," "must proceed by Symbols, by Idols." The only difference between the reverence for true heroes and the "mistaken worship of sham great ones," and, indeed, our only possible means of deciding between them, lies in the *degree* to which the visual form of their respective idols adequately symbolizes an inner substance in which the hero-worshipper sincerely believes.[14] It is for this reason that Carlyle avoids outright condemnation of those cultural practices, such as the "Lionism" of literary celebrities, which conflate greatness with notability or popularity: even these degraded phenomena retain a residual symbolic value in preserving the traces of anthropological forms whose original content has been eviscerated. The very fact that we commonly mistake the outward symbols of clothing for the immanent human qualities which they are thought to represent demonstrates our underlying consent to believe in the existence and enduring value of these qualities, regardless of their misrecognition. In "Goethe's Works," Carlyle pursues this argument through the alternative metaphor of financial currency and its semiotic function in encoding socially approved measures of value:

---

[12]   Ibid., 25.

[13]   Ibid., 46. See also Thomas Gray, "Elegy Written in a Country Churchyard" (1751), in *The Poems of Thomas Gray, William Collins, Oliver Goldsmith*, ed. Roger Lonsdale (London and Harlow: Longman, Green and Co., 1969), 103–141. For a late-twentieth-century allusion to the politics of intellectual obscurity embedded in Gray's elegy, see Tony Harrison, "On Not Being Milton" in *Selected Poems* (Second Edition. London: Penguin Books, 1987), 112.

[14]   See Carlyle, *On Heroes, Hero-Worship and the Heroic in History*, 120–122; and also "Goethe's Works" in *Critical and Miscellaneous Essays* [II], 391.

All these things, I say, the apparel, the counthood, the existing popularity and whatever else can combine there, are symbols; – banknotes, which, whether there be gold behind them, or only bankruptcy and empty drawers, pass current for gold. But how, now, could they so pass, if gold itself were not prized, and believed and known to be somewhere extant?[15]

Here, in suggesting that the relationship between the true substance of heroism and its conventional (symbolic) accoutrements is analogous to the relationship between "gold" and "banknotes," Carlyle fashions a theory of hero-worship precisely in terms of the language of social and economic credit employed in *Alton Locke*. But where Kingsley appears, at first sight, to position the working-class hero beyond the field of visual representation demarcated by the process of social accreditation, Carlyle's anthropological account of the cultural value of heroic "currency" qualifies his celebration of the condition of unknown greatness.

II

In *Alton Locke*, too, heroism and hero-worship are implicated in the theological charge of idolatry. Nowhere is Kingsley's indebtedness to Carlyle more evident than in the novel's relentless pursuit, and zealous unmasking, of the false ideals of heroism into which its narrator and protagonist frequently stumbles. Idolatry is unquestionably Alton's besetting sin, castigated on numerous occasions throughout the text. Its danger is signaled, most graphically, in an episode set in the Dulwich Picture Gallery (Chapter VI), in which his susceptibility to "everything beautiful in form or colour" (69) is attached, first, to a Guido Reni painting of St. Sebastian, and then to Lillian, the middle-class woman who will become the "the idol of my imagination" for most of the ensuing narrative (131). The conspicuous elision of these two figures suggests that a common thread linking Alton's political aspirations with his aesthetic ideals is a tendency to substitute iconic emblems—of suffering or beauty—for the complex desires which stand behind them.[16] Kingsley appears to sociologize this fallibility by grounding Alton's excessive sensitivity to beauty in the material and cultural deprivations of his working-class Protestant upbringing, having Lillian's cousin Eleanor Lynedale—the alternative, wiser choice of female mentor—later conclude: "I should have known how enchanting, intoxicating, mere outward perfection must have been to one of your perceptions,

---

[15]   See "Goethe's Works" in *Critical and Miscellaneous Essays* [II], 392. Carlyle pursues a similar line of argument in regard to the practice of "lionism" in 'Sir Walter Scott": see *Critical and Miscellaneous Essays* [IV], 22–24.

[16]   Richard Menke reads the image of Saint Sebastian as both iconic of Alton's political martyrdom and a "powerful figure for … [his] connection to high culture", thus similarly linking his conflicting desires. See "Cultural Capital and the Scene of Rioting: Male Working-Class Authorship in *Alton Locke*," *Victorian Literature and Culture*, Vol. 28, No. 1 (2000), 93–96.

shut out so long as you had been from the beautiful in art and nature" (373). Yet, curiously, the novel reinscribes the theological terms of Alton's repression by describing his response to the Dulwich Gallery explicitly in terms of idolatry; it is here that he first succumbs to the seductive allure of aesthetic icons—an image of political martyrdom redolent of the "idolatry of painted saints", on the one hand, and an "apparition" evoking "simple admiration—idolatry if you will—of physical beauty," on the other (70–75). The charge of idolatry, moreover, becomes central to the novel's overarching critique of Chartism, and to its attempt to supplant Chartist ideology with the doctrine of Christian Socialism. From his retrospective autobiographical perspective, Alton convicts himself of having superstitiously venerated the aims of the Charter, as if it were "the idol of political institutions," a "talisman" created through "spirit-compelling spells" (110–111). Again, it is left to Eleanor, the character who comes closest to espousing Kingsley's proselytizing agenda, to cement this interpretation of Alton's story: "You regarded the Charter as an absolute end. You made a selfish and a self-willed idol of it. And therefore God's blessing did not rest on it or you" (378). The sin of idolatry, then, is not solely attributed to the social and psychological conditions of Alton's personal development, but also diagnoses a much broader, collective failure of political strategy (of which Alton's individual case is conceived as paradigmatic). Hence, the ideological critique mounted by Kingsley is overtly icono*clastic* in method.

Nevertheless, Kingsley preserves a Carlylean distinction between those idols which are merely fetishized visual signifiers and those which truly "symbolize"— express or embody through their external form—an indwelling substance worthy of worship (or "worthship," to employ Carlylean etymology).[17] The point of the Dulwich Gallery episode, and of what follows thereafter, is not that Alton is wrong to have *worshipped* the symbol of his aesthetic ideals and cultural aspirations (as if it were simply a delusion or blasphemy to exalt a fellow human being in this manner) but that he has chosen the wrong object, an "outward symbol" which is not "a sacrament of the loveliness within … but a hollow mask" (358). Had he been attracted to Eleanor instead of Lillian in this initial encounter, Alton's "idolatry" would most likely have been characterized as a form of "hero-worship," the non-pejorative Carlylean term which appears to encapsulate his abject submission to the former at the end of the novel (an experience of "utter trust, delight, submission, gratitude, awe" [358]), and, similarly, towards Dean Winnstay and the Prussian ambassador earlier in the text. It is clearly not part of Kingsley's authorial agenda to demystify Alton's idolatrous delusions in order to reconstruct him as a figure of autonomous working-class agency. Rather, he is used to demonstrate the Carlylean thesis that the capacity for hero-worship is an essential predicate of true heroism; thus, Alton's demonstrative subordination to his supposed spiritual superiors (who just happen also to be his social superiors)—presumably, an uncomfortable feature of his intellectual development for modern readers—is probably intended

---

17   See Carlyle, *On Heroes, Hero-Worship, and the Heroic in History*, 196.

to illustrate his growing fitness for the role of working-class hero.[18] Kingsley presents the "spiritual history" of his narrator as a process of development from primitive idolatry to more modern, "rational" forms of worship: a type of religious conversion narrative with broader phylogenetic implications (355). Like Carlyle's, Kingsley's iconoclasm is aimed not at the outright destruction of all visual icons, but towards a hermeneutic discrimination between true and false objects of idolatry. Just as the former often emphasized the value of portraiture as a hermeneutic tool in his biographical writings on historical heroes, so Kingsley structures Alton's intellectual development around scenes which foreground the importance of learning how to read pictorial images correctly: not only Guido's *Saint Sebastian*, but also the landscape by Copley Fielding which Alton overhears being discussed at an "intellectual" party in Chapter XXVI, and Raffael's [sic] cartoon *The Miraculous Draught of Fishes,* which enters his phantasmagorical "dream-land" in Chapter XXXVI.[19] For this reason, it is hardly surprising that the novel should also incorporate a literary "portrait" of Carlyle himself in the guise of Alton's early mentor, Sandy Mackaye: both under his proper name and in his fictive persona, Carlyle is one of the true (symbolic) idols whose teachings Alton properly reveres.

III

Carlyle's writings on heroism and hero-worship provided Kingsley not only with the central conceptual vocabulary of *Alton Locke*, but also with a specific historical model for its figuration of the working-class poet. In "The Hero as Man of Letters" (Lecture V of *On Heroes*), Carlyle selects three examples to illustrate the condition of this most characteristically modern heroic type, one of whom is his compatriot Robert Burns. Drawing upon an earlier and much longer essay of 1828, the biography of Burns contained within this lecture could be said to represent one of the most influential renditions of the figure of the working-class

---

[18] Throughout his 1840 lecture-series, Carlyle collapses the possibility of a binary distinction between "hero" and "hero-worshipper" as active and passive/receptive roles by defining the character of each of his chosen heroes precisely in terms of their capacity for worship, or "transcendent wonder," of the presence of God within Nature. Thus, he arrives at such tautological formulations as "only in a World of Heroes was there loyal Obedience to the Heroic". See *On Heroes, Hero-Worship and the Heroic in History*, 9 and 179.

[19] In his "Project of a National Exhibition of Scottish Portraits" (1854)—a prospectus for the future Scottish National Portrait Gallery—Carlyle revealed that one of his "primary wants" as a biographer-historian was to "procure a bodily likeness of the personage inquired after" (see *Critical and Miscellaneous Essays* [IV], 404). He refers to portraits, or to physiognomic details evidently derived from portraits, of several of the subjects featured in *On Heroes*, including Luther, Dante, and Rousseau. For an interesting critical account of the importance of portraiture to Carlyle's representation of the heroic, see Paul Barlow, "The Imagined Hero as Incarnate Sign: Thomas Carlyle and The Mythology of the "National Portrait" in Victorian Britain," *Art History*, Vol. 17, No. 4 (1994), 517–545.

intellectual produced during the nineteenth century. For Carlyle, Burns's heroic struggle against the adverse social conditions of his birth (both the material deprivation inherited through his class position and, equally important, the "spiritual paralysis" suffered as a more general consequence of the climate of eighteenth-century skepticism) casts his Life into the form of "tragedy"—"what we may call a great tragic sincerity"—with a particular admonitory value for aspiring autodidacts.[20] Although each of his three men of letters (the other two being Rousseau and Samuel Johnson) is, in some sense, an illustration of heroic failure, Burns's tragic biography suggests the significantly different tenor of the encounter with representative cultural conditions faced by writers of lower social class. In *Alton Locke*, Kingsley adapts some of the main features of this cautionary narrative, from the corruptions of patronage—a scenario replayed in Alton's relationship with Dean Winnstay—to the "fever of worldly Ambition" embodied by the temptations of "Lionism," with its attendant danger of artistic neglect, through to the climactic martyrdom endured by the poet-hero.[21] None of these features, of course, are unique to the experience of working-class writers, but in the tragic concatenation of their effects, the career of Alton Locke closely follows the Burnsian paradigm as fashioned by Carlyle.

So too, it appears, did the careers of many actual working-class poets and autobiographers of the period. The Lancastrian dialect poet, Samuel Bamford, for instance, claimed in his autobiographical record *Early Days* (1848–49) to have taken Burns "as an example," even imitating his "failings" while "striving to emulate" his "genius." Similarly, Thomas Cooper, the Chartist poet on whom Kingsley is thought to have most closely modeled Alton Locke, acknowledged in his well-known autobiography (published in 1872) a youthful absorption in Burns and Byron, a familiar combination amongst self-educated Radicals of the early-to-mid-nineteenth century.[22] Both Bamford and Cooper were correspondents with Carlyle and most likely familiar with his published accounts of Burns's cultural significance. Kingsley was certainly familiar with these accounts, as is witnessed not only in *Alton Locke*, but more explicitly in his companion essay on working-class poets, "Burns and his School," published in *The North British Review* for November 1851.

---

[20]   See "The Hero as Man of Letters," in *On Heroes, Hero-Worship and the Heroic in History*, 170, 188, 192; and "Burns," in *Critical and Miscellaneous Essays* [I], 199.

[21]   See "Burns" in *Critical and Miscellaneous Essays* [I], 227.

[22]   See *The Autobiography of Samuel Bamford. Volume One. Early Days*, ed. W.H. Chaloner (London: Frank Cass, 1967), 290; and *The Life of Thomas Cooper. Written By Himself*, 2nd ed. (London: Hodder and Stoughton, 1872), 42. On the prevalence of a self-destructive "Burns syndrome" amongst nineteenth-century working-class poets, see Martha Vicinus, *The Industrial Muse: A Study of Nineteenth Century British Working-Class Literature* (London: Croom Helm, 1974), 141, 189. Similarly, Nigel Cross describes Burns as "the most potent literary influence" on working-class poets of the mid-nineteenth century, and "the first writer with whom the working-class intellectual was happy to identify". See *The Common Writer: Life in Nineteenth-Century Grub Street* (Cambridge: Cambridge University Press, 1985), 129.

Here, Kingsley directly identifies Burns as the source, or head, of a body of poets defined by their self-conscious class identity, political "Radicalism," and tragically unfulfilled potential.[23] In making available the possibility of this "heroic" reading of Burns, Carlyle's role in shaping the identity of the working-class literary intellectual during the period of Chartism was considerable. Though routinely lambasted by twentieth-century critics as an undemocratic, authoritarian, even proto-fascistic ideology, the Carlylean doctrine of heroism and hero-worship was, in the nineteenth century, open to interpretation as either a Romantic-transcendental theory of the egalitarian essence of poetic genius or, conversely, an anthropological-historicist account of the representative function of the "great man."[24] Both readings were amenable to appropriation by working-class intellectuals, but it is the former upon which the Burnsian model of the hero as man of letters was based. By proclaiming that "[t]he largest soul of all the British lands came among us in the shape of a hard-handed Scottish Peasant," Carlyle signaled the availability of the category of "hero" to a much wider population than was customary at the time.[25] Indeed, the non-coincidence of genius and rank is a feature of the Burnsian myth, which becomes central to Carlylean thought in general: Burns's famous lines "The rank is but the guinea's-stamp, /The Man's the gowd for a' that" are taken by Carlyle and Kingsley to suggest both a specifically "democratic," class-conscious ideal of the heroic and a metaphysical dialectic of essence and appearance underpinning all of their writings on this subject, as we have seen.[26] In this way, it could be argued that Carlyle's

---

[23] See Kingsley, "Burns and His School", 149–83. For details of their correspondence with Carlyle, see *The Autobiography of Samuel Bamford*, 25–34; and *The Life of Thomas Cooper*, 281–282.

[24] The debate over the politics of Carlyle's theory of heroism and hero-worship, and its relationship to broader trends in nineteenth-century historiography towards the elevation of the "Great Man" or "world-historical individual", has a long and sensitive history, which I do not wish to simplify here. It suffices to say that I am arguing, in this context, against the reduction of Carlyle's theory to a "blind cult of the great man" (see Pamela McCallum, "Misogyny, the Great Man, and Carlyle's *The French Revolution*: The Epic as Pastiche," *Cultural Critique*, Vol. 14 [1989–90], 172), or uncritical affirmation of the "exceptional individual" (Alan Steinweis, "Hitler and Carlyle's "Historical Greatness,"" *History Today*, Vol. 45, No. 6 [1995], 34), and would instead emphasize its representative and anthropological functions, as discussed in Philip Rosenberg, *The Seventh Hero: Thomas Carlyle and the Theory of Radical Activism* (Cambridge, MA: Harvard University Press, 1974), 188–193; and Ruth apRoberts, *The Ancient Dialect: Thomas Carlyle and Comparative Religion* (Berkeley and Los Angeles: University of California Press, 1988), 73.

[25] See "The Hero as Man of Letters" in *On Heroes, Hero-Worship and the Heroic in History*, 188.

[26] Burns's lines (from the song "A Man's a Man for a' that" [1795]), are, indeed, probably the unacknowledged source-text of Carlyle's extended use of the metaphor of financial currency in his lecture series *On Heroes*. See *The Poems and Songs of Robert Burns*, ed. Andrew Lang (London: Methuen & Co., 1896), 580–81. For examples of direct quotation from this text, see Carlyle, "The Hero as Man of Letters," in *On Heroes, Hero-Worship and the Heroic in History*, 194; and Kingsley, *Alton Locke*, 220.

theory privileges (or alternatively fetishizes) Burns as a hero of peasant stock, and thus supposedly an embodiment of essential "man," over more elevated exempla, as it is through such a figure that the necessary gap between an appreciation of the true spiritual worth of the hero and superficial worldly estimations of his value is most vividly portrayed. Hence, Carlyle may have appeared to contemporary readers as specifically legitimizing the potential for a distinct working-class heroic ideal.

IV

Kingsley based his fictional autobiography of Alton Locke, then, upon a recently-established narrative paradigm of the literary career archetypically experienced by the working-class or peasant poet, upon which Carlyle's influence was formative. Burns is certainly prominent in the list of historical precedents for Alton's experience, but more contemporary figures referenced in the novel itself include his fellow Scottish poets John Bethune and William Thom, both of whom fit the mold of tragic suffering and early "martyrdom," as Kingsley details at greater length in "Burns and His School."[27] Alton is periodically reminded (so reminding us) of the lessons to be learned from such figures, yet seems destined to repeat their mistakes. In addition, as noted above, the poet Thomas Cooper, whose career was to follow a rather different, more extended, trajectory is a source for many of the details of Alton's Chartist activism.[28] What Kingsley fashions out of these various models, however, is a considerably more sustained and self-conscious account of the *formation* of a working-class intellectual consciousness than had hitherto been produced. *Alton Locke* is probably the first novel in English to apply the Germanic form of the *Bildungsroman* to represent the maturation of a working-class protagonist, notwithstanding the fact that its author was of unambiguously middle-class origin and professional status. While some authentic Chartist fiction, such as Thomas Martin Wheeler's contemporaneous novel *Sunshine and Shadow: A Tale of the Nineteenth Century* (serialized in *The Northern Star* in 1849–50), was also, at this time, beginning to employ narratives of individual character development in conjunction with ideological polemic and socio-historical analysis, its categorization within the genre of "Bildungsroman" by modern critics tends to be of an altogether looser kind. Certainly, in the case of Wheeler's novel, the unfolding

---

[27]   See Kingsley, "Burns and his School," 174–179. For a discussion of Bethune as a possible model for Alton Locke, see Brian Maidment, *The Poorhouse Fugitives: Self-taught Poets and Poetry in Victorian Britain* (Manchester: Carcanet Press, 1987), 138.

[28]   The most notable source material being Cooper's imprisonment for his role in inciting a riot at a Chartist gathering in Hanley (in the Potteries) on August 15, 1842. For his later account of these events, see *The Life of Thomas Cooper*, 191–213. For a biographical account of Kingsley's friendship with Cooper, and its influence on the composition of *Alton Locke*, see Brenda Colloms, *Charles Kingsley: The Lion of Eversley* (London: Constable, 1975), 101–102. Cooper's presence in the novel is also discussed by Nigel Cross (*The Common Writer*, 154) and Richard Menke ("Cultural Capital and The Scene of Rioting," 91).

experiences of the protagonist Arthur Morton run parallel to, and illuminate, the changing political fortunes of Chartism, but the process of intellectual reflection born out of this history is not projected onto Morton himself in any strong sense.[29]

Contrastingly, from the beginning of Kingsley's narrative, Alton refers frequently to the process of his "self-development," to a "self-imposed toil of intellectual improvement," and "inward thirst for mental self-improvement," which are reflected in both the content of his early educational aspirations and in the very form of the narrative through which these aspirations are recalled (30, 42, 53). In part, the form of this narrative draws upon the broader Victorian genre of "self-help" writing, Alton's youthful desire being to "educate myself and rise in life" (38). Yet the novel is also conceived as a critique of this genre, which aims to demonstrate that the two sides of its equation are by no means mutually beneficial: Alton's intellectual development is shown to be in conflict with his social ambition, an unavowed desire to transcend his class origins. Alton thus becomes conscious, from his retrospective standpoint, of embodying a desire for self-development which does not quite match the criteria for successful "improvement" within the self-help tradition. This form of working-class self-improvement is more likely to entail material suffering than success, adding to "an ever-increasing army of martyrs" on whose behalf Alton wishes his own narrative to speak (42):

> Ay; but where are the stories of those who have not risen – of all the noble geniuses who have ended in desperation, drunkenness, starvation, suicide, because no one would take the trouble of lifting them up, and enabling them to walk in the path which nature had marked out for them? (49)

Though the story of Alton's literary career does not precisely match this description—he is, in fact, lifted out of his "desperation" by the redemptive Eleanor at the end of the novel—there is sufficient similarity to indicate its divergence not only from the Smilesian self-help narrative, but also from the contemporary bourgeois version of the literary Bildungsroman, a genre in which the intellectual apprenticeship of a fictive author is traced from youthful illusions to mature wisdom and broadly successful social integration: Dickens's *David Copperfield* (1849–1850), for instance, could be read as a conflation of these two forms.[30] It is important to note that, unlike the hero of Dickens's novel, Alton never reaches a teleological point of intellectual maturity or worldly success, from which the preceding narrative of his self-development can be surveyed, but instead dies at a young age of typhus-fever on an emigrant voyage to Texas, which even had it been completed would obviously have marked the failure of his accommodation within British society of the 1840s (this eventuality, of course, is not recorded directly in his autobiography).

---

[29] See Thomas Martin Wheeler, *Sunshine and Shadow* in *Chartist Fiction*, ed. Ian Haywood, 65–200 (Aldershot: Ashgate, 1999).

[30] See, most obviously, Samuel Smiles, *Self-Help; with Illustrations of Character and Conduct* (London: John Murray, 1860). Gagnier describes *David Copperfield* as "*the autobiography of the self-made author*" (original emphasis) in *Subjectivities*, 33.

Alton Locke's "history of ... mental growth" is thus poignantly presented as a narrative of truncated development, of intellectual potential unrealized (70). Similarly, in "Burns and His School," Kingsley described the poetry of Burns as "only the *disjecta membra poetae*; hints of a great might-have-been," borrowing a metaphor of the fragmented or mutilated body—the poetic corpus—directly from Carlyle's lecture "The Hero as Poet."[31] For Carlyle, this metaphor makes an analogy with sculpture which expresses the materially-mediated and conditional nature of all artistic production: "The sculptor cannot set his own free Thought before us; but his Thought as he could translate it into the stone that was given, with the tools that were given. *Disjecta membra* are all that we find of any Poet, or of any man."[32] But Carlyle also applies this analogy to the specific conditions of working-class literary production in his writings on Burns: Burns's poetry, he wrote in his 1828 essay, was but "a poor mutilated fraction of what was in him; brief, broken glimpses of a genius that could never show itself complete; that wanted all things for completeness: culture, leisure, true effort, nay even length of life"; and the same figure is repeated, twelve years later, in "The Hero as Man of Letters:" "His writings, all that he *did* under such obstructions, are only a poor fragment of him."[33] These images of fractured or dismembered wholeness suggest the awareness of both writers of the difficulties of adapting the Goethean ideal of *Bildung*—the development of a complex, multiform subjectivity towards a state of harmonious self-integration—to the material circumstances of working-class self-education.[34] In place of organic totality, the developmental narrative of the working-class writer is arrested in the inanimate posture of an unfinished statue— perhaps a broken idol.

Both Carlyle and Kingsley, indeed, explicitly compared the differing developmental trajectories of middle-class and working-class writers, though not always to the disadvantage of the latter. In his essay "Corn-Law Rhymes" (1832), for example, Carlyle offers a rather more positive account of the literary

---

[31]   See Kingsley, "Burns and His School," 154.

[32]   Carlyle, "The Hero as Poet," in *On Heroes, Hero-Worship and the Heroic in History*, 110–111.

[33]   See Carlyle, "Burns," in *Critical and Miscellaneous Essays* [I], 201; and "The Hero as Man of Letters" in *On Heroes, Hero-Worship and the Heroic in History*, 190.

[34]   Critical definitions of the terms *Bildung* and *Bildungsroman* vary in their emphases, but, according to Martin Swales, the former constitutes "the self-realization of the individual in his wholeness", and the latter is "a novel form that is animated by a concern for the whole man unfolding organically in all his complexity and richness ... a total growth process": see *The German Bildungsroman from Wieland to Hesse* (Princeton, NJ: Princeton University Press, 1978), 14–15. Moreover, for Jeffrey L. Sammons, the "concept of Bildung is intensely bourgeois", a product of "the early bourgeois, humanistic concept of the shaping of the individual self from its innate potentialities through acculturation and social experience to the threshold of maturity": see "The Bildungsroman for Nonspecialists: An Attempt at a Classification" in *Reflection and Action: Essays on the Bildungsroman*, ed. James Hardin, 41–42 (Columbia: University of South Carolina Press, 1991).

"development" of Ebenezer Elliot, another poet of the laboring class as he is somewhat inaccurately portrayed, going so far as to suggest that "it is actually, in these strange days, no special misfortune to be trained up among the Uneducated classes, and not among the Educated." Here, virtue is made of a paucity of "cultivation" when set against the dangers of over-refinement associated with a decadent ruling class: even Burns has the advantage over Byron, Carlyle suggests, in respect of his vigorous "natural" growth, a contrast implying a predictably gendered opposition between the rude peasant and effete aristocrat.[35] Similarly, in Kingsley's first novel, *Yeast: A Problem* (1848), a text which rehearses many of the key debates of *Alton Locke*, the intellectual development of its middle-class protagonist, Lancelot Smith, is juxtaposed with the aspirations of the self-educated gamekeeper, Tregarva, an earlier figure of the working-class intellectual. The novel can be read as satirizing the fashionable bourgeois cultural ideal of *Bildung*, and its literary exponents, by reducing it to a seemingly mechanical sequence of hollow gestures:

> Lancelot had found Byron and Shelley pall on his taste, and commenced devouring Bulwer and worshipping *Ernest Maltravers*. He had left Bulwer for old ballads and romances, and Mr. Carlyle's reviews; was next alternately chivalry-mad and Germany-mad; was now reading hard at physical science; and on the whole trying to become a great man, without any very clear notion of what a great man ought to be.[36]

It is through the figure of Tregarva that Lancelot learns to appreciate the true importance of self-development as an individual right to educational opportunities which cannot be restricted by social class. Indeed, he comes to place a "right to develop" at the very center of the unwritten contract between Labor and the modern industrial State: "If man living in civilized society has one right which he can demand it is this, that the State which exists by his labour, shall enable him to develop, or at least not hinder his developing, his whole faculties to their very utmost, however lofty that may be."[37] Thus, far from being synonymous with the whims of bourgeois intellectual fashion, the ideal of self-development becomes an organic imperative—implied within the novel's titular metaphor of political fermentation—which Lancelot recognizes he has no right to "hinder" within the working class. For his part, Tregarva is at pains not to conflate his desire for cultural self-improvement with material social advancement in the manner of the young Alton Locke:

> "I want to rise; I want those like me to rise with me. Let the rich be as rich as they will. – I, and those like me, covet not money, but manners. Why should not the workman be a gentleman, and a workman still? Why are they to be shut out from all that is beautiful, and delicate and winning, and stately?"[38]

---

[35]   See Carlyle, "Corn-Law Rhymes," in *Critical and Miscellaneous Essays* [III], 159–164.
[36]   Charles Kingsley, *Yeast: A Problem* (London: John W. Parker and Son, 1851), 2–3.
[37]   Ibid., 89.
[38]   Ibid., 225.

Elevation within the cultural or intellectual fields, then, does not, and neither should it, necessarily lead to a redrawing of the boundaries of social class, with a concomitant shift in class allegiances, nor apparently to any significant redistribution of material resources. This is a view which undoubtedly corresponds to Kingsley's own position, though it somewhat conceals the tensions which later surface around the same issue in *Alton Locke*.

Referring to *Alton Locke*, in a letter dated January 13th 1851, Kingsley wrote that "[t]he moral of my book is, that the working man who tries to get on, to desert his class and rise above it, enters into a lie, and leaves God's path for his own – with consequences." Further, he specifically objects to the cries of "get on" or "rise in life," which he ascribes to "the very increasing impossibility of being anything but brutes while they struggle below." It is the immiseration of the condition of the working-class, he contends, that produces these manifestations of discontent, which, in turn, threaten to destabilize the boundaries of class society. Conversely, these boundaries would be reinforced by such measures as sanitary reform and the educational provision to working men of "the means of developing their own latent capabilities."[39] Kingsley's eagerness to distinguish between working-class intellectual development and material advancement of the kind promised by the ideology of self-help could, then, be seen to reflect a certain conservative anxiety about the potential fluidity of class identities in modern society, while, at the same time, paying unusual respect to the autonomy of working-class culture. Both sides of this ambivalence should be maintained in any assessment of the ideological character of Kingsley's construction of the working-class intellectual. On the one hand, his hostility to the popular self-help gospels of "getting on" and "rising in life" could be said to condemn Alton Locke to a Burnsian mythography of tragic failure: a state of arrested material development hard to separate entirely from the causes of his cultural deprivation, which, again, may be contrasted instructively with an autobiographical narrative such as *David Copperfield*, belonging to exactly the same historical moment. On the other hand, Kingsley's positive emphasis upon the solidarity of working-class intellectuals, and his assertion of their capacity for immanent cultural development, may carry some genuinely radical implications. If, at one level, the analogy with Burns commits Alton to material poverty and intellectual fragmentation, at another it endorses the possibility of working-class culture developing autonomously from within its own resources. In "Burns and his School," Kingsley wrote of Burns's influence on "working men:"

> He first proved that it was possible to become a poet and a cultivated man, without deserting his class, either in station or in sympathies; nay, that the healthiest and noblest elements of a lowly born poet's mind might be, perhaps certainly must be, the very feelings and thoughts which he brought up with him from below, not those which he received from above, in the course of his artificial culture.[40]

---

[39]   See *Charles Kingsley: His Letters and Memories of His Life, ed. By His Wife*, Vol. I (London: C. Kegan Paul & Co., 1878), 247–248.

[40]   Kingsley, "Burns and His School," 164.

Here, then, the development of "culture" is not to be conceived as the acquisition of an extrinsic, commodified object, reached through upward social struggle, but as a natural process of self-cultivation "from below." This possibility may well be construed as a model for the formation of the "organic intellectual" in something approaching the Gramscian sense of the term, and, contrary to some recent interpretations of *Alton Locke*, Kingsley's fictional exploration of the tensions between class loyalty and social aspiration does not primarily work to undermine such a figure.[41] Rather, this organicist model is a measure by which we are invited to judge the progress of Alton's developmental narrative, its obvious failings as well as its serious aspirations. Indeed, far from dismantling the figure of the organic working-class intellectual, I would argue that Kingsley's *Alton Locke* did much to shape its iconic embodiment in the mid-nineteenth century and beyond.

V

There remain, nevertheless, some troubling questions about both the efficacy and legitimacy of Kingsley's employment of such narrative forms as autobiography, the *Bildungsroman*, and the discourse of self-improvement as means of representing working-class subjectivity, as modern commentary on these genres has tended to suggest. A dominant view, endorsed by such influential critics as Martha Vicinus and Regenia Gagnier, is that these narrative forms unavoidably inscribe a bourgeois mode of subjectivity—introspective, self-interested, and domestic in orientation—that is fundamentally alien and antagonistic to working-class experience. In *The Industrial Muse: A Study of Nineteenth Century British Working-Class Literature* (1974), Vicinus sharply distinguishes between two main strands of Chartist writing—one public and polemical, the other personal and educative in orientation—and sees the latter as signaling the political retrenchment of the movement. In *Subjectivities: A History of Self-Representation in Britain, 1832–1920* (1991), Gagnier accepts this account of the introspective, developmental self (which she labels "the modern literary subject") as a depoliticizing feature of middle-class identity-formation, but then attempts to show how working-class

---

[41] For his definition of the categories of "organic" and "traditional" intellectual, see Antonio Gramsci, *Selections From The Prison Notebooks*, edited and translated by Quintin Hoare and Geoffrey Nowell Smith (London: Lawrence and Wishart, 1971, repr. 2003), 5–23. Evan M. Gottlieb has recently applied these Gramscian terms to a reading of *Alton Locke*, which reduces the novel to "a middle-class fantasy of the working-class's inability to retain its organic intellectuals": see "Charles Kingsley, The Romantic Legacy, and The Unmaking of The Working-Class Intellectual," *Victorian Literature and Culture*, Vol. 29, No. 1 (2001), 58. My disagreements with Gottlieb's reading are extended later in this essay. Though less dismissive than Gottlieb, Richard Menke has also recently presented Kingsley as unsympathetic to the concept of "working-class culture." See "Cultural Capital and the Scene of Rioting," 97.

autobiographical forms have typically differed from this model.[42] Critical histories of autobiography have, indeed, routinely associated the "rise" of the genre during the early nineteenth century with an emerging middle-class cultural hegemony. As David Vincent points out, this coupling is inherently problematic for the status of working-class autobiographies, which began to proliferate during the 1840s, as it raises the question "of whether in embracing literature as a means of discovering itself the working class had sacrificed its cultural independence at the very outset." Thus, "rather than resolving the question of class identity," as the use of autobiographical form could be supposed to attempt, it was the form itself which "highlighted the ambiguity of the early working class culture." Unlike Vicinus and Gagnier, however, Vincent does not interpret the Chartist culture of self-improvement as merely epiphenomenal, a damaging assimilation of bourgeois ideological norms. Rather, he identifies within the 1830s and 40s a working-class discourse of self-improvement developing alongside, though in partial resistance to, the quasi-official middle-class endeavor to promote the "diffusion of useful knowledge" amongst the industrial workforce.[43]

In the case of *Alton Locke*, of course, the generic problem of working-class autobiography is exacerbated by the fact that Kingsley's fictive "autobiography" of a working-class poet is manufactured by a middle-class novelist, thus leaving it open to the charge of reproducing a bourgeois model of subjectivity whilst claiming to speak in an authentically working-class voice. The act of imaginative ventriloquism required for such a venture would seem doubly deceptive, twice removed from its authorial origins: a middle-class simulation of a working-class imitation of a middle-class form.[44] Not surprisingly, even Vincent, generally sympathetic to the developmental discourse of working-class autobiography, reads *Alton Locke* as an attempt to "impose" the author's own heteronomous "definition" of working-class experience onto his narratorial persona.[45] At one level, this is patently true. Nevertheless, it is worth noting the complexity of the process of mediation by which this scenario came about. It seems clear that Kingsley did not simply foist an alien narrative form onto his imaginary "tailor and poet," but rather adapted elements of both content and form from contemporary working-class autobiographies; the list of possible source-texts including Thomas Carter's *Memoirs of a Working Man* (1845), Christopher Thomson's *The Autobiography of an Artisan* (1846–47), Alexander Somerville's *The Autobiography of a Working Man* (1848), and Bamford's two autobiographical volumes, *Passages in the*

---

[42]   See Vicinus, *The Industrial Muse*, 109, 140; and Gagnier, *Subjectivities*, 28, 42–43.

[43]   See David Vincent, *Bread, Knowledge and Freedom: A Study of Nineteenth-Century Working Class Autobiography* (London: Europa Publications Limited, 1981), 37, 135, 159–160, 164, 194–198.

[44]   Menke refers—harshly in my view—to "the feebleness of Kingsley's cross-class ventriloquism": see "Cultural Capital and The Scene of Rioting," 97.

[45]   See Vincent, *Bread, Knowledge and Freedom*, 2.

Life of a Radical (1839–41) and *Early Days* (1848–49).[46] Kingsley had almost certainly read, and was responding critically to, Carter's autobiography, which, as Nigel Cross points out, recounts the experiences of a self-educated tailor, and was commended by its publisher Charles Knight for "the rational and contented tone of mind with which the writer looked upon his own vocation in life:" in this instance, indeed, *Alton Locke* is a more subversive adaptation than its working-class model. Moreover, Somerville, a more politically conscious autobiographer, is referred to by name in Alton's text.[47] *Alton Locke*'s ventriloquism of working-class subjectivity, in other words, is more precisely derived from the pre-existing autobiographical culture of the 1840s than Vincent's notion of external "imposition" would suggest. In turn, Kingsley's narrative can be shown to have had a not insignificant influence on subsequent working-class autobiographies, most notably Cooper's *The Life of Thomas Cooper. Written By Himself* (1872).[48] The ideological effects of *Alton Locke*'s peculiar authorial conceit—amplified by the fact that it was published anonymously (thus without any apparent external mediation) in its first edition—are over-simplified by suggestions that the novel suppresses a putatively authentic working-class voice through a middle-class subterfuge. A more productive model for understanding the possible effects of this conceit may be found in Brian Maidment's observation that, throughout the first half of the nineteenth century, "self-taught writing was almost invariably mediated into public consciousness through the filter of its middle-class supporters."[49] In his authorship of *Alton Locke*, Kingsley could be said to adopt a similar mediatory stance by posing as a vehicle of transmission for working-class self-expression; a role analogous to the editorial and biographical apparatuses constructed for many early-nineteenth-century working-class poets by their middle-class sponsors, though less visible in its agency. The result is at once a purer form of mediation and, by virtue of its self-effacement, a more subtle exercise of control: a dynamic which certainly reproduces the relations of power between poet and patron, but not uncritically so for Kingsley is implicitly claiming to be a more sympathetic

---

[46] For full details of these, and other contemporary, autobiographies, see *The Autobiography of the Working Class: An Annotated Critical Bibliography. Volume 1: 1790–1900*, eds John Burnett, David Vincent, and David Mayall (Brighton: The Harvester Press, 1984). The editors of this volume conclude that the "autobiography of self-improvement" was, in fact, the most "characteristic" form of working-class self-representation during the nineteenth century: "improvement in the moral and intellectual state of the writer", rather than in the form of "upward mobility". They also dispute the assumption that autobiography was an indigenously middle-class literary form ("Introduction", xvi–xvii).

[47] See Thomas Carter, *Memoirs of a Working Man* (London: Charles Knight & Co., 1845), x; Cross, *The Common Writer*, 152; and Kingsley, *Alton Locke*, 278.

[48] For the suggestion that Cooper's autobiography may have been influenced by *Alton Locke*, see Cross, *The Common Writer*, 154. I return to this point later in the essay.

[49] Brian Maidment, "Essayists and Artizans: The Making of Nineteenth-Century Self-Taught Poets," *Literature and History*, Vol. 9, No. 1 (Spring, 1983), 84.

medium of the working-class text than the middle-class patrons who succeed in censoring Alton's poetry within the narrative itself.

The emergence of a recognizable body of working-class autobiographies during the 1840s, however, is not the only contemporary generic context in which the narrative form of *Alton Locke* should be considered. As I have already noted, another genre to which the novel belongs, but in relation to which it is less frequently considered, is that of the *Bildungsroman*, a novelistic form of developmental narrative introduced into British literary culture partly under the auspices of Carlyle's 1824 translation of Goethe's *Wilhelm Meister*. Here, we are on stronger ground in assuming that Kingsley's narrative of working-class "self-development" transposes a specifically bourgeois mode of subject-formation for there is no prior body of working-class fiction (to my knowledge) which the novel can be seen to engage. Indeed, Kingsley goes out of his way to situate Alton's experience within the recently established conventions of the middle-class Bildungsroman hero, cramming the text with allusions to a network of comparable novels. In addition to the more obvious Carlylean sources—*Sartor Resartus* and *Wilhelm Meister* itself—the novel contains direct references to Edward Bulwer Lytton's *Ernest Maltravers* (1837) and William Makepeace Thackeray's *History of Pendennis* (1848–50), two recent and prominent examples of the literary Bildungsroman.[50] The presumptively middle-class reader of the novel is thus invited to chart the course of Alton's intellectual development in the same terms as those of his middle-class male *confrères*. One chapter, entitled "Pegasus in Harness" (XX), for instance, implicitly compares Alton's experience of becoming a "hack writer," forced by economic necessity to "try and serve God and Mammon," with that of Thackeray's Arthur Pendennis, a designedly "unheroic" hero whose career as a journalist reveals some of the moral compromises exacted by modern literary commerce (188). As a hack-writer for the *Weekly Warwhoop*, a fictive caricature of Feargus O'Connor's Chartist newspaper *The Northern Star*, Alton faces not only a similar threat to the integrity of his "moral sense" (215), but also, when required "to sit scribbling off my thoughts anyhow in prose," to his very status as a poet (189). In *Pendennis*, Thackeray had examined the process by which a Romantic poetic sensibility is forced to adjust itself to the mechanical routines of "prose labour," and his emphasis upon the prosaic character of modern authorship (both literally and figuratively speaking) is, in fact, a common motif

---

[50]   For a recent discussion of the two latter novels in relation to the emergence of a distinct genre of narratives of literary development during the 1830s and 1840s, see Richard Salmon, "The Genealogy of the Literary *Bildungsroman*: Edward Bulwer-Lytton and W.M. Thackeray," *Studies in the Novel*, Vol. XXXVI, No. 1 (2004), 41–55. Though introduced in Germany during the first two decades of the nineteenth century, the word "Bildungsroman" was not in itself widely used, either in its country of origin or elsewhere, before the late nineteenth century: it is used here, then, in a slightly anachronistic way to re-translate a body of writing in English influenced by Goethe's foundational text, however indirectly.

of the early-Victorian literary *Bildungsroman*.[51] In this section of the novel, then, Alton is rendered as much an embodiment of the generalized condition of the literary hack as a class-specific Chartist poet. In Chapter XXV, Kingsley takes intertextual reference to the contemporary *Bildungsroman* even further by having Sandy Mackaye actually present Alton with a copy of Bulwer's *Ernest Maltravers* and invite him to draw a moral lesson from its treatment of the figure of Castruccio Cesarini, an Italian poet who goes mad from an obsessive desire for literary celebrity.[52] Alton duly attends to this "fearful story", but in the following chapter, "The Triumphant Author," is shown at the height of his worldly success, attending a social gathering of "great men" of the kind satirized in Bulwer's novel (236). Again, this episode suggests that Alton's narrative draws upon broader cultural sources than the paradigm of working-class intellectual development established by Carlyle: in fact, the destructive consequences of "Lionism" were featured as prominently in the bourgeois literary *Bildungsroman* as in Carlyle's biography of Burns.[53]

Reading *Alton Locke* as a *Bildungsroman*, as we have also seen, enables us to apprehend the ways in which Kingsley's figure of the working-class author *fails* to assimilate the generic conventions of middle-class cultural development. Most notably, the fact that the hero's premature death is recorded at the end of the novel would seem to indicate, as suggested earlier, a violent truncation of the developmental narrative quite unlike the endings of any of its designated intertexts. In accordance with his use of the Burnsian archetype, Kingsley could, in some ways, be said to arrest the development of his hero in the ""Werterean" stage" of youthful sorrows (or its immediate aftermath) from which the middle-class *Bildungsroman* hero—such as his own Lancelot Smith—is usually allowed to emerge. Alton himself categorizes "that peculiar melancholy of intellectual youth" from which he suffers as "Werterism," a "nickname" he ascribes to Carlyle, for whom it signified a partial and transient phase in the process of *Bildung*, not to be confused with the

---

[51]   See William Makepeace Thackeray, *The History of Pendennis. His Fortunes and Misfortunes, His Friends and His Greatest Enemy*, ed. John Sutherland (Oxford and New York: Oxford University Press, 1994), 416, 449–450. In *David Copperfield*, Dickens also foregrounds the prosaic routines of modern literary production, albeit from a different professional standpoint, as reflected in his criticism of Thackeray during the "Dignity of Literature" controversy of 1850. On this aspect of the novel, see Jennifer Ruth, "Mental Capital, Industrial Time, and the Professional in *David Copperfield*," in *Novel: A Forum on Fiction*, Vol. 32, No. 3 (1999), 303–330.

[52]   See Lord Lytton, *Ernest Maltravers* (London: Routledge, 1873), 289.

[53]   Heavily indebted to *Ernest Maltravers*, G.H. Lewes's *Ranthorpe* (1847) is another contemporary novel of literary development preoccupied with the dangers of "Lionism" to the emerging professional author. See George Henry Lewes, *Ranthorpe*, ed. Barbara Smalley (Athens: Ohio University Press, 1974), 47–77. The phenomenon of "Literary Lionism" is described by Harriet Martineau in a review-essay for *The London and Westminster Review*, Vol. XXXII, no. II (April, 1839), 261–281.

mature teaching of Goethe (95).[54] This deviation from generic norms can be taken to imply the necessary incompleteness of working-class intellectual development at the moment of writing, as is suggested in "Burns and His School," yet it also reveals a contradictory preference for external intervention within the process of subject-formation over the immanent unfolding of intellectual potential which Kingsley passionately supported in his critical essays and correspondence. Rather than reaching a position of intellectual maturity through a primarily autonomous self-development, Alton undergoes a spiritual conversion to Christian Socialism at the hands of Eleanor, his true middle-class "idol:" the novel thus meshes the new genres of the *Bildungsroman* and self-developmental autobiography with a much older form of religious conversion narrative—which, ironically, was a more traditional medium for working-class life-writing.[55]

An equally striking example of the way in which Alton's class identity and political affiliation sit uneasily within the developmental paradigm of the *Bildungsroman* can be found in the well-known dream-sequence of Chapter XXXVI ("Dreamland"), an episode directly preparatory to this conversion process and symbolizing its urgent necessity. Here, Kingsley deploys an evolutionary scientific schema of organic development to convey anxieties about the detrimental consequences to individual subject-formation from the kinds of collective political identity espoused through Alton's involvement with Chartism. The sequence betrays a punitive logic by which Alton's preceding quest for intellectual self-improvement unravels in a degenerative nightmare of primeval dissolution. Regressing "to the lowest point of created life; a madrepore," Alton undergoes a horrifying loss of the "individuality" which he has previously craved: "I was not one thing, but many things – a crowd of innumerable polypi; and I grew and grew, and the more I grew the more I divided, and multiplied thousand and ten thousand-fold" (336). This fear of multiplicity, linked by causal effect to the trajectory of growth, suggests a political unconscious at work below the surface form of the *Bildungsroman*. The message would seem to be that individual development is ultimately incompatible with the class aspirations represented by Chartism; that collective growth is a monstrosity, leading to the mere aggregation of the "crowd," on the one hand, and the atomization of individual subjects on the other; and that, hence, Alton's developmental narrative must be symbolically reversed in order for it to be reconstructed along less threatening lines. As may be already apparent, though, Alton's premature death also forecloses the successful completion of this program of ideological reconstruction.

---

[54]   For Carlyle's views on the place of *The Sorrows of Young Werther* (1774) in Goethe's literary development, see "Goethe" (1828), in *Critical and Miscellaneous Essays* [I], 217–224; and "Goethe's Works" in *Critical and Miscellaneous Essays* [II], 430–431.

[55]   For a discussion of the tradition of spiritual autobiography and its significance both to *Alton Locke* and working-class culture, see Vincent, *Bread, Knowledge and Freedom*, 18–29.

VI

Criticism of *Alton Locke* as, in crude terms, a spurious middle-class fabrication of working-class autobiography contains such an obvious element of truth that it has often detracted from the underlying significance and complexity of its contribution to the formation of the working-class intellectual as a modern cultural figure. Recently, for example, Evan Gottlieb has charged Kingsley with "construct[ing] a vision of the working-class intellectual that, appearances to the contrary, is safely apolitical," a "fantasy working-class poet" designed "to justify the reign of the middle class." For Gottlieb, it seems, Kingsley's real purpose is to defuse the radical potential of the "organic" working-class intellectual by exposing his tendency to compromise with the structures of social and economic power which anchor the "traditional" intellectual of the ruling class. He thus conceives of the novel as an attempt to "unmake" the working-class intellectual, rather than to chart the course of his self-formation, as I have suggested. There are two main reasons for questioning this dismissive approach to *Alton Locke*. Firstly, it is a reading which directly conflates Kingsley's authorial stance with Dean Winnstay's censorship of Alton's poetry—a position which is evidently questioned within the text—and also neglects his externally-declared support for working-class cultural autonomy (however equivocal the grounds of this support may be).[56] Secondly, and more fundamentally even, this reading fails to notice the centrality of the organicist model of cultural development to the form of *Alton Locke*, whether it be read primarily within the context of the *Bildungsroman* or the autobiographical discourse of self-improvement. Thus, whilst the Gramscian distinction between "organic" and "traditional" intellectuals is by no means an inappropriate schema through which to view Kingsley's text, we should avoid dichotomizing these labels in ways that fail to acknowledge the novel's part in helping to shape the very terms of intellectual culture from which these labels have emerged. Rather than deducing from Kingsley's own social and professional status—that of the archetypal traditional intellectual, rooted in the quasi-natural social function of the rural clergy—a latent antagonism towards the overt class affiliation of the organic intellectual, a more fluid encounter between these two intellectual types can be observed within the authorial conceit of *Alton Locke*.[57] This novel, one might say, constitutes a traditional intellectual's impersonation, or ventriloquism, of an organic intellectual, not for the effect of ironically undermining the narratorial voice, as was already common within the contemporary genre of fictional autobiography, but in a self-conscious and committed act of moral sympathy—a gesture resembling perhaps Kingsley's famous declaration before a public meeting

---

[56] See Gottlieb, "Charles Kingsley, the Romantic Legacy, and the Unmaking of the Working-Class Intellectual," 51, 55, 57–58, 60–61.

[57] For a biographical account of Kingsley's professional life as an Anglican priest in the rural parish of Eversley, see Colloms, *Charles Kingsley*, 56–87.

in 1849: "I am a Church of England parson ... and a Chartist!"[58] This, of course, is not to deny the possibility that such a gesture works to reinscribe the logic of class distinction which it appears to break down, for example by occluding an assumption of the capacity for ideological disinterest on the part of the real author of the text. Gramsci, indeed, saw all intellectuals as organically related to their material class interests, not exclusively those of working-class origin: in this sense, the term "traditional intellectual" is something of a misnomer, categorizing an organic intellectual function which has become naturalized within the prevailing social order.[59] Nevertheless, I would argue that far from serving to demonstrate the impossibility of the organic working-class intellectual, caught between the conflicting demands of class loyalty and intellectual or social aspiration, *Alton Locke* uses this very dilemma, derived from the example of Carlyle's "tragic" mythography of Burns, to offer powerful support to the cultural dissemination of such a figure.

That Kingsley's novel played a significant role in shaping perceptions of the working-class intellectual throughout the nineteenth century can be shown from the influence which it exerted over writers of varying social backgrounds and class identities across a considerable length of time. Its effects may be felt most strikingly in the autobiographical narrative of a poet who is commonly acknowledged as a major source for the figure of Alton Locke. The career of Thomas Cooper, who began his working-life as a shoemaker and ended it as an itinerant lecturer and Baptist preacher, appears to have been profoundly altered by reading of his "own" experience in *Alton Locke*, abandoning Chartism for a Christianized Socialism a few years after its publication (though without entirely swallowing Kingsley's more orthodox Anglican dogma). During the early 1850s, Cooper also became an author of popular "self-help" narratives and was encouraged by his publishers to capitalize on the success of *Alton Locke* by writing "Chartist novels" in a similar vein. Thus, as Cross has remarked, "*Alton Locke* not only borrowed Cooper's experiences, it also predicted them."[60] To be sure, the case of Cooper does not specifically demonstrate the potency of an organicist myth of the working-class intellectual, nor, in fact, does his long and relatively successful professional career fit with the Romantic martyrology of *Alton Locke*. Yet the role of the organic intellectual as a tragically-unfulfilled ideal can be clearly traced from *Alton Locke* to such late-nineteenth-century representations of the artisan hero as are found in Henry James's *The Princess Casamassima* (1886) and Thomas Hardy's *Jude the Obscure* (1895). In these later novels, the tension between organic class identities,

---

[58]   See Colloms, 116.

[59]   See Gramsci, *Selections From The Prison Notebooks*, 5–7. By contrast, Gottlieb renders "organic intellectual" synonymous with the working-class and "traditional intellectual" with the middle-class, thereby assuming that the two categories are mutually-exclusive.

[60]   See Cross, *The Common Writer*, 154; Vicinus, *The Industrial Muse*, 121; and also *The Life of Thomas Cooper*, 334–336, 350–368.

with their attendant political affiliations, and the desire for cultural and intellectual self-development is heightened into the violent internal schisms which mark the experiences of Hyacinth Robinson and Jude Fawley: both figures of the working-class intellectual alienated from their social origins and from the traditions of bourgeois "culture" alike, and, as such, direct inheritors of the cultural dilemma articulated earlier in the century by Kingsley and Carlyle. Both of these later characters may also serve as illustrations of Kingsley's "unaccredited" heroic type, obscure in worldly status yet rendered increasingly visible through their iconic forms.[61]

Works Cited

apRoberts, Ruth. *The Ancient Dialect: Thomas Carlyle and Comparative Religion*. Berkeley and Los Angeles: University of California Press, 1988.

Bamford, Samuel. *The Autobiography of Samuel Bamford. Volume One. Early Days*, ed. W.H. Chaloner. London: Frank Cass, 1967.

Barlow, Paul. "The Imagined Hero as Incarnate Sign: Thomas Carlyle and The Mythology of The 'National Portrait' in Victorian Britain," *Art History*, Vol. 17, No. 4 (1994), 517–545.

Burnett, John, David Vincent, and David Mayall, eds. *The Autobiography of The Working Class: An Annotated Critical Bibliography. Volume 1: 1790–1900*. Brighton: The Harvester Press, 1984.

Burns, Robert. *The Poems and Songs of Robert Burns*, ed. Andrew Lang. London: Methuen & Co., 1896.

Carlyle, Thomas. *Critical and Miscellaneous Essays*, 5 vols. London: Chapman and Hall, 1899.

———. *On Heroes, Hero-Worship and the Heroic in History*, ed. Carl Niemeyer. Lincoln/London: University of Nebraska Press, 1966.

———. *Wilhelm Meister's Apprenticeship and Travels*. Translated from the German of Goethe, 2 vols. London: Chapman and Hall, 1899.

[Carter, Thomas]. *Memoirs of a Working Man*. London: Charles Knight & Co., 1845.

Colloms, Brenda. *Charles Kingsley: The Lion of Eversley*. London: Constable, 1975.

Cooper, Thomas. *The Life of Thomas Cooper. Written By Himself*. 2nd ed. London: Hodder and Stoughton, 1872.

Cross, Nigel. *The Common Writer: Life in Nineteenth-Century Grub Street*. Cambridge: Cambridge University Press, 1985.

Gagnier, Regenia. *Subjectivities: A History of Self-Representation in Britain, 1832–1920*. New York and Oxford: Oxford University Press, 1991.

---

[61] In attacking the monopolization of higher education by the rich, "against both the spirit and the letter of the foundations", *Alton Locke* (in its first edition) does to Cambridge University what *Jude the Obscure* would later do to Oxford (Christminster) (137).

Gottlieb, Evan M. 'Charles Kingsley, "The Romantic Legacy, and The Unmaking of The Working-Class Intellectual," *Victorian Literature and Culture*, Vol. 29, No. 1 (2001), 51–65.

Gramsci, Antonio. *Selections from the Prison Notebooks*, eds and trans. Quintin Hoare and Geoffrey Nowell Smith. London: Lawrence and Wishart, 1971.

Gray, Thomas. "Elegy Written in a Country Churchyard," in *The Poems of Thomas Gray, William Collins, Oliver Goldsmith*, ed. Roger Lonsdale. London and Harlow: Longman, Green and Co., 1969, 103–141.

Hardin, James, ed. *Reflection and Action: Essays on the Bildungsroman*. Columbia: University of South Carolina Press, 1991.

Harrison, Tony. *Selected Poems*. 2nd ed. London: Penguin Books, 1987.

Haywood, Ian, ed. *Chartist Fiction: Thomas Doubleday,* The Political Pilgrim's Progress *and Thomas Martin Wheeler,* Sunshine and Shadow. Aldershot: Ashgate, 1999.

Kaplan, Fred. *Thomas Carlyle: A Biography*. Cambridge: Cambridge University Press, 1983.

Kingsley, Charles. *Alton Locke, Tailor and Poet. An Autobiography*, ed. Elizabeth A. Cripps. Oxford and New York: Oxford University Press, 1983.

———. 'Burns and His School' *North British Review*, Vol. XVI, No. XXXI (November, 1851), 149–183.

———. *Charles Kingsley: His Letters and Memories of His Life* edited By His Wife, Vol. I. London: C.Kegan Paul & Co., 1878.

———. *Yeast: A Problem*. London: John W. Parker and Son, 1851.

Lewes, George Henry. *Ranthorpe*, ed. Barbara Smalley. Athens: Ohio University Press, 1974.

Lytton, Lord. *Ernest Maltravers*. London: Routledge, 1873.

McCallum, Pamela. "Misogyny, the Great Man, and Carlyle's *The French Revolution*: The Epic as Pastiche," *Cultural Critique*, Vol. 14 (Winter, 1989–90), 153–178.

Maidment, Brian. "Essayists and Artizans: The Making of Nineteenth-Century Self-Taught Poets," *Literature and History*, Vol. 9., No. 1 (Spring, 1983), 74–91.

———. *The Poorhouse Fugitives: Self-taught Poets and Poetry in Victorian Britain*. Manchester: Carcanet Press, 1987.

Martineau, Harriet. "Literary Lionism" *London and Westminster Review*, Vol. XXXII, No. II (April, 1839), 261–281.

Menke, Richard. "Cultural Capital and The Scene of Rioting: Male Working-Class Authorship, in *Alton Locke*" *Victorian Literature and Culture*, Vol. 28, No. 1 (2000), 87–108.

Rosenberg, Philip. *The Seventh Hero: Thomas Carlyle and the Theory of Radical Activism*. Cambridge, MA: Harvard University Press, 1974.

Ruth, Jennifer. "Mental Capital, Industrial Time, and the Professional in *David Copperfield,*" *Novel: A Forum on Fiction*, Vol. 32, No. 3 (1999), 303–330.

Salmon, Richard. "The Genealogy of The Literary *Bildungsroman*: Edward Bulwer-Lytton and W.M. Thackeray," *Studies in the Novel*, Vol. XXXVI, No. 1 (Spring, 2004), 41–55.

Smiles, Samuel. *Self-Help; with Illustrations of Character and Conduct*. London: John Murray, 1860.

Steinweis, Alan. "Hitler and Carlyle's 'Historical Greatness,'" *History Today*, Vol. 45, No. 6 (June, 1995), 33–38.

Swales, Martin. *The German Bildungsroman from Wieland to Hesse*. Princeton, NJ: Princeton University Press, 1978.

Thackeray, William Makepeace. *The History of Pendennis. His Fortunes and Misfortunes, His Friends and His Greatest Enemy*, ed. John Sutherland. Oxford and New York: Oxford University Press, 1994.

Vicinus, Martha. *The Industrial Muse: A Study of Nineteenth Century British Working-Class Literature*. London: Croom Helm, 1974.

Vincent, David. *Bread, Knowledge and Freedom: A Study of Nineteenth-Century Working Class Autobiography*. London: Europa Publications Limited, 1981.

Chapter 10
Alexander Somerville's Rise from Serfdom: Working-Class Self-Fashioning through Journalism, Autobiography, and Political Economy[1]

Julie F. Codell

Alexander Somerville (1811–85) fits well James Epstein's definition of an intellectual as "predominantly functional ... as someone who assumes the role of persuader, consciously producing or conveying ideas to a public."[2] Somerville's writings are frequently cited by scholars of working-class culture and history. His *Autobiography of a Working Man* (1848), published the year of the Chartist march and petition in England and of violent class struggles on the Continent, has long appealed to scholars for its well-articulated political radicalism. Somerville's political views were intimately tied to his widening experiences in school, rural labor, the army, journalism and Victorian politics. E.P. Thompson places Somerville in the "dissenting tradition...precipitated in the English Jacobin Agitation," a diverse group comprised of "immigrants brought up in the Covenanting sects of Scotland;" Thompson calls Somerville "a famous anti-Corn Law publicist [who] was educated as a strict Anti-Burgher in a family of Berwickshire field-labourers."[3]

Somerville's resistance to bourgeois authority, however, was re-fashioned by Somerville himself in subsequent journalistic writings on his own life and on political economy. In the 1850s he represented himself as a journalist and not the rural worker of his *Autobiography* to a combined readership of workers and middle classes. In his nearly obsessive refashionings in the 1850s, Somerville invoked respectability, economic expertise, masculinity, and a denigration of politics that

[1]   I wish to thank Aruna Krishnamurthy for her insightful comments and suggestions on earlier drafts of this essay.

[2]   James Epstein, "'Bred as a Mechanic': Plebian Intellectuals and Popular Politics in Early Nineteenth-Century England," in *Intellectuals and Public Life: Between Radicalism and Reform*, eds Leon Fink, Stephen Leonard, and Donald Reid (Ithaca: Cornell University Press, 1996), 56.

[3]   E.P. Thompson, *The Making of the English Working Class* (New York: Vintage Books, 1966), 51. Somerville's *Autobiography* is a source of information on gender issues in Anna Clark, *The Struggle for the Breeches: Gender and the Making of the British Working Class* (Berkeley: University of California Press, 1995), 32, 64, 227.

helped transform his "radical" rural worker identity into his professional public spokesperson identity. His literary transformation, furthermore, was possible because of popular journalism's opportunities for bourgeoisification, reflecting increased literacy among working classes. Autobiographies' commercialization and popularity offered opportunities to Somerville, to address a public of rural laborers. Political economy offered a platform to reach a wider audience and re-write his life's story through a national role.

I will examine Somerville's identities across autobiography, journalism, and political economy to explore ways in which he shaped a complex, mixed-class identity, full of divided loyalties. Above all, he wrote himself as a national figure—with all the authority and power that role implied. No matter his experiences, Somerville joined his life narrative with British history, interjecting himself into national history as a player, not merely an observer, to create a national, upwardly mobile working-class identity. Whether soldier, rural laborer, journalist, Anti-Corn Law Leaguer, political economist or colonial emigrant, Somerville insisted that his experience served, and at times saved, the nation through two major narrative strategies: "hailing" his readers by their class identities to present them to themselves as a utopian unity of classes and invoking the geography of England, walking readers through imagined towns and countrysides as he analyzed various topics. Such walking united in a virtual tour both urban and rural laborers and ultimately all classes. His virtual walks turned workers' long treks between work and home (told in his *Autobiography*) into an ownership of Britain through political economy, an ownership by the unpropertied workers he encouraged to travel and to explore the wider world.

Somerville began as a rural laborer in a family descended from generations of rural laborers. Rural laborers were the poorest of the English workers and included women and children, from the ages of seven or eight. With "food coarser and less plentiful," housing "more overcrowded and insanitary" and the lowest wages of any workers, their poverty in hard times meant starvation and was unchanged until the end of the century.[4] Often considered unskilled, rural laborers engaged in many skilled trades. Hard workers, like Somerville, sometimes got higher wages or bonuses. Hierarchies of workers were distinguished by small, but crucial differences in wages. Some workers were closer in living standards and ideals to the "petty bourgeoisie" than to working classes as proletariat.[5] Like most rural laborers, by mid-century Somerville sought urban occupations, failing at opening his own establishment, but succeeding in journalism, and, also typically, emigrating to the colonies, in his case to Canada with his family in 1859. But there he could not make a good living from writing, despite his growing conservative political views. (He did not have sympathy with the Fenian attack in Upper Canada, 1866.) He died in poverty in Toronto in 1885.

---

[4]   John Burnett, ed. *Useful Toil: Autobiographies of Working People from the 1820s to the 1920s* (London and New York: Routledge, 1994), 9–10.

[5]   Burnett, 253.

Somerville's writings participated in an emerging and increasingly vocal working-class public presence and readership. As a journalist, he served as an effective spokesperson for laborers and honed his views. Somerville traveled in Ireland first in 1843 and then in 1847 as correspondent for the *Manchester Examiner*. Edward Lengel believes that "Alexander Somerville saw the famine as yet another example of the principle that 'it would be in the natural order of things of an Irish parliament of Irish landlords to legislate for themselves and against their tenantry and the great body of the People.'"[6] Witnessing firsthand the Irish famine shaped his notions about work, domestic life, empire, and social mobility. He supported various radicals, like the Tolpuddle Martyrs, but was always wary of attempts to exploit working class unrest, even by trade unions.[7] He opposed violent resistance from early on in *Dissuasive Warnings to the People on Street Warfare*[8] (1839) and *Public and Personal Affairs*[9] (1839) and was hostile to mobs.[10] He was critical of Chartist calls to violence and in the *Manchester Examiner* in 1847 he attacked the Chartist Land plan as unfeasible.

Somerville had utter faith that his writings would make a difference. *Dissuasive Warnings* was written "to dissuade the Chartists from the use of physical force ... . by argument and demonstration,"[11] in a series of one penny letters (eight pence per dozen). Somerville acknowledged that Chartists were well-intentioned and the crowd exhibited "earnestness and unquestionable courage" planning an insurrection. He refused to blame the working-classes for their feelings and intentions. Rather he wrote "to shew that whatever their honesty, earnestness, and courage may be, that they cannot possibly carry conquest on their side ... all the influence of wealth from the peer to the shopkeeper is against them." He argued that insurrection would lead to "uncontrollable crimes ... commercial ruins ... social wretchedness."[12] Somerville did not condemn the Chartists as he had the middle-

---

[6] From *Letters from Ireland during the Famine of 1847*, ed. K.D.M. Snell (Dublin: Irish Academic Press, 1994), 98; hereafter cited as *Letters*. See Edward G. Lengel, *The Irish Through British Eyes; Perceptions of Ireland in the Famine Era* (Westport, CT and London: Praeger, 2002),102.

[7] See K.D.M. Snell's fine introduction to *Letters from Ireland during the Famine of 1847* (Dublin: Irish Academic Press, 1994), 7–23.

[8] Alexander Somerville, *Dissuasive Warnings to the People on Street Warfare. Letter II, 1839* (London: J. Patten, 1839).

[9] *Public and Personal Affairs, being an enquiry into the physical strength of the people, in which the value of their pikes and rifles is compared with that of the grape-shot, shells, and rockets, of the Woolwich artillery: also, an exposure of treacherous patriots and drunken lawyers who have imposed upon the people, and are connected with Alderman Harmer, and the Weekly Dispatch, the whole comprising a personal narrative* (1839). London: Printed, published, and sold by A. Somerville, 1839.

[10] See Brian Behan's introduction to the 1967 edition of Somerville's *Autobiography*; he cites George Rude's *The Crowd in History* on the constitution of British "mobs."

[11] *Dissuasive Warnings*, 1.

[12] Ibid., 1–2.

class Leaguers, but argued that riots would only hurt them. He then reprinted his letter from Birmingham, claiming to be "an impartial observer" and promising to publish other letters. Journalism for Somerville was a means to educate working classes on how things really worked both as lessons and through his attacks on those he felt were unfairly disguising their real economic motives to blind workers to economic disparities. Once a journalist mixing tract writing and propaganda for the Anti-Corn Law League, he gained a modicum of authority on the subject of political economy. In 1849 he was invited by a publisher to comment on Richard Cobden's defense of his national budget.[13]

Somerville's *Autobiography of a Working Man* (hereafter cited as *Autobiography*) sold well and was reprinted in 1854, 1855, and 1863 (in Canada), and recently in 1951 and 1967. The title, like many working-class autobiographies' titles, is somewhat sensationalistic and self-fashioning, creating an essence of himself as forever working class, despite the upward change in his social and economic fortunes by the time it was published. One cannot imagine a title including class, job, or gender in the autobiographies of John Stuart Mill, John Ruskin, or Harriet Martineau, for example. As many scholars of life writing note, autobiographical writing is as rhetorical as any literary form, despite presumptions of its purpose to record historical "fact." His book's title puts it into a class of literary genre.[14] Calling his book "autobiography," Somerville asserts a middle-class subjectivity of self-reflection not conventionally tied to the "working man" part of his title. He articulated a complex mix of political radicalism with social conventions of domesticity and the work ethic. Somerville's self-fashioned identities were split between his literary and his laborer selves, produced in the clash between his lifelong proximity to working-class life and his distance from it as the author-journalist.

Somerville's *Autobiography* was a highly detailed account of his harsh rural life from childhood in the Lothians through early adulthood. He went to school, his parents ambitious for their children (including their girls) to be literate and improve their lot. His experiences in Victorian institutions, however, formed his awareness of, and resistance to, class oppression. Because of his poverty he suffered abuse in school and learned to hate class privilege there. In the army, he learned to hate war. He wrote for working-class readers primarily, but was aware that middle-class readers would read his book, too, and addressed them, as well. His self-awareness was built on pillars of middle-class hegemony—family life, work ethic, and charity toward the weaker or poorer. For him working was a social dividing line between deserving and undeserving poor. His views of the Irish famine are harsh regarding Irish who don't work, disregarding underlying conditions of Irish depravation.

---

[13] "Mr. Cobden's Defence of his National Budget," *Financial Reform* (1849), 1.

[14] See Regenia Gagnier, *Subjectivities: A History of Self-Representation in Britain, 1832–1920* (Oxford: Oxford University Press, 1991), 4–6, on rhetorical and generic issues in Victorian working-class autobiographies.

Somerville's radical views were tempered by identifications with the work ethic and family life; his family was rural, "progressive," close, and supportive. One of the most cited points of the book is how his grandparents in the eighteenth century and his own family carried a window around from hovel to hovel as they followed harvests and the agricultural labor cycles, so they and their children could read.[15] His rhetorical power is evident in many passages.[16] He readily drew on literary genres of autobiography and epistolary forms in his first person narrative *Notes from the Farming Districts*, 1842 (serialized in the *Morning Chronicle*), written as a letter of his journey. He incorporated his and others' letters in his tracts, using letters as historical and factual documentation to support his arguments. His frequent reprints of newspaper articles as tracts and pamphlets reflect the economy of his publications, recycled to be cheaper and more available for wider circulation.

The strength of Somerville's resistance to authority and abuse is most evident in the beatings he got at school, his intervention when stone masons beat a laborer (he hated intra-class conflict as much as inter-class conflict), and the near-fatal flogging he got in the army, the most dramatic and often–cited event of his life, even today. British military discipline was harsher than on the Continent.[17] Flogging aroused particular opposition. During agitation for Parliamentary reform in 1831, Private Somerville of the Royal Scots Greys was flogged with the cat o'nine tails after writing a letter to the *Weekly Dispatch* against the use of soldiers to fight the populace in Birmingham during the "Captain Swing" unrest, 1830–31, recalling the earlier Peterloo Massacre of civilians. He removed his shirt and was tied up:

> Simpson took the cat as ordered, at least I believe so; I did not see him, but I felt an astounding sensation between the shoulders, under my neck, which went to my toe nails in one direction, my finger nails in another, and stung me to the heart, as if a knife had gone through my body. The sergeant major called in a loud voice "one". I felt as if it would be kind for Simpson not to strike in the same place again. He came on a second time a few inches lower, and then I thought the former stroke was sweet and agreeable compared with that one. The sergeant major counted 'two'. The 'cat' was swung twice around the farrier's head again, and he came on somewhere about the right shoulder blade, and the loud voice of the reckoner said 'three.'[18]

---

[15] Edward Royle, *Modern Britain: A Social History, 1750–1997* (London: Arnold 1997), 164; Gagnier, 140.

[16] For example: "a row of shabby-looking tile sheds ... about twelve feet by fourteen, and not so high in the walls as will allow a man to get in without stopping. ... without ceiling, ... without a floor save the common clay; without a cupboard ... no grate but the iron bars ... with no partition of any kind save what the beds made; with no window save four small panes on one side" (*Autobiography*, 7). Here his repetition of "without" and "no" underscores the depravation.

[17] French who joined the British Army deserted it because of its brutal punishments.

[18] *Autobiography*, 195.

This incident, complete with satiric understatement in the narrative ("I felt as if it would be kind for Simpson ..."), made Somerville legendary. Refusing rum or submission to his superior officer's bullying, he suffered one hundred lashes (the punishment of two hundred was reduced for fear he would die a martyr) without crying out despite 5400 wounds. His flogging recounted in the press became a cause célèbre to fellow soldiers and urban and rural workers. The case came before Parliament and the King; crowds provoked officers of the regiment. Somerville became a hero and bought his release from the army in 1832. After business failures, he joined the British Legion in Spain where he fought in Spain's civil war, 1835–37, and left as a lieutenant with a bullet lodged in his arm.

The *Autobiography* stops at April 1834. Somerville never intended to publish it, but wrote it for his son. But "Personal circumstances which need not be further explained here, have changed this purpose. Public circumstances have also had an influence to decide the author on present publication."[19] Perhaps the need for money and some urging to publish his life as a model of working-class experiences and views prompted him to publish. But he cites a "conspiracy of trades' unionists and political lunatics, in 1834, in which the author was solicited to take a part, which he did not take." He knew "that calamities of direst peril impended over the lives of some of the highest personages in the kingdom," referring to a threat to kidnap the Cabinet. In his view he was sworn to save the constitution. He ends his life story with this incident that occurred ten years before the book's publication, perhaps to encourage readers to see him more as a patriot than a radical.

He even claimed that he withheld publication of his autobiography in the tumultuous year of 1848, "until several chapters were added on the delusions of our working classes."[20] Perhaps it is no surprise that he stopped his story in 1834 and did not fill in the blanks by its 1848 publication, at which time he was no longer a rural laborer, but a fulltime journalist and political writer. Somerville's Preface modifies the identity that emerges from the autobiography. Even before his narrative begins, his preface shapes his public image as patriotic, constitutional and civic-minded. He wrote his life to "be of use to warn working men of the perils into which they are led by leaders whom they cannot control," and to make the details of his childhood and rural labor "satisfactory reading, and not obtrusive of puerilities, or of private affairs which have no public uses."[21] There is much in the *Autobiography* that is radical and radicalizing, but the Preface foregrounds a cooler, more respectable narrative voice. Before publication, he removed "many of the reflections on men, on facts, on opinions or on principles," to present a story without political comments. This apology seems meant to disguise disingenuously the inherent political implications of his life's experiences. His Preface highlights the flogging incident and promises the book will reveal "what his motives were," but this is never clarified.

---

[19]   Ibid., 13.

[20]   Alexander Somerville, *Cobdenic Policy, the Internal Enemy of England* (London: R. Hardwicke, 1854), 88.

[21]   Somerville, *Autobiography*, 13.

Somerville's tone is full of Victorian uplift, despite his harsh life. As Vincent notes, Somerville's "faith in progress was founded on four pillars:" [22]

> Universal enfranchisement, railways, electric telegraphs, public schools (the greatest of the moral levers for elevating mankind named last—because last to be advocated, which should have been first); these are some of the elements of a moral faith, believing in the universal brotherhood of mankind, which I daily hold and never doubt upon; which I believe will as certainly be realised, as I believe that *good*, and not *evil*, was the object of all creation, and is the end of all existence.[23]

Somerville returned to the flogging incident repeatedly. In *Public and Personal Affairs* he tried to redirect the public's interpretation of his flogging "which gained for me a temporary notoriety"[24] through reports in the *Weekly Dispatch*. In *Cobdenic Policy, The Internal Enemy of England. The Peace Society, Its Combativeness. Also, a Narrative of Historical Incidents*, published in London in 1854, Somerville re-writes himself and the flogging incident. He deployed the iconic incident of the flogging as both a sign and a symptom of his dual roles as a public intellectual and member of the laboring classes, making these identities inextricably intertwined. In *Public and Personal Affairs*, he takes up his life after 1834, including service in Spain, which becomes a turning point. This service was marked by bravery, promotions, and complete identification with his military role and became a vantage point from which to criticize his earlier self and re-write his flogging. The meaning and presumed rarity of military flogging became important to both his revision of the incident and to his attacks on Cobden and the Peace Society.

This book was identified as about patriotism and England's national security and here Somerville elided his life and British history, appealing to readers' masculinity as a bond:

> Young Man of England! –
> You are son of the palace, son of the cottage, offspring of every social degree between. No rank is too exalted, no home too humble, to give birth and growth to manliness. In the field, in the workshop, and in mines ... in ship, on sea, in ports and marts of commerce; in the town, in the country; in cottage, garret, mansion; from hornbook at school to degrees at university; on the roughest roads of toil and smoothest ways of fortune; in office of command, in duty of obedience, your inherent honour teaches you to be, and to know when you are – what you were born to be – a Man of England ... Every corner of the island, and each island of the British group owns you; your mother soil is Britain – eldest daughter of Freedom, – and still the freest, most stable industrious, trustworthy, dignified, and in her sons, the most chivalric of all the nations of the earth. You are guardian of her honour; your duty and fidelity are her life. The only danger

---

[22] Vincent, 198.

[23] *Autobiography*, 361.

[24] *Public and Personal Affairs*, 3.

which besets your inherent faith and fidelity to her, and therein lieth her greatest peril, is your being seduced from natural duty by teachers of sedition. ...[25]

Here Somerville erases class difference beneath uniform masculine, British virtues—honor ("inherent," no less), chivalry, a mother country—in preparation for defending England against a seductress of sedition.

The seductress is no less than the combined Quaker Peace Society and Cobden who have tossed out the "apple of discord" (note the classical reference) by their political dissent and sympathy with Continental revolutions. Somerville draws on his experience of civil war in Spain to expose the nature of violent upheaval. Cobden and the Peace Society produced anti-military pamphlets citing Somerville's flogging without his approval or even notification. They claimed that flogging was a regular punishment of soldiers. Outraged, he wrote his own pamphlets and appealed to politicians, including Lord Palmerston, who read Somerville's patriotic letter to a cheering Parliament. Somerville appealed to the legal system to get these pamphlets stopped, claiming they harmed his sales of subscriptions to his literary work on the eve of his departure for Canada. In addition to a vicious attack on Cobden as an exploiter of the poor, Somerville attacked John Bright, Liberal MP from Manchester, and aligned himself with the aristocracy against the commercial classes.[26] Somerville rewrote his flogging experience in *Cobdenic Policy*:

> The book was written not to dissuade men from entering the army, or other defensive service of the country, but to warn soldiers not to lend themselves to the emissaries of political intrigue, as I had unfortunately done, and bitterly repented having done (time, 1832); to warn young men in civil life not to be misled by the blockheads who plotted, or talked approvingly of the plots of 'physical force,' as the means to effect their political ends.[27]

The letter-writing which resulted in his flogging now becomes the "one grave error of my life—breach of military duty" which taught him "so far as political authorship has been my business, to occupy a position of practical usefulness on the side of lawful authority, social order, and the tranquil progress of this great industrial nation. There have been no exceptions to this rule."[28] He even renounced employment on Bright's newspaper that advocated European revolutions and refused "the proprietorship and editorial pay in a first class Pro-Corn Law newspaper, proposed to me by Mr. Cobden, on behalf of the Anti-Corn Law League, rather than be a hypocrite."[29] Somerville's animosity was fueled by his sense of being personally exploited by Cobden who employed him to write but severely censored his writings.

---

[25]   *Cobdenic Policy*, 3.

[26]   Ibid., 7–10.

[27]   Ibid., 10–11.

[28]   Ibid., 17.

[29]   Ibid.

Describing his father as a "religiously devout" farm laborer who taught his children "to pay respect to all who were set in authority over them,"[30] Somerville returned to autobiography to set the stage for rewriting his flogging. It was punishment for disobedience and made his father feel that Somerville ignored his father's teachings. Somerville offered his readers a surprising lesson: "regimental flogging did me good. It made me observant and thoughtful. It gave me an acquaintance with political persons, schemes, and plots which otherwise I should have never known. Through it I learnt the hollowness and worthlessness of many 'patriots,' so-called, and self-styled."[31] In the revision, Somerville was "induced" by "older men in the regiment" to write his letter, "a momentary act of insubordination;" he praised the officers during his court martial but did not give up names of others involved in his political activity.[32] In this way, Somerville can maintain both his solidarity with other laborers and at the same time rewrite himself as obedient, unseditious, patriotic, and worthy of a role in national history. Perhaps to repair his military record, he volunteered to serve in Spain and includes verbatim letters commending his service there.[33] During riots, arson, and upheaval in 1837, Somerville tried to dissuade workers from street violence, telling them they were wasting "time and opportunity ... for self-improvement and mutual benefit in things useful and practicable, by occupying their minds with such revolutionary schemes."[34] His final message is a distrust of politics which, he argued, sidetracked unions from issues of wages and hours into political riots.

In chapter three of *Cobdenic Policy*, Somerville identified himself as a journalist. Attacking Cobden, Somerville moved from satire ("he retained all his early petulance, all his early intolerance of other political writers than himself") to hyperbole: "he is not a common man. He is leader of the most dangerous political faction that ever under the semblance of innocence comprehended ulterior objects pregnant with national peril—the society for effecting a national disarmament."[35] In his diatribe he embedded an epistolary mode, citing private letters from Cobden to him to reveal his own sympathy "with a reasoning conservatism" never antagonistic to "established institutions."[36]

Somerville's pseudonym, "One who has whistled at the Plough," truly described him in his view; he had a rule "not to write as that which I was not," as Cobden wanted him to do.[37] However, he did write articles privately for Bright who

---

[30]   Ibid., 20.

[31]   Ibid.

[32]   Ibid.

[33]   His *Narrative of the British Legion in Spain* in 1837 was published weekly for four months.

[34]   Ibid., 24.

[35]   *Cobdenic Policy*, 36.

[36]   Somerville reprinted a great number of private letters in *Cobdenic Policy* to record his experiences with the League.

[37]   *Cobdenic Policy*, 42.

published them as written by a farmer; while attacking Bright for this, Somerville certainly indicts himself, unleavened by the fact that these articles were privately submitted. Somerville's writings for the League did not always get reimbursed, and he eventually sued the League in 1852 for money owing him for his services as journalist and League historian in 1846. He was even briefly imprisoned for a League debt of £45 owed to a printer on behalf of the League which did not pay his bail.

In these conflicted experiences recounted and revised within a combination of epistles and journalism as personal yet public, "objective" modes, Somerville represented himself differently from his autobiographical rural laborer identity which he yet retained as a residual justification for this writing to help or protect other laborers. His penny *National Wealth Tracts* published twice a month were intended "to render Political Economy intelligible and agreeable to those classes of society who know least of it. Those who produce much and consume little, and those who consume much and produce little," implying that the upper classes are as ignorant of the subject as the workers.[38] His leveling moves up and down. Writing that "All men are in one sense capitalists," he raised the workers into ownership, while evaporating class connotations of the term. He continued to define them conventionally, however, and to address them directly as those "who possess a store of commodities more than sufficient to the supply of their own wants."[39] Then he addressed laborers, also redefining and expanding this category from a classed one to a universal human nature, as he did with "capitalist":

> All men are in one sense labourers. ... at present addressed under this head are such as possess no capital beyond strength and skill. ... It is as indispensable to the social well-being, to the moral advancement, to understand the naturally economic principles which govern wages, upon which principles the first step must be taken to rise about the condition of working for wages ... to become self-employers, or to provide commodities for others to work upon. [40]

As a journalist, Somerville defined "public opinion," a new concept generated by and reflected in the press. He distinguished between "that wholesome public opinion recognized in the British constitution and protected by our laws" from "the whimsical 'popular voice,' unstable as the wind, but equally certain as the wind to return to the same quarter with returning causes of change…demagogues, with the response of their unthinking crowds; the 'popular voice' of demagogues, whether professing peace, or more honestly announcing sympathy with war."[41] Somerville's comments imply a working-class crowd, which he admonishes to have confidence in British institutions and join the "wholesome" public opinion.

---

[38]   *Somerville's National Wealth Tracts*, No. 1, "Capital and Labour" (London: C. Gilpin, 1848), 1.

[39]   Ibid.

[40]   "Capital and Labour," ii.

[41]   *Cobdenic Policy*, 27.

To this end Somerville himself printed his 1839 *Dissuasive Warnings to the People on Street Warfare* "almost universally circulated in the provincial newspapers .... translated into Welsh, and in Welsh and English ... sent among the iron and coal workers of South Wales."[42] He believed this tract read by even "the most ignorant" slowed down extremists, especially when accompanied by "pictorial illustrations of Shrapnell shells exploding among a crowd"[43] which he believed dissuaded Chartist leaders from violence. Somerville ended this chapter asserting his position "on the side of public morality, peace, law, order and industrial humanity,"[44] in contrast to the swindling land scheme of Feargus O'Connor, editor of the *Northern Star*, whom Somerville attacked in writing.

The most remarkable interpellation of his readers, however, is his imaginary journey through Britain in which he invited the "General Reader" to follow him

> through the green lanes into the meadow, the corn-fields and the farm yards, over the stiles, across brooks, up to the village, through the church-yards, among the cottage houses, into the wooded parks, around the mansions; upon the railways and highways, into the towns, the factories, workshops, saleshops, warehouses, banks, dock, ships; upon the rivers and the sea-tides; on share again and down into the mines; again among the ringing hammers, the clamouring looms, and the heaving pistons, and the world of wheels; and to the working man's town habitation, and out again to the green meadows to moralise, and to the library to write of capital and labour.[45]

This extraordinary passage blends Somerville's life with British industrial and labor histories through the geography of Britain: workers finding jobs throughout the countryside and noisy factories and witnessing the trajectory of goods (railways, highways, shops and warehouses, ships and the sea) that with their labor become the wealth of Britain. Somerville hailed readers as a third category, presumably overlapping with "capitalist" and "laborer." Readers were manly, owners of Britain, and both marked by class and above class. Paths of goods, workers and capitalists converge in his imaginary tour. Somerville's life followed most of these paths in the countryside, towns, cities, and in the meadows where he learned to read and aspired to write and in the library where he studied and where his writings were available to all readers. Libraries, like factories, were part of his vision of production-consumption cycles which embrace symbolic, as well as material capital. Somerville's tracts offer an imagined secular pilgrim's progress toward shared ideas of political economy that he hoped to make as palpable as the shared British landscape, virtually owned by all, including unpropertied workers.

Somerville's entry into discourse through literary genres (autobiography, tracts, the press) moved him into other social classes' discourses, suggesting fluid

---

[42]   Ibid., 29.
[43]   Ibid.
[44]   Ibid., 30–31.
[45]   "Capital and Labour," ii.

Victorian working class identities. For Somerville, workers made history by defining a class space that brought experience into play with discourse through political economy's palpable lessons and scientific laws. Imaginatively traversing the geographies of Britain in hailing his readers—embracing urban streets, the countryside, and towns—Somerville's writings define a utopian space where classes meet in literacy and readership. As James Epstein notes,

> spatial practice bears a metaphorical resemblance to the agency, the transformations that readers enact on a written text; walking like reading is a creative, even subversive, social activity. Accordingly, the trajectories of space and place are themselves storied, narratives of lived activity and practice. This is potentially important since spatial practice and spatial imaginings, the struggles to dislodge the authority of place, suggest a way to think about interactions between text and practice, between form and the cultural production of meaning.[46]

Somerville aligned his and others' experiences with upward mobility, social restraint, and constitutional authority, didactic strategies he believed enabled workers to control their means of production, bodies and spaces. He presented all Britain as open, available and free for anyone to traverse. Walking Britain made workers citizens, and therefore owners of all spaces, rural and urban, public and private, work and domicile. Britain was their collective property embodied, as he knew firsthand, in workers' long treks to find work and between work and home. He transformed these treks into workers' ownership of Britain.

The workings of economics was often obscured for laborers, despite their dire circumstances. David Vincent argues that

> It is doubtful, for instance, whether any member of Alexander Somerville's family economy was fully aware of his or her daily or even annual wage. In return for the notional rent of their tied cottage the family had to perform certain tasks for the farmer throughout the year, and although some members were occasionally paid case wages for certain types of labour, they usually worked as a single economic unit.[47]

Vincent underscores "the intricate pattern of adjustment, assistance and dependence presented in Somerville's account of the functioning of his family economy."[48] Many working class autobiographers dwelt in detail on their hardships, but if they saw some purpose in their labor, they accepted their situation, though grudgingly. E.P. Thompson notes how complex it is to determine what the "average" rural

---

[46]   James Epstein, *In Practice: Studies in the Language and Culture of Popular Politics in Modern Britain* (Palo Alto: Stanford University Press, 2003), 107.

[47]   David Vincent. *Bread, Knowledge, and Freedom: A Study of Nineteenth-Century Working Class Autobiography* (London and New York: Methuen, 1981), 79–80, referring to *Autobiography*, 21.

[48]   Vincent, 83. See *Autobiography*, 11–12.

laborer earned for many reasons.[49] Many laborers were paid in garden plots or in kind (in addition to or in place of wages). Their earnings were affected by game laws and poaching, taxes, tithes and poor-rate. Enclosures meant fewer cottagers could keep cows, something that offered independence from their employers.[50]

The family economy included the children's education, a symbolic capital to help them improve their lot. Somerville did not go to school until he was eight because his family lacked adequate clothes and were sensitive to their appearance in public. His clothes were still ragged compared to other children's, and he suffered beatings and bullying.

This family economy, then, was a combination of meager material capital and a social consciousness of their condition; they attempted to save face and present some semblance of respectability.[51] Somerville was introduced to books by other rural workers so his aspirations were not entirely unique. Such aspirations led him to seek middle-class employment as a librarian, or forester, or shop owner, all of which failed.[52]

Somerville produced a series of pamphlets, "Somerville's Manchester School of Political Economy" ("Edited by 'One who has Whistled at the Plough'"), published in London by W. Strange, in Manchester by Abel Heywood and W. Irwin, in Edinburgh by J. Menzies, and in Liverpool by Philip and Son. Some of these publishers were associated with political radicalism.[53] Somerville wrote several short tracts on political economy for working-class readers, many written while he promoted the Anti-Corn Law League. What ties his writings together is his belief in political economy as directly related to his and other workers' experiences, circumstances, *and* improvement. He considered political science an inductive science,[54] advocating that those who produce should enjoy the products of their toil. The three propositions of political economy are

---

[49] Thompson (262) cites Somerville's interview in *The Whistler at the Plow*, 1852, with Joseph Carter. Between 1823–30 Carter earned £64 a year from a squire, but had to pay as much as £20 a year for three helpers, something the squire "did not shew" in his accounts.

[50] Thompson, 216–217.

[51] He attended a school where the quality of the teacher overcame the apparent disadvantage of not being associated with the church: "it was not a parish school; but he had a local fame as a good teacher" (*Autobiography*, 20).

[52] Piece work and part-time work permitted him to earn extra money to encourage his aspirations (*Autobiography*, 373–374). See Vincent, 149–150.

[53] Abel Heywood (1810–93) was a publisher, radical and mayor of Manchester. Heywood created a penny reading room in Manchester which led him to publish a newspaper. Despite his radicalism, his business succeeded and he entered public life, first as commissioner of police in 1836. He was elected to the Manchester council in 1843, becoming alderman in 1853 and twice mayor (1862–1863, 1876–1877). He stood unsuccessfully for Parliament for the Liberal Party in 1859 and 1865.

[54] See "Capital and Labour," 9.

that mankind do not labour for the love of toil, but that they may enjoy the products of their labour. ... that all obstacles to production, or to the commercial exchanges which increase the value of industrial production, should be removed by science. ... that all laws which confer the power of consumption upon classes of persons, or classes of *capital*, without imposing on them or *that capital*, the offices of productiveness, or *utile* public service, are laws which diminish, and do not replenish, the general store of wealth.[55]

He believed that producers should partake "of the abundance, which their toil, genius, and productive capital bring forth."[56] He even suggested that rent increases, which he did not consider productive, be put into a national bank to be useful to all.[57]

His tracts were filled with pedagogical explanations. Somerville's writings on political economy made him what we now call a public intellectual, who makes complex ideas comprehensible to the general public. He even published a series of children's "Penny Tales" contrasting children at play with children working in factories. He ended his first National Wealth Tract with a geographical tour of Britain as necessary to understanding political economy. He addressed an imaginary reader named "Peter," for whom "Princes shall be your companions, and, at least, one person out of each class of society as the representative of that class; and one other from each class of economic errors, as the representative of that error," along with books by Adam Smith, Louis Blanc, Feargus O'Connor, Robert Owen, Richard Cobden and Colonel Thompson.[58] Finally, he invented a story of "Sally Grey" who breaks her cup, ruining the treacle she sells as an example of the economics of production and consumption.[59]

Invited to comment on Cobden's speech in 1849, Somerville used an accessible epistolary form that framed Cobden's speech with Somerville's criticism of it.[60] Addressing Cobden's false modesty, Somerville proceeded to comment on "one or two passages which might lead to misapprehension on the part of some who are unacquainted with the measure propounded by the Financial Reformers,"[61] referring to their proposal to cut military spending back to expenditures of 1835. Somerville explained the proposed cut of ten million pounds in concrete terms of "commodities which comprise national wealth being food, clothing, lodging,

---

[55]   *Somerville's Manchester School of Political Economy*, No. 3 (Manchester: Abel Heywood and W. Irwin, June–August, 1850), 180.

[56]   Ibid.

[57]   Ibid., 182–183.

[58]   "Capital and Labour," 11.

[59]   Ibid., 12–20. He promised the next tract would expose moral issues inherent in the pleasure business; "Capital and Labour," 20.

[60]   Alexander Somerville, *Financial Reform. Mr. Cobden's Defence Of His National Budget. Letter To The Publisher, By "One Who Has Whistled At The Plough."* (Liverpool: Matthews Printer, n.d.)

[61]   Ibid., 1–2.

furniture, fuel, locomotion, money, and the other instruments of production and exchange; together with books and other accessories of intellectual enjoyment; and a lesser or greater amount of these in a nation constituting, as it undeniably does, a lesser or greater amount of prosperity, power and happiness"[62] would all be reduced ten-fold by Cobden's cut. He promised to explicate in a forthcoming *Somerville's Monthly Register* "a familiar exposition and illustration of such economical subjects, so that even in the circle of the fireside, the child who begins to drink from its mother's knowledge, clinging to her little story now as it hung upon her breast before, may have a tale of political economy which it can comprehend and delight in to remember."[63]

Somerville's writings suggest relationships among discourses of life writings, journalism and political economy as venues for working class mobility and open expression. His views on Cobden, the Corn Laws, and class conflicts attack middle-class economic manipulation of workers to sustain the wealth of the former and subordinate the latter, often revolving around the Corn Laws and the Anti-Corn Law League. The Manchester School of Economics and the Anti-Corn-Law League culminated sixty years of free trade debates.[64] After the Napoleonic Wars, corn prices almost halved, causing panic among farmers. Lord Liverpool's government introduced the Corn Laws in 1815 to keep prices of wheat up to benefit landowners and farmers. The Corn Laws were intended to stabilize wheat prices at 80/- per quarter. No foreign grain could be imported until domestic grain reached that price. Some MPs thought limiting purchases to British sources would lower prices. But the laws caused violent fluctuations in food prices and encouraged hoarding which harmed domestic industry and foreign markets. Landowners benefited as Parliament represented them, since owning land was required for politicians.

The increased cost of food depressed the domestic market for manufactured goods because people spent their earnings on food, devastating the Lancashire cotton industry and raising the price of bread. The government failed to remedy the situation, provoking public meetings, protests and riots in 1815. Revised laws in 1828 only partially solved the dilemma. The 1832 Reform Act enfranchised much of the middle class, including industrial middle classes, so manufacturers had more power to pressure Parliament. Economic depression in the 1830s encouraged free traders; increased industry required more free trade to create incentives to put capital into railways and expand transportation. But Whig governments of 1830–4 and 1835–41 were challenged by Chartists, the Anti-Poor Law movement, the Ten Hour Movement, and the Anti-Corn-Law League. Between these years, Conservatives under Robert Peel sought a union of land and industry, but Leaguers criticized the aristocratic parliament.

---

[62] Ibid., 3.

[63] Ibid., 4.

[64] Adam Smith's *Wealth of Nations*, 1776, advocated free trade for developing a nation's "natural economy," especially an industrial one.

Many believed repeal of Corn Laws and tariffs for free trade would lead to more markets, expanded employment, lower bread prices, increased agricultural efficiency and productivity and international peace through trade. The League's leaders included Richard Cobden, MP for Stockport in 1841, and John Bright, MP for Durham in 1843 and for Manchester in 1847. The Anti-Corn-Law League sought working-class support. Some League supporters were interested in the Complete Suffrage Union to widen its electorate. Working-class members included the Sheffield Mechanics' Anti-Bread-Tax Society and Ebenezer Elliott, Sheffield's "Corn Law Rhymer."[65] Disorders in 1842 ended Chartists' and Leaguers' hopes for class reconciliation. The League then focused on rural areas and electors, exploiting divisions between landowners and tenants.

Somerville writing under the pseudonym, "The Whistler at the Plough," well-known to his readers, contributed a series of anti-Corn Law articles aimed at agricultural readers to the *Morning Chronicle* after 1842.[66] Cobden recruited Somerville among others to observe and write about the social and political scene in the countryside; they were paid by the League. Somerville's widely read articles were later published as a book, *The Whistler at the Plough*, in 1852. Somerville disavowed support of the League in light of its manipulation of workers in the interests of manufacturers, industrialists and commerce.

Somerville's curious role inside and against the League parallels his conflicted representations of himself and his universalizing and dilution of the dialectical binary of capitalist and labor. Two of Somerville's themes were that workers deserve to have money to save and spend as they want, and that moral and social issues, not simply money, constitute political economy: "it is preferable to leave capital in the hands of those to whom it belongs, to the whole number ... in every community, or nation" who "will add to it, more zealously if left in their own hands as private property, than if taken out of their own hands and made public property" with the exception of a tax for military defense.[67] He considered people's private possessions as public/national wealth and repeatedly condemned those who "consume without producing ... the greater the number of rich persons, who could use commodities, and by using put them out of existence without producing others, or without devoting their money as capital to produce others, the poorer would the nation become."[68] Using money properly was civic and patriotic. Somerville elides private and public to illuminate his criticism of the well-to-do and to defend the poor as economical, thrifty, contributors to national wealth, and active players in the nation's well-being, a role he claimed for himself at every turn. But the "influence of personal conduct on the condition of the producing classes" was

---

[65]   Artisans in Sheffield supported the League, and working-class hostility to the law was strong in Sheffield's trade unions. For the history of the Corn Laws, see http://www.historyhome.co.uk/.

[66]   Somerville's visit to the headquarters of the Corn Law League in Manchester is described in *The Whistler at the Plough* (1852), 79–82.

[67]   "Capital and Labour," 5.

[68]   Ibid., 9.

only one part of "that mysterious anomaly – a nation whose rich people increase in number, many of whose poor people deepen in poverty."[69] He did not simply accept the popular Victorian equation between good money management and good character as a solution to economic inequities.[70]

Somerville demarcated a line between politics and economics, refusing "to become a traitor to what I believed to be economic truths—principles in political economy which I had arrived at before I heard the name either of Cobden or of Bright—and to become a hypocrite in working out a plot against the unsuspecting agricultural classes," as when he refused Cobden's request to write anti-Corn Law articles for a pro-Corn Law paper.[71] Somerville denied that his knowledge of political economy was the result of "pollution" by middle-class manufacturing politics. His unsullied political economy then became the faith by which his identity and credibility can serve the "agricultural classes," a service by which he sustained his past identity as rural worker. Writing about his journalistic interviews with the poor in the countryside, Somerville created his own version of political economy mixed with journalism—paying interviewees, giving income he earned from their stories back to them, never lodging or eating at the expense of local people, and not taking bribes.[72]

Somerville was constantly presenting himself as sacrificing his personal gain to improve workers' lot. Writing for Bright's paper, he described ways that employers avoided the Act of Parliament's law for shortening workers' hours. He was told not to comment on such things, so he decided to write his own tracts: "In short, of all the materials which formed national wealth, I presumed to teach that the *human material* was first and all-important. This, in Manchester, was political heresy."[73] Somerville claimed his purpose in writing *National Wealth Tracts* "was to counteract the feverish and revolutionary spirit which ... was then so prevalent and dangerous."[74] His tracts made him unpopular with the Free Traders: "My theories, also, for the cure of commercial panics, not being very complimentary to those capitalists, to whom a commercial panic is a harvest, formed another cause of their disfavour."[75] He insisted that readers "judge if the public benefit, rather than my own popularity, and consequent profit as a writer, was not their object."[76]

Political economy was a means to sustain both sides of his subjectivity. It helped him define himself and his class beyond their status as laborers. Political economy was a means for working classes to raise themselves up as a class.

---

[69]   Ibid.
[70]   This equation is the focus of the writings of Samuel Smiles, for example.
[71]   *Cobdenic Policy*, 39.
[72]   Ibid., 40.
[73]   Ibid., 83.
[74]   Ibid., 88.
[75]   Ibid., 83.
[76]   Ibid., 88.

Advocating political economy instead of violence to improve workers' lots, he condemned Leaguers' attempts to politically manipulate workers. He distinguished himself from the League because he believed that only landowners would benefit from urban growth, national industry, external commerce and increasing national wealth.[77] Somerville explicitly and conscientiously attacked Victorian social hierarchies while advocating the means—work, family support, education, and political economy—to move up into those hierarchies, without replicating middle-class complacency and callousness. He perceived middle-class behavior as expressed in political, economic and physical brutalities (war, beatings in school), oppressive payment schemes for workers' wages, child labor, and poor living conditions. He presented himself as exemplary of social mobility without a loss of his laborer self. Political economy permitted him to cross class borders back and forth in his writings.

Political economy was a solution to problems of poverty and tenancy for Somerville grown from his experiences and early travels to Ireland. Somerville created his own personal economy; while many travelers and officials went heavily armed in Ireland during the famine and advised Somerville to do the same, he "armed" himself with bread and cheese to give to hungry people who might accost him. Initially the British government responded generously to the crisis, but in 1847 it failed to address the famine and subsequent diseases (which befell Somerville, too) unprecedented in earlier Irish famines. Somerville hoped to convince the British public of the horrors of Ireland's famine and Britain's lack of political and economic understanding because of ruthless Irish landlords, high rents, and political uses of their land to force clearances and evictions, all paid for by English taxpayers (he was even more hostile to them than to English landowners). He allowed his subjects to speak in their own voices. His views on political economy (he rejected Malthus) rooted in his life were enhanced by his rhetorical use of sharp contrasts to expose inequities: beautiful landscape against Irish peasants evicted in winter.

Political economy as a combined moral and economic system appealed to Somerville as "the very essence of humanity, benevolence and justice" needed to aid Ireland,[78] although he freely used the terminology of race regarding Saxons and Celts, foreshadowing his imaginary unity of all Britons: "the aptitude for commercial enterprise, ... becomes the Saxon inheritance, and would become the inheritance of any race if that race were fairly set in motion."[79]

Somerville knew that citizenship conferred on workers would transform not just their behavior, but also the perception of them among the other classes. He remarked that "the greater the number of men enfranchised, the smaller is the

---

[77]   Ibid., 43.

[78]   Lengel, 108–109.

[79]   Alexander Somerville, *Letters from Ireland during the Famine of 1847*, ed. K.D.M Snell (Dublin; Portland, OR: Irish Academic Press, 1994), 177–178. He noted that some Irish peasants starved themselves to buy arms while refusing to pay rents (*Letters* 54–55).

number of 'blackguards.'"[80] He used political economy to encourage workers to identify with their circumstances *and* to improve their lot. Political economy could raise their consciousness to understand their situation in political and economic terms necessary to change the materiality of their circumstances.

Journalism enabled Somerville to see the wider world beyond rural laboring life. Peter Gurney's study of Thomas Frost (who also wrote an autobiography and worked in journalism) examines a case parallel to Somerville's. Gurney comments on the liberation by submission (a point borrowed from Pierre Bourdieu) to examine

> the possible effects of employing the dominant language and writing for money on an individual from a subaltern class like Frost. ... Criticizing those commentators who have simply celebrated working-class resistance to the dominant language, exemplified by the use of "low" or vulgar discourse, Bourdieu has emphasized the liberating effects submission to the dominant language can have for subaltern individuals and groups. ... Frost himself handled and later made sense of the dialectic of resistance and submission and how that dialectic exerted a shaping influence on his literary productions or discourse. Frost used the written word to improve his situation and his life opens a window onto a relatively unexplored but profoundly important aspect of working-class culture ... the complex experience of social mobility in a society characterized by fairly impermeable class boundaries, particularly the boundary between the working and middle classes. As Savage and Miles have pointed out, there was a two-hundred-to-one chance against a skilled worker's son entering the established middle class before World War One, so Frost is certainly a rare and atypical figure. But it is precisely his marginality that can help illuminate the wider society within which he sought recognition and acceptance.[81]

What Gurney says about Frost applies to Somerville whose life was similar to Frost's in its professional trajectory, ideological accommodations and self-fashionings. While these are only two cases, they raise the issue of just how marginal they were, as well as how effective they were in reaching a working-class public. John Burnett argues that the working poor when describing their lives convey an "uncomplaining acceptance of conditions of life and work" which seem to us "brutal, degrading and almost unimaginable," yet described with "patient resignation to the facts of life."[82] They put personal relationships above their work. Geographical mobility to find work was sometimes a matter of choice, as some workers wanted new experiences and broader horizons.[83] But many workers were

---

[80]   *Autobiography*, 132. See John Plotz, *The Crowd: British Literature and Public Politics* (Berkeley: University of California Press, 2000), 132, for the changing nature of crowds in the public space in the 1830s.

[81]   Gurney, "Working-Class Writers and the Art of Escapology in Victorian England: The Case of Thomas Frost," *Journal of British Studies*, Vol. 45 (January, 2006), 53.

[82]   Burnett, *Useful Toil*, xiv.

[83]   See E.J. Hobsbawn, *Labouring Men: Studies in the History of Labour* (London: Weidenfeld and Nicolson, 1964), 34ff.

"barely conscious of class beyond recognition" of differences between themselves and the master. Burnett argues that workers "constructed their own exclusive world, remote from the acquisitive accumulative impulses of the Victorian economy ... they were both excluded, and excluded themselves, from public life. ... inhabited an inner, secret life which perpetuated traditional values and patterns of behaviour, essentially of rural origin, into the new urban industrial society."[84]

Somerville and his family were not isolated, but sought increasing participation, despite inexorable hard labor, economic difficulties, and lack of education.[85] Regenia Gagnier argues that Victorian subjectivity, something taken for granted by middle-class male authors, had to be justified for working-class authors for whom it was not a given. From his autobiography on, Somerville claimed historical agency. Asked by conspirators because of his "reputation which I had acquired (forced upon me, I should say)"[86] by the flogging affair to join a plan to kidnap government officials, Somerville wrote letters to newspapers warning workers to avoid being in the streets on the appointed day of the procession but did not expose the plan. Many avoided the procession, so Somerville felt he had frustrated the plot (he did write to Lord Melbourne about the plot). In his *Autobiography*, he confessed to these secret writings "In the hope of teaching working men a lesson ... of the danger their mad-headed leaders have placed then in."[87] He closed his text with a promise that his knowledge of the conspirators would die with him. As in the flogging incident, Somerville remained mum on names of other workers involved in these events.

Mark Hearn and Harry Knowles cite Bourdieu's notion of the struggle for recognition, defined as "personal identity and value as a citizen," as a "fundamental dimension of social life" through which workers seek "honour in the sense of reputation and prestige" to accumulate symbolic capital.[88] Hearns and Knowles suggest biography as a means to weave textures of individual lives into discourses of social history in a "dialogue of the self and the social" that refuses to reduce either of these or consider them distinct, instead of dialectically interlocked.[89] For Somerville journalism permitted him a chance to join his personal (*Autobiography*) with the social (political economy) to make sense of his and others' lives. Autobiography haunted all of Somerville's writings as a means to write himself into Britain's larger history. He claimed to have affected history—he stopped a riot, stung the Leaguers, etc.—by virtue of his dual roles as a laborer and as an upwardly mobile middle-class writer.

---

[84]   Burnett, xix.

[85]   John Burnett, ed. *Destiny Obscure: Autobiographies of Childhood, Education and Family from the 1820s to the 1920s* (London: Routledge, 1982), xvii.

[86]   *Autobiography*, 273.

[87]   Ibid., 282–287.

[88]   Hearn and Knowles, "Struggling for Recognition: Reading the Individual in Labour History," *Labour History*, Vol. 87 (November, 2004), 1.

[89]   Ibid., 3.

Journalism alone—not the army, trade union, or politics—was the only institution through which he could exercise his abilities. Journalism offered Somerville Victorian ideologies of literary activity—individualism, public voice, didactic intentions, signatorial identity, name as trademark, and the myth of creative genius. Somerville's overarching obsessive autobiographical references intruded upon everything he wrote to create a body of literature that could be called autoethnographic, a mode of life narrative that "writes back" to the dominantly middle-class genre. As Michael Sheringham argues: "We do not remember alone, and our story is that of our place and time,"[90] drawing on shared experience embedded in social contexts. Mary Louise Pratt defined autoethnography as a mode in which "colonized subjects undertake to represent themselves in ways that engage with the colonizer's own terms."[91] She argued that processes of "transculturation" change generic modes of life writing, through collaboration and appropriation, to produce hybrid forms of collective narrative. Such literary encounters offer revisions of genres that then require new reading practices.

These ideas suggest ways of understanding Somerville's autobiographical obsessions as resistance to middle-class (especially Leaguers) attempts to "colonize" workers to fit their agenda. He recycled autobiography into journalism sprinkled with palpable life stories (e.g., Sally Grey, children's stories, individual workers telling their lives, and imaginary tours of Britain that echo his own travels in the British countryside and cities). He engaged the colonizers' own terms, not only in his literary style and content but in his more combative replies to Leaguers and editors who presumed to tell him how to confront his "betters."

In 1913 Canadian author William Sandison wrote an article on Somerville in *Border Magazine*,[92] complete with illustrations and portraits of Somerville. Sandison presented Somerville as a man who shunned the martyr's role following the flogging and surveyed his publications, including those written in Canada, his establishment of the *Canadian Illustrated News* until 1864, his writings on the 1866 Fenian troubles in Canada, and his intention to write his memoirs and expose those responsible for his letter to the press in 1832, which Somerville never did (trunks with the manuscripts supposedly disappeared). Political economy could not save Somerville from his many business failures, his obsessive defensiveness and dying in poverty in Toronto, but his work did carve out a space for his reputation on two continents and two centuries. His *Autobiography* reprinted in 1951 and 1967 and a play about him, *Somerville the Soldier* by Donald Campbell (1978), focused on the flogging incident, about which Somerville had so much to tell and retell.

[90]   I wish to thank my colleague Julia Watson for her suggestions on relations between autoethnography and autobiography. See Michael Sheringham, "Memory," in *Encyclopedia of Life Writing*, ed. Margaret Jolly (London: Fitzroy Dearborn, 2001), 597.

[91]   Mary Louise Pratt. *Imperial Eyes: Travel Writing and Transculturation* (London: Routledge, 1992), 7.

[92]   Vol. 18, No. 207 (March, 1913), 1–9.

Works Cited

Bourdieu, Pierre. *In Other Words: Essays Towards a Reflexive Sociology.* London, 1990.

Burnett, John, ed. *Useful Toil: Autobiographies of Working People from the 1820s to the 1920s.* London and New York: Routledge, 1994.

———. *Destiny Obscure: Autobiographies of Childhood, Education and Family from the 1820s to the 1920s.* London: Routledge, 1982.

Campbell, Donald. *Somerville the Soldier, a Play.* Edinburgh: P. Harris, 1978.

Clark, Anna. *The Struggle for the Breeches: Gender and the Making of the British Working Class.* Berkeley: University of California Press, 1995.

Epstein James. *In Practice: Studies in the Language and Culture of Popular Politics in Modern Britain.* Palo Alto: Stanford University Press, 2003.

———. "'Bred as a Mechanic': Plebian Intellectuals and Popular Politics in Early Nineteenth-Century England," in *Intellectuals and Public Life: Between Radicalism and Reform,* eds Leon Fink, Stephen Leonard, and Donald Reid. Ithaca: Cornell University Press, 1996, 53–73.

Frank, Christopher. "'Let But One of Them Come before Me, and I'll Commit Him': Trade Union, Magistrates, and the Law in Mid-Nineteenth-Century Staffordshire," *Journal of British Studies,* Vol. 44, No. 1 (January, 2005), 64–91.

Gagnier, Regenia. *Subjectivities: A History of Self-Representation in Britain, 1832–1920.* Oxford: Oxford University Press, 1991.

Gurney, Peter, "Working-Class Writers and the Art of Escapology in Victorian England: The Case of Thomas Frost," *Journal of British Studies,* Vol. 45, No. 1 (January, 2006), 51–71.

Hearn, Mark and Harry Knowles, "Struggling for Recognition: Reading the Individual in Labour History," *Labour History,* Vol. 87 (November, 2004), 1–9.

Hobsbawn, E.J. *Labouring Men: Studies in the History of Labour.* London: Weidenfeld and Nicolson, 1964.

Krishnamurthy, Aruna. "'More than Abstract Knowledge': Friedrich Engels in Industrial Manchester," *Victorian Literature and Culture,* Vol. 28, No. 2 (2000), 427–448.

———. "'Assailing the Thing': Politics of Space in William Cobbett's Rural Rides," Cardiff Corvey: *Reading the Romantic Text,* Issue 7, No. 1 (December, 2001), 1–15. <http://www.cf.ac.uk/encap/corvey/articles/cc07_n01.html>.

Lengel, Edward G. *The Irish Through British Eyes; Perceptions of Ireland in the Famine Era.* Westport, CT and London: Praeger, 2002.

———. "A 'Perverse and Ill-Fated People': English Perceptions of the Irish, 1845–52," *Essays in History,* Vol. 38 (1996). <http://etext.lib.virginia.edu/journals/EH/EH38/Lengel.html>.

Plotz, John. *The Crowd: British Literature and Public Politics.* Berkeley: University of California Press, 2000.

Royle, Edward. Modern *Britain: A Social History, 1750–1997*. London: Arnold 1997.

Savage, Mike, and Andrew Miles. *The Remaking of the British Working Class, 1840–1940*. London: Routledge, 1994.

Somerville, Alexander. *The Autobiography of a Working Man*. London: C. Gilpin, 1848. (Also: London: Turnstile, 1951; ed. John Carswell. London: Macgibbon and Kee, 1967).

———. *Book Of A Diligent Life*. Montreal: John Lovell, 1869.

———.*Canada, a Battle Ground about a Kingdom in America*. Hamilton, Canada West, ON: Printed for the author by Donnelley & Lawson, 1862.

———. *A Chapter on the Men of the League, being a note from the factory districts, which must not be overlooked by those interested in agriculture*. Scotland: np, 1843.

———. *Cobdenic Policy, the Internal Enemy of England*. London, R. Hardwicke, 1854.

———. *Conservative Science of Nations (preliminary instalment) being the first complete narrative of Somerville's diligent life in the service of public safety in Britain*. Montreal and Toronto: J. Lovell, 1860.

———. *Dissuasive Warnings to the People on Street Warfare. Letter II, 1839*. London: J. Patten, 1839.

———. *Financial Reform. Mr. Cobden's defence of his national budget. Letter to the publisher, by "One who has whistled at the plough."* Liverpool: Matthews printer, n.d.

———. *Free Trade and the League: a biographic history of the pioneers of freedom of opinion, commercial enterprise, & civilisation, in Britain, from the times of serfdom to the age of free trade in manufactures, food, and navigation*. Manchester, J. Ainsworth, 1853.

———. *History of the British Legion, and War in Spain, with an Appendix, containing every officer's name, rank, and service, that was in the expedition*. London, James Pattie, 1839. Also Manchester: J. Ainsworth, 1853.

———. *A Journey to Harmony Hall, Hampshire with some particulars of the socialist community* ... [England: np, 1842 (Variant ed.)].

———. *A Letter to the Farmers of England on the Relationship of Manufactures and Agriculture*. London: J. Ridgway, 1843.

———. *Letters from Ireland during the Famine of 1847*, ed. K.D.M Snell. Dublin; Portland, OR: Irish Academic Press, 1994 (orig. pub. 1847).

———. *The Life of Roger Mowbray*. London: Darton, 1853.

———. *Living for a Purpose: or, the Contrast*. London: Darton and Hodge, 1865.

———. *A Narrative of the British Auxiliary Legion: with incidents, anecdotes, and sketches of all parties connected with the war in Spain, from a journal of personal observation*, Glasgow: Muir, Gowans & Co., 1838.

———. *Narrative of an Eventful Life: A Contribution to the Conservative Science of Nations*. Hamilton, ON: np, 1863.

————. *Narrative of the Fenian Invasion of Canada with a map of the fields of combat, at Limestone Ridge.* Hamilton, ON: Joseph Lyght, 1866.

————. *Notes from the Farming Districts, no. XVII; a journey to Harmony Hall in Hampshire, with some particulars on the socialist community, to which the attention of the nobility, gentry, and clergy, is earnestly requested* ... England: np, 1842.

————. *The O'Connor Land Scheme Examined and Described from its Formation to the Present Time: by one who has whistled at the plough and Mr. Joshua Hobson* ... London: B.D. Cousins, 1847.

————. *Personal Experiences in Executing Lord Palmerston's Foreign Policy.* London: np, 1850.

————. *Public and Personal Affairs, being an enquiry into the physical strength of the people, in which the value of their pikes and rifles is compared with that of the grape-shot, shells, and rockets, of the Woolwich artillery: also, an exposure of treacherous patriots and drunken lawyers who have imposed upon the people, and are connected with Alderman Harmer, and the Weekly Dispatch, the whole comprising a personal narrative (1839).* London: Printed, published, and sold by A. Somerville, 1839.

————. *Somerville's Financial Reform Catechism. No. 1: The Soldier's Kit.* London: Bateman & Hardwicke, 1849.

————. *Somerville's Manchester School of Political Economy.* English Serial Publication: Periodical Monthly: Manchester: Abel Heywood and W. Irwin, June–August, 1850.

————. *Somerville's National Wealth Tracts. No. 1, Capital and labour.* London: C. Gilpin, 1848.

————. *The Whistler at the Plough containing travels, statistics, and descriptions of scenery and agricultural customs in most parts of England: with letters from Ireland: also "Free trade and the League;" a biography history.* Manchester: J. Ainsworth, 1852; London: W. French, 1853. (Also London: Merlin Press, 1989; and Fairfield, NJ: A. Kelley, 1952.)

————. *The Working Man's Witness against the London Literary Infidels*, No.1. London: np, 1858.

Thompson, E.P. *The Making of the English Working Class.* New York: Vintage Books 1966.

Vincent, David. *Bread, Knowledge and Freedom: A Study of Nineteenth-Century Working Class Autobiography.* London and New York: Methuen, 1981.

Chapter 11
Politeness and Intertextuality in Michael Faraday's Artisan Essay-circle[1]

Alice Jenkins

The year after Faraday's death in 1867, his fellow-Royal Institution scientist John Tyndall wrote, in a hyperbolic and wholly misleading comment which might nonetheless have mightily gratified the Faraday of fifty years earlier: "Faraday could not write otherwise than as a gentleman."[2] This essay explores one of the means by which Faraday practiced writing 'as a gentleman' and suggests that the history of early nineteenth-century artisan writing has not yet taken sufficient account of the assimilative and aspirational in working-class intellectualism.

Class mobility has long been a key element of the construction of Michael Faraday as a figure in popular and literary culture. Samuel Smiles's 1859 *Self-Help*, for instance, described Faraday as "the son of a blacksmith, [who] now occupies the very first rank as a philosopher, excelling even his master, Sir Humphrey Davy, in the art of lucidly expounding the most difficult and abstruse points in natural science."[3] Apprenticed to a bookbinder at fourteen, Faraday had very little formal education but began to acquire scientific knowledge in his teens by reading among the books brought in for binding, attending evening lectures, and later working as Chemical Assistant first to Davy, then to William Brande, professor of chemistry at the Royal Institution. Through his twenties, while he was undertaking this scientific apprenticeship, he adopted a variety of self-improvement techniques constituting what Iwan Rhys Morus has called "a concerted campaign of betterment."[4] He was active in a variety of self-help scientific and educational groups, including the City Philosophical Society, run by the silversmith John Tatum from his house in Dorset Street in London.[5]

[1]   I am very grateful to Aruna Krishnamurthy, Frank A.J.L. James and Catherine Steel for helpful comments on earlier versions of this essay.
[2]   John Tyndall, *Faraday as a Discoverer*. 5th ed. Repr. Kessinger, 2004.
[3]   Samuel Smiles, *Self-Help; with Illustrations of Character, Conduct, and Perseverance*, ed. Peter W. Sinnema (Oxford: Oxford World's Classics, 2002), 24.
[4]   Iwan Rhys Morus, *Frankenstein's Children: Electricity, Exhibition, and Experiment in Early Nineteenth-Century London* (Princeton: Princeton University Press, 1998), 19.
[5]   For an account of Faraday's involvement with the CPS see Frank A.J.L. James, "Michael Faraday, the City Philosophical Society and the Society of Arts," *Royal Society of Arts Journal*, Vol. 140 (1992), 192–199.

Faraday took care to ensure that his self-presentation was appropriate to the circles in which he wanted to move; he followed a course in elocution and made a close study of the oratorical techniques used by the public lecturers to whom he had access. To ensure that his written as well as his spoken English was clear, well-constructed and socially acceptable, Faraday founded a writing group in July 1818 along with four other ambitious young Londoners: Edward Deeble, Edward Barnard, Thomas Deacon, and J. Corder. Of these four, Barnard is the best-documented. He came from a well-to-do artisan family; his father was a highly successful silversmith. The others, especially Deacon and Corder, are much more difficult to trace; however, the fact that they were allowed to join the group may suggest that their backgrounds were not significantly different from the others'. It seems reasonable to identify the essay-circle as at least predominantly an artisan self-improvement group, one of the many fora existing in the capital at that time in which new possibilities for social mobility and cultural enfranchisement were being explored—where, in short, working-class intellectuals were developing.

For a year and a half the group met every two months, each contributing an essay, poem or letter to be copied into the group's book for criticism by the others. Over the eighteen months of its existence, the circle produced forty-seven texts, ranging from substantial 2,500 word essays to a comic poem of 17 quatrains. Although by 1818 Faraday had been working in elite scientific circles for five years, neither his contributions to the "Mental Exercises" nor those of the other members deal with topics in the physical sciences, though they do sometimes address matters which contemporary writers tended to classify as belonging to the "sciences of the mind." The group seems to have felt that moral subjects were the most appropriate to their project of literary upward mobility, but not to have been able to stick for long to the very high-minded vein of the initial months.

The 50,000-word manuscript of the group's work, titled "A Class Book, for the Reception of Mental Exercises," is now preserved in the Faraday archives of the Royal Institution and an edition has been recently published by Liverpool University Press. The texts produced by this London essay-circle can helpfully be included in the study of early nineteenth-century working-class writing. The circle's bi-monthly exercises offer important evidence about the intellectual aspirations, tastes and politics of non-radical artisans in this period, a social group which has been somewhat neglected in the history of working-class literacy.

Evidence of the writing of this social group is scarce and often incomplete; this complicates the task of contextualizing the writings produced by Faraday's essay-circle. I shall suggest later that the essay-circle does not readily fit dominant critical models of working-class writing in the period, because these have generally been derived from the study of writers committed to radical (or, less often, anti-radical) politics. Faraday and his friends barely show interest in the political questions of their time; to compare them to writers like Samuel Bamford, William Cobbett, or Christopher Thomson, would be to misrepresent their literary and social ambitions. The members of the essay-circle hoped to produce texts which, rather than belonging among contemporary artisan writing, looked to the literature of a higher social class and a more polite and conventional voice. Accordingly, this essay will explore the aims and practices of Faraday's essay-circle through an account of its intertextual relations with canonical writers.

At first, these relations were characterized by considerable anxiety. The members of the essay circle evidently felt a good deal of diffidence about themselves as authors, and took pains to limit their individual responsibility for their work. At the most formal level, the group deliberately obscured authorship in the sense of personal accountability for the texts they produced. The book opens with a set of eight procedural rules, the last of which insists on personal authorial responsibility: "as entire liberty is allowed in the choice of the subject, and the manner of treating it; so, also, none be considered as involved in the observations of another, or accountable except for his own productions."[6] But this guarantee of individual rights and duties seems to have been unnecessary, because the group went to some trouble to suppress individualism from their texts. Members signed their work with initials only (in many cases apparently pseudonymous), or simply left it unsigned. Attribution is made especially difficult by their practice of delegating to a scribe the copying up of each two-month period's crop of writing, so that handwriting is no guide to authorship. Although the group's complicated approach to authorship poses methodological problems for the historian, it also provides a useful contrast to the emphasis in modern criticism of nineteenth-century working-class writing on autobiography and confessionality. Further, the sense of collective identity that results from the concealment of individual attribution has the effect of strengthening the group's voice as representing a little-heard segment of artisan writers.

The attempts the group's members made to minimize the importance of attribution are indicative of their sense of identity and purpose as authors. Although a few of the texts they produced refer to particular incidents or allusions which single one member out from the others, on the whole the members did not aim to write in a highly individualized way. Stylistically, their goal was to adopt a polite manner which they seem to have understood as a generic way of writing, in the polished surface of which individuality or personal difference would have appeared as a flaw. And the content of their writing, equally, tends—at first, particularly—to be general, philosophical, and designed to resemble known successful models rather than to fulfill an impulse to autobiographical expression. Though first-person writing is not uncommon in the group's work, it is not at all clear in many instances that 'I' refers to any particular group member; rather it often seems to refer to an assumed authorial persona or the voice of perceived social wisdom. These practices make identifying Faraday's contributions less than straightforward, though among the few scholars who have commented on these materials, there is consensus that

---

[6]   *Michael Faraday's Mental Exercises: An Artisan Essay-Circle in Regency London*, ed. Alice Jenkins (Liverpool: Liverpool University Press, 2008), p. 40.

two substantial essays on imagination and judgment are his.[7] The collective or conventional first person is one of the techniques the group's members used to negotiate a respectful stance towards the canonical styles to which they aspired. It allowed them to get past their sense of their personal unreadiness or unfitness as authors, and to enter the sphere of writing—even the comparatively private sphere of a circulated manuscript. The effects of strengthened legislation against sedition, and of active prosecution of authors and publishers may also have had a significant effect on the essay-circle members' decisions about what to write and how to construct themselves as authors, as I shall discuss later.

The most explicit evidence for the group's authorial intentions comes early in the "Mental Exercises," where the members write in earnest and high-minded rhetoric about their purposes and their sense of what one calls "the imperious duty" of mental self-improvement.[8] Though later offerings included anecdotes, poems and puzzles, the first crop of bi-monthly writings consisted entirely of essays, all addressing elevated themes such as "Honour," "Argument," and "Hope," and several stressing the importance of the kind of project on which they were embarking. The essay "On Study" is typical of the approach adopted during the group during this, its most serious phase: it proposes some general and impersonal reflections on the definitions of key terms and exhorts the reader to "the formation of a habit of reasoning" and methodical thought.[9] But almost throughout the essay, the tone is distant and discursive. Only the final paragraph makes any allusion to the existence of the group itself:

> Now it is the humble endeavour of a few individuals, to secure to themselves a portion of the good that belongs to a well regulated and disciplined mind; and to expand their views, and render them distinct, by urging themselves into an active and delicate perception of things. It is believed, that by practising the mind in attention, and progression; a habit of industry and improvement will be formed. – The rules, or regulations, which preceed these remarks, are supposed to be sufficient to ensure the advantages resulting from method, without in any way confining exertions; and whatever opinion may be formed of the plan, still we may without vanity say that it merits praise, since it has humility for its character and improvement for its object.[10]

The writer of this essay takes elaborate grammatical precautions, including use of weighty passives ("it is believed", "the rules [...] are supposed") and third-person plural narration ("to secure to themselves") to avoid identifying either himself or his reader as personally involved in the self-improvement process he urges.

7   See L. Pearce Williams, *Michael Faraday: A Biography* (London: Chapman and Hall, 1965), 81, 93.

8   *Michael Faraday's Mental Exercises*, 44.

9   Ibid., 45.

10   Ibid., 45–46.

Only in the penultimate clause does a first-person form emerge from the mass of distancing constructions, and even this is a rather remote "we."

By contrast, the first of the essays which we can confidently attribute to Faraday uses much more active and colorful constructions, though it addresses a related subject. "On Imagination and Judgement" follows the same pattern as "On Study" in opening with general reflections and closing with a more pointed reference to the group's project, but an important difference is that Faraday acknowledges the difficulties as well as the advantages of self-improvement. The chief difficulty he explores is that of finding a place in which to begin: Faraday explains that this problem undermines the confidence of all self-improvers and his own confidence as a writer. Noting that the difficulty of making a beginning afflicts everyone on first becoming aware of the immensity of human knowledge, Faraday concludes that the same problem is at work in his unease with the formal requirements of essay-writing:

> We feel it necessary that our first essay should be in the style of a preface and therefore not having the choice of a subject the mind is compell'd to enter though unwillingly into the first attempt while the very circumstances which should be the spur to our exertions are the means which retard the accomplishment of so easy a task.[11]

The first person plural here might be an attempt to speak for the group, or for an imagined constituency of self-improvers beyond the bounds of the group. Or it might refer to Faraday himself, in a rhetorical move which could be read as both self-concealing and self-aggrandizing. The concern with making form and content agree (prefatory essays must address prefatory subjects) suggests that Faraday hopes to make his writing match a pre-existing standard of expression, one in which his own present confusion is impermissible and all but unspeakable. His stylistic aspiration is thus at odds with his evident interest in his own experience as an autodidact. In the final sentences of the essay, however, Faraday manages to reconcile the two by looking towards a future in which he (along with the rest of the group) will have adopted a polite style so thoroughly as to lose the fear of its fitting his thoughts badly:

> We shall trace with pleasure the visible alteration in the style and substance of our essays we shall be delighted with the ease with which we perform what at first appeared so formidable. – I expect to read this paper at no distant period with a triumphant pleasure at my success [...][12]

I want to suggest that the shifting, unstable relationship between "I" and "we" in this essay is a mark of an uncertainty about identity which characterizes the "Mental Exercises." In the remainder of the essay I will explore this uncertainty in

---

[11]   Ibid., 55.
[12]   Ibid., 55.

terms of a series of possible identities affecting much of the writing in the MS: first two of the large-scale identities which we might expect to provide a framework for the group, and then some intertextual relationships based on defining levels of identification between the group's members and other writers.

Let us start with the large-scale identities offered by religious and class affiliation. Three members at least—Barnard, Deacon and Faraday—were from families belonging to the Sandemanian church, and this religious connection profoundly colors the group's textual aspirations and productions, though not in immediately predictable ways. The Sandemanian church was an offshoot of the Church of Scotland. Robert Sandeman, whose father-in-law John Glas founded this Protestant sect in Scotland, migrated to England in the mid-eighteenth century and then to America, where churches following his practice survived until the 1890s. Sandeman's followers emphasized a near-literalist interpretation of the Bible and sought to separate themselves to a considerable degree from the rest of society, often intermarrying, for example. Since the nineteenth century, biographers and historians have been much interested in the effects of Faraday's Sandemanianism on his scientific and personal life, though sometimes this interest has been superficial. The most comprehensive treatment of the topic to date is Geoffrey Cantor's 1991 biography. But the role played by Sandemanianism in the making of Faraday as working-class intellectual—that is, the intersection between his religious and class identities—has not received much attention. The "Mental Exercises" gave Faraday and his fellow Sandemanians among the essay-circle an opportunity to write about moral topics outside the social and generic bounds of their religion, and they seem to have used the implicit permission to experiment that the essay-circle provided to assume a pose of worldliness without transgressing religious barriers. So rather than writing in directly religious genres, modelling their work on the landmarks of Dissenting literature, addressing religious themes, or frequently quoting Scripture, the members of the essay circle preferred to adopt a sophisticated manner in which religious principles appeared in the guise of a concern with individual moral judgement and a tendency to treat social and psychological questions as matters of character and principle. It may be relevant to Faraday's experimentation in the "Mental Exercises" that he did not make his confession of faith in the Sandemanian church until 1821, a couple of years after the essay-circle folded, and may until that point have felt he had some license to discuss moral matters in a way that was not explicitly religious.

As well as religion, a second large-scale identity available to the members of the group was based on class; but the urbane pose adopted by the group has the effect of heavily suppressing the presence of class identity in their work. Indeed, as an instance of artisan writing in the early nineteenth century, the "Mental Exercises" are at first sight notable for their refusal to engage in class politics, indeed for a disdain for popular politics altogether. This, as I have suggested, makes the task of interpreting the essay circle and its writings within currently-available critical frameworks rather problematic. The study of nineteenth-century working-class British literature has often focused on autobiography and radical writing, both of which fit well into a historicist critical model which reads them in the context of contemporary social conditions and political movements. Neither genre, however, reflects the kind of writing Faraday and his circle were producing. In particular, the absence of class-based radicalism in the texts in the "Mental Exercises" means that they are not easily accommodated by many of the critical models developed since E.P. Thompson's *Making of the English Working Class*, despite Thompson's citing the Sandemanians among the Dissenting sects in which the roots of nineteenth-century working-class intellectualism were located.[13] More recent scholarship on conservative and counter-revolutionary writing of the early nineteenth century has provided a picture of a much more diverse Romantic engagement in contemporary politics, but the work of the essay-circle does not fit well with anti-radical writing either. On the whole, rather than presenting any programmatic or activist politics, the "Mental Exercises" evince attitudes much like those which Kevin Gilmartin describes as "implicit and deeply embedded habits of deference and national feeling that undoubtedly contributed to the prevention of revolution in Britain;" though as I shall indicate shortly, interesting and suggestive counter-examples occur from time to time in the manuscript.[14]

Considered in a rather crude way, the essay-circle's emphasis on adopting the classical models of the previous century might be interpreted as a reaction of economically- and socially-successful artisans against the developing working-class consciousness traced by E.P. Thompson. On the other hand, the collectivity of the enterprise, the emphasis on group rather than individual identity, and the acknowledgement that literary and socio-economic endeavor are related might suggest that the essay-circle should be seen as reflective of a growing class-consciousness indeed, but one that eschews political critique in favor of economic assimilation. This is not to say that the "Mental Exercises" are not concerned with ideology. In some ways, indeed, they could be cited as an example of conscious embourgeoisement. The topic of self-improvement is directly addressed several times in these texts, usually with reference to acquiring "superior" mental habits ("superior" is a favorite word of this group). The members seem to have measured their improvement in greater politeness, polish, and civility, the acquisition of the manners and style of a gentleman, as well as in the sturdier qualities of mental discipline, skill in argument and discrimination. Though the essay-circle was itself a collective and clearly a social endeavor, its textual productions show almost no interest in the lives or conditions of workers outside the group. In this respect the essay-circle's self-*improvement* activities are significantly different from the self-*help* practiced by artisan groups in this period and later in the century. The historian Eric Hopkins distinguishes between nineteenth-century working-class self-help aimed at co-operative social provision and employment protection, and

---

[13]   E.P. Thompson, *The Making of the English Working Class* (Harmondsworth: Penguin, 1984), 35, 55.

[14]   Kevin Gilmartin, *Writing Against the Revolution: Literary Conservatism in Britain, 1790–1832* (Cambridge: Cambridge University Press, 2007), 9–10.

"the conventional form of Victorian self-help", which involves "individual endeavour, raising one's self by one's own boot straps, getting on by solid endeavour."[15] Faraday's essay-circle seems to have subscribed much more to the latter than the former model of working-class organization. Sandemanians were exhorted to be "exclusive," to have nothing to do with the religious practices of other churches or their members, and to be apolitical.[16] If three or more of the group's members were influenced by, if not actually bound by, Sandemanian doctrine, this may have contributed to the group's apparent lack of interest in external affairs. Certainly the essay-circle's members express no identification with the poor or the laboring classes and very little even with the labor aristocracy of skilled artisans from which several of them originated.

In this respect, Patrick Joyce's model of 'populism', though derived chiefly from later nineteenth-century writing, is in limited ways more appropriate to the work of the essay-circle than Thompson-influenced class-based models. Joyce sees populism as "a set of discourses and identities which are extra-economic in character, and inclusive and universalising in their social remit in contrast to the exclusive categories of class."[17] Though the group wholly ignores the political critique at the heart of the radical populism described by Joyce, nonetheless it displays in a weaker form some of the elements of this populism, particularly its universalist tendency. Paradoxically, the 'exclusivism' of Sandemanianism results in a kind of universalism as the members focus their interests not on groups or sections of the population but on the individual (especially in essays approaching toward the philosophy of mind) and on the construction of a decontextualized, depoliticized universal moral being. The group's social views are exemplified by a passage in an essay "On Tradesmen" which identifies trade as the occupation of every citizen rather than that of an identifiable sector of the nation:

> there are few who can say they have never in their lives, engaged in any sort of dealing for the sake of gain, if it be the artist, the man of literature, or the man of science each will vend some time or other the produce of his hands, or his intellectual labor, [and] it will be seen that all are so engaged (unless thro' the prevention of indolence) from the monarch down to the lowest subject.[18]

The attempt to group all sellers of labor as 'tradesmen' does not express a political commitment to leveling or reforming class structures; rather it is a way of evading social categories by applying moral ones. The essay urges that "tradesmen" be judged as individuals, based on their characters, their behavior, filial obedience,

---

[15]   Eric Hopkins, *Working-class Self-Help in Nineteenth-Century England: Responses to Industrialization* (London: University College London Press, 1995), 3.

[16]   Geoffrey Cantor, *Michael Faraday: Sandemanian and Scientist* (Houndmills: Macmillan, 1991), 6.

[17]   Patrick Joyce, *Visions of the People: Industrial England and the Question of Class, 1848–1914* (Cambridge: Cambridge University Press, 1991), 11.

[18]   *Michael Faraday's Mental Exercises*, 139.

financial prudence and social habits. The writer is not at all concerned with the mechanisms of trade, the place of tradesmen in the national economy, or the rights and wrongs of contemporary trade practices.

As in this example, the members of the essay-circle generally eschewed discussing current affairs, often using conventionality in thought or expression to avoid topicality. In particular, where they touched on subjects of power or social hierarchy they often tried to adopt a tone of worldly sophistication which permitted general reflections without topical reference. The writer of the brief essay "On Laws," for example, avoids political analysis by assuming a universal (and banal) consensus in attitudes to legislation:

> all agree that laws are useful; all find pleasure in making them for others; and, all dislike the constraint they impose on themselves. [19]

The purpose of this essay is not to discuss legislative practice, still less to identify faults in the legal system: it is to complain about the other members' failure to submit their essays on time. In this context, it would be an over-reading to interpret such free-floating pronouncements as politically engaged, not least because they do not identify the group or any member with any section of society. The writings produced by the group almost never mention class or other large-scale interests other than that of the nation as a whole: they generally take English patriotism for granted and focus ideological comments mainly on individual character.

However, isolated and rather surprising exceptions to this general lack of political engagement indicate that the essay group was not so immune to contemporary political debate as they might have wished to suggest. In particular, brief comments about kings and kingship suggest that one member at least of the group was willing to express somewhat subversive views, and that the others were willing at least to countenance them. In a single treasonous sentence in a collection of 'Memoranda', the group jeopardized its anti-engagement habit:

> The Son of Napoleon is more legitimate on the throne of France than the present Dynasty on that of England.[20]

Why should one of this socially conservative group of artisans have expressed such a subversive view of the Hanoverians? Faraday is the only one of the group to whose political views beyond the MS book we have access; and he was in this period noticeably unconcerned with large-scale politics. Geoffrey Cantor details the Sandemanian tradition of loyalty to the civic authorities and obedience to the monarch, whether he be "a just king or a despotic ruler."[21] However, though the group's political thinking may well reflect the Sandemanian tradition of disregard for worldly bodies and events, nonetheless a rare but important vein of criticism of

---

[19]   Ibid., 143.
[20]   Ibid., 120.
[21]   Cantor, 93.

George III or the Prince Regent runs through the "Mental Exercises." An important example comes in an essay "On Prematurely Forming Opinions of Characters" which immediately precedes a poem by another group member on the death of Princess Charlotte. This essay urges the unfairness of condemning "as a democrat, a leveller, one who wishes ill to his Country" a man who

> questioned the power of the king under some peculiar circumstances, and considered that a Monarch is but a Man, who is elevated to his rank by the general consent of his fellows not to debauch himself with the luxuries which his high station could command; but to be an example to others, the arm of power for the administration of the laws, and the fulfilling of justice.[22]

The writer of this essay distances himself from these opinions by giving their proponent a classical name, but this rather flimsy device does not disguise the writer's ill-ease at the dangers from suspicion and the assumption of guilt by association in politically turbulent times. "We often see the man condemned, who has not been tried, because he appears to doubt whether the opinions advanced are consistent with reason; and merely differing is made a sufficient crime to be punished by misrepresentation."[23] As usual, the writer strives to present the problem as a moral rather than a political one: but the liberalism of the defence of difference, and the possible radicalism of the appeal to reason over conformity, suggest a surprising moment of political engagement for at least one member of the group; and perhaps a tolerance for such engagement or its expressions among the others who allowed the essay to go into the book.

That this essay group should have shown a comparative lack of interest in the class politics with which many of the celebrated early nineteenth-century artisan writers—Samuel Bamford, for instance—were chiefly concerned is unsurprising for two reasons, one general, the other particular. First, the group was writing during a time of harsh repression of radical political expression, amid outbreaks of political violence including, in August 1819, the Peterloo massacre. Already-severe legislation against subversive politics was being tightened: the late eighteenth-century Combination Acts, which criminalized societies dedicated to political reform, were still in force, and in 1819 the passing of the Seditious Meetings Act and the other 'Gag' Acts further obstructed gatherings of pro-reform organizations. Publishers and pamphleteers were subject to severe penalties for promulgating seditious material. In the last month of the essay-circle's existence, for instance, the radical London artisan publisher Richard Carlile was convicted of seditious libel for publishing accounts of the Peterloo massacre and imprisoned for six years. In this climate, it is easy to see why the respectable and ambitious artisans forming this essay-circle might have sought to keep overt politics out of their writings. And second, the Sandemanians in the group would probably have been particularly reluctant to express sympathy with radical politics, given their tradition of what

---

[22]   *Michael Faraday's Mental Exercises*, 122.
[23]   Ibid.

Cantor calls "a non-factional form of conservatism,"[24] often leading them to eschew engagement in public affairs.

But the views of the essay-circle were not entirely individualist. Though the members did not express interest in collective or class politics, they used literary emulation as a method of engaging with the world beyond the circle. They tried to adopt the styles of writers they admired, or more often to write in a voice that seemed to them public and general rather than private and idiosyncratic, since these qualities suggested social outsiderhood. In attempting to match their own taste to that of respected models, the members were obliged to take part—to some extent—in contemporary debates, albeit largely those in the realm of aesthetics or the science of mind. When they addressed topics such as the pleasures and uses of the imagination,[25] for instance, they were negotiating a relationship for their own writing with the great canonical writers of the eighteenth century who had written on the same subject, particularly Addison and Akenside, and at the same time they were venturing into a set of arguments being staged in the scientific and moral literature of their own time.

In this engagement with canonical writers, especially the eighteenth-century essayists, the members of the essay-circle were characteristic of their class and their period. Paul Thomas Murphy's work on the development of a working-class literary criticism argues that reinvestigation of the traditional canon, and re-presentation of a selection of canonical writers to new readers were important parts of the project of some working-class editors and publishers in the first half of the nineteenth century. While expensive anthologies such as the six volumes of *Elegant Extracts* published around 1810 would have been beyond the means of most artisan readers, many of the Augustan writers included in such collections (especially Addison, Steele, Pope, Johnson, and Sterne) were also being republished in cheaper compilations. Through republications, these classic authors were kept current in early nineteenth-century artisan culture, and were made available in gobbet form to readers like the essay-circle members who lacked a formal literary education. Addison and Steele were cited by authorities on rhetoric such as Hugh Blair as models of various kinds of composition, and by Isaac Watts, whose book on the *Improvement of the Mind* had a profound influence on Faraday's conception of self-improvement, as "having had a considerable share in furnishing the present age with knowledge and politeness."[26] Among the members of the essay-circle, we have external evidence only of Faraday's literary taste, but he at least was certainly given to reading and copying out such gobbets from eighteenth-century writers, especially Pope, Johnson and Addison, as his Common Place Book indicates.

---

24 Cantor, 95.

25 *Michael Faraday's Mental Exercises*, 62–68.

26 Isaac Watts, *The Improvement of the Mind [...]*. 1741 (Whitefish: Kessinger, 2004), 45; see Faraday's *Correspondence*, for his description of Watts as "great in all the methods respecting the attainment of Learning." *The Correspondence of Michael Faraday*, 6 vols, ed. Frank A.J.L. James (London: Institution of Electrical Engineers, 1991), I, 3.

He knew the *Rambler* well enough to make a brief index of his favorite passages; the *Spectator* is also excerpted and indexed in the Common Place Book.[27] The strong presence of these early- and mid-eighteenth century writers in Faraday's reading reflects both their availability and their high standing in self-improvement literature. The fact that their style was now noticeably outdated may have suggested that to emulate them would be to add gravitas to one's own writing, and gravitas, far more than any other quality except for clarity, seems to have been what the essay-circle was hoping to acquire. Accordingly, they emulated.

The most egregious instance of literary emulation in the "Mental Exercises" is the wholesale plagiarism of an anecdote from Benjamin Franklin's *Narrative of the Late Massacres in Lancaster County*. A passage of around three hundred words is lifted from Franklin and copied, minus some of its punctuation, into a very early essay "On Honour."[28] It would be extremely interesting to know whether this copying was detected or confessed, and, if revealed, whether it was regarded by the other members as culpable or as legitimately imitative, or perhaps even as a kind of elegant anthologizing. Much later in the group's life, a member cited another Franklin text, this time his letter "On Early Marriage," in an essay titled "Marriage is Honourable in All." The Franklin letter would have been fairly easily available to the members of the essay circle, having just appeared in a selection of *The Private Correspondence of Benjamin Franklin* [...] published in London in 1817.[29] The writer of the essay "Marriage is Honourable in All," unlike the author of "On Honour," is careful to mention Franklin by name, and the quotation, though not marked off by inverted commas, is separated from the earlier part of the essay by a paragraph break. Should we read this more sophisticated management of citation as evidence that the members developed a more proprietorial attitude to their own and hence to others' writing as they grew in confidence? The early nineteenth-century literary critic Nathan Drake, author of an early nineteenth-century collection of essays on the *Spectator*, *Rambler* and *Idler*, would have seen the shift away from copying as a sign of growing politeness: "it is the description indeed of a liberal, as distinguished from a servile imitation, that it is studious only of the principle and spirit of its model [...] without straining the resemblance to a mechanical conformity."[30] In modern terms, we might argue that the explicit citation (unlike the copying) is a sign of a more conversational and hence more empowered relationship with past authors, as well as of a conscious participation in the world of letters.

---

[27]   Michael Faraday, *Common Place Book*, 2 vols, Institution of Engineering and Technology archives. Special Collections MS2, 176, 8, 395.

[28]   *Michael Faraday's Mental Exercises*, 48.

[29]   Benjamin Franklin, *The Private Correspondence of Benjamin Franklin. Comprising a Series of Letters on Miscellaneous, Literary and Political Subjects*, 2 vols (London: Colburn, 1817), I, 7–9.

[30]   Nathan Drake, *Essays, Biographical, Critical, and Historical [...]*, 3 vols, 1805 (London: Suttaby, 1810), II, 430.

Faraday appears to have been the most confident of the essay group in the direct use of earlier writers. His very first essay for the group opens with an epigraph from Pope: appropriately, the famous couplet on authorial responsibility from the *Essay on Criticism*:

> In every work regard the writer's end
> Since none can compass more than they intend.[31]

In its context in Pope's *Essay*, the couplet reproves over-exacting critics, urging them to give credit for good artistic intentions despite small failures in execution. Intertextuality, however, frequently works against rather than with the meaning of the original, and instead of expounding and elaborating on Pope's point, Faraday reverses the meaning of the lines so that they speak to the situation of the writer rather than the critic. In the context of Faraday's essay, contrary to Pope's original meaning, the lines emphasize the need for ceaseless striving to form rational intellectual habits. Faraday wants them to mean something like: "'writers (and self-improvers) must be vigilant to keep up their good efforts, because otherwise their performance will not come near to their aspirations'. He turns Pope's argument for generosity into an anxious reminder of the ever-present possibility of failure.

Learning to use earlier authors may have been a measure of the group's growing maturity as writers. But it was in their engagements with contemporary authors that their confidence was most rigorously tested. The most topical item in the "Mental Exercises" is a poem of six couplets "On the Death of the Princess Charlotte:"

> Britons repine, and melt in sorrows tears,
> Yes Albion weep, your brightest hope is fled
> For lovely Charlotte joins the band of Dead;
> With her youth, Beauty, loveliness are gone
> And hapless Britons left in gloom forlorn,
> Without a youthful race to wear the Crown.[32]

In writing on this theme, the author was joining a wave of professional and amateur poets contributing in newspapers and periodicals to the national mourning for the death of the twenty-one-year-old Charlotte. This poem's mythologizing method is in keeping with what Stephen Behrendt has identified as the "ornate and laboriously allusive" style characterizing many of the elegies for the Princess.[33] For this reason, it is not possible to be certain whether the choice of allegorical manner was intended to express genuine patriotic support for the House of Hanover, or to secure the success of the poem by anchoring it to accepted literary models and a publicly-validated voice. The second possibility does not necessarily imply

---

[31] *Michael Faraday's Mental Exercises*, 51.

[32] Ibid., 124.

[33] Stephen C. Behrendt. *Royal Mourning and Regency Culture: Elegies and Memorials of Princess Charlotte* (London: Macmillan, 1997), 89.

the first. Conservatism in form and conservatism in politics cannot be assumed to be closely associated in the work of an unpracticed or unconfident writer. The writer's adoption of a conventional and unexceptional poetic voice might suggest that the poem is an exercise rather than an ideological statement. Alternatively, the conventional sentiment which the poem expresses in its (would-be) conventional way might be read as only incidental to the writer's project, and less interesting both to the poet and to us as readers of working-class writing than the fact of an effort toward public expression in a public style on a public event.

I want to suggest, then, after this very brief discussion of their contents, that the "Mental Exercises" pose some interesting problems for the critic of early nineteenth-century working-class writing. Despite the counterexamples I have mentioned, the "Exercises" elude dominant models of critical investigation of artisan texts by their general reluctance to address contemporary political topics. Instead they demand to be judged aesthetically, because aesthetic standards are the ones that the group themselves wanted to meet. But the members' inexperience as writers means that the classical Augustan aesthetic virtues of clarity, elegance, and politeness often lead them into a conventionalism we might even identify as mimicry. If we look for personality or sincerity in these texts, we must seek it not in direct narration, nor in the matching of pace and tone to fluctuations of intensity of argument which we might expect to find in more practiced writers, but in the goals of the project itself and in the gradual emergence of a sense of ownership of those goals, which expresses itself in growing playfulness and formal experimentation as the writers move away from the dominance of the essay form.

James Chandler argues at the opening of his study of *England in 1819* that at this post-Waterloo period, literature was "where (in every sense) the action was – where the work of cultural specification, historical determination, and national constitution seemed crucially to be going on."[34] This national and cultural centrality of literature drew figures (including many of those we now acknowledge as the great writers of their time) into writing, who might easily have given their energies to success in other pursuits. Perhaps something of this irresistible impetus towards literature is involved in the work of Faraday's essay-group. A strictly utilitarian, economic, self-help-minded reading of the group's motives for writing would miss the excitement and enthusiasm which are evident in some of their productions. The fact that the group had very little to say about the political and topical matters which drew most of Chandler's figures into literature does not mean that they were not, in their way, engaging with the contemporary dynamic model of "literature" itself.

Works Cited

Anon., ed., *Elegant Extracts. Being a Copious Selection of Instructive, Moral, and Entertaining Passages, from the Most Eminent Writers*, 6 vols. London: Sharpe, 1810[?].

---

[34]   James Chandler, *England in 1819: The Politics of Literary Culture and the Case of Romantic Historicism* (Chicago: University of Chicago Press, 1998), 46.

Behrendt, Stephen C. *Royal Mourning and Regency Culture: Elegies and Memorials of Princess Charlotte*. London: Macmillan, 1997.

Blair, Hugh. *Lectures on Rhetoric and Belles Lettres*, 1783, eds Linda Ferreira-Buckley and S. Michael Halloran. Carbondale: Southern Illinois University Press, 2005.

Cantor, Geoffrey. *Michael Faraday: Sandemanian and Scientist*. Houndmills: Macmillan, 1991.

Chandler, James. *England in 1819: The Politics of Literary Culture and the Case of Romantic Historicism*. Chicago: University of Chicago Press, 1998.

Drake, Nathan. *Essays, Biographical, Critical, and Historical* [...], 3 vols, 1805. London: Suttaby, 1810.

Faraday, Michael. *The Correspondence of Michael Faraday*, 6 vols, ed. Frank A.J.L. James London: Institution of Electrical Engineers, 1991.

———. *Common Place Book*, 2 vols, Institution of Engineering and Technology archives. Special Collections MS2.

Faraday, Michael, et al. *Michael Faraday's Mental Exercises: An Artisan Essay-Circle in Regency London*, ed. Alice Jenkins. Liverpool: Liverpool University Press, 2008.

Franklin, Benjamin. *The Private Correspondence of Benjamin Franklin. Comprising a Series of Letters on Miscellaneous, Literary and Political Subjects*, 2 vols. London: Colburn, 1817.

Gilmartin, Kevin. *Writing Against the Revolution: Literary Conservatism in Britain, 1790–1832*. Cambridge: Cambridge University Press, 2007.

Gooday, Graeme. "Faraday Reinvented: Moral Imagery and Institutional Icons in Victorian Electrical Engineering," *History of Technology*, Vol. 15 (1993), 190–205.

Hopkins, Eric. *Working-Class Self-Help in Nineteenth-Century England: Responses to Industrialization*. London: University College London Press, 1995.

James, Frank A.J.L. "Michael Faraday, the City Philosophical Society and the Society of Arts," *Royal Society of Arts Journal*, Vol. 140 (1992), 192–199.

Joyce, Patrick. *Visions of the People: Industrial England and the Question of Class, 1848–1914*. Cambridge: Cambridge University Press, 1991.

Morus, Iwan Rhys. *Frankenstein's Children: Electricity, Exhibition, and Experiment in Early Nineteenth-Century London*. Princeton: Princeton University Press, 1998.

Murphy, Paul Thomas. *Toward a Working-Class Canon: Literary Criticism in British Working-Class Periodicals, 1816–1858*. Columbus: Ohio State University Press, 1994.

Schaffer, Simon. "The History and Geography of the Intellectual World," in *William Whewell: A Composite Portrait*, eds Menachem Fisch and Simon Schaffer. Oxford: Clarendon, 1991, 201–232.

Smiles, Samuel. *Self-Help; with Illustrations of Character, Conduct, and Perseverance*, ed. Peter W. Sinnema. Oxford: Oxford World's Classics, 2002.

Smith, Crosbie. "The Genius of Michael Faraday," *Notes and Records of the Royal Society of London*, Vol. 46 (1992), 317–324.

Taylor, John. *The Pocket Lacon. Comprising Nearly One Thousand Extracts from the Best Authors*, 2nd ed. London: Cox, 1837.

Thompson, E.P. *The Making of the English Working Class*. London: Gollancz, 1963. Harmondsworth: Penguin, 1984.

Tyndall, John. *Faraday as a Discoverer*. 5th ed.. Repr. Kessinger, 2004.

Watts, Isaac. *The Improvement of the Mind [...]*, 1741. London: n.p., 1837. Whitefish: Kessinger, 2004.

Williams, L. Pearce. *Michael Faraday: A Biography*. London: Chapman and Hall, 1965.

Chapter 12
Playing at Poverty:
The Music Hall and The Staging
of the Working Class

Ian Peddie

"It's Nice to Be Common Sometimes"
—Daisy Hill

In 1935, the year in which Daisy Hill's yearning to be free of middle-class constrictions first appeared, the music hall was in its final death throes. The rise of cinema and later television had done for the music hall just as the halls had sounded the death knell for free-and-easies and song-and-supper rooms whence they emerged. Nevertheless Hill's song, written and composed by George Ellis, registers more than an evolution in live entertainment; as it implies an ideological impulse beyond a nostalgic longing for "the good old days," the song implicitly gestures towards the transformation of the image of the working class that had occurred on the music hall stage. At its core this reconfiguration, the origins of which may have begun as early as the 1860s, was crucial in damping down any vestigial antithetical political agitation remaining in the wake of the Chartist movement. At the same time, in their role as a stage for redefining existing social structures, the music halls effectively became a platform for propaganda. The dynamics that informed the correlation between these two issues were essential to the universalizing process to which the working class was subject and in which the role of music hall was central. But the influencing of social and political visions was far more subtle and profound than it may at first appear. The patronizing noblesse oblige of popular Victorian novels, to take one example, may have been suitable for the parlor but it simply acknowledged the presence of despair and misery. Instead, and with no little irony, because the reassertion of hierarchy necessitated the complicity of the working class, any rationale for inequality in the social landscape had to take into consideration the vast numbers hierarchy would inevitably emasculate. In ways both insidious and shrewd, those condescendingly referred to as the "salt-of-the-earth" were invited to participate in the refashioning of their own image, or, to paraphrase E.P. Thompson, the working-class audience in the music hall was "present at its own making."[1] What all this meant was that

---

[1]   E.P. Thompson, *The Making of the English Working Class* (New York: Vintage, 1966), 9.

by 1935 Daisy Hill could safely assume that implications arising from the notion of what being "common" actually entailed were understood and shared for reasons other than the uniformity of the audience's social rank. At stake here, of course, were issues beyond questions of gentility: the staged manipulation of the image of the working class functioned to ensure that the meanings disseminated actually became part of the social identities of the working classes.

Hill's assertion unwittingly makes sense because it points to the internalization of distinctions similar to those which the working classes would have to accept were they to accede to the reconfiguring of their images. From this perspective, populist images of the music hall as an escapist and ideologically neutral form of leisure marked by communal entertainment "of the People, for the People, by the People" were important means of concealing agendas that sought to eradicate the politics of class antagonism in favor of the maintenance of deference and hierarchy.[2] So often and in so many ways was the alleged innocuous essence of the music hall articulated that Max Beerbohm, one of its most famous critics, came to think of the music hall as "Demos's Mirror."[3] Beerbohm, as Barry J. Faulk points out, considered music hall entertainment synonymous with English character, and he also viewed it as an exemplar of public organic expression and populist taste.[4] According to Beerbohm, music hall entertainments "have grown, feature for feature, from the public's taste," a belief that invites the conclusion that "they are things which the public itself has created from its own pleasure," and consequently "they know no laws of being but those which the public gives them."[5] The notion that the music hall offered authentic working-class expression was widespread and ensured that as a form of entertainment it was an important site of struggle. After all, as many critics have pointed out, Britain was a nation built upon "cohesive inequality," and there were many willing to invest time and effort in ensuring it remained that way.[6] Behind such sentiments, however, lay the

---

[2]   W. Macqeen-Pope, *The Melodies Linger On: The Story of the Music Hall* (London: W.H. Allen, Nd), 3.

[3]   Beerbohm saw the music hall as a mirror on life: "There is no nonsense about the Halls, no pretence. The mirror is held up, and in it the face of Demos is reflected, whole and unblurred. Thus for those who, like myself, have the misfortune to hate humbug, a Hall is preferable to a theatre. It has an air of honest and freshness not to be found in a theatre. It is nearer to life. The average song, maybe, does not distort life less than the ordinary play; but, at least, it distorts life exactly as the public likes to see life distorted. It shows us, in fact, what are the tastes and sentiments of the public. It is an always trustworthy document. And, in this sense, it is near to life." *More Theatres, 1898–1903* (London: Rupert Hart-Davis, 1969), 274.

[4]   *Music Hall & Modernity: The Late-Victorian Discovery of Popular Culture* (Athens: Ohio University Press), 30.

[5]   Beerbohm, *More Theatres*, 273.

[6]   Philip Williamson, "The Doctrinal Politics of Stanley Baldwin" in *Public and Private Doctrine: Essays in British History Presented to Maurice Cowling*, ed. Michael Bentley (Cambridge: Cambridge University Press, 2002), 198.

dilemma of the experience of class and, crucially, how it would be represented. Ensuring that the "common" was interpreted as a shared and palatable affirmation of Hill's song was the result of a process of social shaping and reinforcement through which the meaning and image of what constituted appropriate notions of working class were contested. Consequently, songs such as "It's Nice to Be Common Sometimes" owed their very existence to the fact that by the time they appeared so much of the entertainment the music halls identified as threatening to the social order, especially anything approximating to class conflict, had either been purged or appropriated and reconfigured to the point where it had been emptied of much of its original potency.

From this perspective, there is no more important figure than that of the cockney, or more specifically that of the costermonger, who by the opening of the twentieth century had been repeatedly staged and completely reinvented.[7] The costermonger as a figure of some independence, with his own barrow from which he sold vegetables, and his historic antipathy towards figures of authority, no doubt elicited much consternation in a Victorian world extremely concerned with exercising paternalistic social control. While these reasons alone made costermongers a target for propaganda, their presence and visibility, with their own distinctive uniforms which later gave rise to the exaggerated attire of Pearly Kings and Queens, ensured that theirs was an image whose effacement and subsequent replacement with a sanitized, staged mockney would prove especially useful. Again, at the risk of laboring a point, this process required the mobilization of narratives that sought to redefine the image of the working class in terms of the political and social aspirations of an establishment cadre; and, any such narratives would also have to function as a template the working class could be invited to adopt. For those who conceived of Britain as a layered social hierarchy contingent upon the maintenance of established categories for its very survival, here was a moment that granted a useful opportunity to reinforce social divisions while simultaneously offering the working classes the illusion that they too had a participatory role in society.

Fundamental to this process were the critics and commentators who saw the music hall and its entertainers as the essence of Englishness. To envisage things in this way necessitated an ideological commitment that banished Henry Mayhew's charges, made in *London Labour and the London Poor* (1851), that the halls were vulgar and coarse; instead, the largely post-1900 cultural shift that imbued "a decidedly low-brow practice" with more significant meaning is invariably explained as a response to the growing commercialism—and implicit connotations of associated artistic banality—that affected the music hall as the twentieth century approached.[8] In this hypothesis, the middle class emerges as a

---

[7]   The term is derived from "costard," which is an apple, and "monger," one who sells.

[8]   Barry J. Faulk, *Music Hall and Modernity* (Athens: University of Ohio Press, 2004), 24.

kind of philistine buffer between the working class, producers of art synonymous with organic "national" expression, and intellectuals, who are beleaguered by middle-class conformism. Appealing though this reading is, it runs the risks of partially removing intellectuals from the political aspects involved in attributing to the working classes ownership of a form of entertainment some intellectuals argued was indistinguishable from the national character. But intellectual privileging of working-class music-hall entertainment was not only a transparently self-serving strategy, it was a form of appeasement, a way of diluting the reality of inequality and reasserting the primacy of hierarchy.

Crucial to this enterprise was the poet and critic T. S. Eliot, whose homage to the music-hall singer Marie Lloyd (1870–1922) elevated her to a synechdocal, representative role of near-angelic status, where "'Marie Lloyd,' as the poet imagined her, comes to stand in *for* the working class."[9] In so doing, Eliot took his place among a long line of critics for whom music-hall entertainers were the true purveyors of an essential and immutable working-class essence. In ways both ingenious and incredulous, critics as diverse as George Orwell, G.H. Mair, and Max Beerbohm have been quick to assert that, as the latter put it, "there is not one peculiarity of our race, good or bad, that is not well illustrated in the Music Halls."[10] At stake here were not merely issues of authenticity: instead an idealized image of the working class realized through its allegedly representative entertainers suggested a sense of anxiety that fostered a desire to co-opt an idealized image of the working class as an ally against the deadening effect of mass consumer society. Hence cultural custodians like Eliot, whose interest in the working-class at times bordered on salacious, revealed an investment in reproducing and sanctioning a working-class that typifies their concept of not what the working-classes might be but what they wanted it to be. The threat posed by the rise of a new commercial lower-middle class, of which the carbuncular clerk of "The Waste Land" is Eliot's archetypal example, suggests that the championing of music hall as the touchstone of working-class experience effectively hid an agenda desirous of what it implicitly purported to oppose: a still more stratified society.[11]

---

[9]   Ibid., 44. See also Eliot's "Marie Lloyd," in *Selected Prose of T.S. Eliot*, ed. Frank Kermode (New York: Farrar, Strauss and Giroux, 1975), 172–174, where the poet asserts his belief in Lloyd's "moral superiority" over other performers. "It was her understanding of the people and sympathy with them, and the people's recognition of the fact that she embodied the virtues which they genuinely most respected in private life, that raised her to the position she occupied at her death. And her death is itself a significant moment in English history. I have called her the expressive figure of the lower classes. There is no such expressive figure for any other class. The middle classes have no such idol: the middle classes are morally corrupt" (173).

[10]   *More Theatres*, 276.

[11]   Useful discussions of the Victorian and Edwardian lower middle class include G.L. Anderson, "The Social Economy of Late-Victorian Clerks," in *The Lower Middle Class in Britain 1870–1914*, ed. Geoffrey Crossick (New York: St. Martin's Press, 1977), 113–133, and Rae Harris Stoll, "The Unthinkable Poor in Edwardian Writing," *Mosaic* (December, 1982), 23–45.

Such significant attempts to exercise influence over the social landscape were contingent upon the assumption that the importance of the music hall as a site of class struggle owed much to its socially diverse audience. The fact that audiences were, as one critic points out, "never homogenous" underlines the relevance of the staging of class just as it amplifies how significant it was that the audience received and interpreted the appropriate social messages.[12] For those invested in promoting a social agenda, the opportunity to transmit selected class values and attitudes in front of a hierarchically diverse audience must have been of inestimable importance. That an elemental contrast between working-class and middle-class attitudes towards the music hall existed is not in doubt. According to Dagmar Kift, the values propagated in the mid-Victorian music hall, those of "hedonism, ribaldry, sensuality, the enjoyment of alcohol, the portrayal of marriage as a tragic-comic disaster, and the equality of sexes at work and leisure" were all "diametrically at odds with those propagated by and attributed to the Victorian middle class."[13] While these were the broad frames of reference that governed social approaches to the music hall, they also encouraged the kind of consistent intervention in music hall programmes that can only be read in terms of class interest. A useful example in this respect is the case of the popular entertainer Charles Godfrey, whose song sketches of Crimean War veterans moved patrons to "volcanic excitement and thunders of applause."[14] Yet towards the end of the nineteenth century, Godfrey was censored in the West End when another of his songs from his Crimean War set, "On Guard," a song about poverty, met with "complaints from the better seats."[15] This suggested that while it was acceptable to invoke patriotism illuminating the neglect of former soldiers was another thing altogether. Considered in the aggregate, these examples intimate a pattern of intent that dovetails with the evolution of the music hall as a medium through which hierarchy and social standing could be defended. Viewed from the standpoint of the working classes, the dilution of class antagonism in the music halls was deepened as the halls became an increasingly commercial venture and their potential as a pulpit for propaganda became evident.[16]

The core assumptions that informed these ideas, the reassertion and maintenance of hierarchy, a social vision consistent with traditions of rank and station, and fear of social conflict between capital and labor, were invariably interpreted

---

[12] Dave Russell, *Popular Music in England, 1840–1914* (Montreal: McGill-Queen's University Press, 1987), 91.

[13] Dagmar Kift, *The Victorian Music Hall: Culture, Class and Conflict* (Cambridge: Cambridge University Press, 1991), 176.

[14] Quoted in Kift, 4.

[15] Quoted in Russell, 90.

[16] Useful on the commercial aspects of music hall ownership is Penelope Summerfield, "The Effingham Arms and the Empire: Deliberate Selection in the Evolution of Music Hall in London" in *Popular Culture and Class Conflict, 1590–1914: Explorations in the History of Labour and Leisure*, eds Eileen Yeo and Stephen Yeo (Brighton: Harvester Press, 1981), 209–240.

through the dominant metropolitan culture. Hence while few critics disagree that the music hall possesses impeccably working-class roots, fewer still oppose the truism that London was the fulcrum of the music hall. The fact that the music hall largely began in London and was subsequently disseminated in the provinces has important implications not least because so much of music hall entertainment defined itself with this proviso in mind. Not surprisingly in this light, many of the provincial artists hoping to "make it" on the London music-hall circuit relied for effect upon provincial stereotypes popular in "the smoke." Typical in this respect was George Formby senior (1875–1921), who was wont to introduce himself to London audiences as "George Formby fra' Wigan" to which he added the rejoinder, "I've not been in England long ..." Born James Booth in Ashton-under-Lyne, Lancashire, the illegitimate son of an illiterate mother, after a dreadful childhood Formby became a comedian known for his dry wit. Ironically, however, perhaps he is best known for a distinctive cough, which he would excuse with "it's not the cough that carries you off, it's the coffin they carries you off in," which was always guaranteed to raise a laugh. But the cough was no act: Formby died of tuberculosis. His London appearances centered around his adoption of the persona of a gormless northerner, John Willie, a provincial notable for his failed attempts at "Playing the Game in the West" (End) as one of his song titles has it. The game that had to be played was, in effect, a form of reassertion of identity consistent with the attitudes of social acquiescence that became an increasing feature of the halls as the twentieth century approached. Read in this way, Formby's naïve provincial invites the kind of paternalism that critics such as Laurence Senelick has suggested is the defining feature of the music hall.[17] No doubt similar conclusions might be applied to the legions of provincial entertainers who trod the boards in London. The authenticity of many of the portrayals they offered might best be judged in the light of a couple of representative acts. First, the Scots singer and comedian Harry Lauder (1870–1950), who was one of the most famous of all music hall performers. Allegedly described by Winston Churchill as "Scotland's greatest ever ambassador," Lauder actually first appeared as an Irish comic singing "Calligan-Call Again." Just as quickly as he dropped his Irish persona, however, Lauder became the stereotypical Scot; replete with kilt, tam and walking stick, he is perhaps most famous for "Roamin in the Gloamin" and "I Love a Lassie." But for all his considerable success the identity Lauder created has always been contentious, not least during his heyday. One of the most striking comments on his act came during his 1917 tour to Australia, where an anonymous correspondent challenged not only the image Lauder was projecting but also the extent to which that image influenced Lauder's imitators. As "a typical Lowlander of the towns, corresponding to the London Cockney," the reviewer asserted, "there is no good reason why it [a kilt] should be worn by Lauder."[18] But while the persistence of

---

[17]   Laurence Senelick, "Politics as Entertainment: Victorian Music-Hall Songs," *Victorian Studies*, Vol. 19, No. 2 (1975), 149–180.

[18]   Quoted in Paul Maloney, *Scotland and the Music Hall, 1850–1914* (Manchester: Manchester University Press, 2003), 179.

the stereotypical vision of the Scot Lauder created particularly rankled, it is the interpretation of the staged Scot in terms of a metropolitan comparison that proves most revealing. Dismissing the presence of "kilt jokes or songs" as "cockney rubbish," the reviewer concluded that "comic songs from London" which made reference to Scots were invariably written by "the slum-brained type of Cockney song-writer."[19] Compelling correlations of this ilk exist in myriad forms, not least in the person of Chas W. Whittle, who "gained his major success not with the proud "My Girl's a Yorkshire Girl," but "Let's All Go Down the Strand."[20]

While such examples indicate the dominance London exerted over music-hall entertainers, it would be wrong to conclude that the situation was uniform. Away from the capital, many provincial music-hall entertainers built their reputations upon the fact that they were part of the local community. Edward "Ned" Corvan (1829–1865) was "a favourite everywhere" on Tyneside, not least because his "localized pieces spoke to the experience of workers."[21] Corvan, who did odd jobs and played the violin at the Victoria Theater before his singing career blossomed, actively resisted the collaborationist pressures at work from the mid-nineteenth century onwards. The "quiescence" of working-class music after the Chartist decades of the 1840s, marked by "a transition from protest, street music and spontaneous sing-song to formalised performance in choirs and brass bands," and where "the outlines of a qualitatively distinct workers' music culture become even mistier" in hindsight makes Corvan's resistance seem all the more admirable.[22] Yet because "music-hall was a participatory form of activity," then Corvan's success must be read in terms of the class homology he engendered with his audience.[23] Establishing himself as vox populi for the class identity he shared with onlookers, Corvan articulated a sense of solidarity his audience understood well, as the following verse from "The Funny Time Comin'" indicates:

> There's a funny time comin' lads,
> A funny time comin'
> We'll hae ne shippin maisters then,
> I' the funny time comin';
> We'll hae nae cutlashes on the Quay,
> The bairns and wives to anger;
> We'll hae a better North Shields M---r,
> Ony wait a little langer. [24]

---

[19]   Ibid., 180.

[20]   Russell, 98.

[21]   Dave Harker, "The Making of the Tyneside Concert Hall," *Popular Music*, Vol. 1 (1981), 49.

[22]   Richard Middleton, "Articulating Musical Meaning/Re-constructing Musical History/Locating the 'Popular,'" *Popular Music*, Vol. 5 (1985), 19.

[23]   Gareth Stedman Jones, *Languages of Class: Studies in Working Class History, 1832–1982* (Cambridge: Cambridge University Press, 1983), 224.

[24]   Quoted in Harker (1981), 51.

Opposition to the "maisters," who, as the singer in "Astrilly [Australia] or The Pitmen's Farewell" points out "keeps us striking,'" would have found the same kind of favorable reception as that of "The Rise in Coals," a song decrying an increase in the price of winter fuel:

> The snaw fell doon fast, an' poor folks seem'd shy,
> Clos'd up I' thor hyems as the storm pelted by;
> An they wished roond their nooks such times soon wad pass,
> For provisions had risen an' they'd saved little brass,
> And as money an' firin' was meltin' away,
> Thor seemed nowt but caud dops for us poor sons of clay,
> The women folks flew ti' fill thor coal holes,
> To the depoe but hand them they've raised wor small coals.
> O What a price for sma' coals, how they've raised wor sma' coals.[25]

The almost Dickensian opening of this song quickly gives way to the kind of serious social critique that marks so much of Corvan's best work. In the final verse, the dishonest tactics of the unscrupulous coal-merchants are implicitly contrasted with honest "toil" of the pitmen who dig the coal:

> They ken hoo ti swindle poor folks wi' thor loads,
> Pretendin' thor raised, and that snaw stopped the roads,
> But a pitman tell'd me ti stop up sic jaw,
> For it niver rained hailstones nor snawed doon belaw.
> An' he says if thou'll teeyke advice fra a feul,
> When thors a greet vast o' weather, get thaw holes a chock full
> An while thou's warmin' thaw shins by the fire, as the snaw
> Drops doon through the loom, think o' the pitmen belaw.
> For they toil hard and sair for sma' coals, how they toil for sma' coals.[26]

As an organic intellectual of some importance, Ned Corvan understood the value of recording events from the perspective of those not usually quoted. "When 'eer owt happens in the toon," he pledged in the song "£4 10s Or, the Sailor's Strike," "aw'll take maw pen and write it doon."[27] And so he did, as the following verse, taken from "The Queen Has Sent a Letter, or The Hartley Calamity" (1862) indicates:

> The collier's welfare, as he toils, more interest might command
> Among the wealthy owners and rulers of the land.
> Are they like beasts of burthen, as Roebuck once did rave,
> Will government in future strive the collier's life to save?
> Why should the worn-out collier amid his abject gloom
> Eke out the life his Maker spared to share the pauper's doom?[28]

---

[25]   Quoted in Middleton, 28.
[26]   Ibid., 28–29.
[27]   Quoted in Harker, 51.
[28]   Ibid., 53.

This was written to commemorate the mining disaster at New Hartley in 1862, where a shafthead collapse entombed and subsequently killed many miners; one cannot help wondering if there is a sense of irony in a song that begins with "Bless the Queen of England" and ends with the above-quoted verse. Corvan's defense of collective, communal, working-class interests was reinforced by local circumstances that were difficult to understand by those from outside the area. Given that the shared identities upon which so much of his work depends were coming under increasing pressure as the influence of the London music hall burgeoned, the appearance in his repertoire of parodies of cockney songs, many of which he wrote as a consequence of seeing London entertainers performing in Newcastle, indicates that he too had begun to look over his shoulder.

Ned Corvan had good reason to be worried. After a spell as a publican in the late 1850s, he returned to the music hall, though by now many of the small halls had gone under in the face of pressure from commercial chains just as local artists were losing out to London stars. "What had happened," Dave Harker asserts, "was that big capital had seen a promising investment, and had bought up most of the 'machine tools.'" Thus when Corvan appeared at the Tyne Theater, "*even in spite of his sustained popularity*, he was continuously made to play second fiddle . . . to the imported, London-based stars, to the foreign attractions like the Christy Minstrels and, most decisively of all, to the culture and ideology of the proprietors."[29]

Although examples of genuine working-class expression continued during this period, so much of the evidence suggests that as the nineteenth century progressed the music hall became a tool to endorse the prevailing social order as well as the desires of those at the apex of the social hierarchy. Joe Wilson, Ned Corvan's contemporary and fellow Geordie, is a useful example of how ideologically subtle some of the significant changes that affected the music hall actually were. While Wilson was often regarded as a working-class radical, Dave Harker has shown that he was "really useful in helping to popularize the values, attitudes and ideas espoused by the bourgeoisie, and by those who aspired to that status."[30] In fact, while Wilson's style panders to prevailing notions of respectability and his belief in temperance, his work offers little or no concession to those too desperate to worry about the state of their boots nor those driven to drink by circumstance. In "Bad Beuts" the social ostracism Wilson suggests awaits those afflicted with worn footwear is as certain as the social order is immutable. After all, as the song has it, "it's the way o' the world if a chep's hard up."[31]

Such attitudes nurtured a social vision far removed from the collective identities so important to Ned Corvan. For Joe Wilson, who ironically once played

---

[29]   Ibid., 54.

[30]   Dave Harker, "Joe Wilson: 'Comic Dialectical Singer' or Class Traitor?" in *Music Hall: Performance and Style*, ed. J.S. Bratton (Milton Keynes: Open University Press, 1986), 127.

[31]   "What That Man Might Heh Been," <http://www.geocities.com/matalzi/priests18. html#songs>. Accessed December 9, 2006.

at a benefit concert for his fellow Geordie, the self-help culture, which he seems to have been completely captivated by, leads to his condemnation of alcohol and those who use it:

> Thor once wes a time-when i' bizniss his-sel,
> He held a fine place I' the toon,
> An' bore a gud nyem as a nice sort o' man
> That few, varry few wad run doon;
> But the hyem that he had wassint peaceful aw've heard,
> He'd trubbles that cuddint be seen,
> So he flew te the drink-an' it myeks a chep sad,
> When he thinks what that man might heh been.
> He had wealth-as a scholar he gain'd greet renoon,
> An' respect frae the foaks that he knew;
> But noo, man, he's poor, for the money he had
> Like chaff on a windy day flew;
> He drinks day an' neet- but he's not biv his-sel,
> For thor's cases like this daily seen,
> An' hoo often ye'll hear iv a cumpny the words
> Wiv a sigh, "What that man might hev been![32]

Inasmuch as it records a standard fall from grace, "What That Man Might Heh Been," is a fairly typical example of Wilson's many temperance pieces. Typically, in this song and in others too, Wilson admits no other explanation for alcoholism save that vaguely intimated kind of moral failure which Victorians attributed to those they routinely condemned as inadequate. On the other hand, while articulations of the social order emphasizing respectability became ten-a-penny in Victorian Britain, the claims to authenticity implicit in the vernacular idiom Wilson uses make his songs a particularly useful barometer of prescient embourgeoisment.

One might, then, interpret the likes of Joe Wilson as a kind of bridging figure spanning the distance between the antithetical radicalism of Ned Corvan and the more overtly pro-establishment "coster" entertainers that emerged in the latter decades of the century. This particular vision of the music hall, which Martha Vicinus characterized as a movement from a "class to a mass entertainment," was a gradual process that entailed the appropriation and manipulation of working-class images and minds.[33] Once under way, this progressive rearticulation of the politics of music hall songs could be deployed to buttress dominant ideologies in limitless ways. Particularly towards the end of the nineteenth century, music hall narratives, for instance, played an important role in legitimizing the British empire to a Glasgow audience many of whom no doubt saw their own country as a victim of English imperialism. Hence expressions of loyalty to the British Empire in this respect reveal how widespread invitations to identify with British imperialist

---

[32]   Ibid.

[33]   Martha Vicinus, *The Industrial Muse: A Study of Nineteenth Century British Working Class Literature* (New York: Barnes and Noble, 1974), 238.

goals masked the reassertion of class hierarchy at home. If those Scots "ready tae fecht [fight] for auld England" as one song put it, bear testimony to the powerful internal and cultural hegemony England was asserting north of Hadrian's Wall, they also suggest allegories of class of a strength similar to those that encouraged the suppression of antithetical opinion in the music halls of England.[34] Piecemeal and at times arbitrary though these processes of change were, it is worth pausing to remind ourselves that they required a remarkable ideological journey from the militant opposition of songs such as "The Funny Time Comin,'" where hierarchy is abolished as "the lads" vow to make the "shipping maisters ... work like other men," to songs such as the Scot William C. McPhie's imperial triumphalism wherein "Britain's flag has risen over Afric's sunny plains," and Scots "with their bayonets fixed soon put Britannia's foes to rout".[35]

Behind these questions, which not surprisingly have inspired considerable debate, lay the extension of capitalism, for while it may be that "in the 1860s many of the songs sung in the working-class halls were still anti-aristocratic and populist in tone" it is also the case that capitalist entrepreneurs and institutions provided the means through which the working-class could be manipulated and shaped.[36] In fact, music halls were vulnerable to profit-seeking capitalists as well as those authorities attempting to encourage and control the kind of behavior they believed should be promoted. Even though "opportunities for relatively autonomous working-class experience were still created and used . . . these were under mounting pressure from other social groups with a stake in shaping working-class culture."[37] Equally, no doubt in a further attempt to control song content, it was not unknown for hall owners to employ songwriters. But these were far from the only reasons why the music hall was one of the key ideological battlegrounds of the nineteenth and early twentieth centuries.

Criticism of the music halls also came from a combination of the pressure applied by reformers, often in the guise of temperance groups, who associated the halls with drinking, prostitution, and other examples of debauchery and vice. At the same time, the withholding of entertainment licenses could be and was used as a disciplinary measure against halls associated with behavior to which licensing boards objected. In conjunction with the erosion of political comment of an anti-establishment stripe from the halls, these changes became key elements in the reconfiguration of what was deemed acceptable in the music hall. Among a number of influential directives, "House Rules," which demanded that performers eschew derogatory remarks towards the royal family as well as members of parliament, closed off another avenue of expression. Not surprisingly in this light, as the social composition of the audience became more varied in the later decades of the nineteenth century—though established hierarchy was still visible in the

---

34   Quoted in Maloney, 165.
35   Quoted in Harker, "The Making," 51; Quoted in Maloney, 166.
36   Stedman Jones, 231.
37   Summerfield, 209.

form of seat price segregation—the content of entertainment in the halls began to reflect social ideologies and visions consistent with establishment values. Little by little, in the aggressive, interventionist attempts to preserve and reassert what many saw as an organic hierarchy crucial to Britain's very existence, the impact of the politics to which the audience was exposed "continued over the course of decades to grow into a creed."[38] But advocating a sense of national identity around the promotion of Empire and one's duty to it fostered more than the advancement of patriotism as a civic responsibility; because it conceals class distinctions under the umbrella of imperial obligation, this conception of "duty" implies unquestioning acceptance of one's "lot" or station in life. Ideas that repeatedly presented hierarchy as sacrosanct and class position as immutable fostered the ingredients with which entertainers could manipulate the visions and images of the working class to the point where the working class was presented with an idealized image of itself. As we have seen, granting the working class an essentialist authenticity of experience, as intellectuals and others did, offered an added layer of legitimacy. However important though all these issues were perhaps the most crucial figure in the rearticulation of the working-class image was that of the staged cockney, especially the persona of the costermonger.

As I noted earlier, the relative autonomy and cohesion of the costermonger community, with its own working hours, meant that costers appeared to be under the command of no one, an issue that, given the Victorian propensity towards vigorous attempts at social control, must have made them an especially appealing target for music hall appropriation. The nature of their profession, especially their visibility and mobility, also made them ideal for the dissemination of political opposition through the sales of broadsides. According to Penelope Summerfield, costermongers "composed many of their own broadsides" wherein they "asserted their political identity in songs opposing restrictive legislation.[39] But there was another reason, no less political, why the coster image was so dramatically altered. Certainly from the 1860s onward, the influence of theatrically trained performers meant that the regional artists, many of whom represented local class interests, were eased out of the halls. If there was a hint of Victorian Darwinism to this theatrical evolution, it could be explained away as a contest between authenticity and acting. After all, the changing composition of the hall audiences, which included an increasing number of patrons whose viewing experiences were defined by the theatre, invited such a conclusion. Accordingly, the audience "decided that class relationships were of less importance than dramatic expertise" and, as "primarily men [sic] of the theater" they "didn't expect to admire performers for the 'authenticity' of their origins as much as for their acting power."[40] It was this kind of subtle shift in emphasis, with pathos replacing authenticity as the benchmark of quality, that opened the way for

---

[38]   Senelick, 155.

[39]   Summerfield, 232.

[40]   John Stokes, *In the Nineties* (Chicago: University of Chicago Press, 1989), 90.

the appropriation of the costermonger image and subsequent rearticlation of the working class.

Alfred Peck Stevens (1839–1888), better known as Alfred Vance or "The Great Vance," was one of the earliest artists to exploit the coster image. Theatrically trained, Vance established his cockney credentials in the 1860s with such "rorty sketches of real life" as "The Ticket of Leave Man," "Costermonger Joe," and "The Chickaleary Cove."[41] The latter, in which the performer affected a curious Jewish articulation, now seems more mockney than Cockney:

> I'm a Chickaleary bloke, with my one—two—three—
> Vitechapel was the willage I was born in;
> To catch me on the hop,
> Or on my tibby drop,
> You must vake up wery early in the mornin'.
> I've got a rorty gal, also a knowing pal,
> And merrily together we jog on.
> And I doesn't car a flatch
> So long as I've a tach,
> Some pannum in my chest—and a tog on!"[42]

In the parlance of the time, one is inclined to cry "well fancy that!" And this, after all, may well be the intended response because this song, with its later references to back-slang ("yenom" = money) and other Cockney fixtures such as "dipping blokes" (pickpockets), is fairly typical of the genre. For all these reasons, it appears difficult to agree that the song's "cockney dialect" is "an assertion of local solidarity and pride."[43] Nonetheless, "The Chickaleary Bloke" and songs of a similar sentiment began to resonate powerfully as they contributed to the changing image of the costermonger. And as there were no shortage of performers willing to impersonate what was becoming a standard version of the stage costermonger, the evolving image became "a desired image created by the music hall and perpetuated by the music hall's feeding upon itself" rather than being a representation founded in the reality of costermonger London.[44] No one contributed more to this process than "the Coster's Laureate," Albert Chevalier (1861–1923).

Chevalier was a character actor who initially thought the halls beneath him. But a period of unemployment quickly removed any inhibitions he may have held about "playing down" in the halls. He made his debut at the Tivoli Theatre in 1891 singing among other songs, "The Future Mrs. 'Awkins" and "Knocked 'Em in the

---

[41] Chance H. Newton, *Idols of the Halls* (Wakefield: E.P. Publishing, 1975 [1928]), 23.

[42] Quoted in Newton, 25.

[43] J.S. Bratton, *The Victorian Popular Ballad* (Totowa: Rowan and Littlefield, 1975), 99.

[44] Derek B. Scott, "The Music-Hall Cockney: Flesh and Blood, or Replicant?" *Music and Letters*, Vol. 83, No. 2 (May, 2002), 256.

Old Kent Road (Wotcher!)." Both of these songs assume only a tenuous pretence towards realism; in the former the singer attempts to woo "sweet Lizer" on the romantic basis that if she dies "an old maid" then she will "only 'ave erself to blame." "Knocked 'Em in the Old Kent Road," which purports to describe typical coster behavior, continues in a similar lexicon:

> Last week down our alley came a toff
> Nice old geezer with a nasty cough
> Sees my missus, takes 'is topper off
> In a very gentlemanly way
> Wot cher! all the neighbors cried
> Who yer gonna meet, Bill
> Have yer bought the street, Bill?
> Laugh! I thought I should've died
> Knocked 'em in the Old Kent Road
> Ev'ry evenin' at the stroke of five
> Me and the missus takes a little drive
> You'd say, Wonderful they're still alive
> If you saw that little donkey go
> When we starts the blessed donkey stops
> He won't move, so out I quickly lops
> Pals start whackin' him, when down he drops
> Someone says he wasn't made to go
> Wot cher! all the neighbors cried
> Who yer gonna meet, Bill
> Have yer bought the street, Bill?
> Laugh! I thought I should've died
> Knocked 'em in the Old Kent Road. [45]

"I was there," H. Chance Newton wrote of "Chivvy's" debut, "and well remember the deep impression Chevalier's quaint and semi-pathetic manner and his finished acting made upon the usually rollicking Tivolians."[46] Clearly, as Derek B. Scott points out, Chevalier "was important to the growing respectability of the halls."[47]

Chevalier, in fact, was important in so many ways because his songs underscored and naturalized the established hierarchy in significant ways. At a time when a growing number of lower-middle class clerks were aspiring to rise in the class system—and Leonard Bast in E.M. Forster's *Howards End* became the archetypal example—lines of class demarcation, which were an important means of establishing benchmarks of gentility, were underscored at every opportunity. So thoroughly had the ground in fact been prepared that as the twentieth century opened it mattered little to critics such as Max Beerbohm that Chevalier's costermonger

---

[45]   <http://lyricsplayground.com/alpha/songs/k/knockedemintheoldkentroad.shtml>. Accessed May 15, 2007.

[46]   Quoted in Newton, 121.

[47]   Scott, 250.

was "unfaithful to the Old Kent Road."[48] What was of concern to the same critic was Chevalier's over-acting, or more correctly his didactic delivery. After commending Chevalier's for his lyrics, Beerbohm then castigates his manner and delivery, concluding that "his points do not need such an unconscionable amount of hammering, to drive them home for us."[49] In other words, Beerbohm's anxiety centers on a fear that Chevalier's act runs the risk of undermining the ideological goals it is designed to serve. But given the rapturous reception some of Chevalier's more famous sketches received, it appears that Beerbohm failed to grasp the extent to which the audience had already been taught how to perceive such acts. Such perceptual frameworks were reinforced through sketches such as "The Coster's Serenade" (1890), a song constructed around a staged glimpse at courtship. Here Chevalier first establishes his undying love for "'Arriet" and then proceeds to take her on a mawkishly sentimental trip enlightened by what must have been the customary Cockney attractions:

> You ain't forgotten yet that night in May,
> Down at the Welsh 'Arp, which is 'Endon way;
> You fancied winkles and a pot of tea.
> 'Four-'alf', I murmured, 'is good enough for me'.
> 'Give me a word of 'ope that I may win.'
> You prods me gently with the winkle pin.
> We was as 'appy as could be that day
> Down at the Welsh 'Arp, which is 'Endon way.
> Oh! 'Arriet, I'm waiting, waiting for you my dear.
> Oh! 'Arriet, I'm waiting, waiting alone out here.
> When that moon shall cease to shine,
> False will be this 'eart of mine;
> I'm bound to go on lovin' yer, my dear,
> (spoken) D'ye 'ear? [50]

Ensuring the survival of hierarchical privilege and the social codes and attitudes that gave rise to them, to which this verse makes a strong contribution, necessitates the repeated demonstration of exactly what separates the classes and why those distinctions should be preserved. And what could be more natural in this respect than language, the incorrect usage of which marked the offender out as vulgar? An important denominator in ascertaining degrees of gentility was the "dropped aitch," which at times even functioned as an indicator of social origin. In fact, as P.N. Furbank points out, "the privileging of an artificial and ideal metropolitan accent ... put Cockney, the dialect of the humbler inhabitants of the metropolis, in a special position. If regional dialects were to be 'corrected,'" he goes on,

---

[48] *More Theatres*, 436.

[49] Ibid., 437.

[50] Quoted in *Best Music Hall and Variety Songs*, ed. Peter Gammond (London: Wolfe Publishing, 1972), 27.

"this one was nearest to hand ... and accordingly the one most likely to figure as the archetype of 'incorrectness.'" From this premise it was but a short step "to selecting some feature of Cockney as a shibboleth distinguishing the gentleman from the non-gentleman."[51]

At the time Chevalier was performing commentators saw the development of his stage coster in terms of "a fully-rounded theatrical type or 'mask.'" But the act that accompanied the song was also an important feature of the mask: "The verse finishes, the coster turns, toys with his hat, in one quick movement the billycock has struck ten attitudes, and then the shoulders are squared, the elbows stick out, and the foot leaps forward before the straightened leg into that inimitable coster stride."[52] These exaggerated affectations, which formed an important part of the image of the costermonger Chevalier was projecting, reached their apotheosis in "My Old Dutch," his most popular song. This was the song around which Chevalier created an act of unbelievable sentimentality. Martha Vicinus describes the staging of the song thus:

> 'My Old Dutch' began with a pantomime act: the curtain would open showing the front of a workhouse with its entrances marked 'Men' and 'Women'. Chevalier would enter arm in arm with 'my old Dutch', and the guardian would separate the two, gesturing to the appropriate doors. With a look of horror, Chevalier would say 'You can't do this to us – we've been together for forty years', and break into song.[53]

While Vicinus is correct to argue that "Chevalier's emotional scene pandered to his audience's expectations in a way that made rigid, and ultimately false, the emotions he expressed," that he could expect spectators to take this kind of thing seriously is indicative of his skill in manipulating the audience and the image of coster.[54] Nonetheless, as I have tried to argue, the song's success depends upon the fact that the ground upon which it could be accepted had already been prepared. A couple of representative verses and the chorus run as follows:

> I've got a pal,
> A reg'lar out an' outer,
> She's a dear good old gal,
> I'll tel yer all about 'er.
> It's many years since fust we met,
> 'Er 'air was then as black as jet,
> It's whiter now, but she don't fret,

---

[51]   P.N. Furbank, *Unholy Pleasure or The Idea of Social Class* (Oxford: Oxford University Press, 1985), 102.

[52]   D.F. Cheshire, *Music Hall in Britain* (Rutherford: Fairleigh Dickinson University Press, 1974), 66.

[53]   *The Industrial Muse*, 275.

[54]   Ibid, 275. J.S. Bratton provides a compelling argument that "My Old Dutch" was meant to be taken seriously. See *The Victorian Popular Ballad*, 100.

Not my old gal!
We've been together now for forty years,
An' it don't seem a day too much;
There ain't a lady livin' in the land
As I'd 'swop' for my dear Old Dutch!
There ain't a lady livin' in the land
As I'd 'swop' for my dear Old Dutch!
I calls 'er Sal,
'Er proper name is Sairer,
An' yer may find a gal
As you'd consider fairer.
She ain't a angel - she can start
A jawin' till it make yer smart;
She's just a woman bless 'er 'eart,
Is my old gal![55]

Described by Chance Newton as a "famous domestic monologue," it is difficult to see this song as anything other than jejune. Nevertheless, at the time it was written and performed arguments as to its didactic purpose were seriously entertained.[56] For instance the reformer Laura Ormiston Chant, felt that "My Old Dutch" expressed "the finest sentiments of the human heart ... in a language understood by the people," while Lewis Carroll was moved to record that Chevalier's influence on public taste "is towards refinement and purity."[57] To what extent these opinions are in any way representative is virtually impossible to tell. What such comments do alert us to, however, is the presence of emotionally paternalistic attitudes towards the working class; by the same token, the implication that the working class could understand only a limited register provides its own rationale for the manipulation of the costermonger: it is done for working class's own good. Hidden behind these various forms of noblesse oblige is a congruity of thought and attitude much of which to one extent or another turns upon the preservation of hierarchy, station, and authority; the affinity between allegorized visions of life and the social order reinforced this compact. At issue, of course, is the duplicitous yet paradoxically impressive extent to which those in a position to exert influence understood that "the social order was not simply 'out there' in social and economic structures, but 'in here,' being actively constructed in the imaginative life of audiences ..."[58] This was the kernel of knowledge that set in motion the staged sublimation of working class interests and their replacement by "compensatory" claims that theirs was the only true authentic British experience.

Throughout the critical canon that comprises music hall historiography, representations that affirm the logic of working-class experience as organically

---

[55] Quoted in *Best Music Hall and Variety Songs*, 86.

[56] Newton, 122.

[57] Quoted in Vicinus, 275; Quoted in Cheshire, 67.

[58] Patrick Joyce, *Visions of the People: Industrial England and the Question of Class 1848–1914* (Cambridge: Cambridge University Press, 1991), 225.

authentic invariably work at one level or another to camouflage and deny vestigial class agitation. By the very same process, hierarchy was reinforced and station and rank re-asserted. Hence it comes as no surprise to find that "political music-hall songs never really attacked the system as such."[59] Instead, they were used to buttress a system wherein Conservative values dominated. As one critic put it, the music hall was a place in which "Toryism must be seen as a theatrical convention as traditional and as unquestioned as the comedian's red nose."[60] The extent to which social aspiration was viewed as a subject fit only for scorn corroborates such apposite conclusions. Yet the fact that many members of the working class saw class as immutable belies how much ideological reinforcement was required for such a position to be reached. In this ideological aim the music hall had few peers; as a means of reinforcing social distinctions it fostered a myth of British community contingent upon the acceptance of one's "lot" or "place." These were lessons that in one way or another were repeated so frequently that they became second nature.

Aspirations towards working-class social advancement were universalized as a topic suitable solely for scorn long before the arrival of *Me and My Girl*, that 1930s lesson in adherence to one's social station. Written by Douglas Furber, Arthur Rose, and Neol Gay, this musical enshrined as fit only for parody working-class pretensions to what Lewis Carroll referred to as "refinement." The plot is familiar: the death of Lord Hareford precipitates the news that he had fathered an illegitimate child, who becomes the heir to his fortune and his title. To the horror of Hareford's friends and relatives, the heir is Lambeth costermonger Bill Snibson. Worse still, Snibson's girlfriend, Sally, is a cockney. Predictably, the plot centers upon attempts to make Snibson into a gentleman and Sally a lady, a desire the servants at Hareford Hall condemn as impossible. Eventually, after much confusion, assorted cockney characters, complete with Pearly King and Queen (an exaggerated version of the distinctive buttoned costumes worn by costers), teach the upper-class characters a song and dance, "The Lambeth Walk." But in the context of the staged image of the working class, one cannot help but wonder whether the immensely popular "Lambeth Walk" is the corollary of decades of social manipulation. Is this song really anything other than the working class reverting to its "rightful place," a position to which legions of music hall entertainers had invited it to assume? In much the same way that Daisy Hill's contention "it's nice to be common sometimes" lauded the alleged simplicity of working class life, "The Lambeth Walk," where everything was "free and easy" and you could "do as you darn well pleasy," made much of the notion that cheerful cockneys could sometimes teach the toffs a thing or two.[61]

But, as we have seen, this was a concession contingent upon the working class accepting the place assigned to it by those who sought to purge the music halls of

---

[59]   Kift, 41.

[60]   Senelick, 165.

[61]   "The Lambeth Walk,"<http://www.lyricsfreak.com/m/me+and+my+girl/the+lambeth+walk_10177677.html>. Accessed May 12, 2007.

class antagonism and political agitation. Those who presented the staged image of the working class, those who played at poverty, were a crucial element in a process that arguably at some level involved a shift in working-class attitudes from the social agitation found in the early music hall to the collaborationist acquiescence of its final years. And this was a process that is inscribed in the lyrics of the periods in question; it entailed a move from the antagonism of Ned Corvan's "Sum people's born wi' silver spoons i' thor gobs, but it strikes me mine's been a basin o' soop" ("The Soop Kitchin"), to the acceptance of one's lot in *Me and My Girl*, where Sally Smith, Bill Snibson's sweetheart, is encouraged to "take it on the chin, cultivate a little grin and smile!" ("Take it on the Chin").[62]

Works Cited

"Knocked 'Em in the Old Kent Road." <http://lyricsplayground.com/alpha/songs/k/knockedemintheoldkentroad.shtml>. Accessed 15 May 15, 2007.

"Take it on the Chin." <http://www.lyricsfreak.com/m/me+and+my+girl/take+it+on+the+chin_10177679.html>. Accessed April 1, 2007.

"The Lambeth Walk." <http://www.lyricsfreak.com/m/me+and+my+girl/the+lambeth+walk_10177677.html>. Accessed May 12, 2007.

"The Soop Kitchin." <http://www.geocities.com/matalzi/priests16.html#The%20Tyneside%20Chorus>. Accessed April 1, 2007.

"What That Man Might Heh Been." <http://www.geocities.com/matalzi/priests18.html#songs>. Accessed December 9, 2006.

Anderson, G.L. "The Social Economy of Late-Victorian Clerks," *The Lower Middle Class in Britain 1870–1914*, ed. Geoffrey Crossick. New York: St. Martin's Press, 1977.

Beerbohm, Max. *More Theatres, 1898–1903*. London: Rupert Hart-Davis, 1969.

Bratton, J.S. *The Victorian Popular Ballad*. Totowa: Rowan and Littlefield, 1975.

Cheshire, D.F. *Music Hall in Britain*. Rutherford: Fairleigh Dickinson University Press, 1974.

Eliot, T.S. "Marie Lloyd," in *Selected Prose of T.S. Eliot*, ed. Frank Kermode. New York: Farrar, Strauss and Giroux, 1975.

Faulk, Barry J. *Music Hall & Modernity: The Late-Victorian Discovery of Popular Culture*. Athens: Ohio University Press, 2004.

Furbank, P.N. *Unholy Pleasure or The Idea of Social Class*. Oxford: Oxford University Press, 1985.

Gammond, Peter, ed. *Best Music Hall and Variety Songs*. London: Wolfe Publishing, 1972.

Harker, Dave. "Joe Wilson: 'Comic Dialectical Singer' or Class Traitor?" in *Music Hall: Performance and Style*, ed. J.S. Bratton. Milton Keynes: Open University Press, 1986.

---

[62] <http://www.geocities.com/matalzi/priests16.html#The%20Tyneside%20Chorus>. Accessed April 1, 2007; <http://www.lyricsfreak.com/m/me+and+my+girl/take+it+on+the+chin_10177679.html>. Accessed April 1, 2007.

————. "The Making of the Tyneside Concert Hall," *Popular Music*, Vol. 1 (1981).

Jones, Gareth Stedman. *Languages of Class: Studies in Working Class History, 1832–1982*. Cambridge: Cambridge University Press, 1983.

Joyce, Patrick. *Visions of the People: Industrial England and the Question of Class 1848–1914*. Cambridge: Cambridge University Press, 1991.

Kift, Dagmar. *The Victorian Music Hall: Culture, Class and Conflict*. Cambridge: Cambridge University Press, 1991.

Macqeen-Pope, W. *The Melodies Linger On: The Story of the Music Hall*. London: W.H. Allen, n.d.

Maloney, Paul. *Scotland and the Music Hall, 1850–1914*. Manchester: Manchester University Press, 2003.

Middleton, Richard. "Articulating Musical Meaning/Re-constructing Musical History/Locating the 'Popular,'" *Popular Music*, Vol. 5, 1985.

Newton, Chance H. *Idols of the Halls*. Wakefield: E.P. Publishing, 1975.

Russell, Dave. *Popular Music in England, 1840–1914*. Montreal: McGill-Queen's University Press, 1987.

Scott, Derek B. "The Music-Hall Cockney: Flesh and Blood, or Replicant?" *Music and Letters*, Vol. 83, No. 2, May, 2002.

Senelick, Laurence. "Politics as Entertainment: Victorian Music-Hall Songs," *Victorian Studies*, Vol. 19, No. 2, 1975.

Stokes, John. *In the Nineties*. Chicago: University of Chicago Press, 1989.

Stoll, Rae Harris. "The Unthinkable Poor in Edwardian Writing," *Mosaic*, December, 1982.

Summerfield, Penelope. "The Effingham Arms and the Empire: Deliberate Selection in the Evolution of Music Hall in London," in *Popular Culture and Class Conflict, 1590–1914: Explorations in the History of Labour and Leisure*, eds Eileen Yeo and Stephen Yeo. Brighton: Harvester Press, 1981.

Thompson, E.P. *The Making of the English Working Class*. New York: Vintage, 1966.

Vicinus, Martha. *The Industrial Muse: A Study of Nineteenth Century British Working Class Literature*. New York: Barnes and Noble, 1974.

Williamson, Philip. "The Doctrinal Politics of Stanley Baldwin," in *Public and Private Doctrine: Essays in British History Presented to Maurice Cowling*, ed. Michael Bentley. Cambridge: Cambridge University Press, 2002.

Index